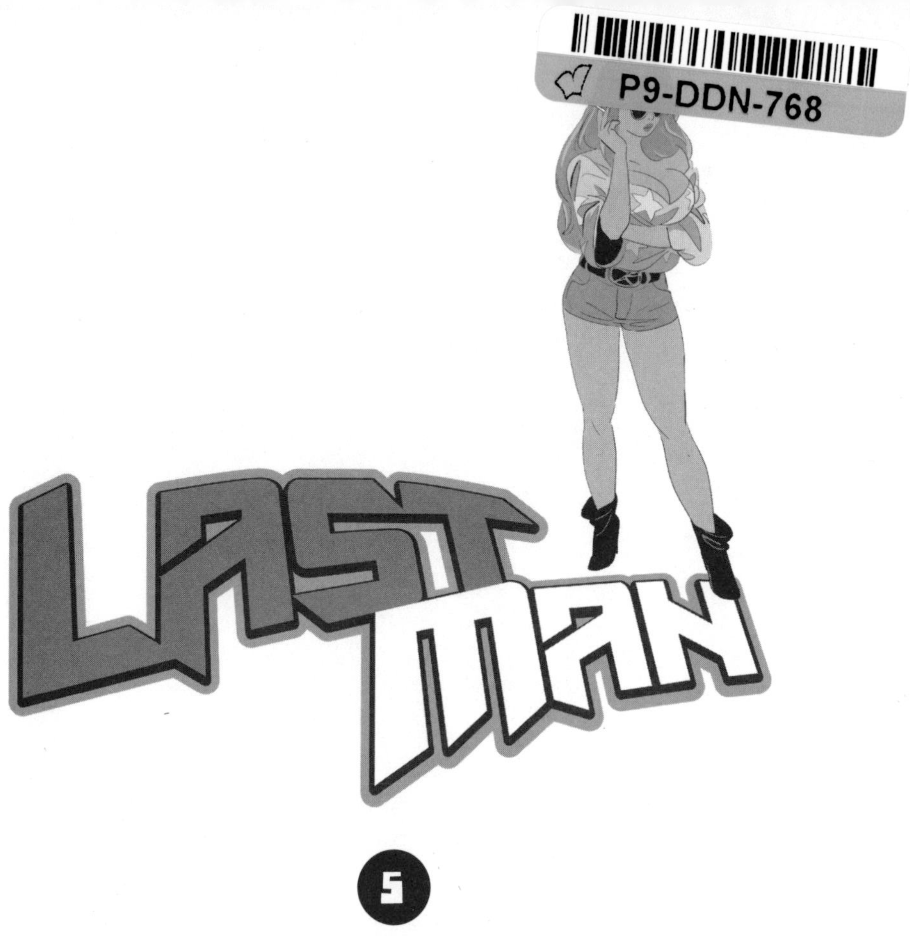

LAST MAN

5

The Order

Balak + Sanlaville + Vivès

:01
First Second
New York

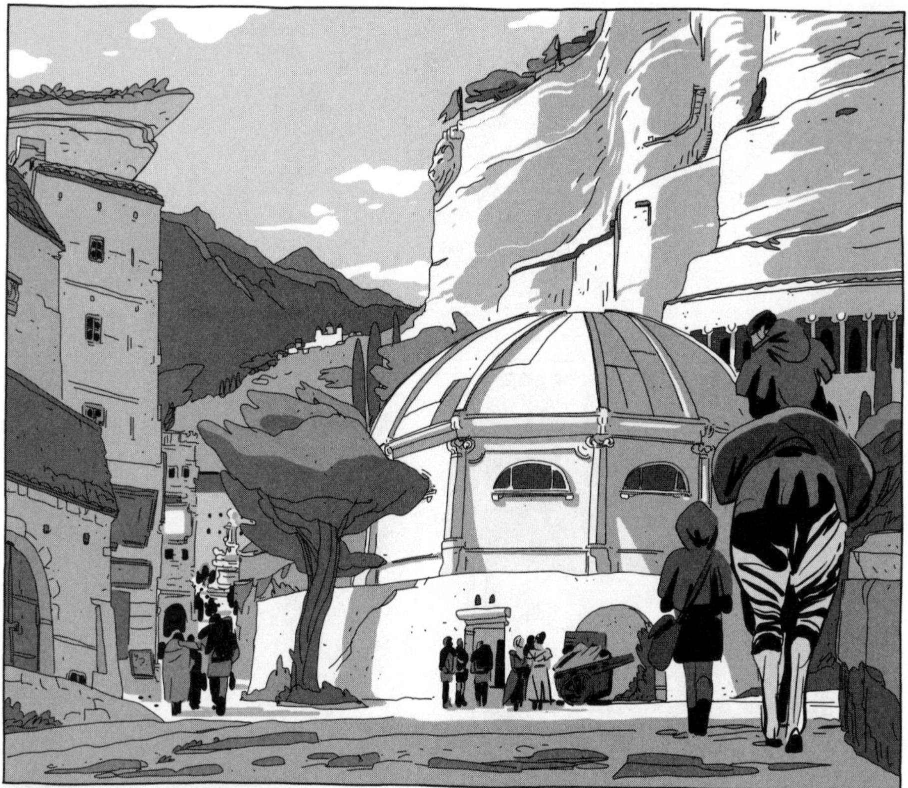

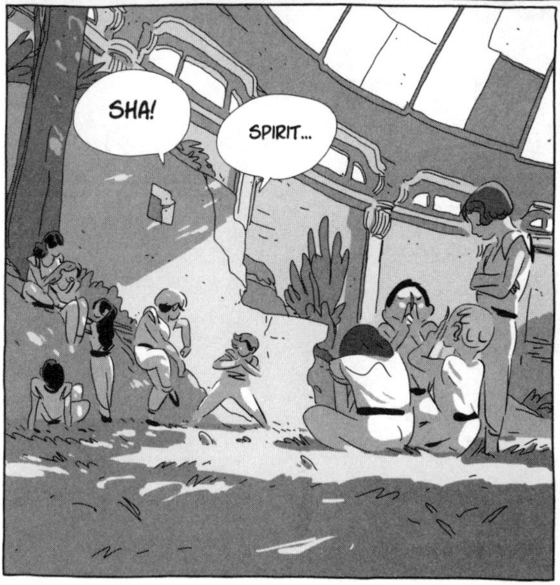
SHA!
SPIRIT...

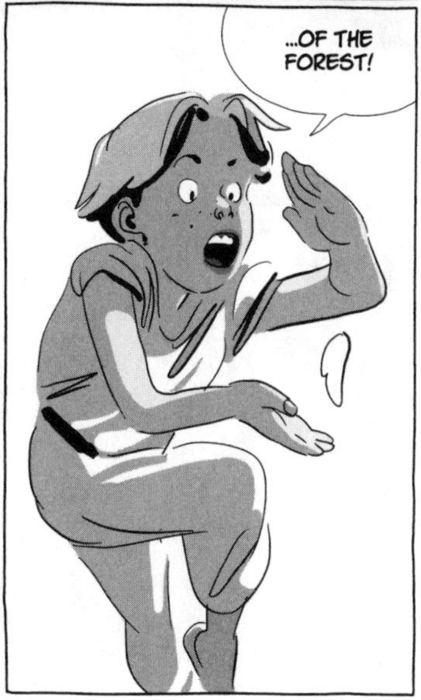
...OF THE FOREST!

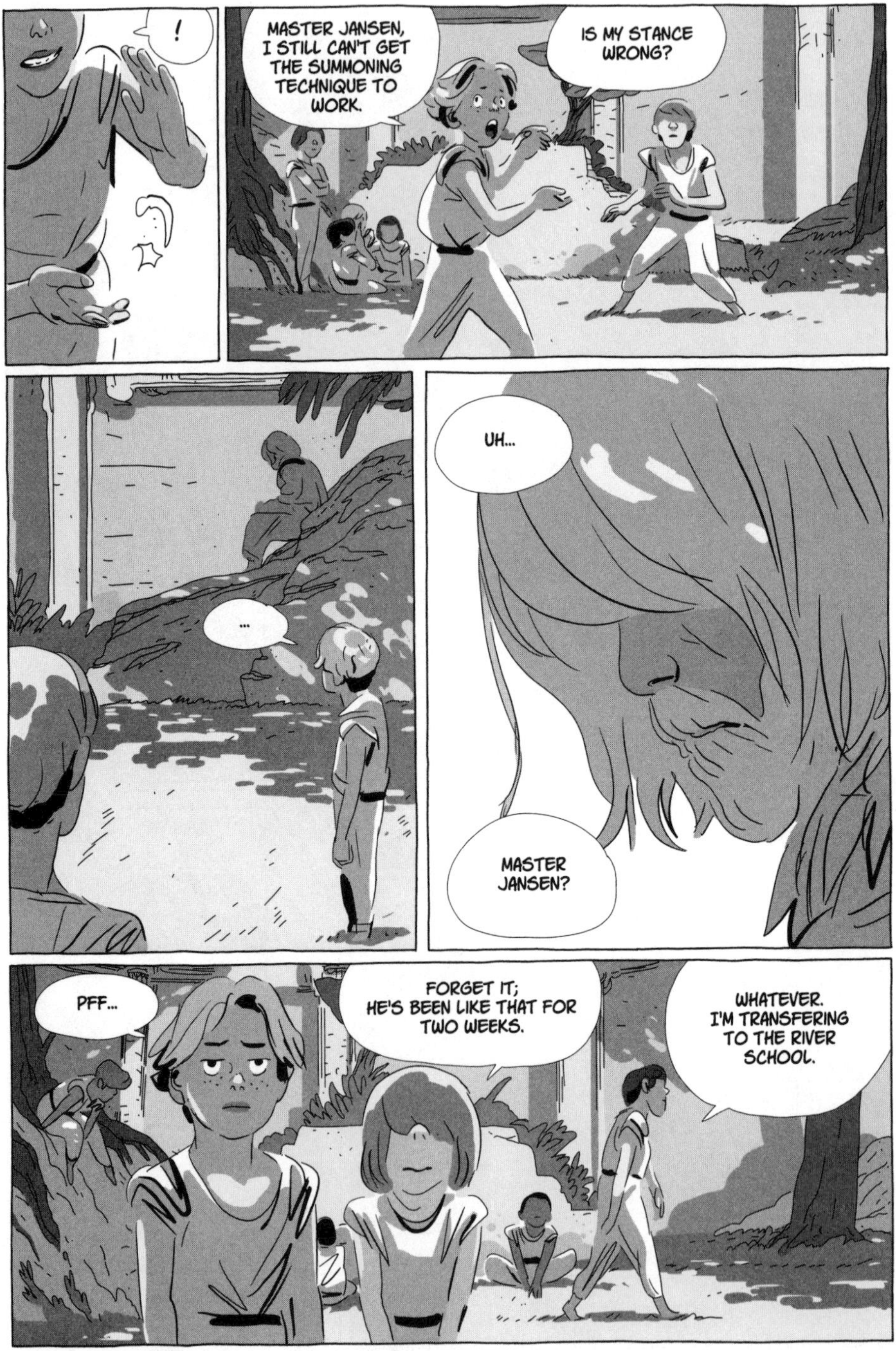
!
MASTER JANSEN, I STILL CAN'T GET THE SUMMONING TECHNIQUE TO WORK.
IS MY STANCE WRONG?
...
UH...
MASTER JANSEN?
PFF...
FORGET IT; HE'S BEEN LIKE THAT FOR TWO WEEKS.
WHATEVER. I'M TRANSFERING TO THE RIVER SCHOOL.

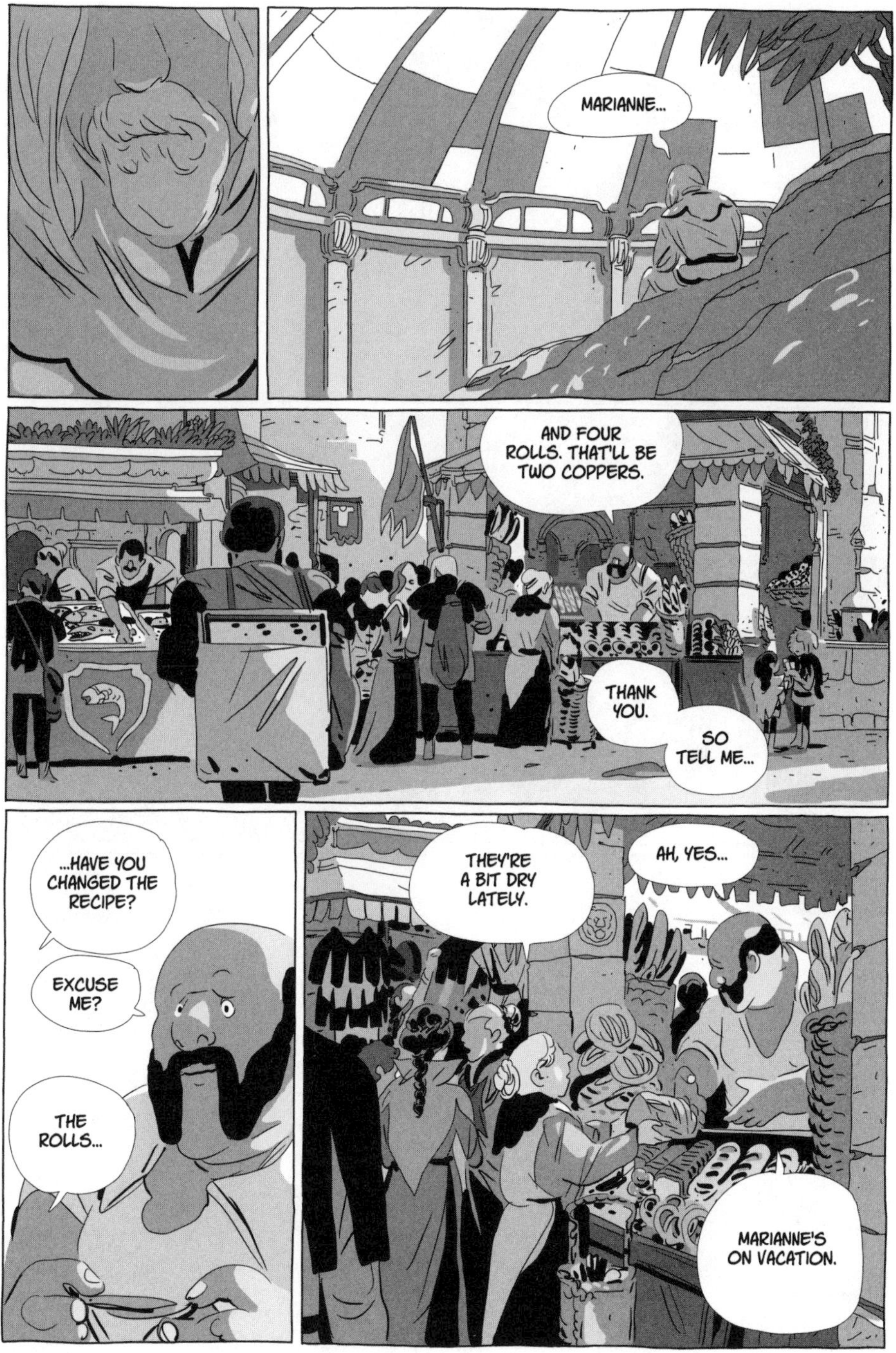
MARIANNE...
AND FOUR ROLLS. THAT'LL BE TWO COPPERS.
THANK YOU.
SO TELL ME...
...HAVE YOU CHANGED THE RECIPE?
EXCUSE ME?
THE ROLLS...
THEY'RE A BIT DRY LATELY.
AH, YES...
MARIANNE'S ON VACATION.

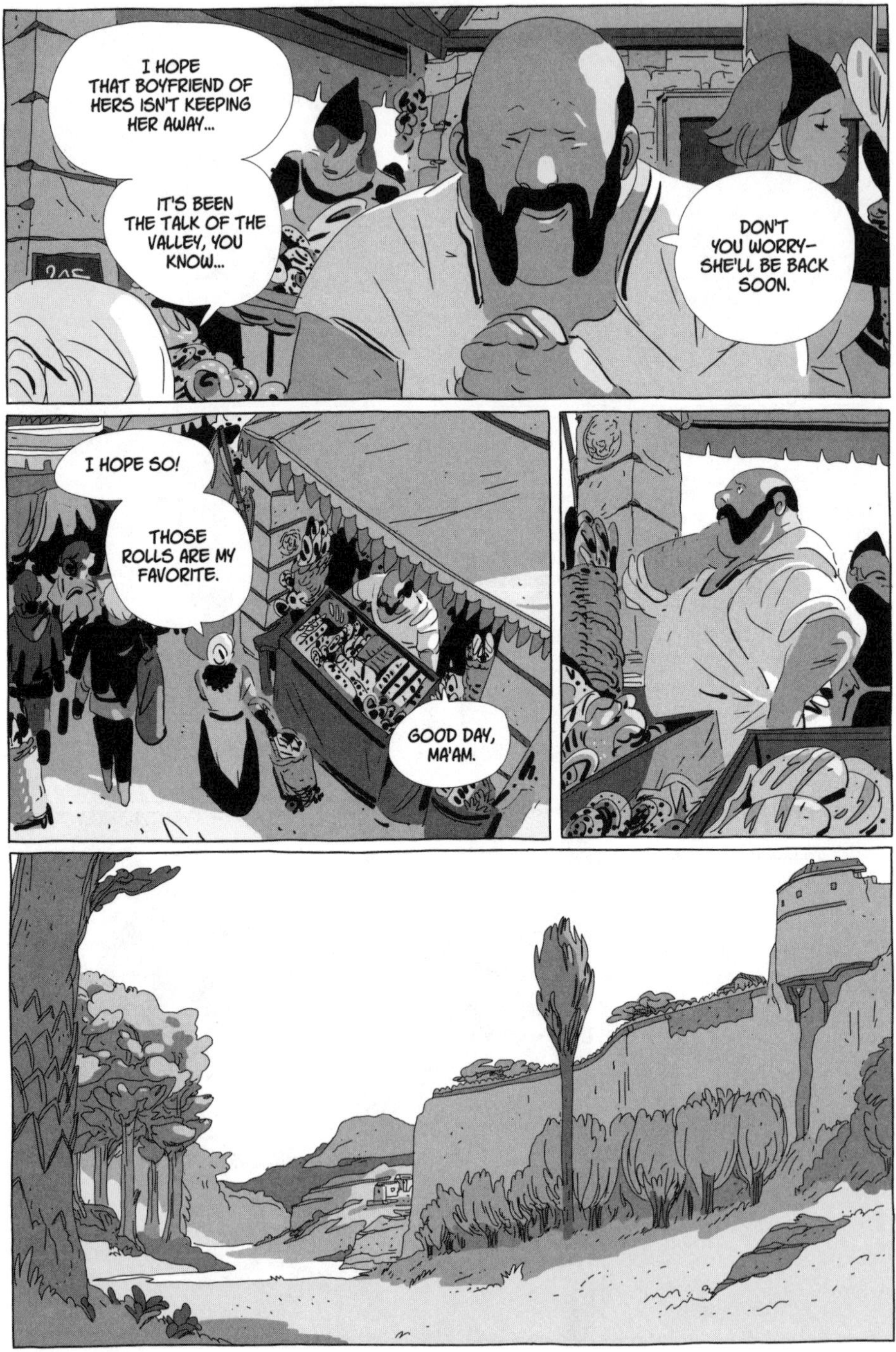
I HOPE THAT BOYFRIEND OF HERS ISN'T KEEPING HER AWAY...
IT'S BEEN THE TALK OF THE VALLEY, YOU KNOW...
DON'T YOU WORRY— SHE'LL BE BACK SOON.
I HOPE SO!
THOSE ROLLS ARE MY FAVORITE.
GOOD DAY, MA'AM.

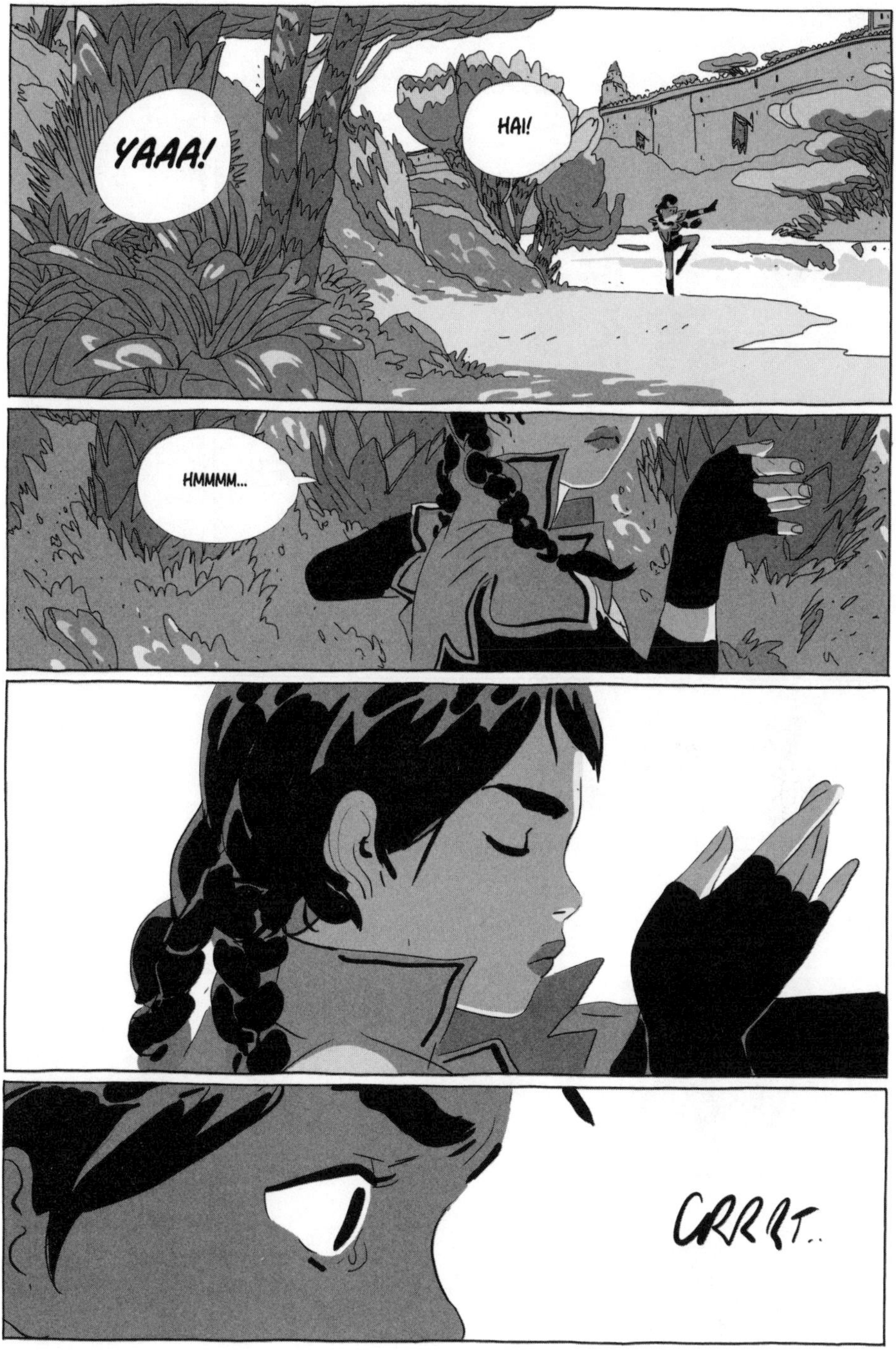
YAAA!
HAI!
HMMMM...
CRRRT..

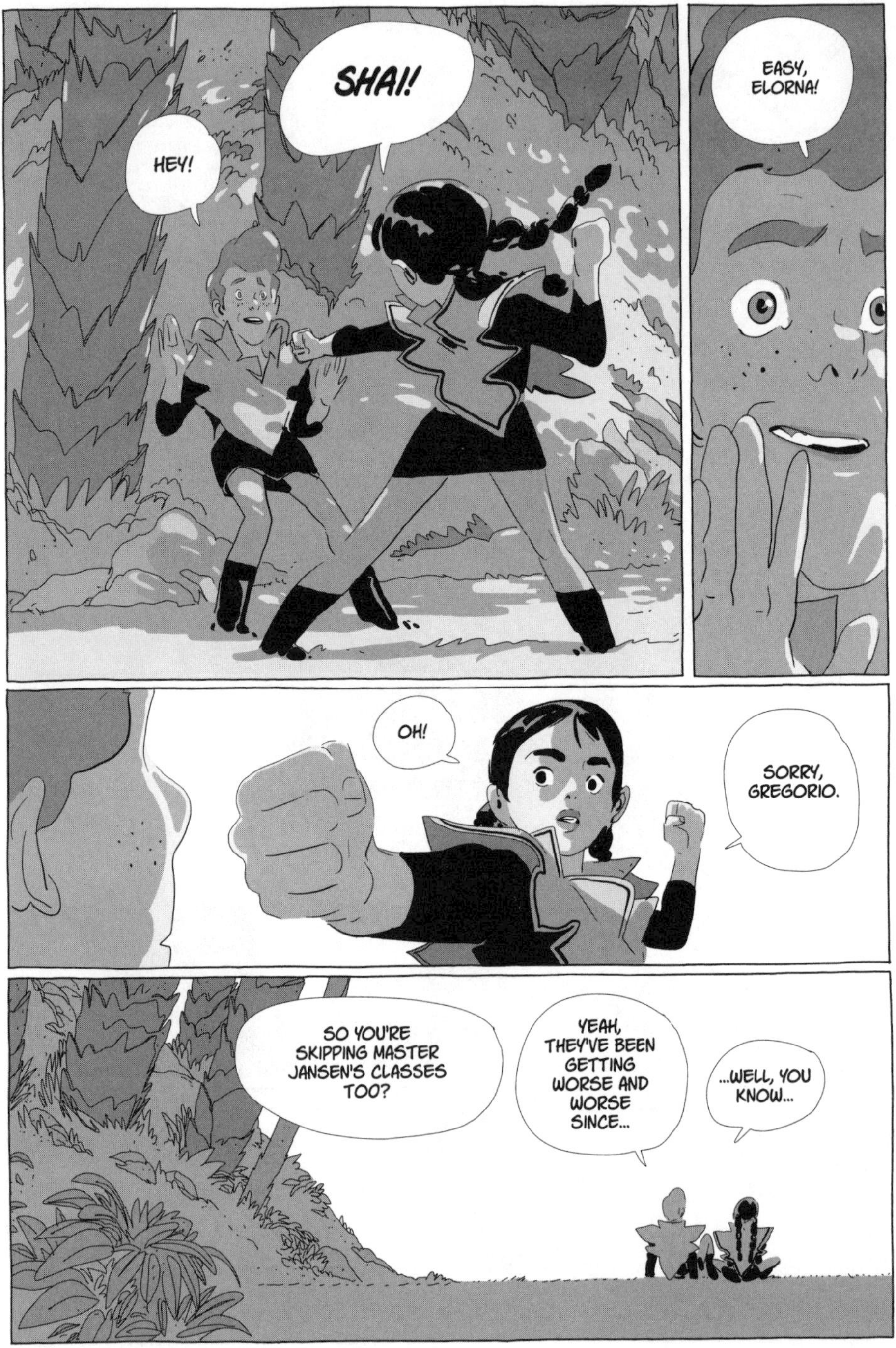
HEY!
SHAI!
EASY, ELORNA!
OH!
SORRY, GREGORIO.
SO YOU'RE SKIPPING MASTER JANSEN'S CLASSES TOO?
YEAH, THEY'VE BEEN GETTING WORSE AND WORSE SINCE...
...WELL, YOU KNOW...

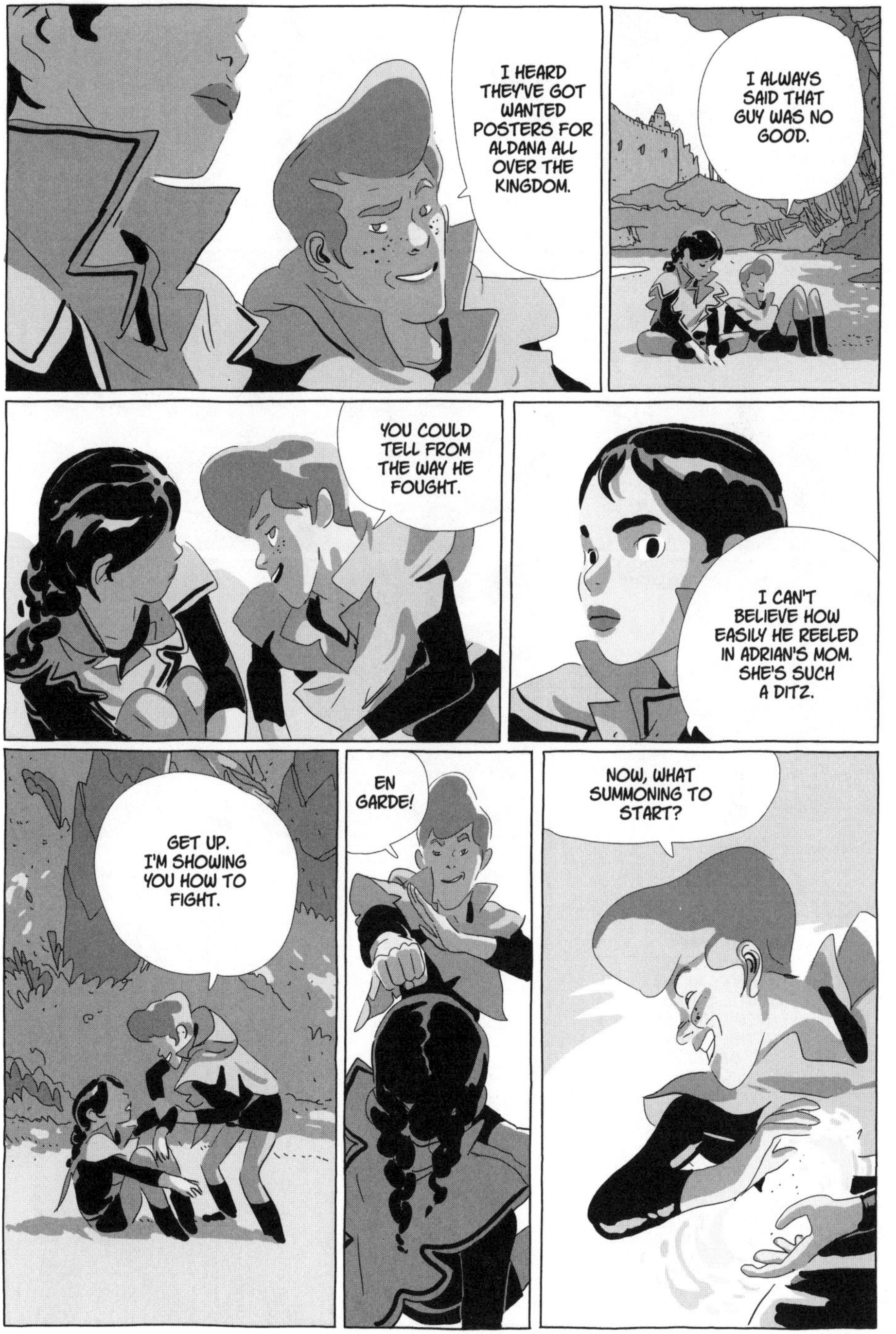
I HEARD THEY'VE GOT WANTED POSTERS FOR ALDANA ALL OVER THE KINGDOM.
I ALWAYS SAID THAT GUY WAS NO GOOD.
YOU COULD TELL FROM THE WAY HE FOUGHT.
I CAN'T BELIEVE HOW EASILY HE REELED IN ADRIAN'S MOM. SHE'S SUCH A DITZ.
GET UP. I'M SHOWING YOU HOW TO FIGHT.
EN GARDE!
NOW, WHAT SUMMONING TO START?

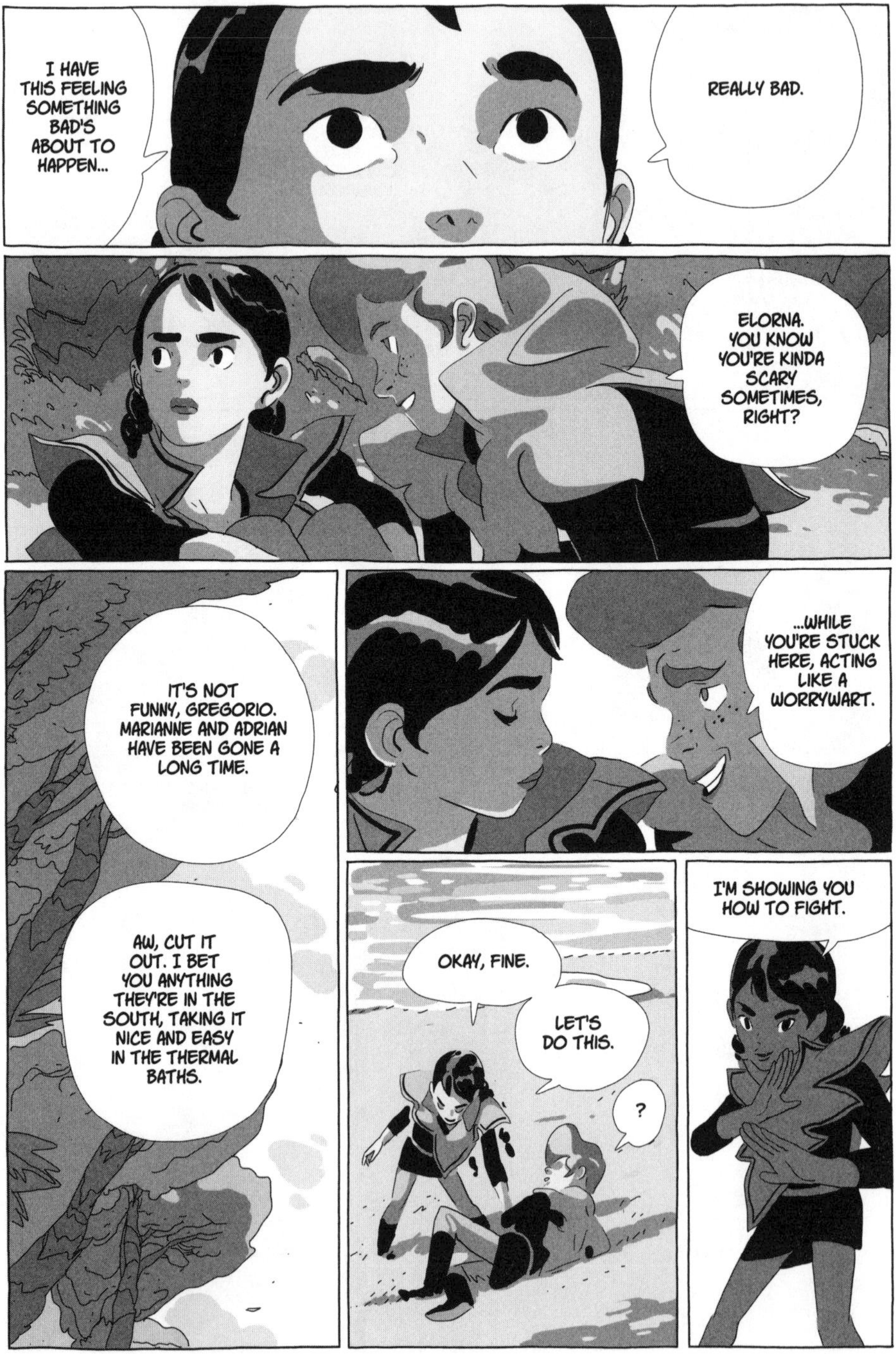
I HAVE THIS FEELING SOMETHING BAD'S ABOUT TO HAPPEN...
REALLY BAD.
ELORNA. YOU KNOW YOU'RE KINDA SCARY SOMETIMES, RIGHT?
IT'S NOT FUNNY, GREGORIO. MARIANNE AND ADRIAN HAVE BEEN GONE A LONG TIME.
AW, CUT IT OUT. I BET YOU ANYTHING THEY'RE IN THE SOUTH, TAKING IT NICE AND EASY IN THE THERMAL BATHS.
...WHILE YOU'RE STUCK HERE, ACTING LIKE A WORRYWART.
OKAY, FINE.
LET'S DO THIS.
?
I'M SHOWING YOU HOW TO FIGHT.

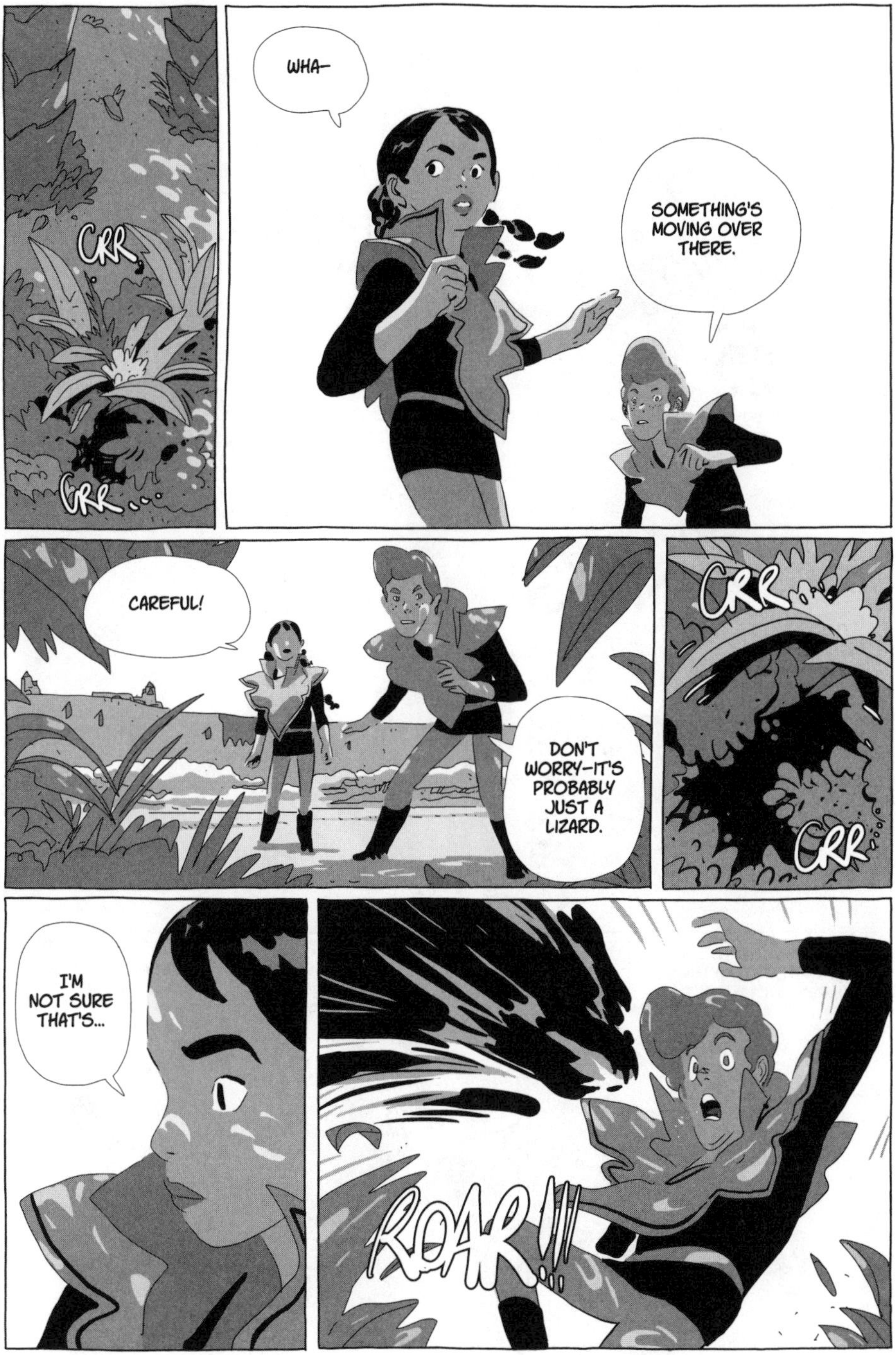

CRR
CRR...
WHA-
SOMETHING'S MOVING OVER THERE.
CAREFUL!
DON'T WORRY–IT'S PROBABLY JUST A LIZARD.
CRR
CRR
I'M NOT SURE THAT'S...
ROAR!!!

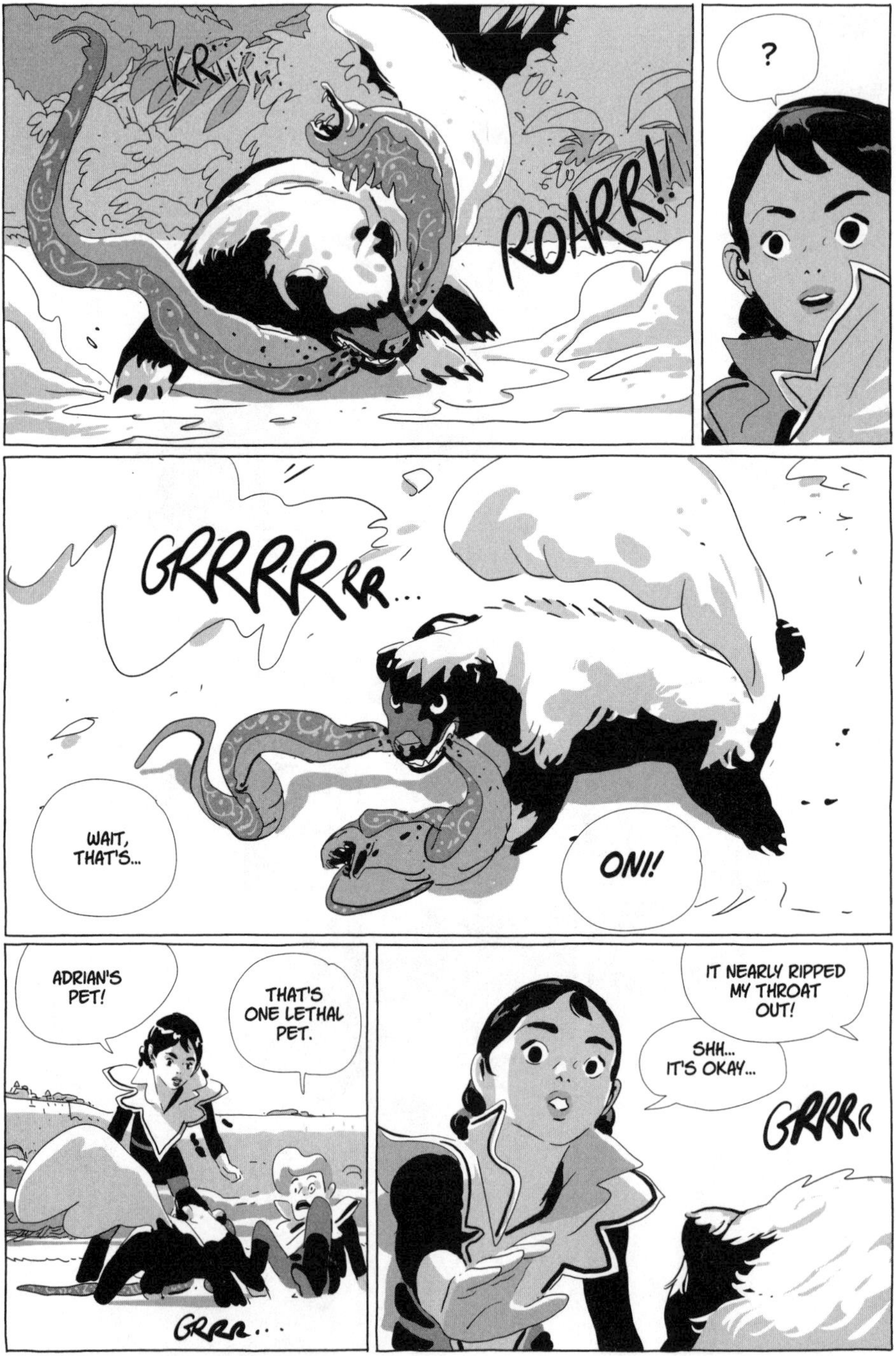
KRIIK...
ROARR!!
?
GRRRRRR...
WAIT, THAT'S...
ONI!
ADRIAN'S PET!
THAT'S ONE LETHAL PET.
GRRR...
IT NEARLY RIPPED MY THROAT OUT!
SHH... IT'S OKAY...
GRRRR

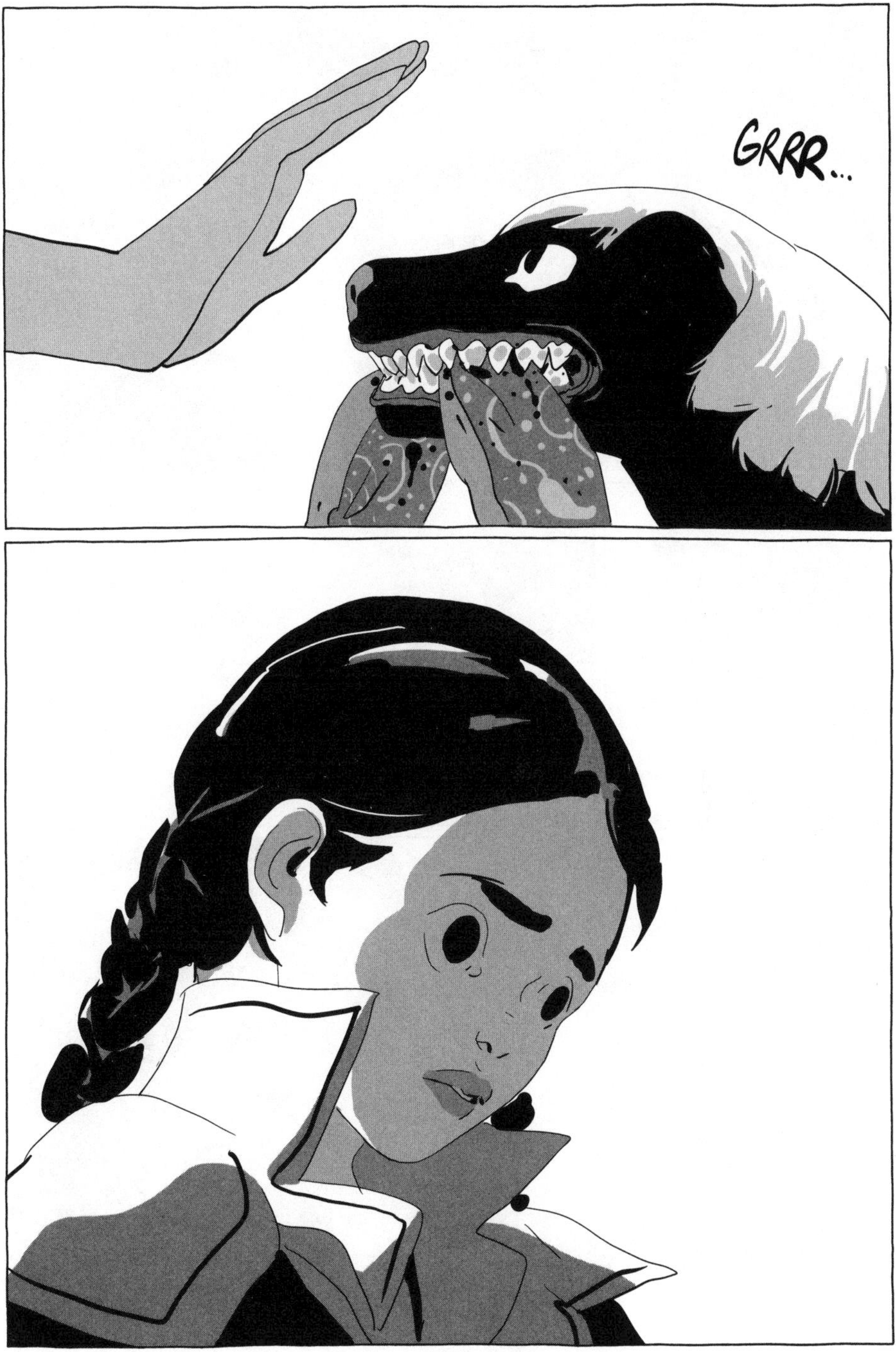
GRRR...

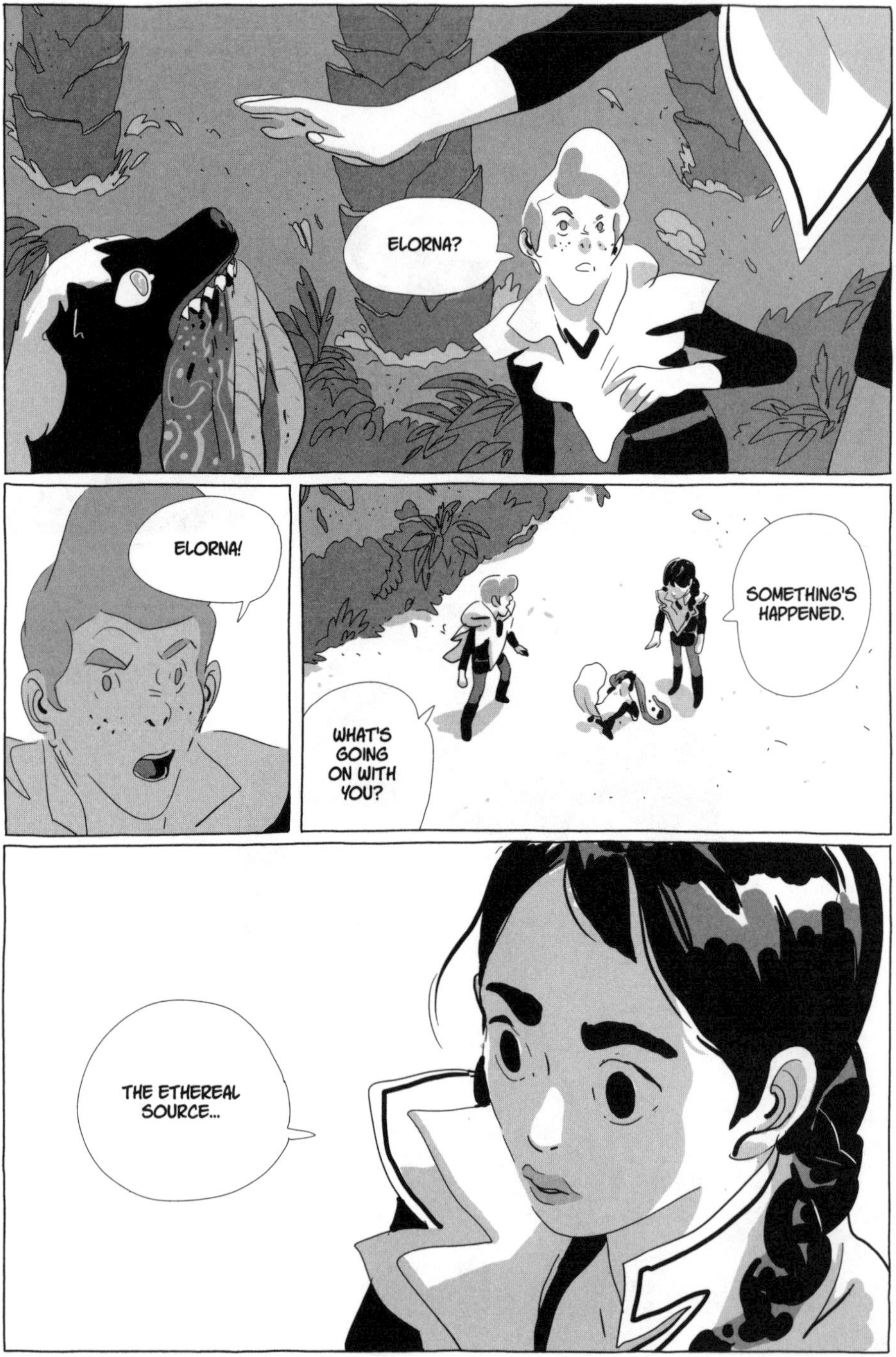
ELORNA?
ELORNA!
SOMETHING'S HAPPENED.
WHAT'S GOING ON WITH YOU?
THE ETHEREAL SOURCE...

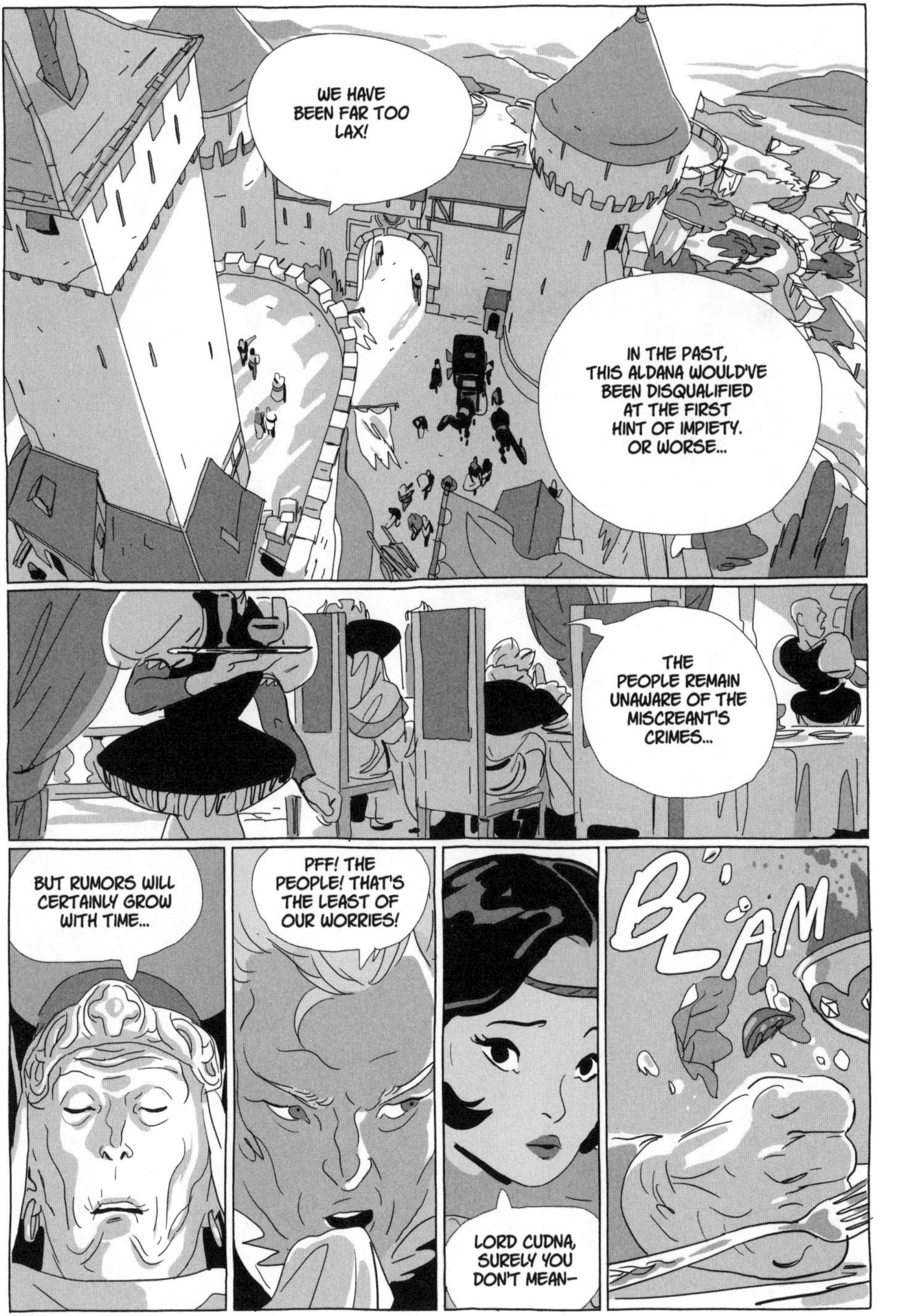
WE HAVE BEEN FAR TOO LAX!
IN THE PAST, THIS ALDANA WOULD'VE BEEN DISQUALIFIED AT THE FIRST HINT OF IMPIETY. OR WORSE...
THE PEOPLE REMAIN UNAWARE OF THE MISCREANT'S CRIMES...
BUT RUMORS WILL CERTAINLY GROW WITH TIME...
PFF! THE PEOPLE! THAT'S THE LEAST OF OUR WORRIES!
LORD CUDNA, SURELY YOU DON'T MEAN—
BLAM

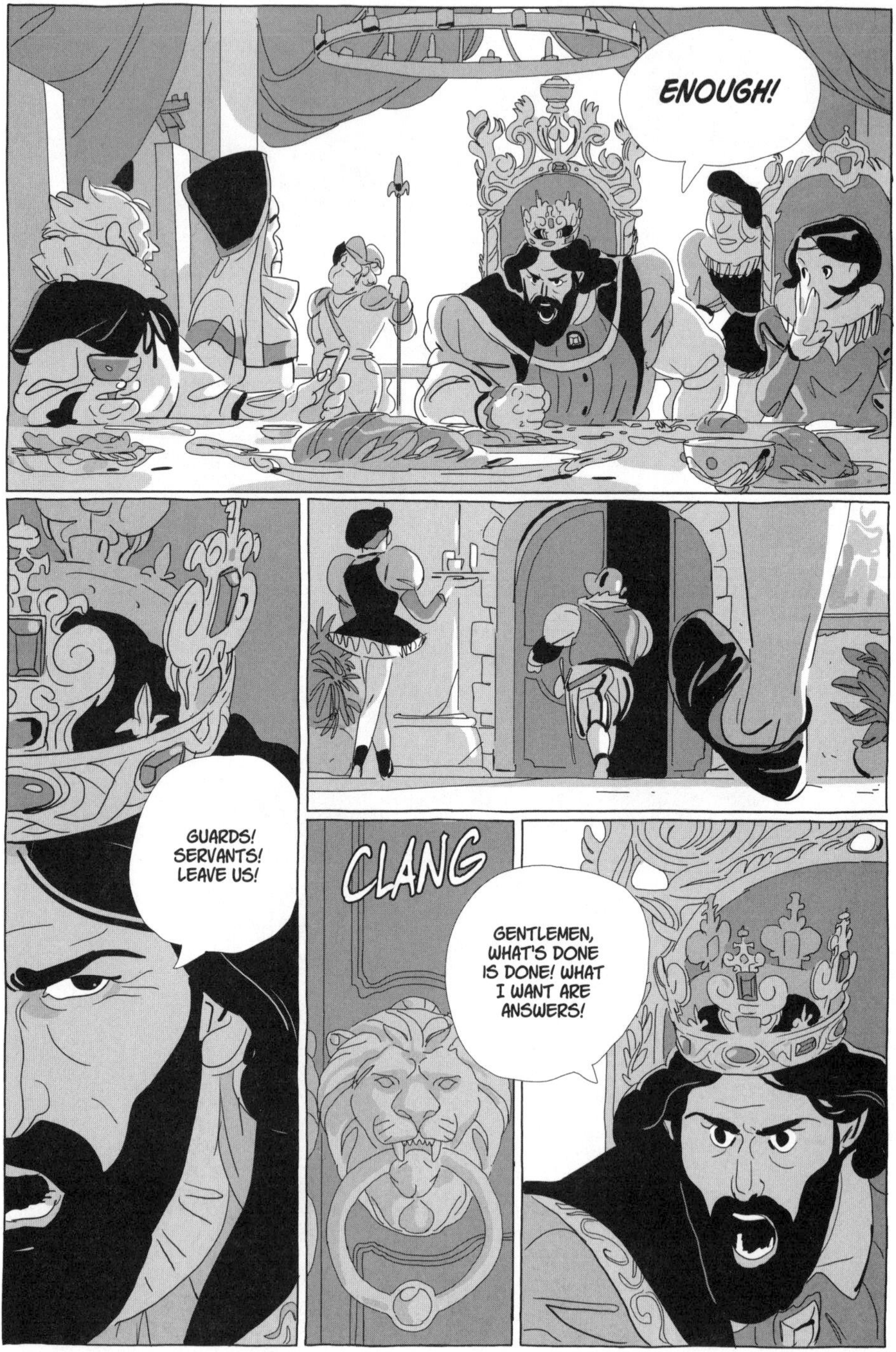
ENOUGH!
GUARDS! SERVANTS! LEAVE US!
CLANG
GENTLEMEN, WHAT'S DONE IS DONE! WHAT I WANT ARE ANSWERS!

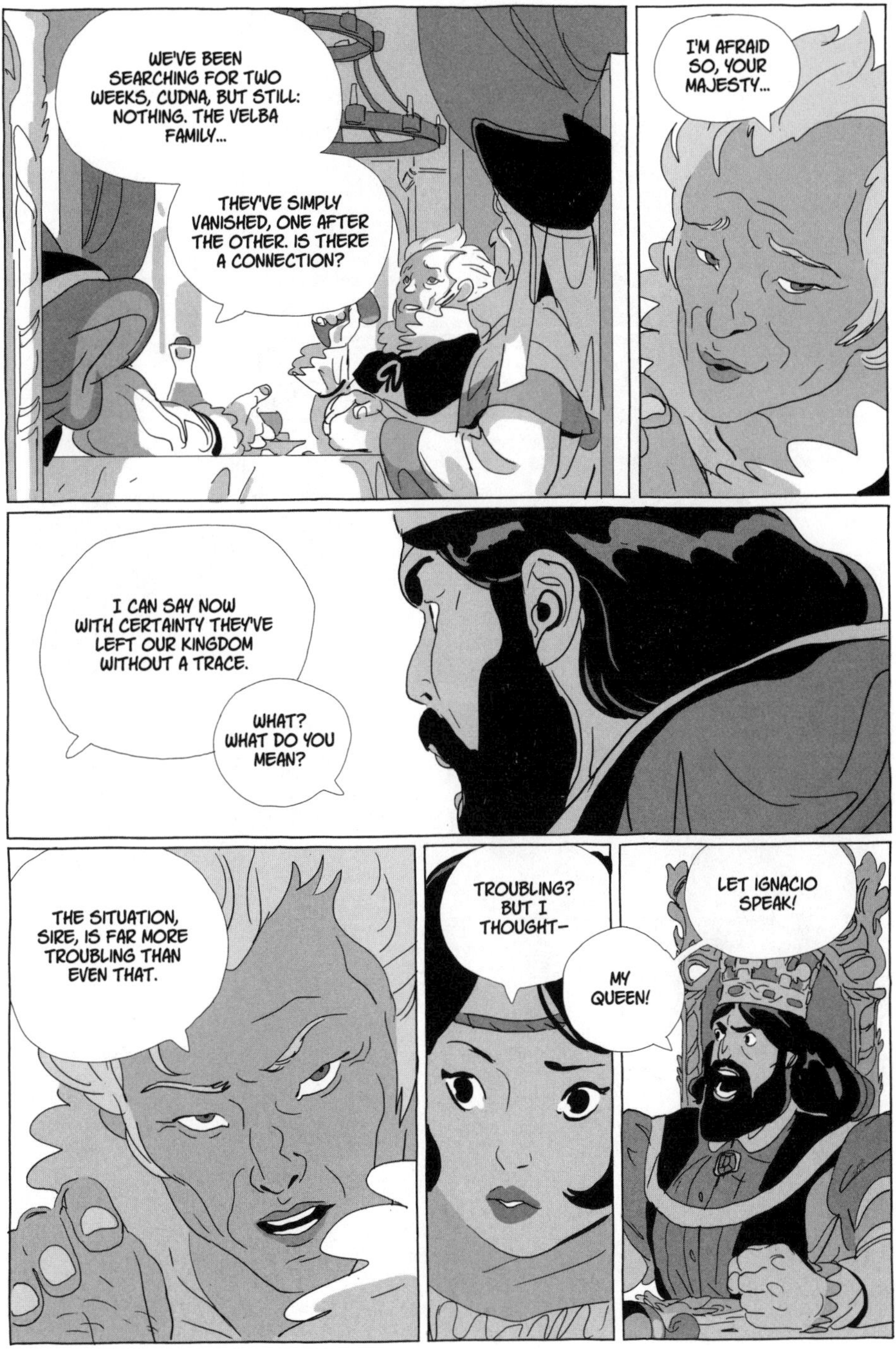
WE'VE BEEN SEARCHING FOR TWO WEEKS, CUDNA, BUT STILL: NOTHING. THE VELBA FAMILY...
THEY'VE SIMPLY VANISHED, ONE AFTER THE OTHER. IS THERE A CONNECTION?
I'M AFRAID SO, YOUR MAJESTY...
I CAN SAY NOW WITH CERTAINTY THEY'VE LEFT OUR KINGDOM WITHOUT A TRACE.
WHAT? WHAT DO YOU MEAN?
THE SITUATION, SIRE, IS FAR MORE TROUBLING THAN EVEN THAT.
TROUBLING? BUT I THOUGHT-
MY QUEEN!
LET IGNACIO SPEAK!

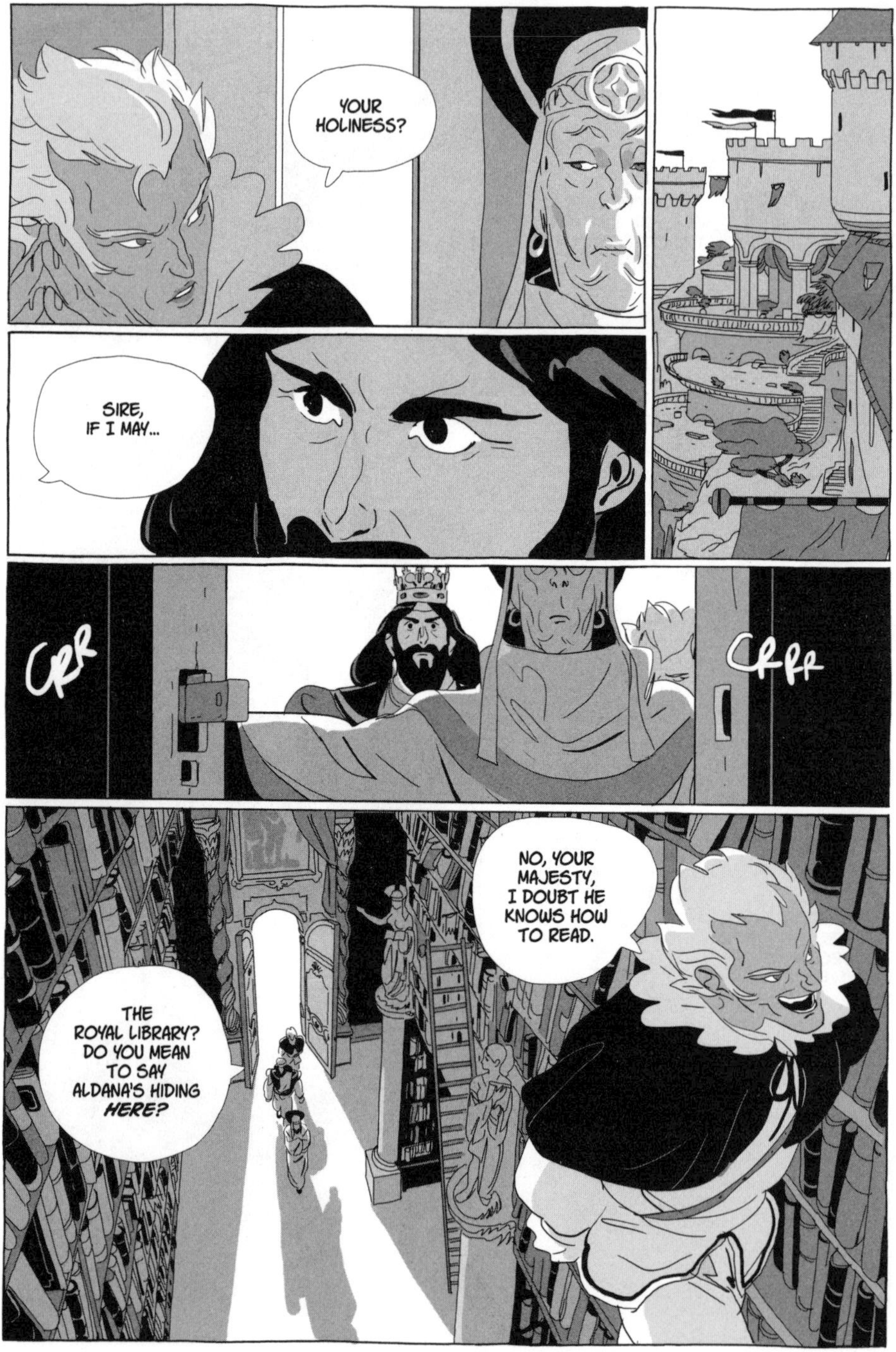
YOUR HOLINESS?
SIRE, IF I MAY...
CRR
CRRR
THE ROYAL LIBRARY? DO YOU MEAN TO SAY ALDANA'S HIDING ***HERE?***
NO, YOUR MAJESTY, I DOUBT HE KNOWS HOW TO READ.

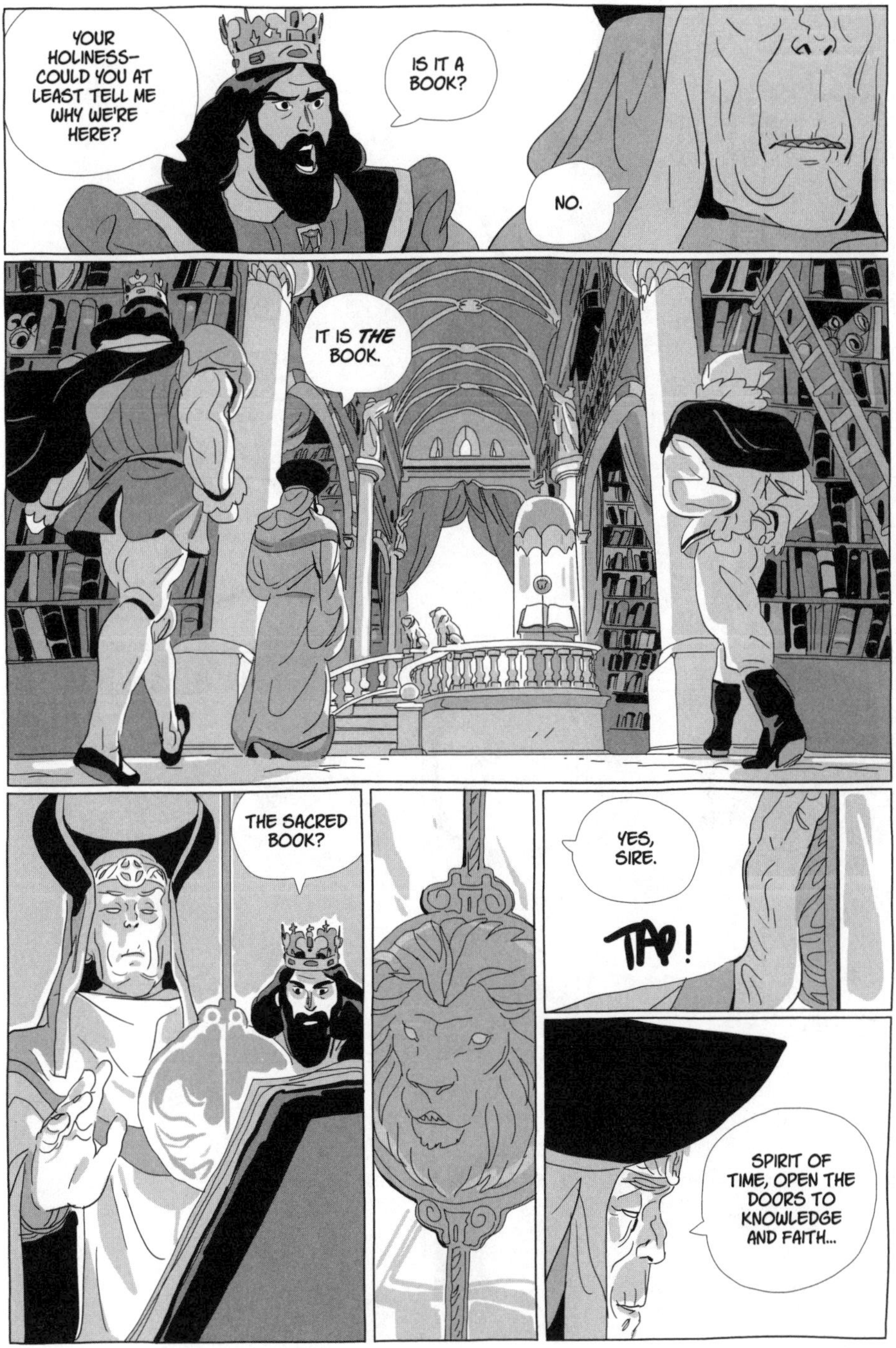
YOUR HOLINESS— COULD YOU AT LEAST TELL ME WHY WE'RE HERE?
IS IT A BOOK?
NO.
IT IS *THE* BOOK.
THE SACRED BOOK?
YES, SIRE.
TAP!
SPIRIT OF TIME, OPEN THE DOORS TO KNOWLEDGE AND FAITH...

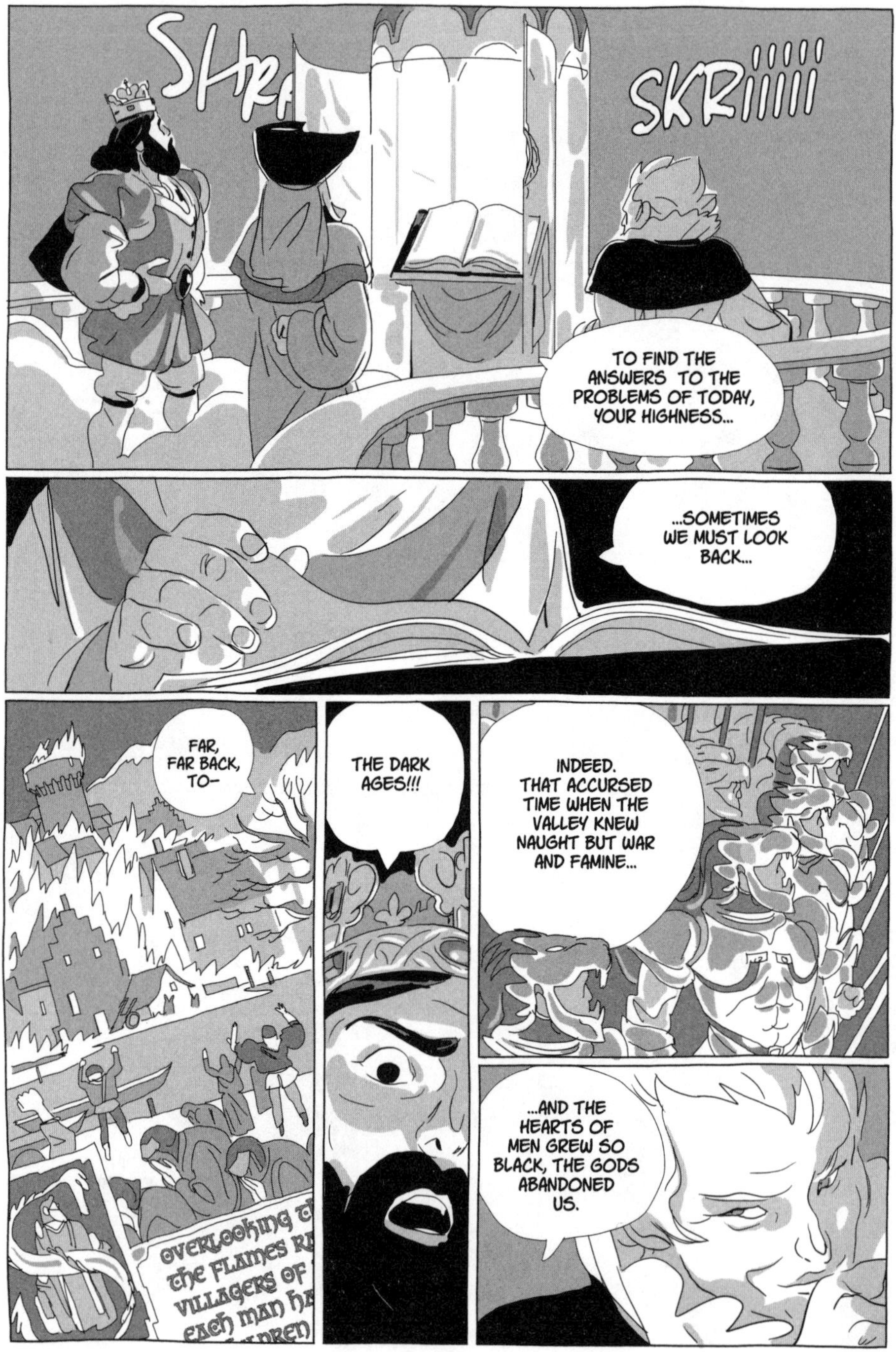
SHRA
SKRIIIIII
TO FIND THE ANSWERS TO THE PROBLEMS OF TODAY, YOUR HIGHNESS...
...SOMETIMES WE MUST LOOK BACK...
FAR, FAR BACK, TO–
OVERLOOKING
THE FLAMES
VILLAGERS OF
EACH MAN
THE DARK AGES!!!
INDEED. THAT ACCURSED TIME WHEN THE VALLEY KNEW NAUGHT BUT WAR AND FAMINE...
...AND THE HEARTS OF MEN GREW SO BLACK, THE GODS ABANDONED US.

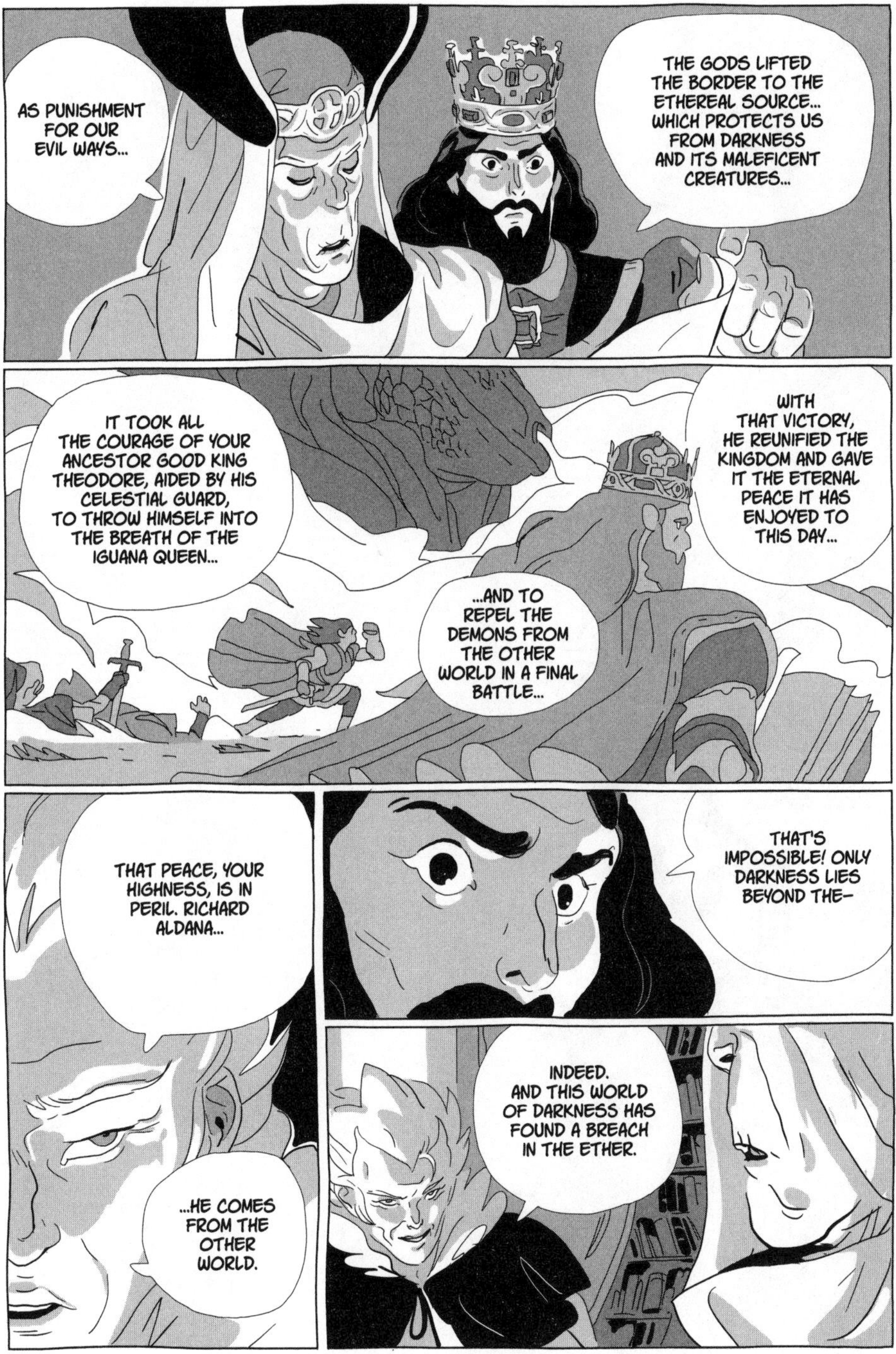

AS PUNISHMENT FOR OUR EVIL WAYS...
THE GODS LIFTED THE BORDER TO THE ETHEREAL SOURCE... WHICH PROTECTS US FROM DARKNESS AND ITS MALEFICENT CREATURES...
IT TOOK ALL THE COURAGE OF YOUR ANCESTOR GOOD KING THEODORE, AIDED BY HIS CELESTIAL GUARD, TO THROW HIMSELF INTO THE BREATH OF THE IGUANA QUEEN...
...AND TO REPEL THE DEMONS FROM THE OTHER WORLD IN A FINAL BATTLE...
WITH THAT VICTORY, HE REUNIFIED THE KINGDOM AND GAVE IT THE ETERNAL PEACE IT HAS ENJOYED TO THIS DAY...
THAT PEACE, YOUR HIGHNESS, IS IN PERIL. RICHARD ALDANA...
...HE COMES FROM THE OTHER WORLD.
THAT'S IMPOSSIBLE! ONLY DARKNESS LIES BEYOND THE–
INDEED. AND THIS WORLD OF DARKNESS HAS FOUND A BREACH IN THE ETHER.

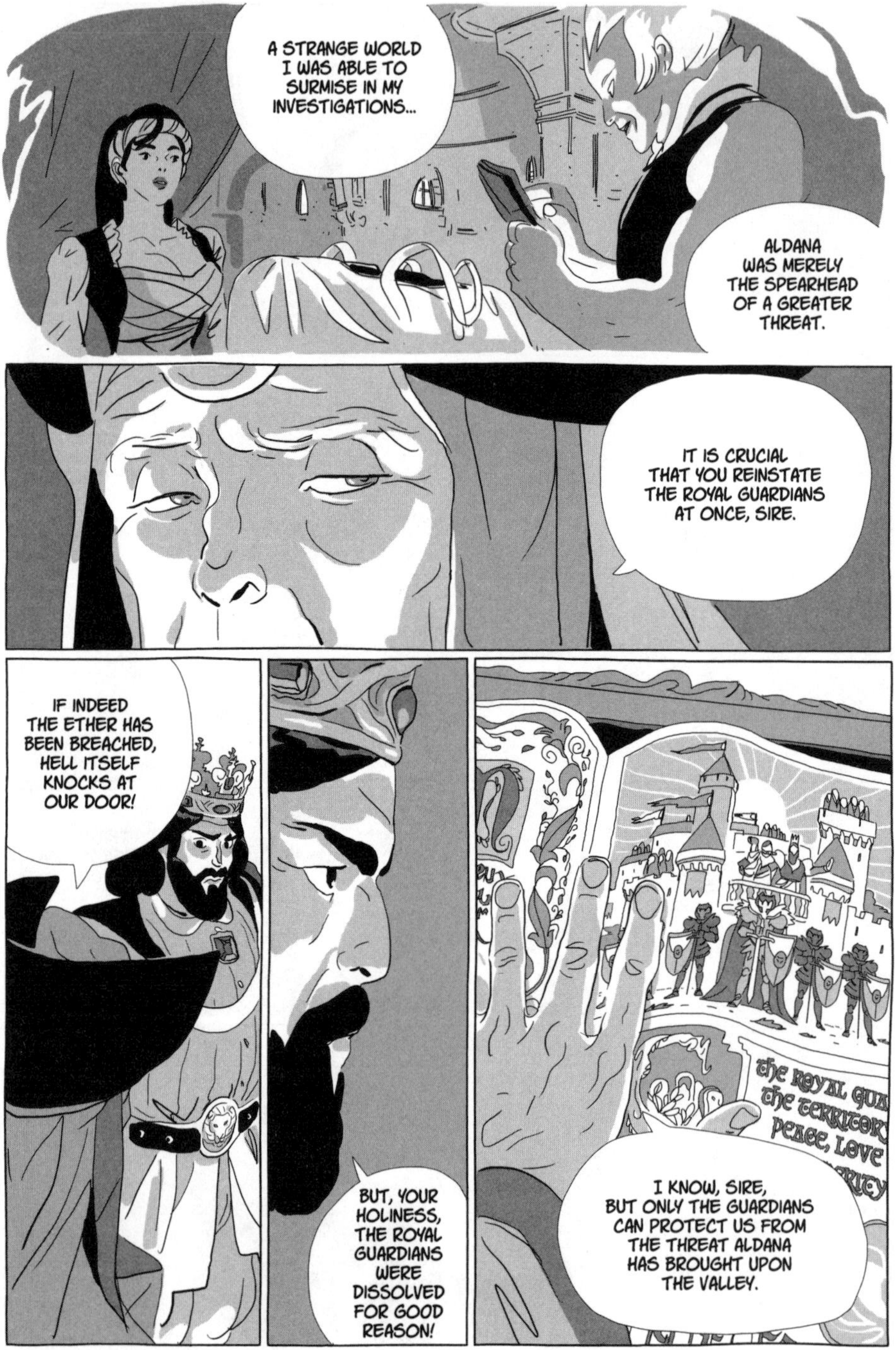
A STRANGE WORLD I WAS ABLE TO SURMISE IN MY INVESTIGATIONS...
ALDANA WAS MERELY THE SPEARHEAD OF A GREATER THREAT.
IT IS CRUCIAL THAT YOU REINSTATE THE ROYAL GUARDIANS AT ONCE, SIRE.
IF INDEED THE ETHER HAS BEEN BREACHED, HELL ITSELF KNOCKS AT OUR DOOR!
BUT, YOUR HOLINESS, THE ROYAL GUARDIANS WERE DISSOLVED FOR GOOD REASON!
I KNOW, SIRE, BUT ONLY THE GUARDIANS CAN PROTECT US FROM THE THREAT ALDANA HAS BROUGHT UPON THE VALLEY.

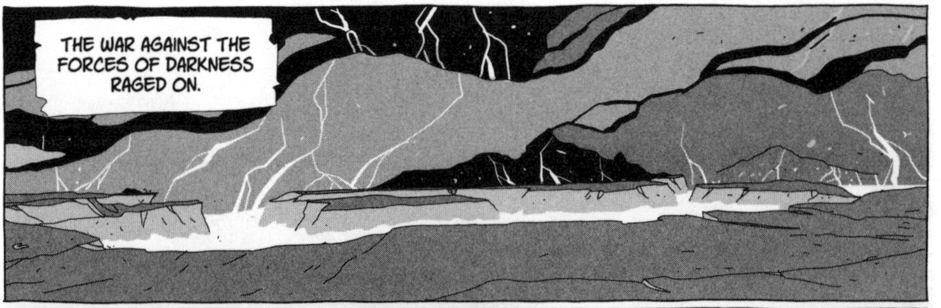
THE WAR AGAINST THE FORCES OF DARKNESS RAGED ON.
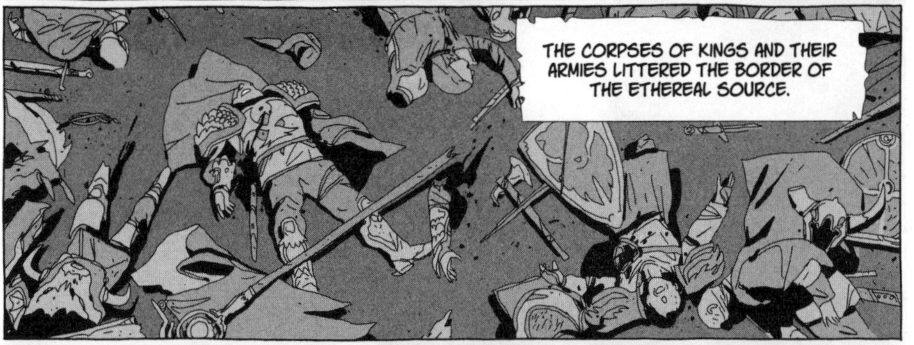
THE CORPSES OF KINGS AND THEIR ARMIES LITTERED THE BORDER OF THE ETHEREAL SOURCE.
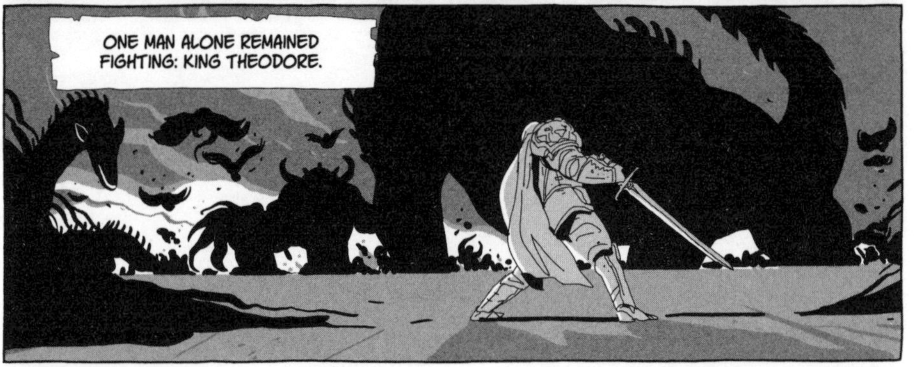
ONE MAN ALONE REMAINED FIGHTING: KING THEODORE.
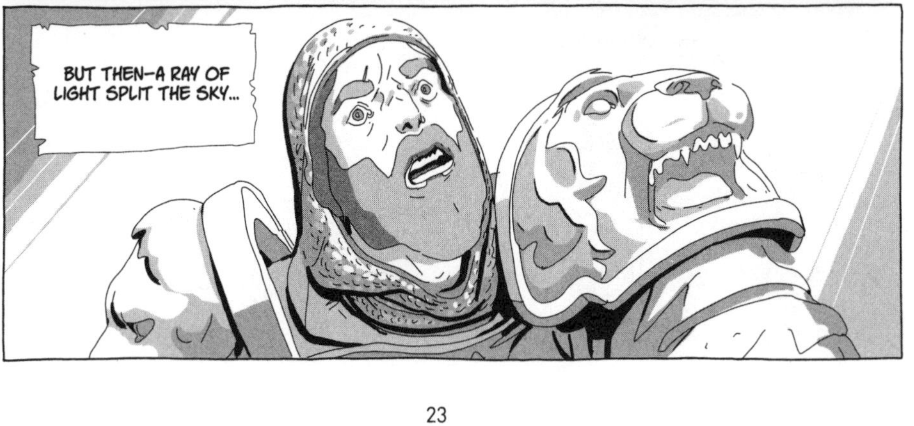
BUT THEN—A RAY OF LIGHT SPLIT THE SKY...

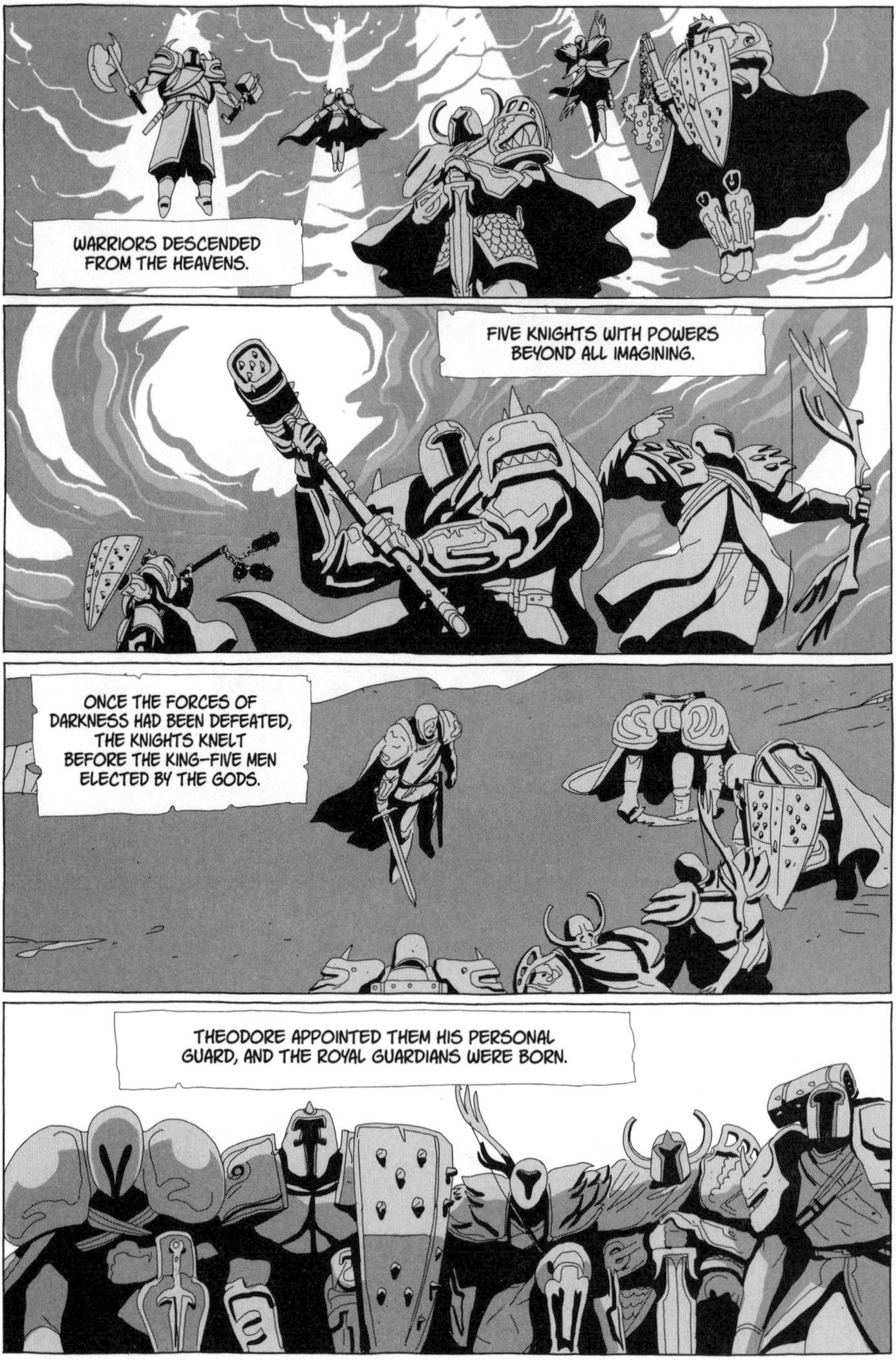
WARRIORS DESCENDED FROM THE HEAVENS.
FIVE KNIGHTS WITH POWERS BEYOND ALL IMAGINING.
ONCE THE FORCES OF DARKNESS HAD BEEN DEFEATED, THE KNIGHTS KNELT BEFORE THE KING—FIVE MEN ELECTED BY THE GODS.
THEODORE APPOINTED THEM HIS PERSONAL GUARD, AND THE ROYAL GUARDIANS WERE BORN.

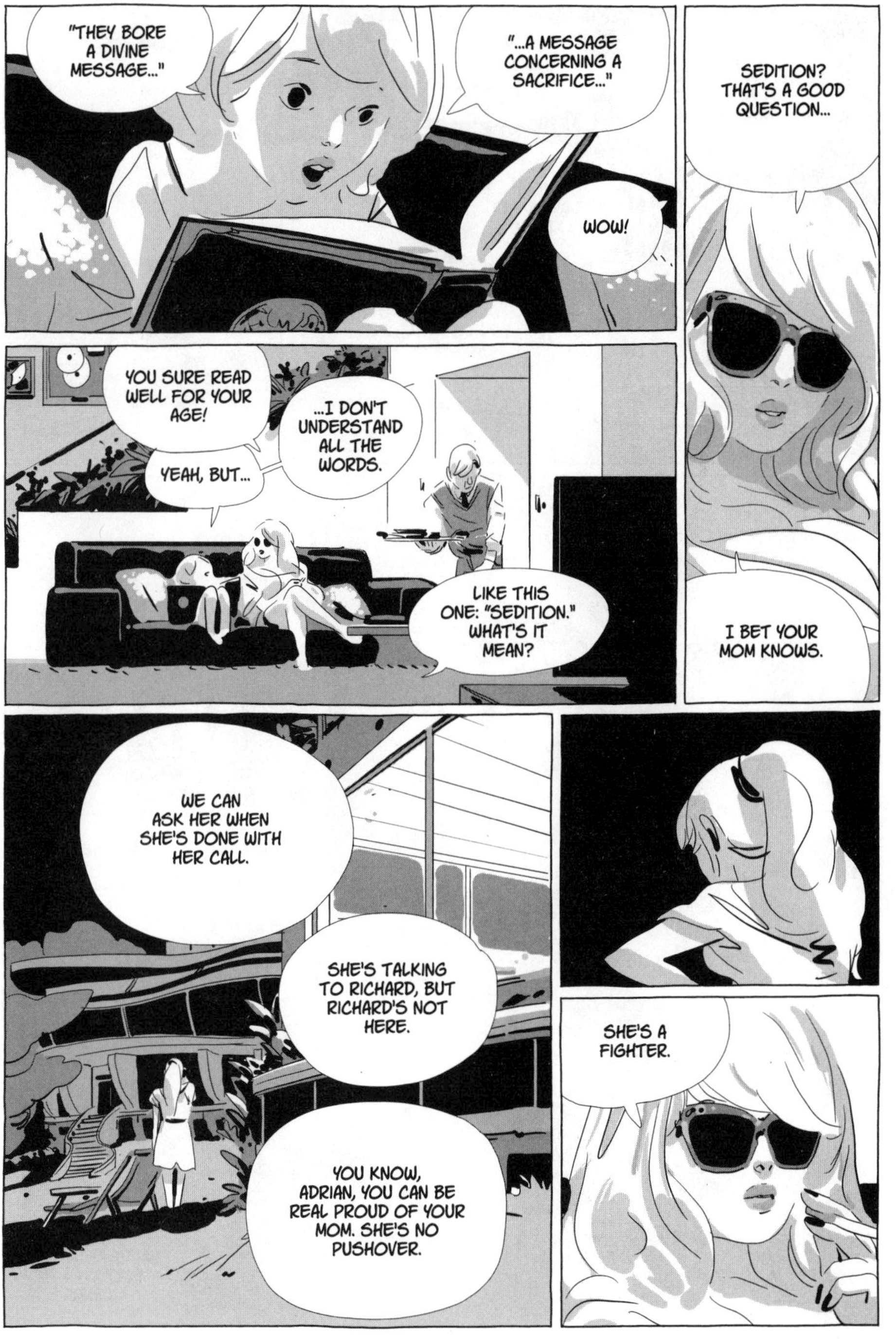
"THEY BORE A DIVINE MESSAGE..."
"...A MESSAGE CONCERNING A SACRIFICE..."
WOW!
SEDITION? THAT'S A GOOD QUESTION...
YOU SURE READ WELL FOR YOUR AGE!
YEAH, BUT...
...I DON'T UNDERSTAND ALL THE WORDS.
LIKE THIS ONE: "SEDITION." WHAT'S IT MEAN?
I BET YOUR MOM KNOWS.
WE CAN ASK HER WHEN SHE'S DONE WITH HER CALL.
SHE'S TALKING TO RICHARD, BUT RICHARD'S NOT HERE.
YOU KNOW, ADRIAN, YOU CAN BE REAL PROUD OF YOUR MOM. SHE'S NO PUSHOVER.
SHE'S A FIGHTER.

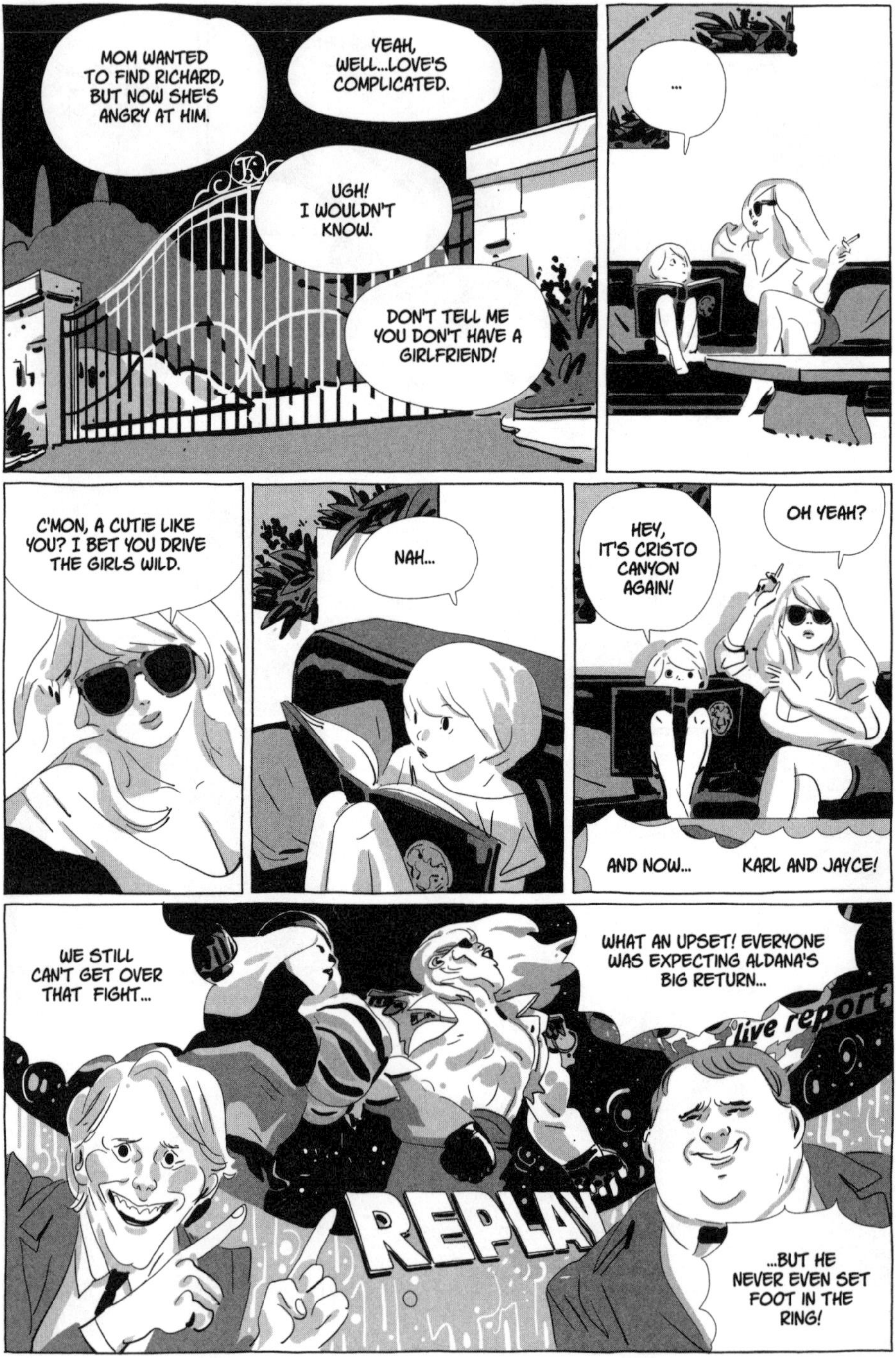
MOM WANTED TO FIND RICHARD, BUT NOW SHE'S ANGRY AT HIM.
YEAH, WELL...LOVE'S COMPLICATED.
UGH! I WOULDN'T KNOW.
DON'T TELL ME YOU DON'T HAVE A GIRLFRIEND!
...
C'MON, A CUTIE LIKE YOU? I BET YOU DRIVE THE GIRLS WILD.
NAH...
HEY, IT'S CRISTO CANYON AGAIN!
OH YEAH?
AND NOW...
KARL AND JAYCE!
WE STILL CAN'T GET OVER THAT FIGHT...
WHAT AN UPSET! EVERYONE WAS EXPECTING ALDANA'S BIG RETURN...
live report
REPLAY
...BUT HE NEVER EVEN SET FOOT IN THE RING!

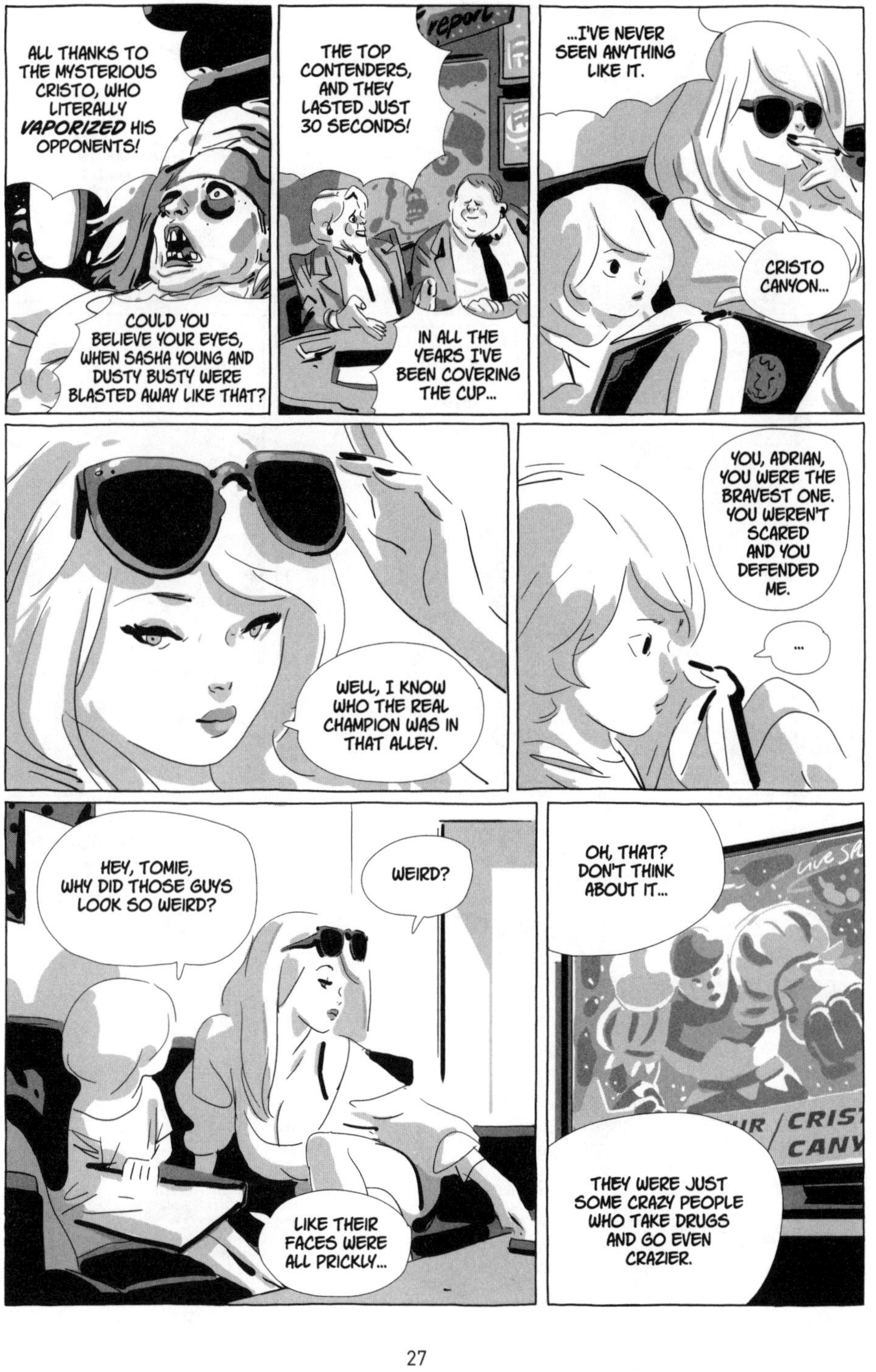
ALL THANKS TO THE MYSTERIOUS CRISTO, WHO LITERALLY ***VAPORIZED*** HIS OPPONENTS!
COULD YOU BELIEVE YOUR EYES, WHEN SASHA YOUNG AND DUSTY BUSTY WERE BLASTED AWAY LIKE THAT?
report
THE TOP CONTENDERS, AND THEY LASTED JUST 30 SECONDS!
IN ALL THE YEARS I'VE BEEN COVERING THE CUP...
...I'VE NEVER SEEN ANYTHING LIKE IT.
CRISTO CANYON...
WELL, I KNOW WHO THE REAL CHAMPION WAS IN THAT ALLEY.
YOU, ADRIAN, YOU WERE THE BRAVEST ONE. YOU WEREN'T SCARED AND YOU DEFENDED ME.
...
HEY, TOMIE, WHY DID THOSE GUYS LOOK SO WEIRD?
WEIRD?
LIKE THEIR FACES WERE ALL PRICKLY...
OH, THAT? DON'T THINK ABOUT IT...
THEY WERE JUST SOME CRAZY PEOPLE WHO TAKE DRUGS AND GO EVEN CRAZIER.

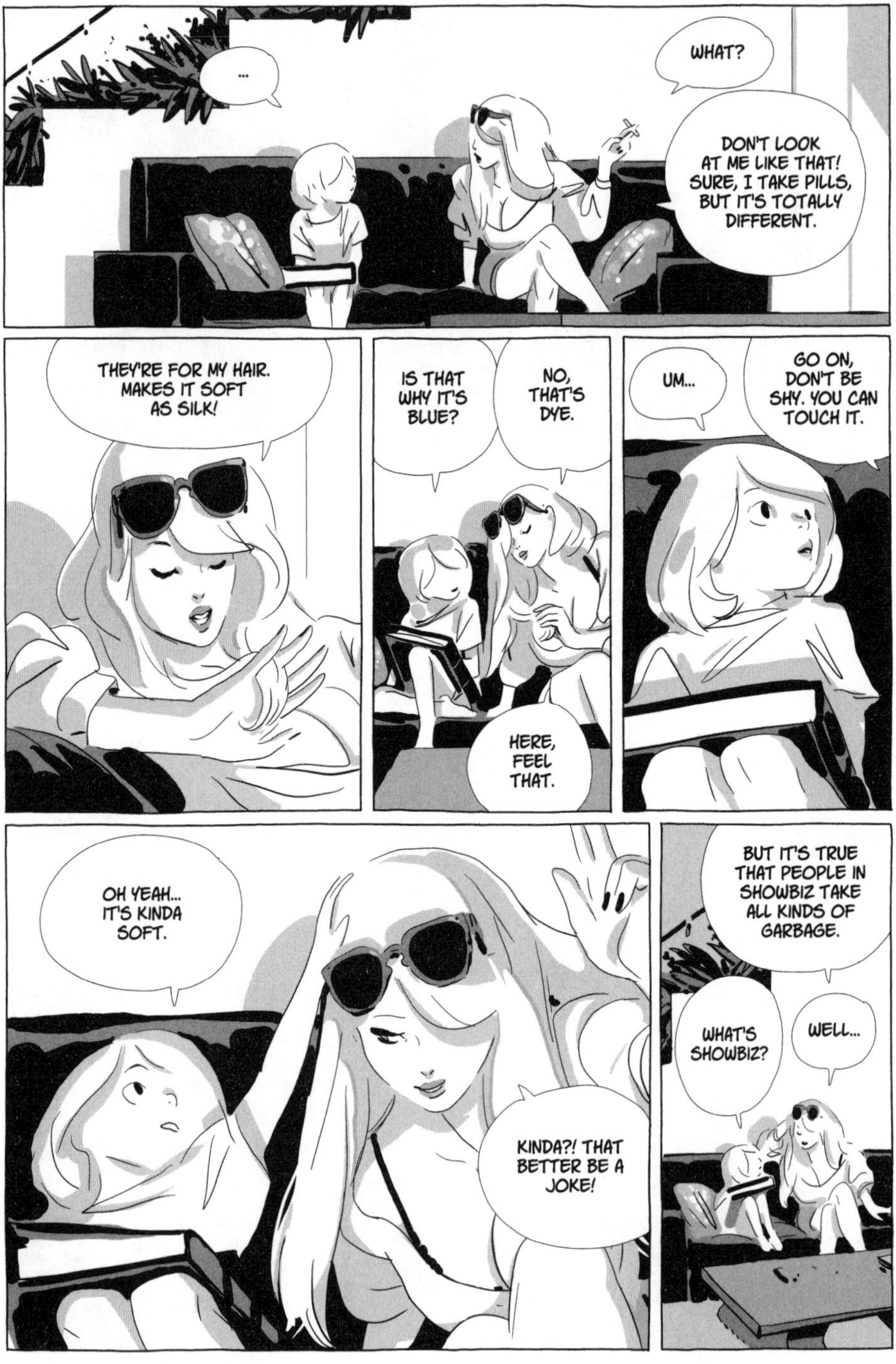
...
WHAT?
DON'T LOOK AT ME LIKE THAT! SURE, I TAKE PILLS, BUT IT'S TOTALLY DIFFERENT.
THEY'RE FOR MY HAIR. MAKES IT SOFT AS SILK!
IS THAT WHY IT'S BLUE?
NO, THAT'S DYE.
HERE, FEEL THAT.
UM...
GO ON, DON'T BE SHY. YOU CAN TOUCH IT.
OH YEAH... IT'S KINDA SOFT.
KINDA?! THAT BETTER BE A JOKE!
BUT IT'S TRUE THAT PEOPLE IN SHOWBIZ TAKE ALL KINDS OF GARBAGE.
WHAT'S SHOWBIZ?
WELL...

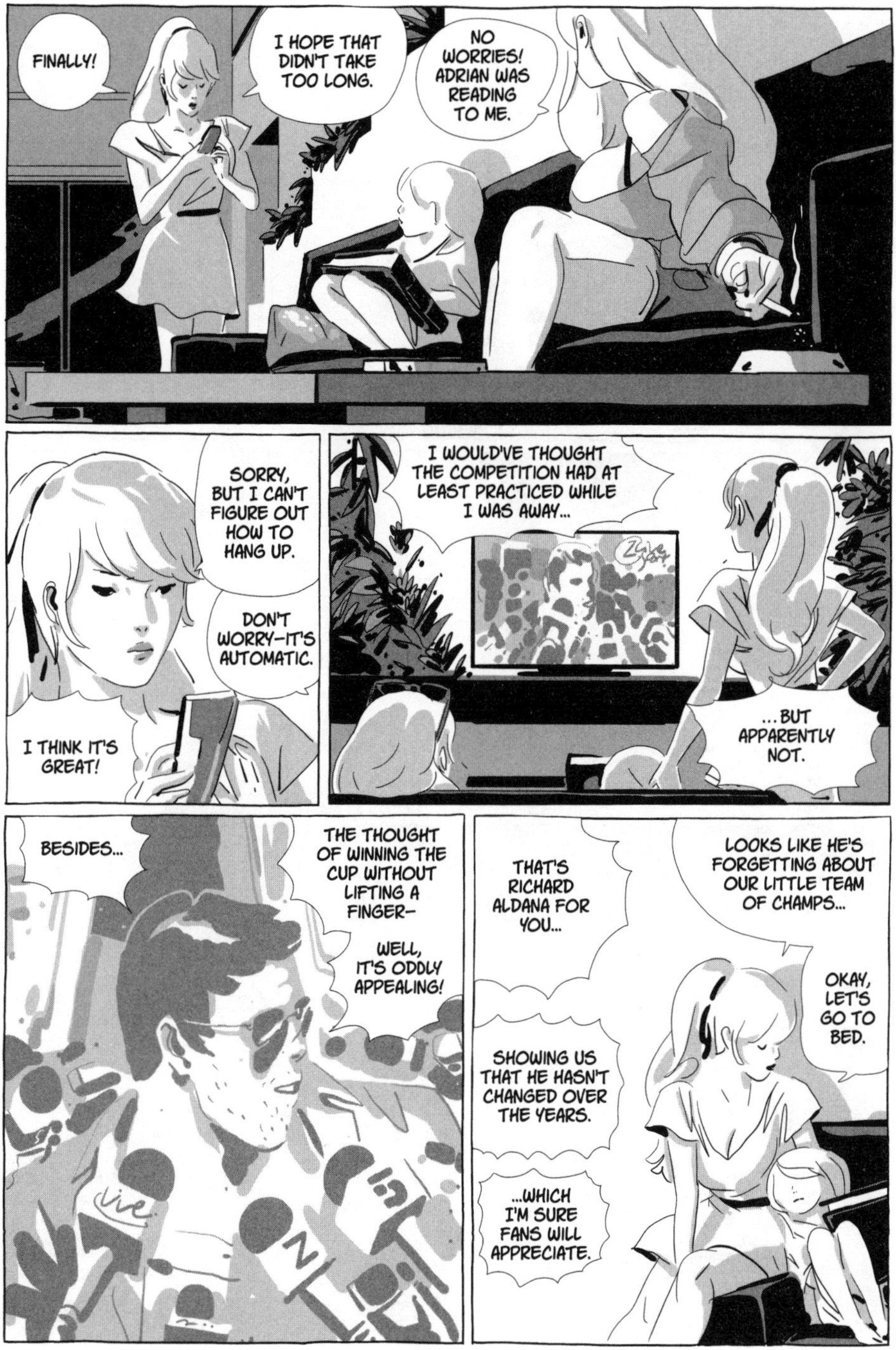
FINALLY!
I HOPE THAT DIDN'T TAKE TOO LONG.
NO WORRIES! ADRIAN WAS READING TO ME.
SORRY, BUT I CAN'T FIGURE OUT HOW TO HANG UP.
DON'T WORRY–IT'S AUTOMATIC.
I THINK IT'S GREAT!
I WOULD'VE THOUGHT THE COMPETITION HAD AT LEAST PRACTICED WHILE I WAS AWAY...
...BUT APPARENTLY NOT.
BESIDES...
THE THOUGHT OF WINNING THE CUP WITHOUT LIFTING A FINGER–
WELL, IT'S ODDLY APPEALING!
THAT'S RICHARD ALDANA FOR YOU...
LOOKS LIKE HE'S FORGETTING ABOUT OUR LITTLE TEAM OF CHAMPS...
SHOWING US THAT HE HASN'T CHANGED OVER THE YEARS.
...WHICH I'M SURE FANS WILL APPRECIATE.
OKAY, LET'S GO TO BED.

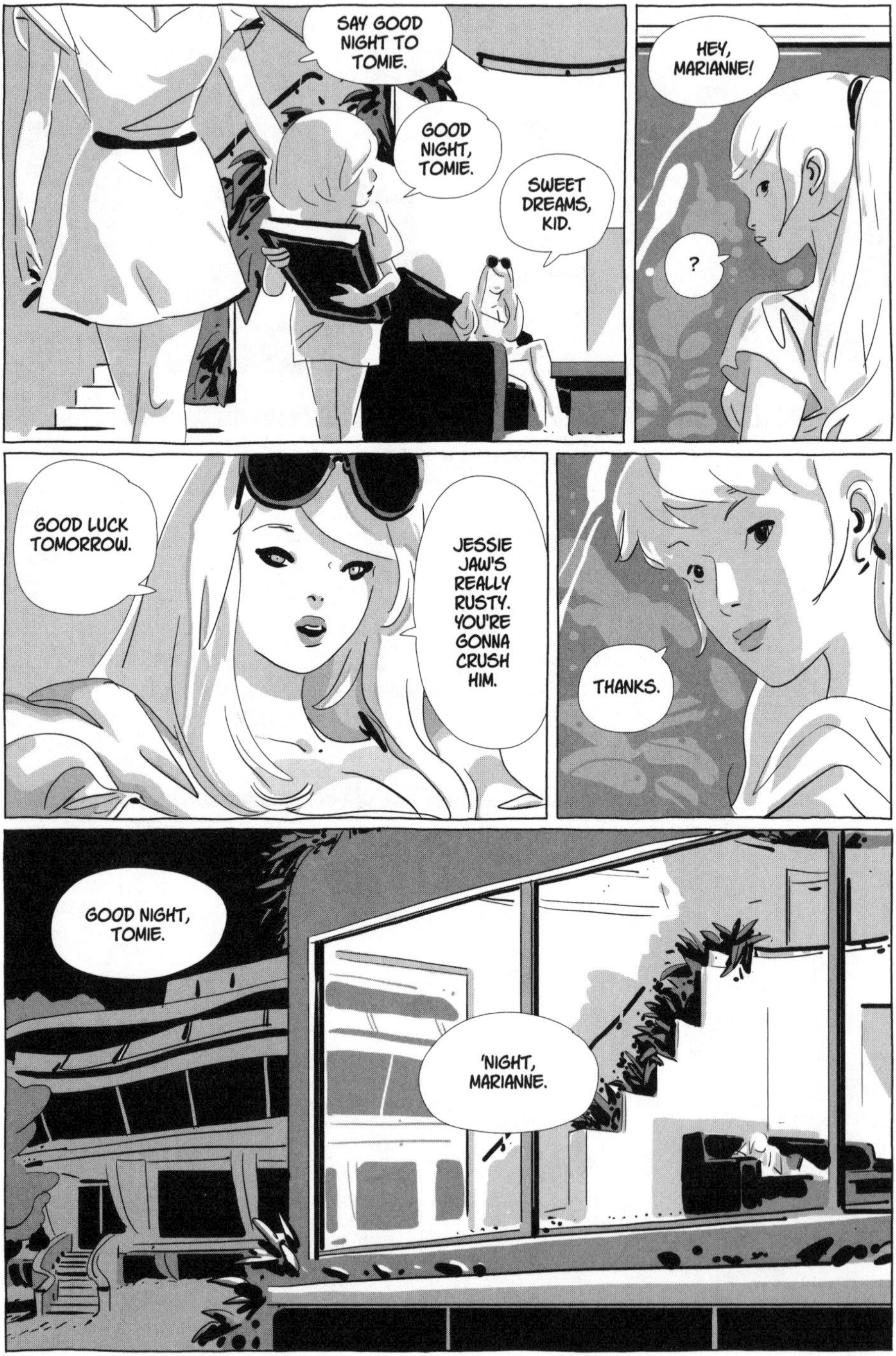
SAY GOOD NIGHT TO TOMIE.
GOOD NIGHT, TOMIE.
SWEET DREAMS, KID.
HEY, MARIANNE!
?
GOOD LUCK TOMORROW.
JESSIE JAW'S REALLY RUSTY. YOU'RE GONNA CRUSH HIM.
THANKS.
GOOD NIGHT, TOMIE.
'NIGHT, MARIANNE.

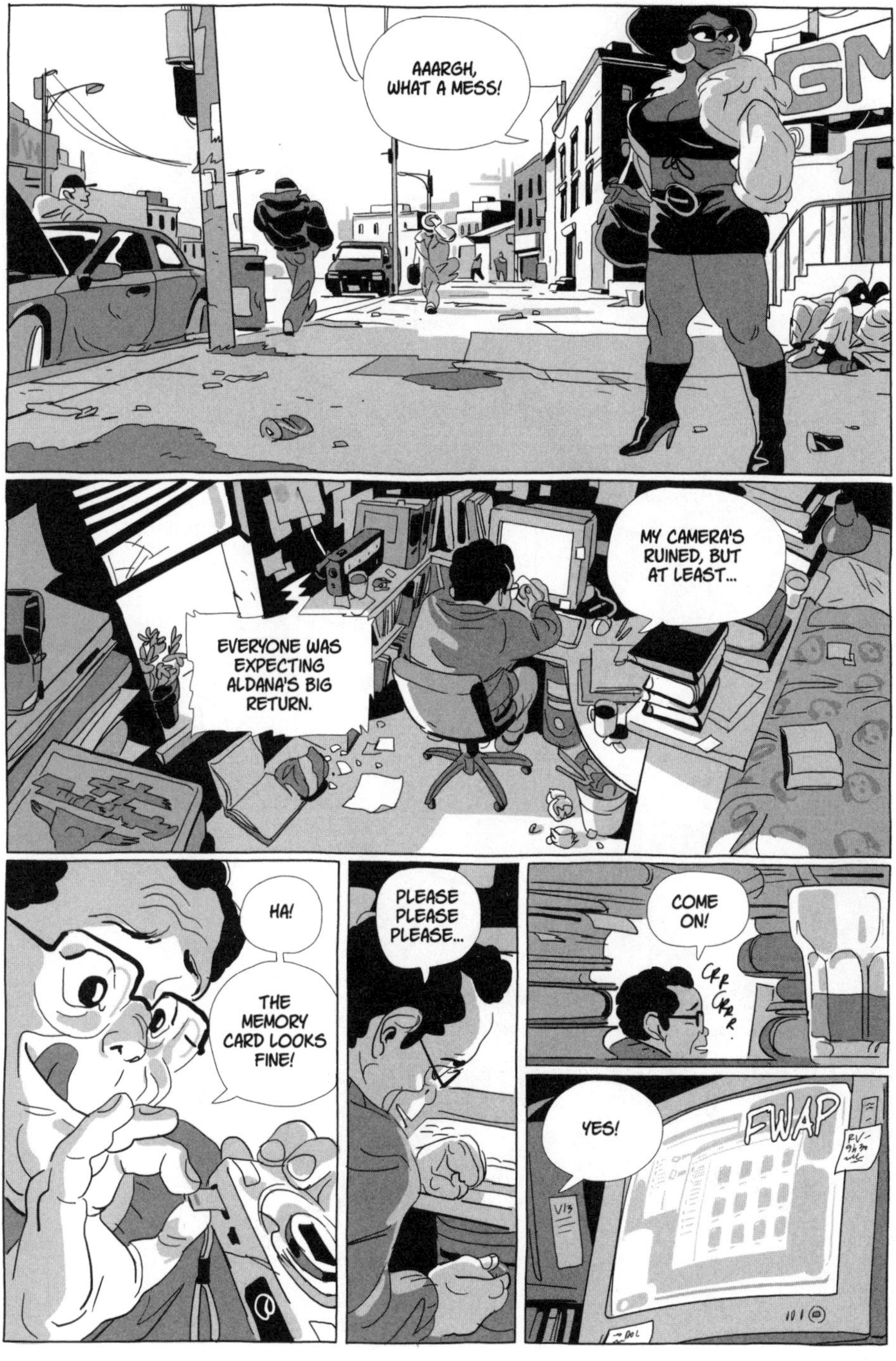
AAARGH, WHAT A MESS!
EVERYONE WAS EXPECTING ALDANA'S BIG RETURN.
MY CAMERA'S RUINED, BUT AT LEAST...
HA!
THE MEMORY CARD LOOKS FINE!
PLEASE PLEASE PLEASE...
COME ON!
CRR CRR
YES!
FWAP

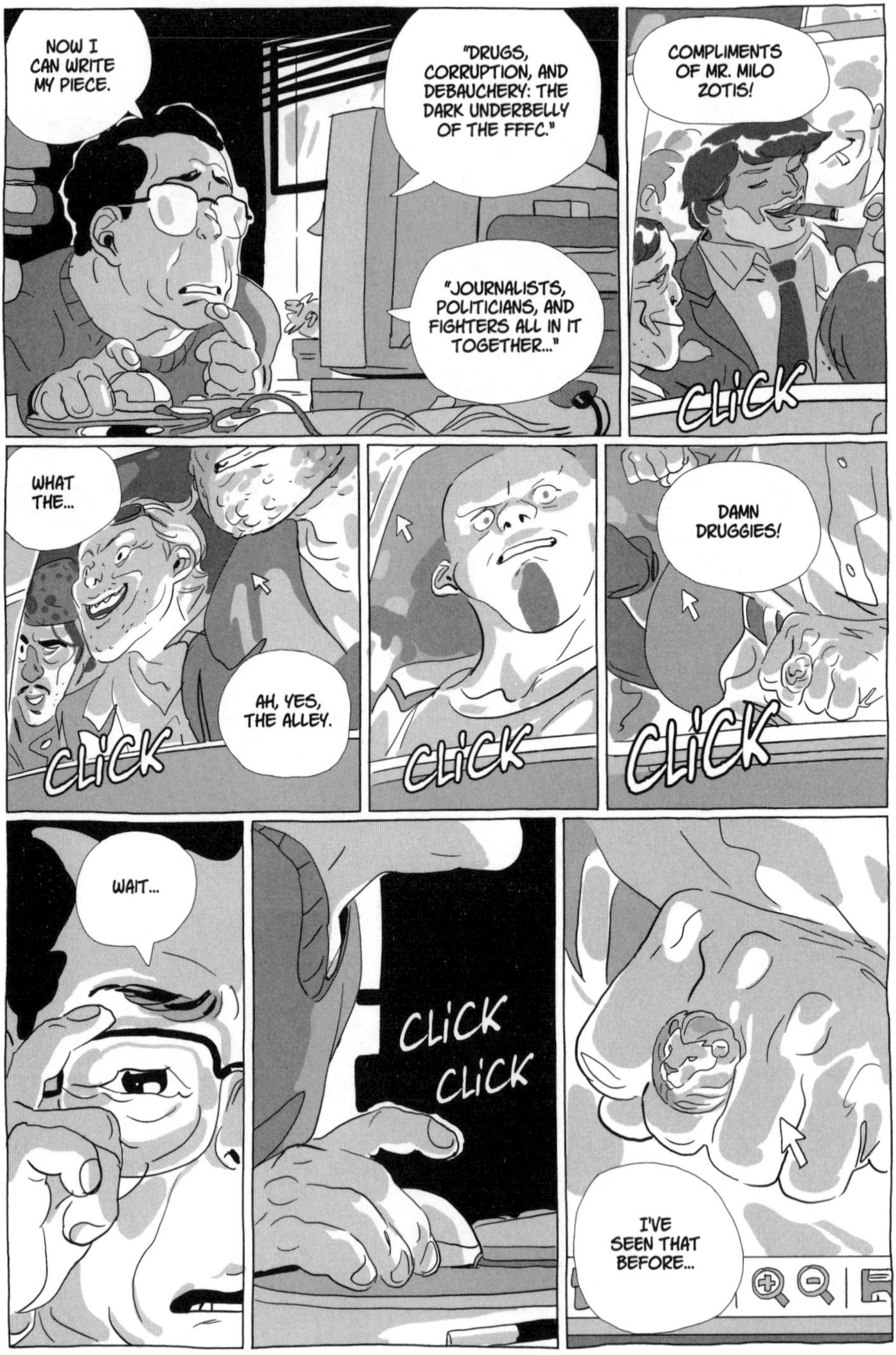
NOW I CAN WRITE MY PIECE.
"DRUGS, CORRUPTION, AND DEBAUCHERY: THE DARK UNDERBELLY OF THE FFFC."
"JOURNALISTS, POLITICIANS, AND FIGHTERS ALL IN IT TOGETHER..."
COMPLIMENTS OF MR. MILO ZOTIS!
CLICK
WHAT THE...
AH, YES, THE ALLEY.
CLICK
CLICK
DAMN DRUGGIES!
CLICK
WAIT...
CLICK
CLICK
I'VE SEEN THAT BEFORE...

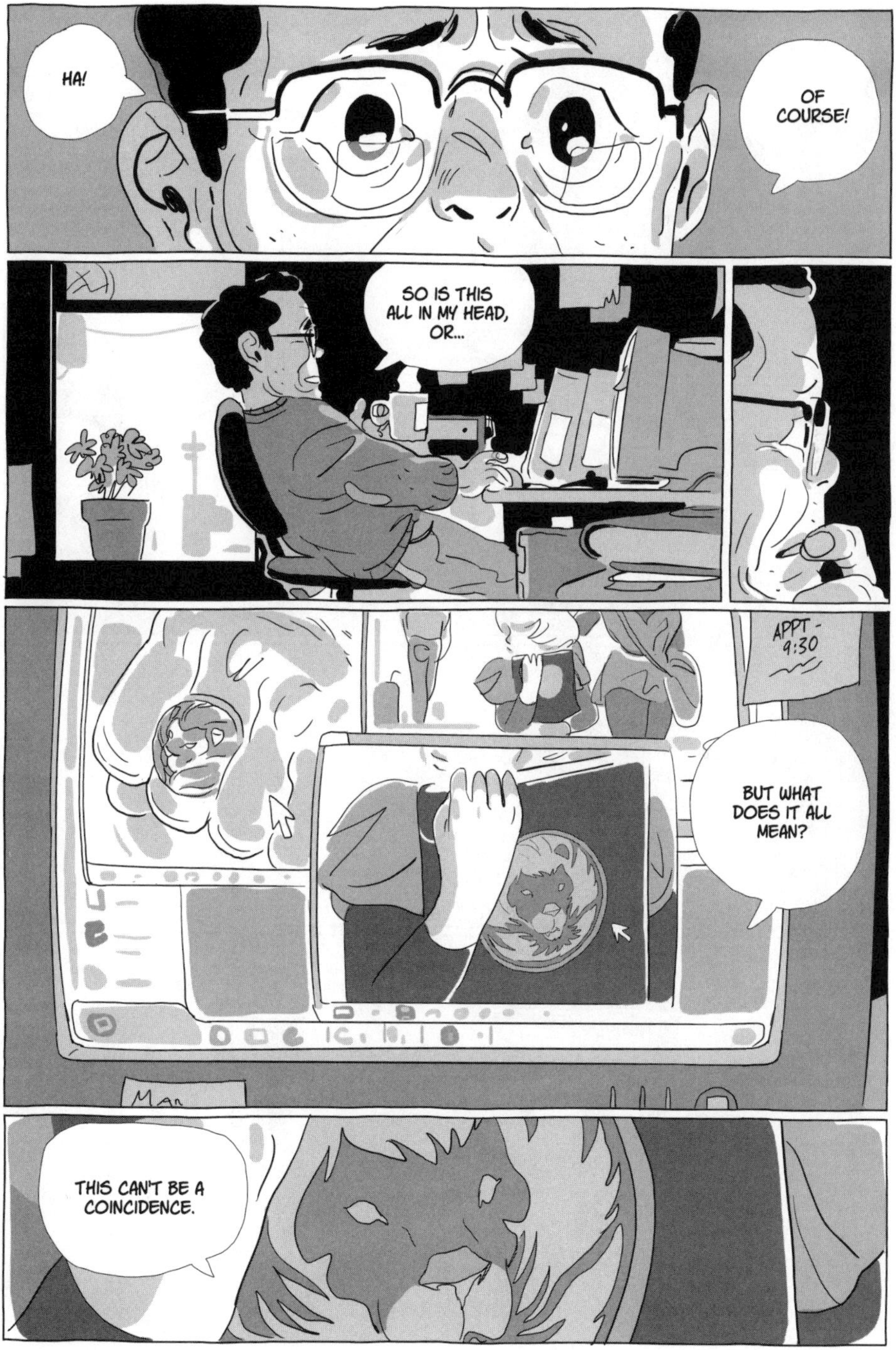
HA!
OF COURSE!
SO IS THIS ALL IN MY HEAD, OR...
APPT - 9:30
BUT WHAT DOES IT ALL MEAN?
THIS CAN'T BE A COINCIDENCE.

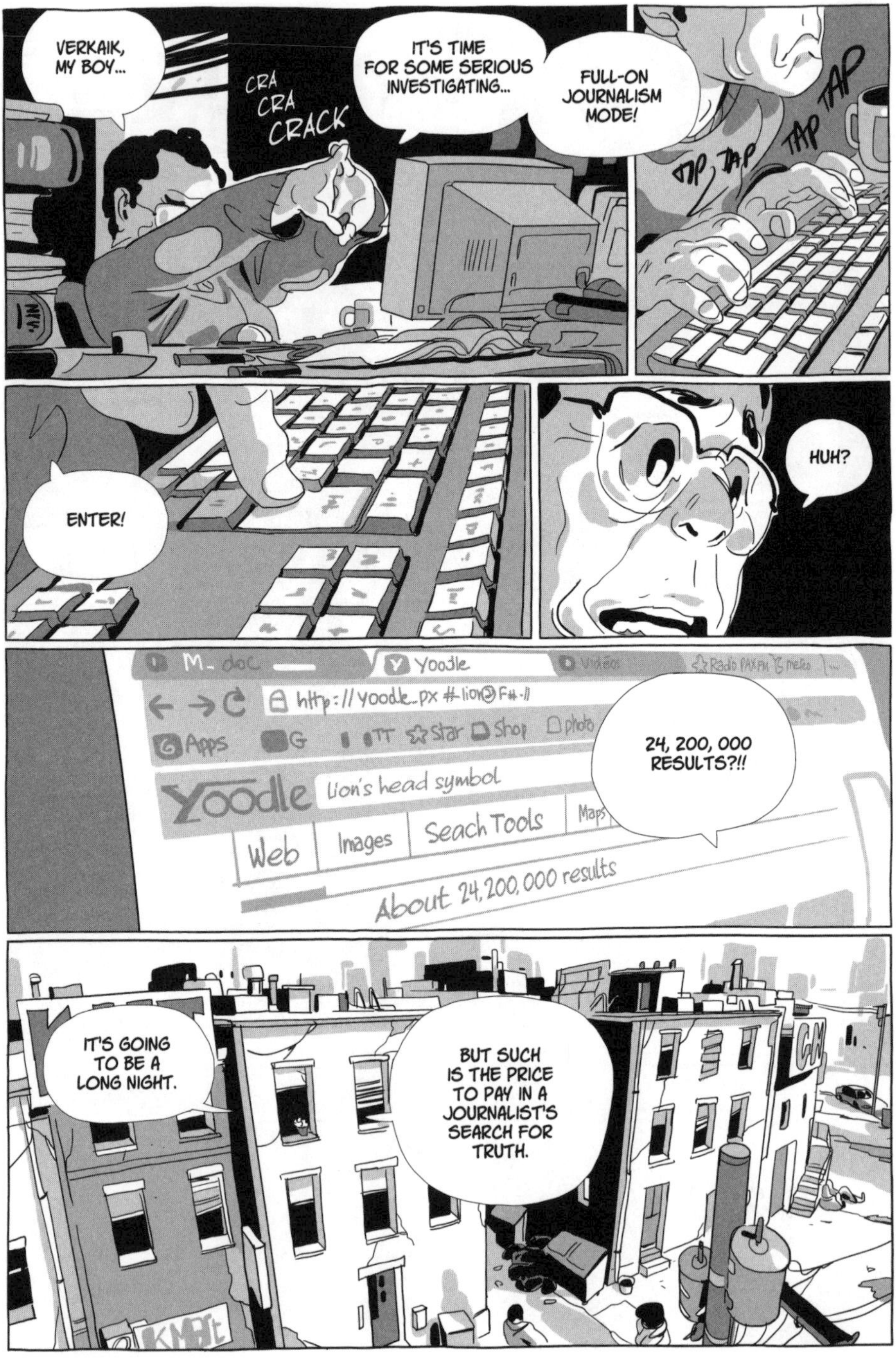
VERKAIK, MY BOY...
CRA CRA CRACK
IT'S TIME FOR SOME SERIOUS INVESTIGATING...
FULL-ON JOURNALISM MODE!
TAP TAP TAP TAP
ENTER!
HUH?
Yoodle
lion's head symbol
Web
Images
Seach Tools
Maps
About 24,200,000 results
24, 200, 000 RESULTS?!!
IT'S GOING TO BE A LONG NIGHT.
BUT SUCH IS THE PRICE TO PAY IN A JOURNALIST'S SEARCH FOR TRUTH.

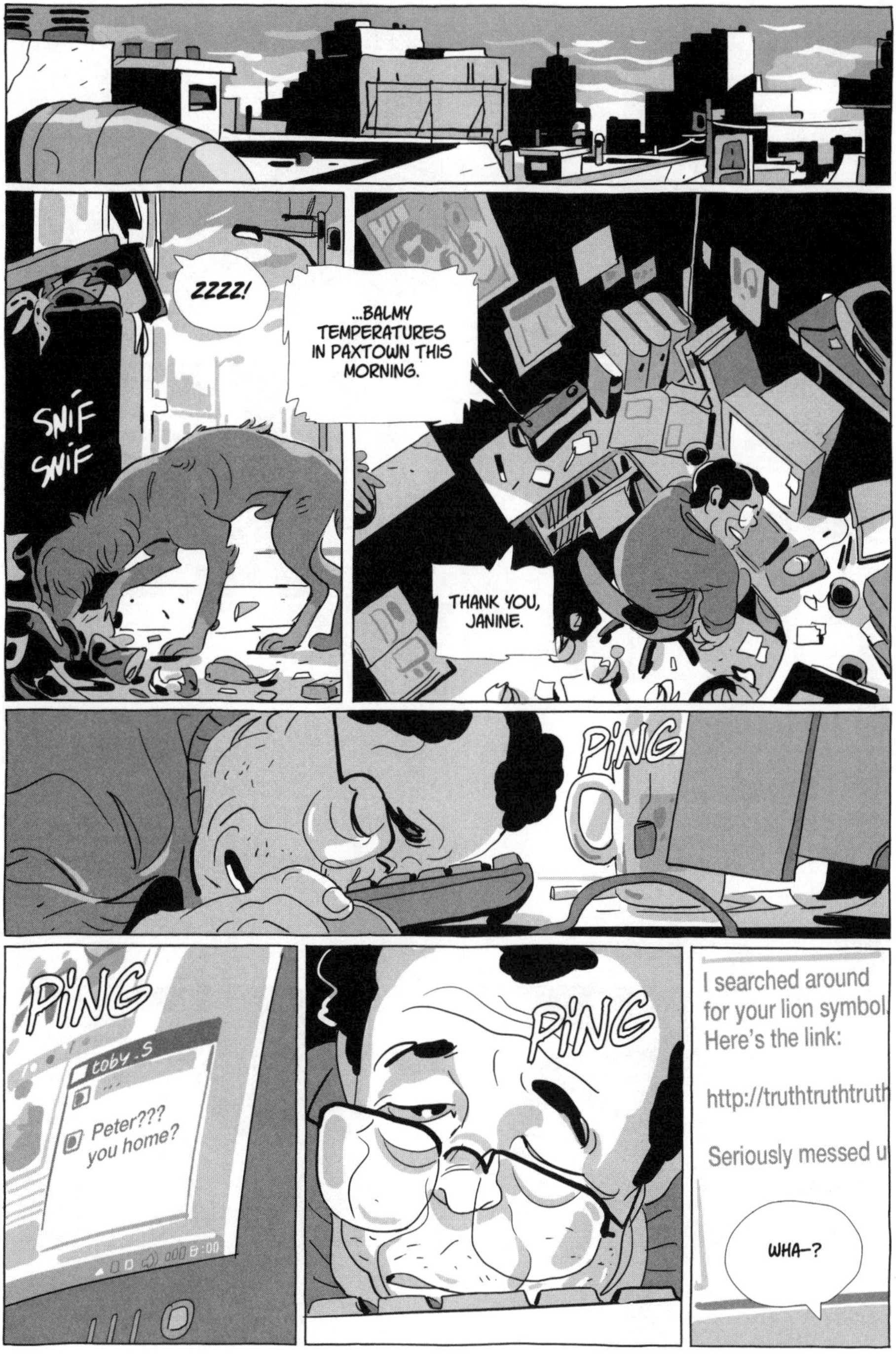
ZZZZ!
...BALMY TEMPERATURES IN PAXTOWN THIS MORNING.
SNIF SNIF
THANK YOU, JANINE.
PING
PING
toby.S
Peter??? you home?
PING
I searched around for your lion symbol. Here's the link:
http://truthtruthtruth
Seriously messed u
WHA-?

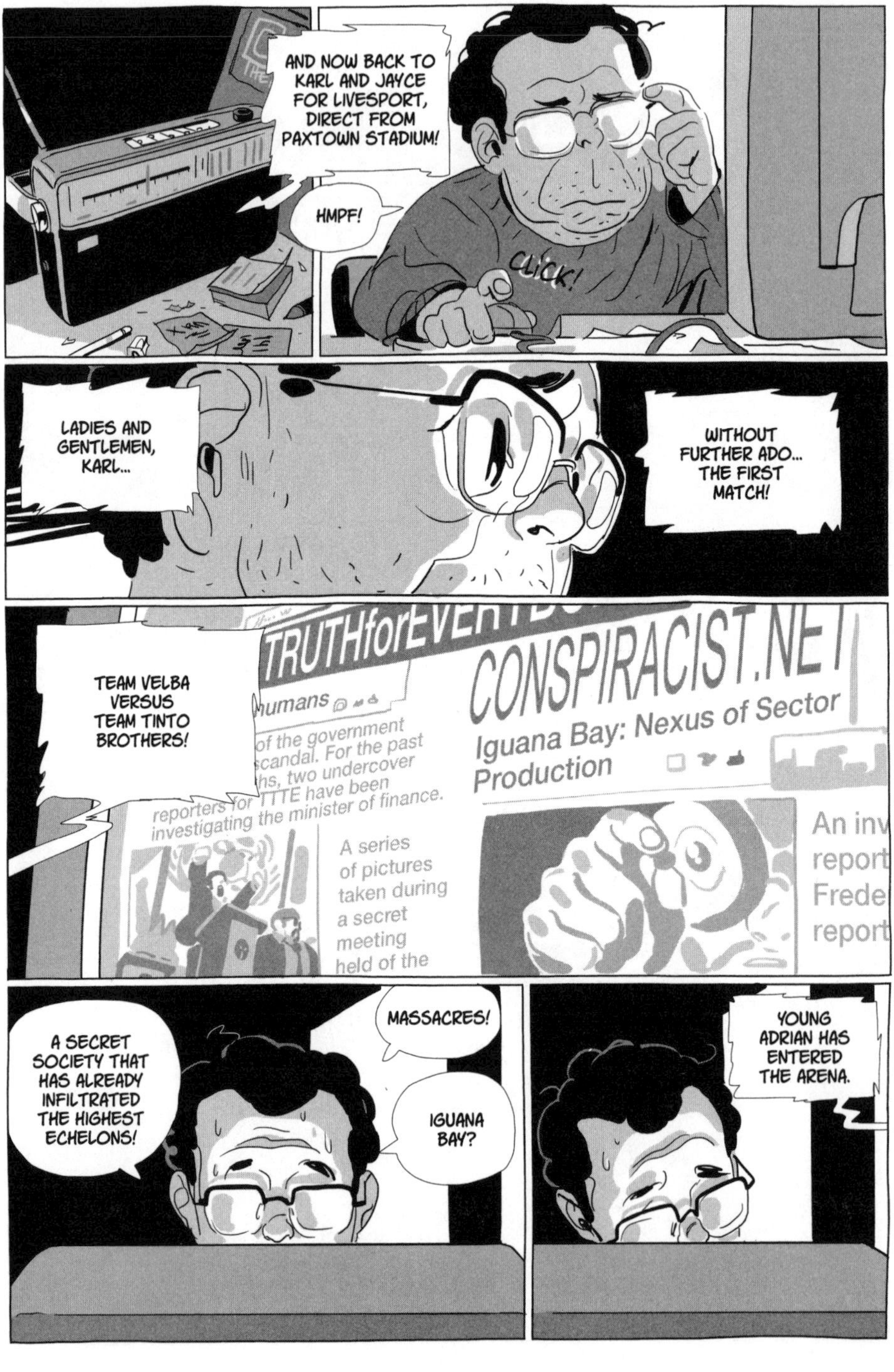
AND NOW BACK TO KARL AND JAYCE FOR LIVESPORT, DIRECT FROM PAXTOWN STADIUM!
HMPF!
CLICK!
LADIES AND GENTLEMEN, KARL...
WITHOUT FURTHER ADO... THE FIRST MATCH!
TEAM VELBA VERSUS TEAM TINTO BROTHERS!
CONSPIRACIST.NET
Iguana Bay: Nexus of Sector Production
reporters for TTTE have been investigating the minister of finance.
A series of pictures taken during a secret meeting held of the
A SECRET SOCIETY THAT HAS ALREADY INFILTRATED THE HIGHEST ECHELONS!
MASSACRES!
IGUANA BAY?
YOUNG ADRIAN HAS ENTERED THE ARENA.

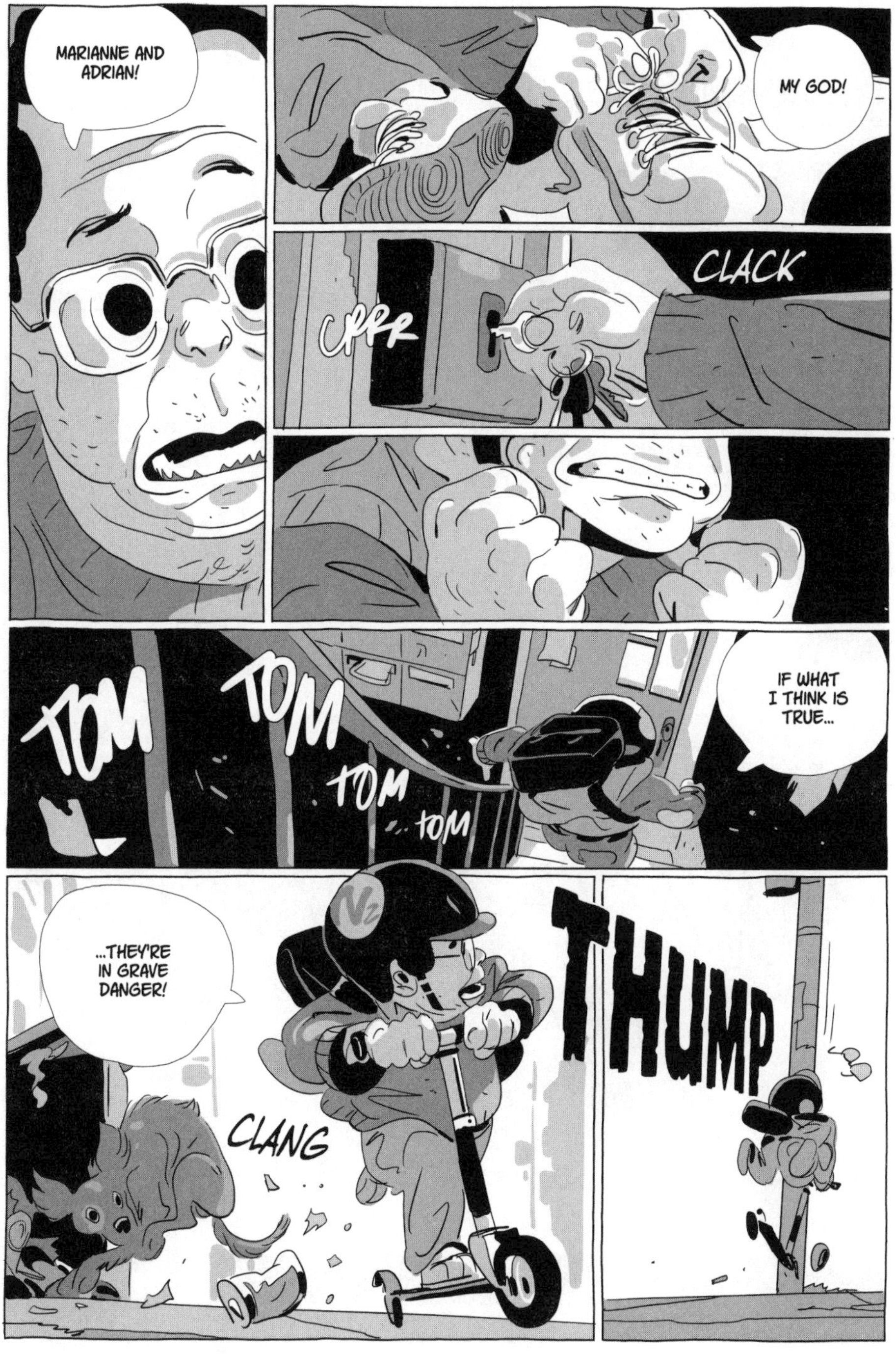
MARIANNE AND ADRIAN!
MY GOD!
CRRR
CLACK
TOM
TOM
TOM
TOM
IF WHAT I THINK IS TRUE...
...THEY'RE IN GRAVE DANGER!
CLANG
THUMP

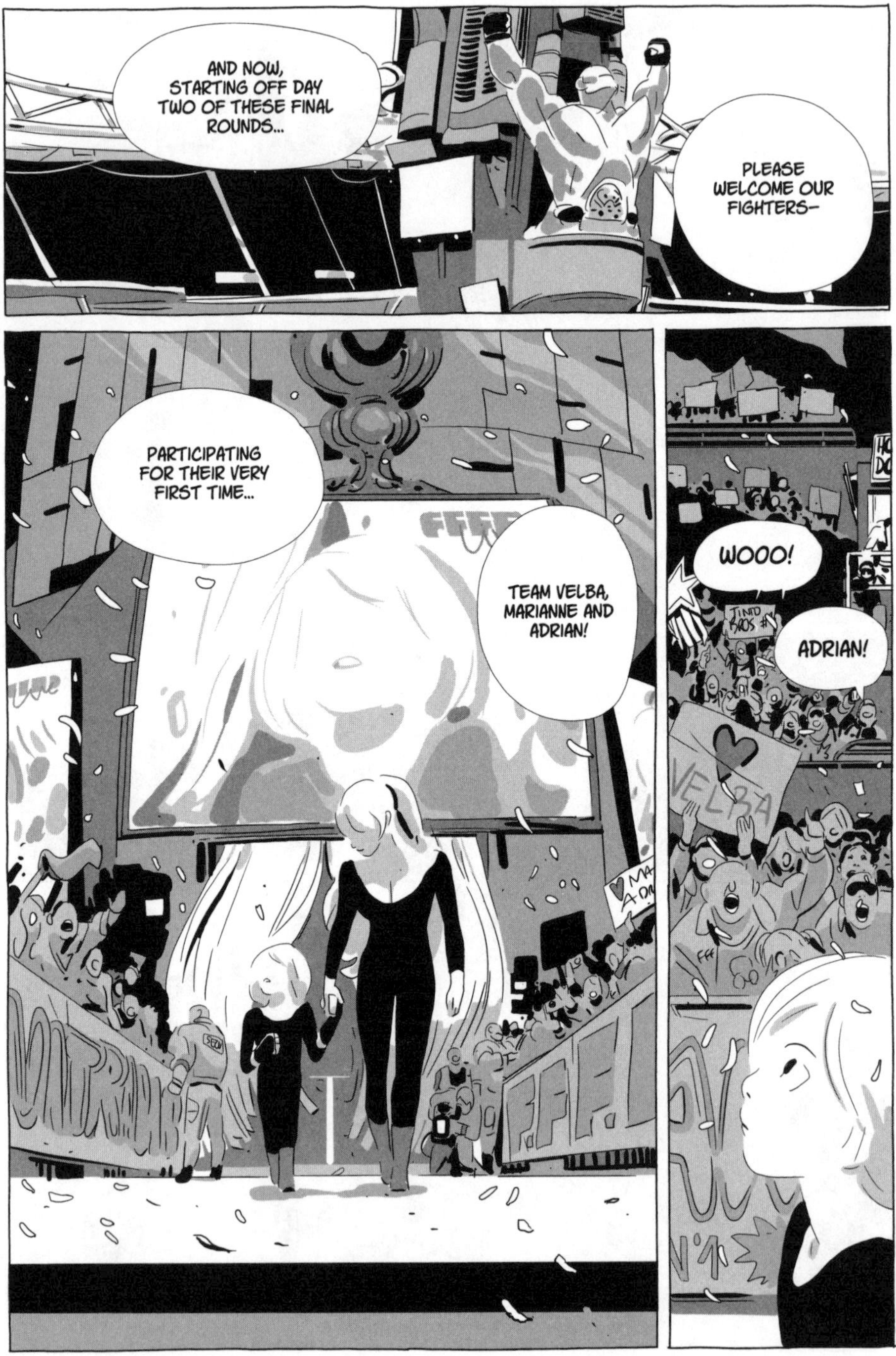
AND NOW, STARTING OFF DAY TWO OF THESE FINAL ROUNDS...
PLEASE WELCOME OUR FIGHTERS–
PARTICIPATING FOR THEIR VERY FIRST TIME...
TEAM VELBA, MARIANNE AND ADRIAN!
WOOO!
ADRIAN!
VELBA

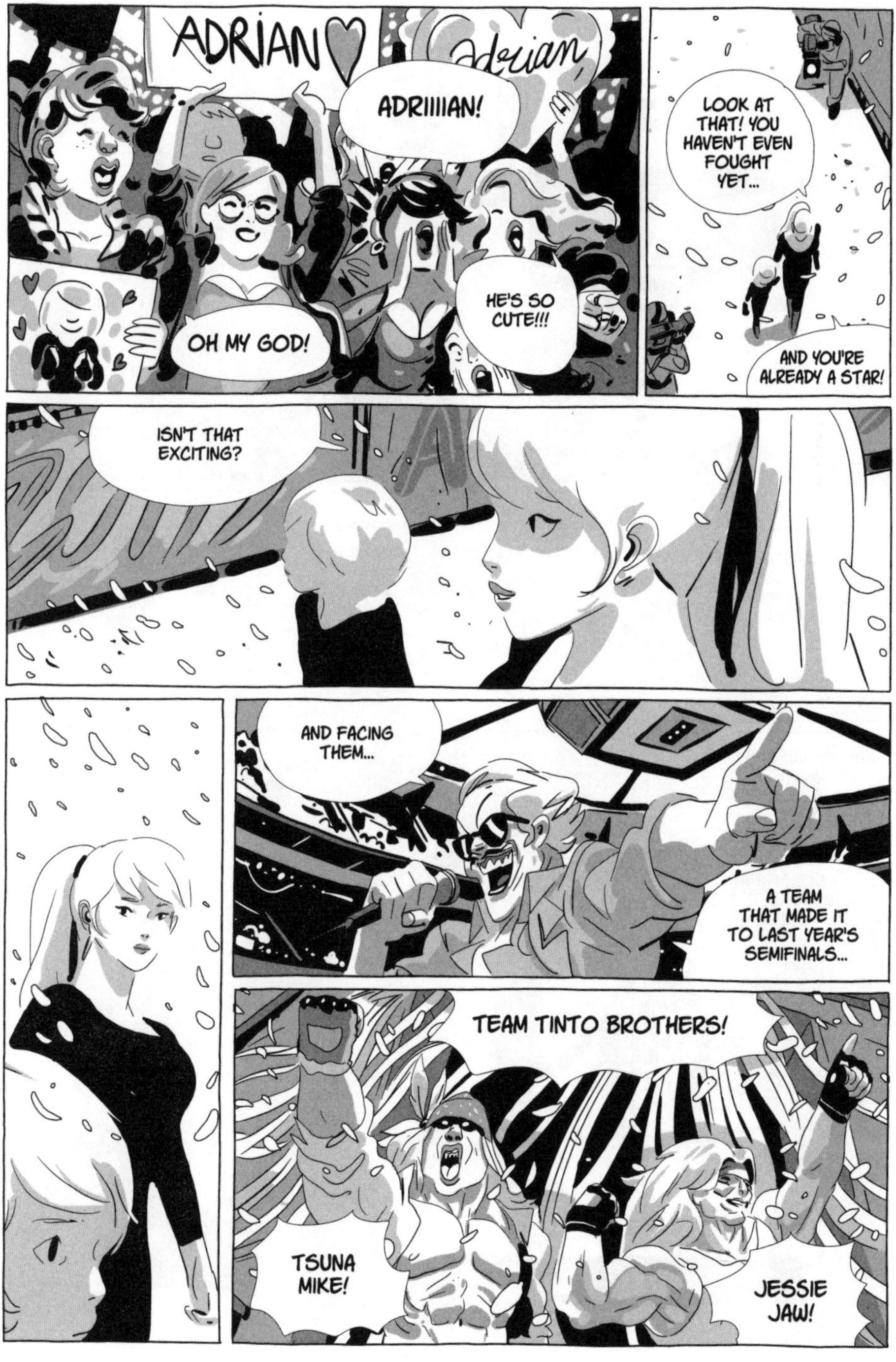
ADRIAN
Adrian
ADRIIIIAN!
OH MY GOD!
HE'S SO CUTE!!!
LOOK AT THAT! YOU HAVEN'T EVEN FOUGHT YET...
AND YOU'RE ALREADY A STAR!
ISN'T THAT EXCITING?
AND FACING THEM...
A TEAM THAT MADE IT TO LAST YEAR'S SEMIFINALS...
TEAM TINTO BROTHERS!
TSUNA MIKE!
JESSIE JAW!

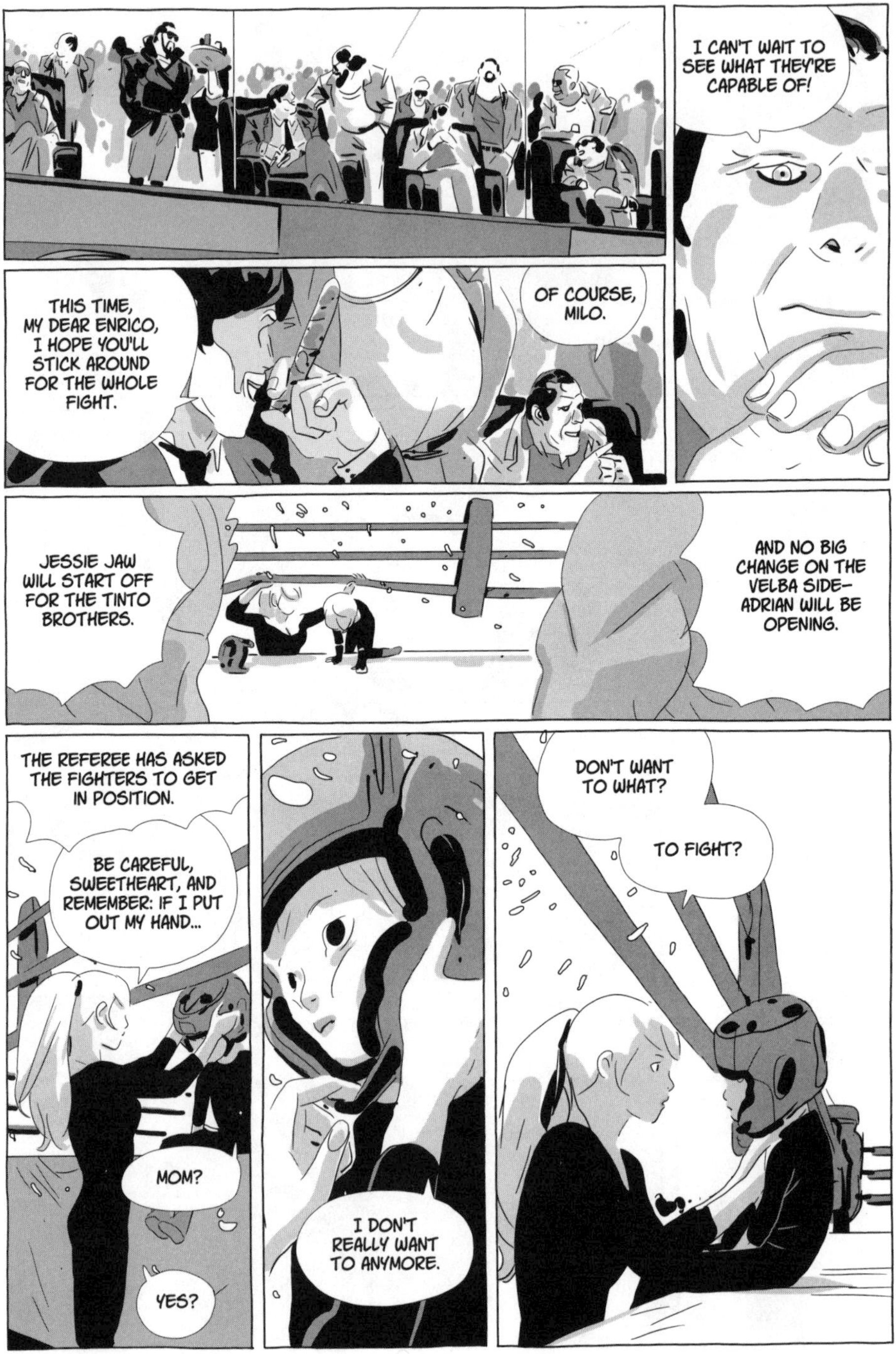
I CAN'T WAIT TO SEE WHAT THEY'RE CAPABLE OF!
THIS TIME, MY DEAR ENRICO, I HOPE YOU'LL STICK AROUND FOR THE WHOLE FIGHT.
OF COURSE, MILO.
JESSIE JAW WILL START OFF FOR THE TINTO BROTHERS.
AND NO BIG CHANGE ON THE VELBA SIDE- ADRIAN WILL BE OPENING.
THE REFEREE HAS ASKED THE FIGHTERS TO GET IN POSITION.
BE CAREFUL, SWEETHEART, AND REMEMBER: IF I PUT OUT MY HAND...
MOM?
YES?
I DON'T REALLY WANT TO ANYMORE.
DON'T WANT TO WHAT?
TO FIGHT?

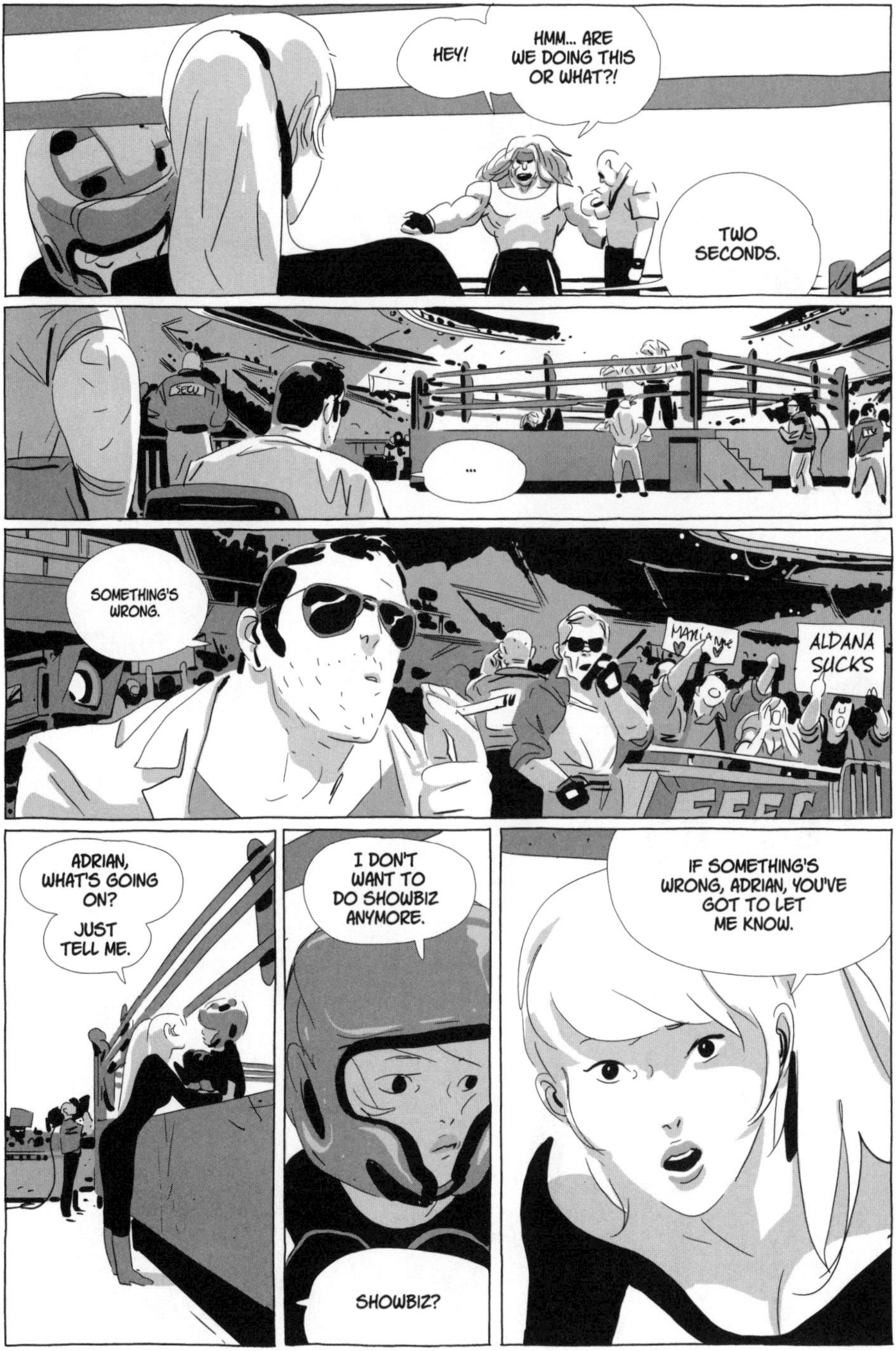
HEY!
HMM... ARE WE DOING THIS OR WHAT?!
TWO SECONDS.
...
SOMETHING'S WRONG.
ALDANA SUCKS
ADRIAN, WHAT'S GOING ON?
JUST TELL ME.
I DON'T WANT TO DO SHOWBIZ ANYMORE.
SHOWBIZ?
IF SOMETHING'S WRONG, ADRIAN, YOU'VE GOT TO LET ME KNOW.

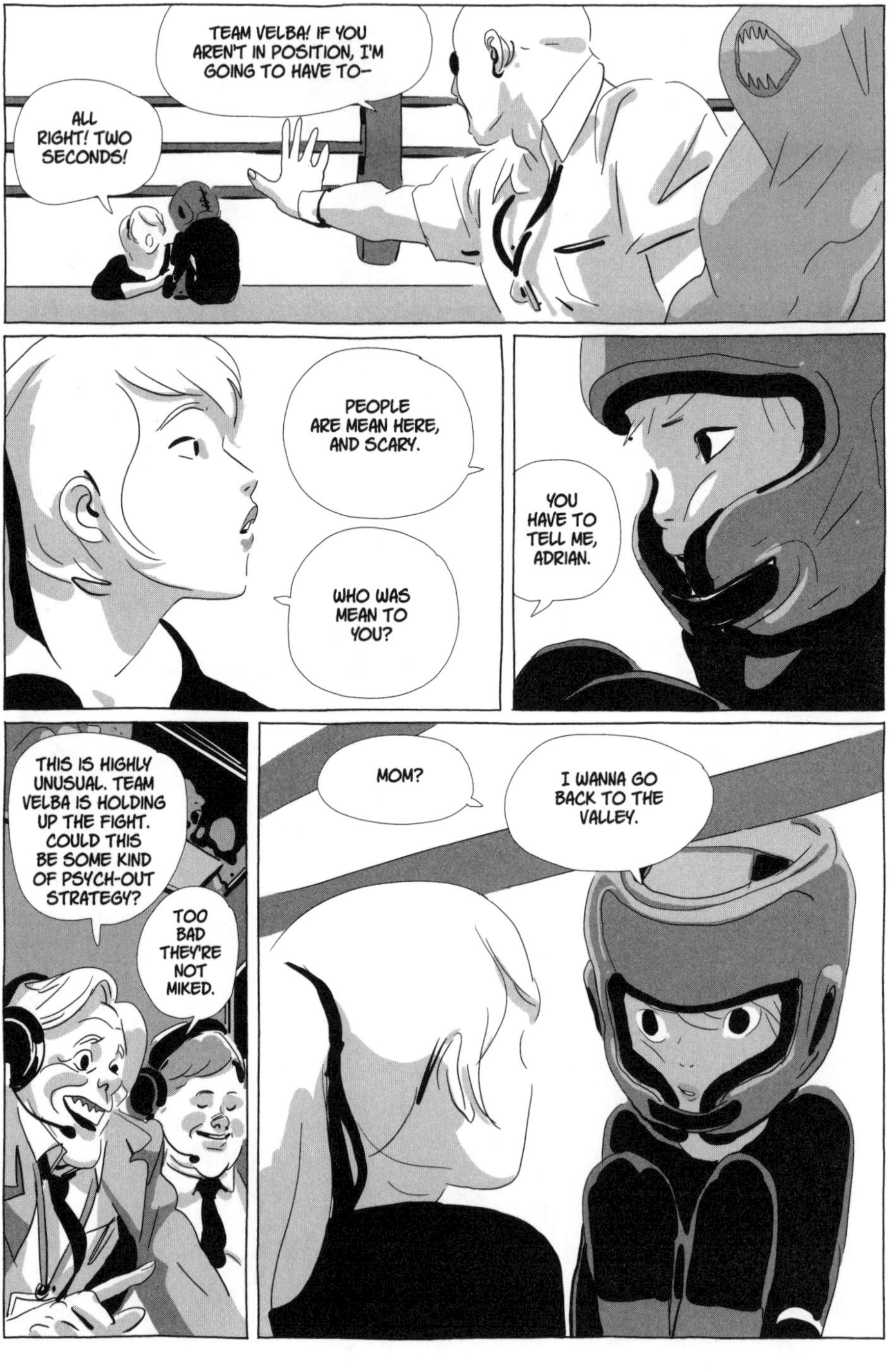
TEAM VELBA! IF YOU AREN'T IN POSITION, I'M GOING TO HAVE TO–
ALL RIGHT! TWO SECONDS!
PEOPLE ARE MEAN HERE, AND SCARY.
WHO WAS MEAN TO YOU?
YOU HAVE TO TELL ME, ADRIAN.
THIS IS HIGHLY UNUSUAL. TEAM VELBA IS HOLDING UP THE FIGHT. COULD THIS BE SOME KIND OF PSYCH-OUT STRATEGY?
TOO BAD THEY'RE NOT MIKED.
MOM?
I WANNA GO BACK TO THE VALLEY.

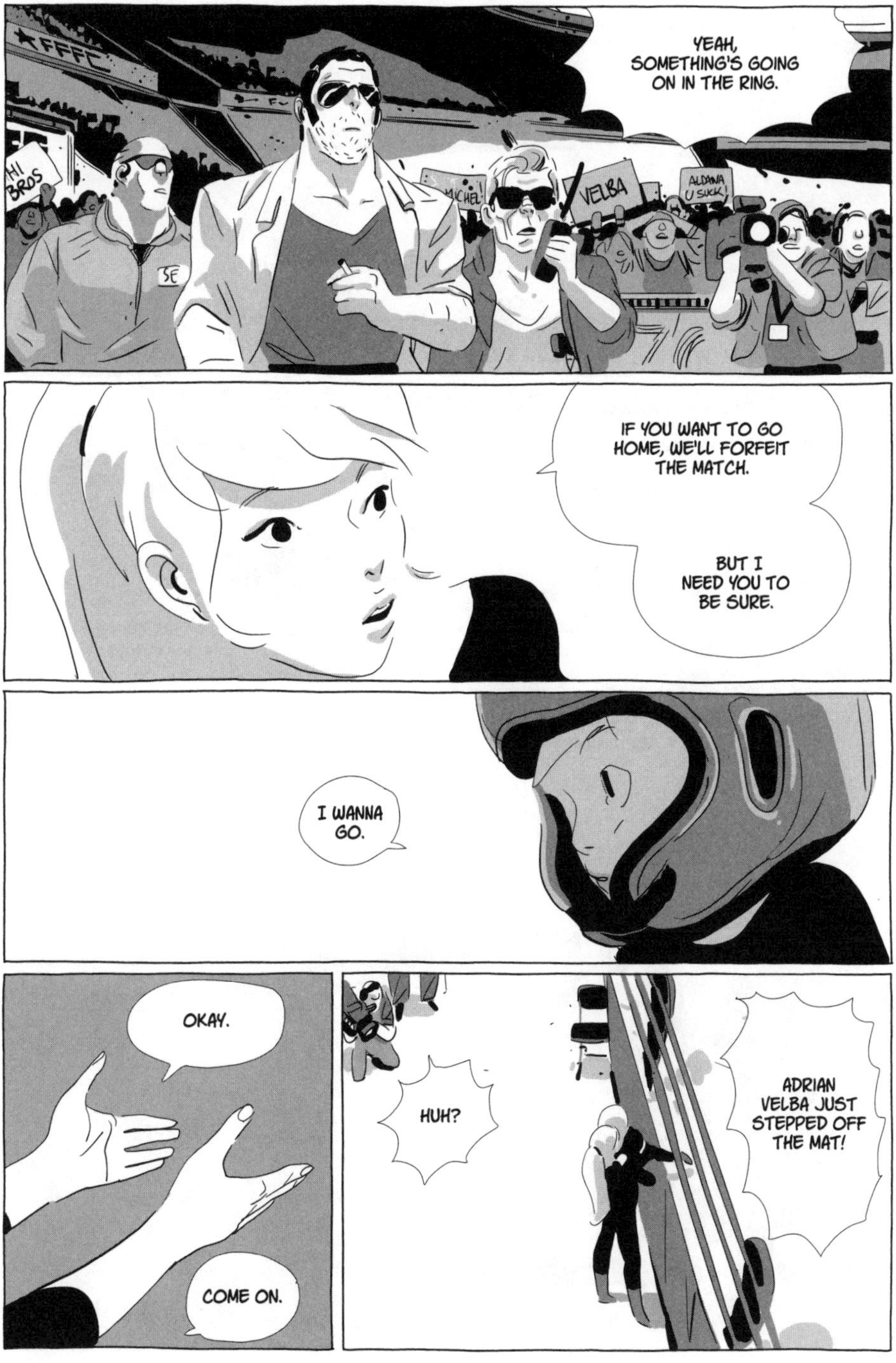
YEAH, SOMETHING'S GOING ON IN THE RING.
HI BROS
MICHEL!
VELBA
ALDANA U SUCK!
IF YOU WANT TO GO HOME, WE'LL FORFEIT THE MATCH.
BUT I NEED YOU TO BE SURE.
I WANNA GO.
OKAY.
COME ON.
HUH?
ADRIAN VELBA JUST STEPPED OFF THE MAT!

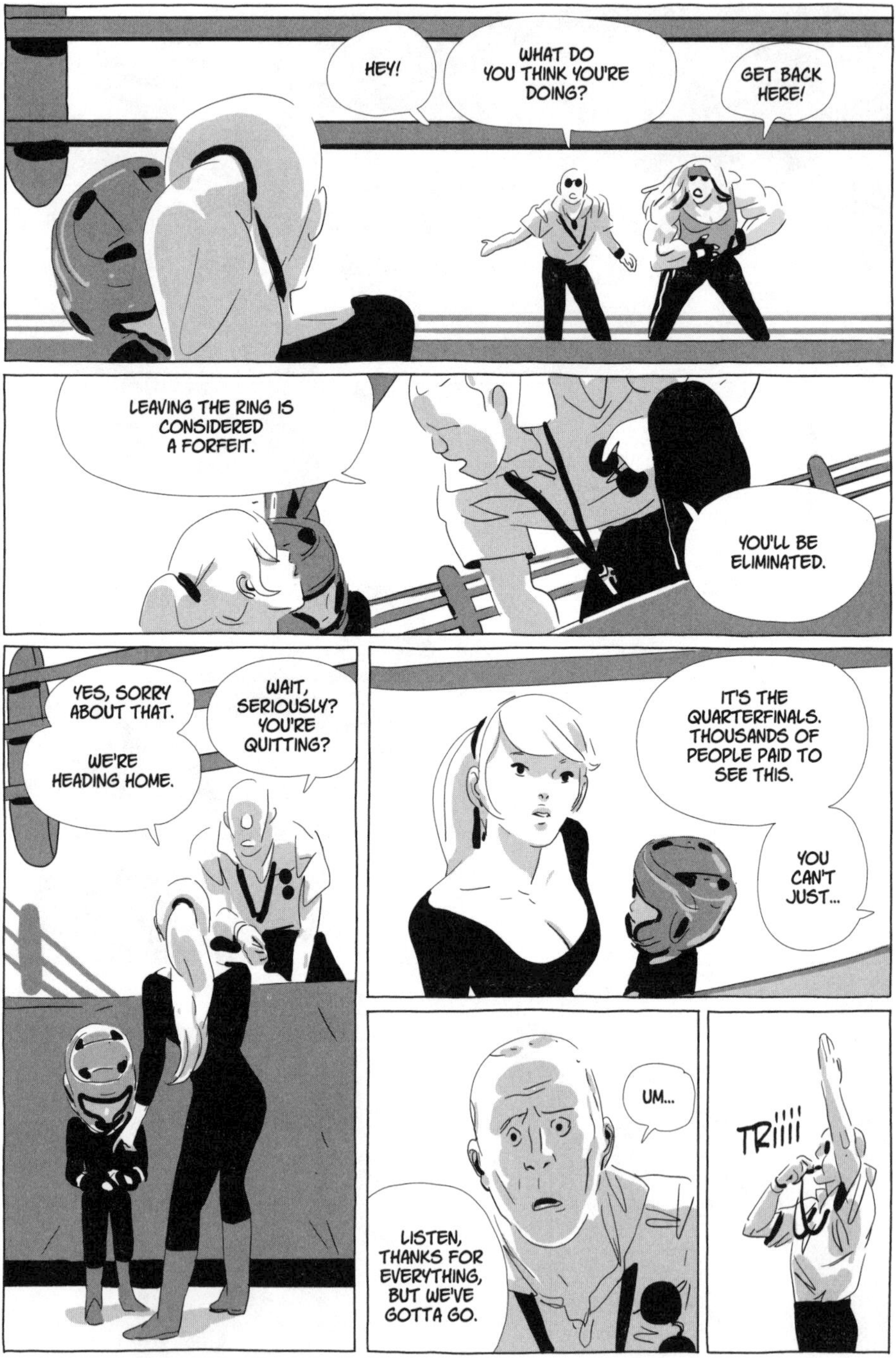
HEY!
WHAT DO YOU THINK YOU'RE DOING?
GET BACK HERE!
LEAVING THE RING IS CONSIDERED A FORFEIT.
YOU'LL BE ELIMINATED.
YES, SORRY ABOUT THAT.
WE'RE HEADING HOME.
WAIT, SERIOUSLY? YOU'RE QUITTING?
IT'S THE QUARTERFINALS. THOUSANDS OF PEOPLE PAID TO SEE THIS.
YOU CAN'T JUST...
UM...
LISTEN, THANKS FOR EVERYTHING, BUT WE'VE GOTTA GO.
TRiiii

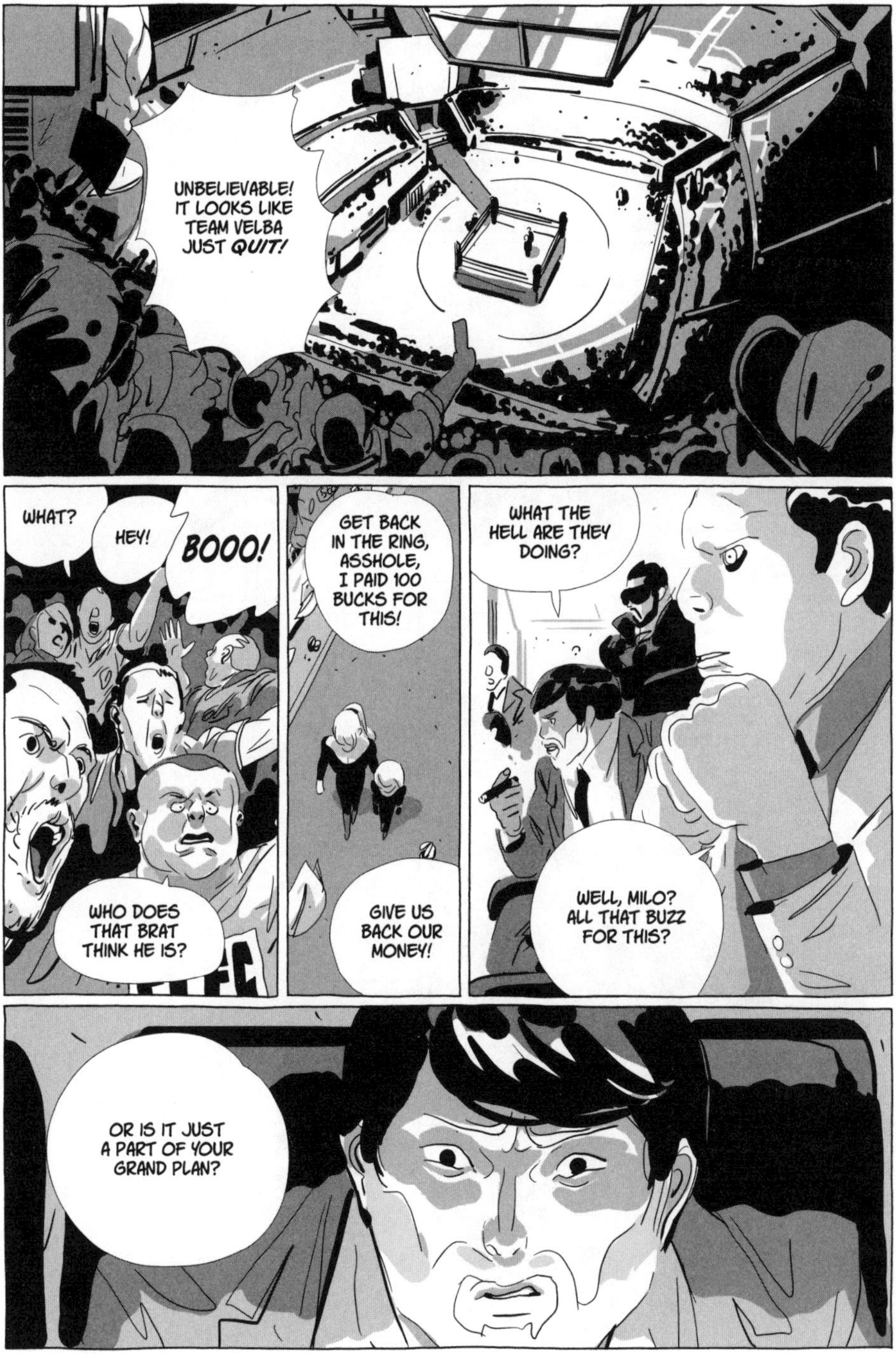
UNBELIEVABLE! IT LOOKS LIKE TEAM VELBA JUST *QUIT!*
WHAT?
HEY!
BOOO!
WHO DOES THAT BRAT THINK HE IS?
GET BACK IN THE RING, ASSHOLE, I PAID 100 BUCKS FOR THIS!
GIVE US BACK OUR MONEY!
WHAT THE HELL ARE THEY DOING?
?
WELL, MILO? ALL THAT BUZZ FOR THIS?
OR IS IT JUST A PART OF YOUR GRAND PLAN?

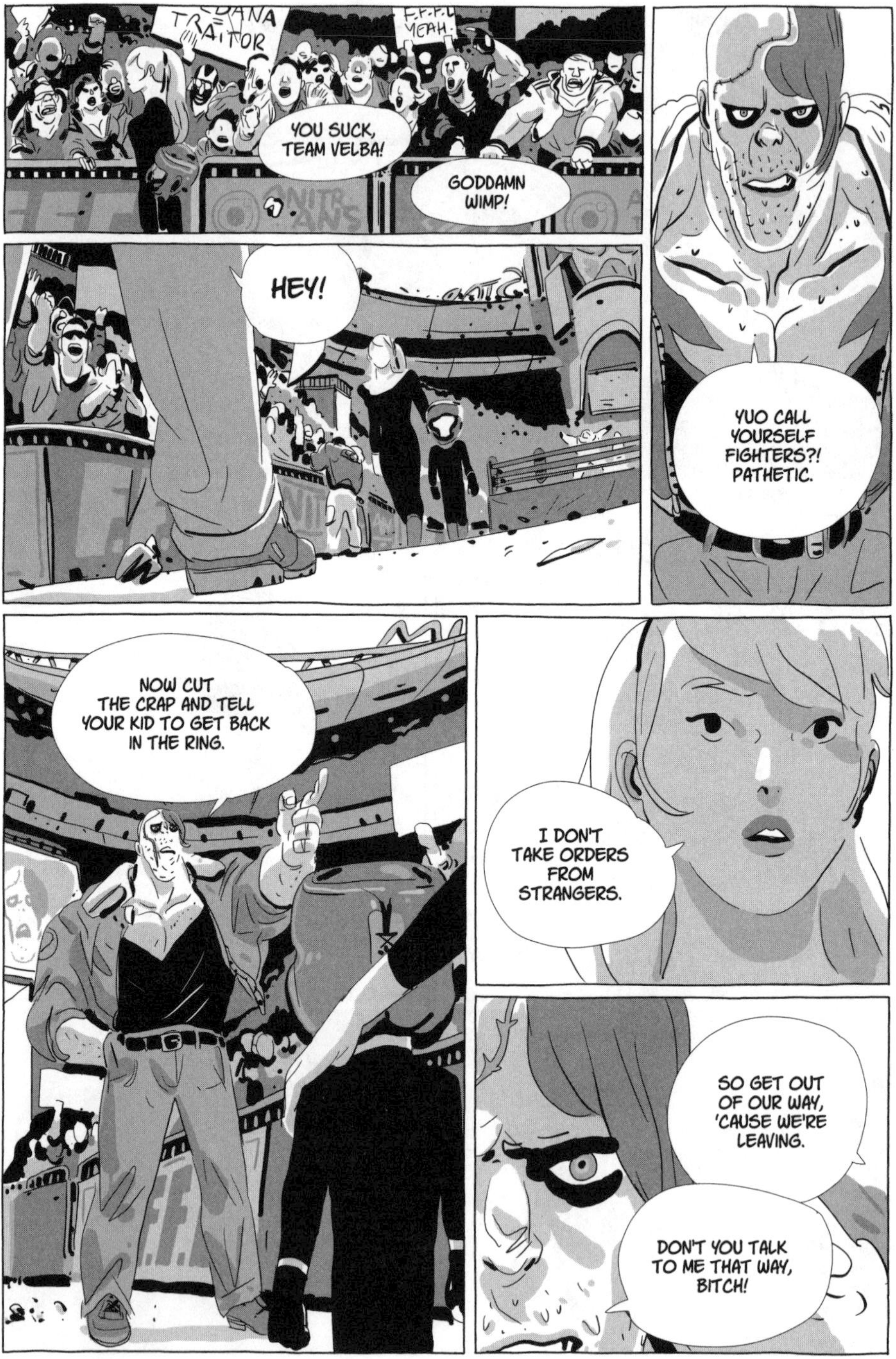
TRAITOR
YOU SUCK, TEAM VELBA!
GODDAMN WIMP!
HEY!
YUO CALL YOURSELF FIGHTERS?! PATHETIC.
NOW CUT THE CRAP AND TELL YOUR KID TO GET BACK IN THE RING.
I DON'T TAKE ORDERS FROM STRANGERS.
SO GET OUT OF OUR WAY, 'CAUSE WE'RE LEAVING.
DON'T YOU TALK TO ME THAT WAY, BITCH!

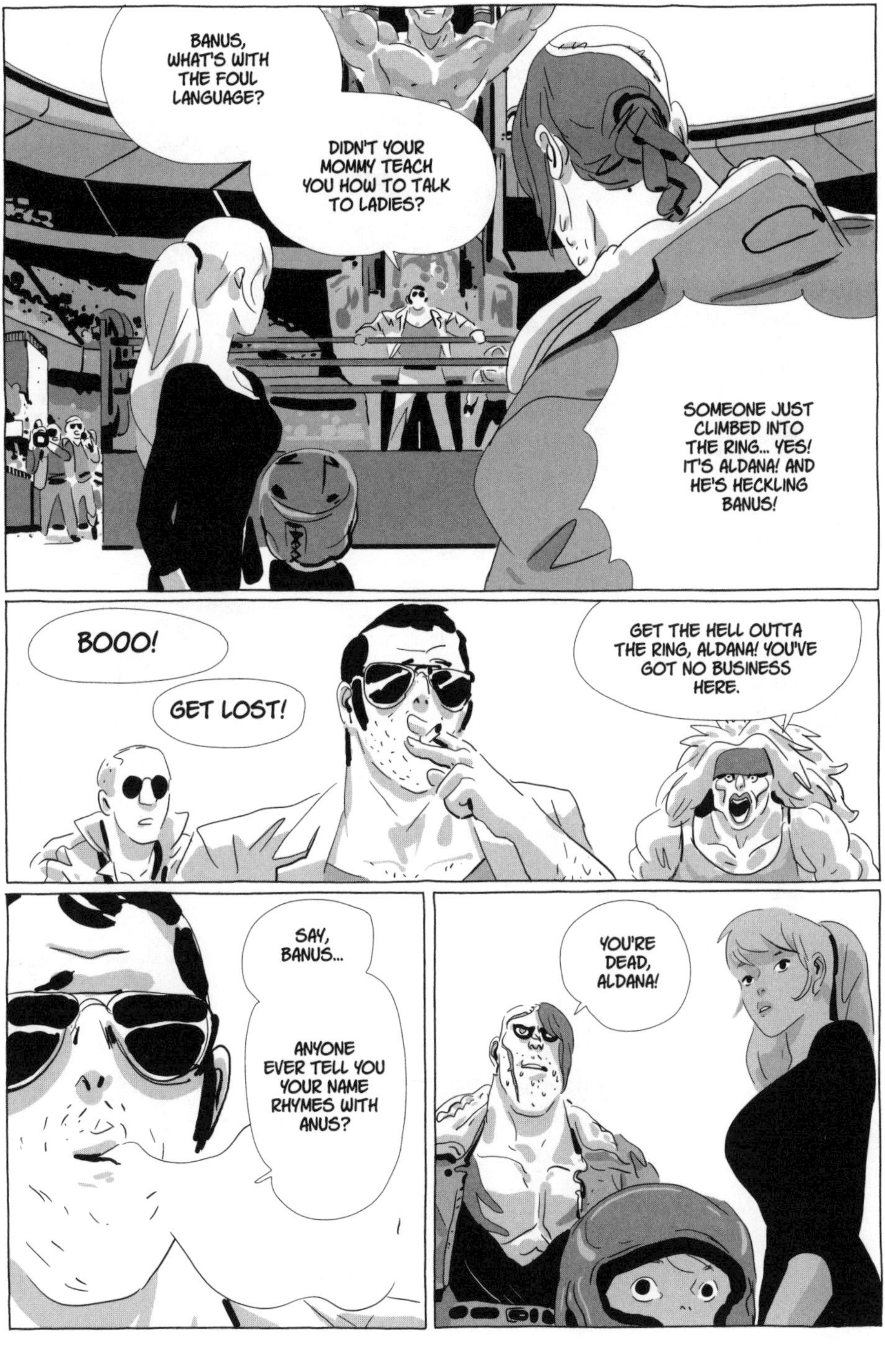
BANUS, WHAT'S WITH THE FOUL LANGUAGE?
DIDN'T YOUR MOMMY TEACH YOU HOW TO TALK TO LADIES?
SOMEONE JUST CLIMBED INTO THE RING... YES! IT'S ALDANA! AND HE'S HECKLING BANUS!
BOOO!
GET LOST!
GET THE HELL OUTTA THE RING, ALDANA! YOU'VE GOT NO BUSINESS HERE.
SAY, BANUS...
ANYONE EVER TELL YOU YOUR NAME RHYMES WITH ANUS?
YOU'RE DEAD, ALDANA!

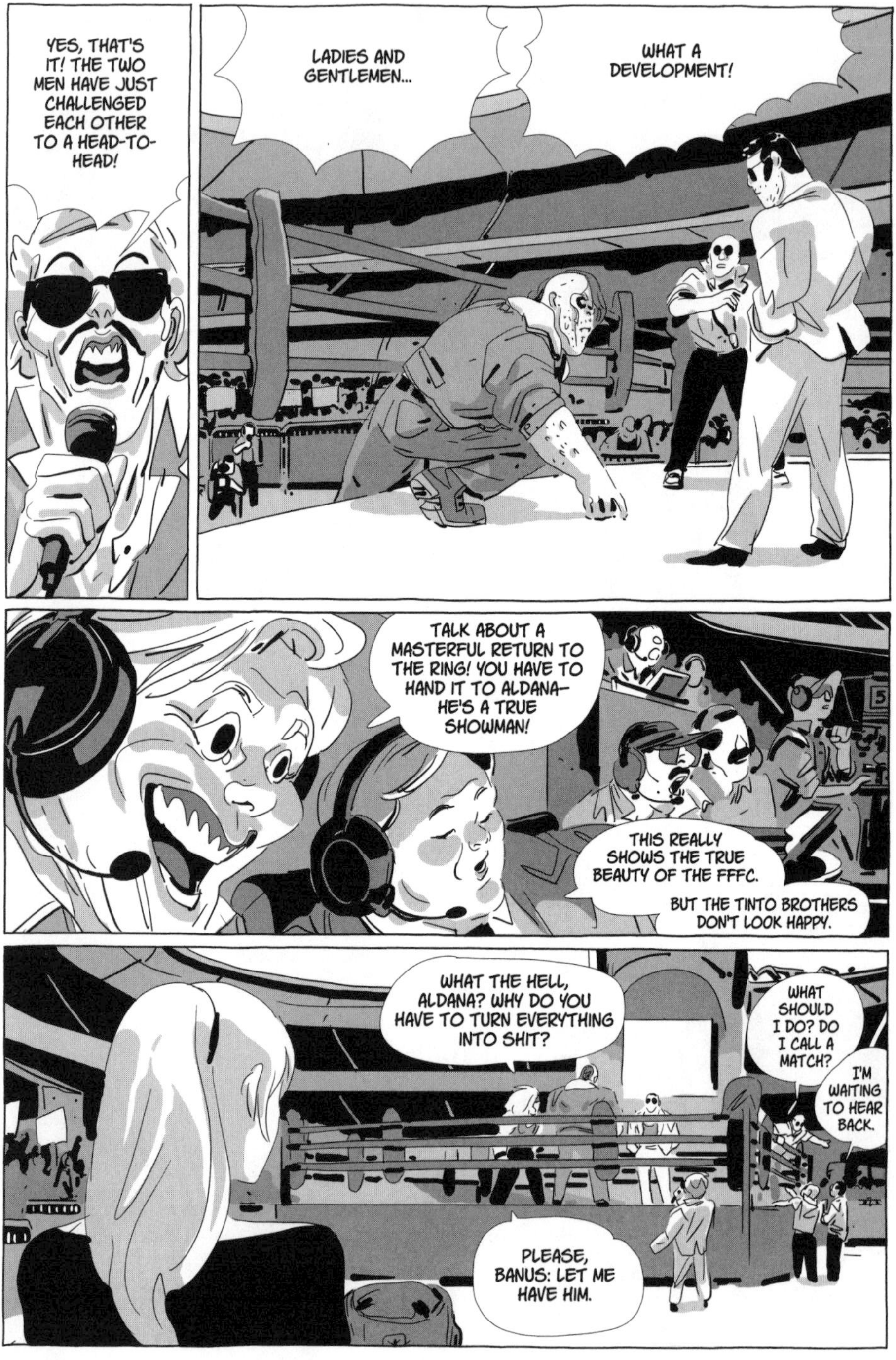
YES, THAT'S IT! THE TWO MEN HAVE JUST CHALLENGED EACH OTHER TO A HEAD-TO-HEAD!
LADIES AND GENTLEMEN...
WHAT A DEVELOPMENT!
TALK ABOUT A MASTERFUL RETURN TO THE RING! YOU HAVE TO HAND IT TO ALDANA— HE'S A TRUE SHOWMAN!
THIS REALLY SHOWS THE TRUE BEAUTY OF THE FFFC.
BUT THE TINTO BROTHERS DON'T LOOK HAPPY.
WHAT THE HELL, ALDANA? WHY DO YOU HAVE TO TURN EVERYTHING INTO SHIT?
WHAT SHOULD I DO? DO I CALL A MATCH?
I'M WAITING TO HEAR BACK.
PLEASE, BANUS: LET ME HAVE HIM.

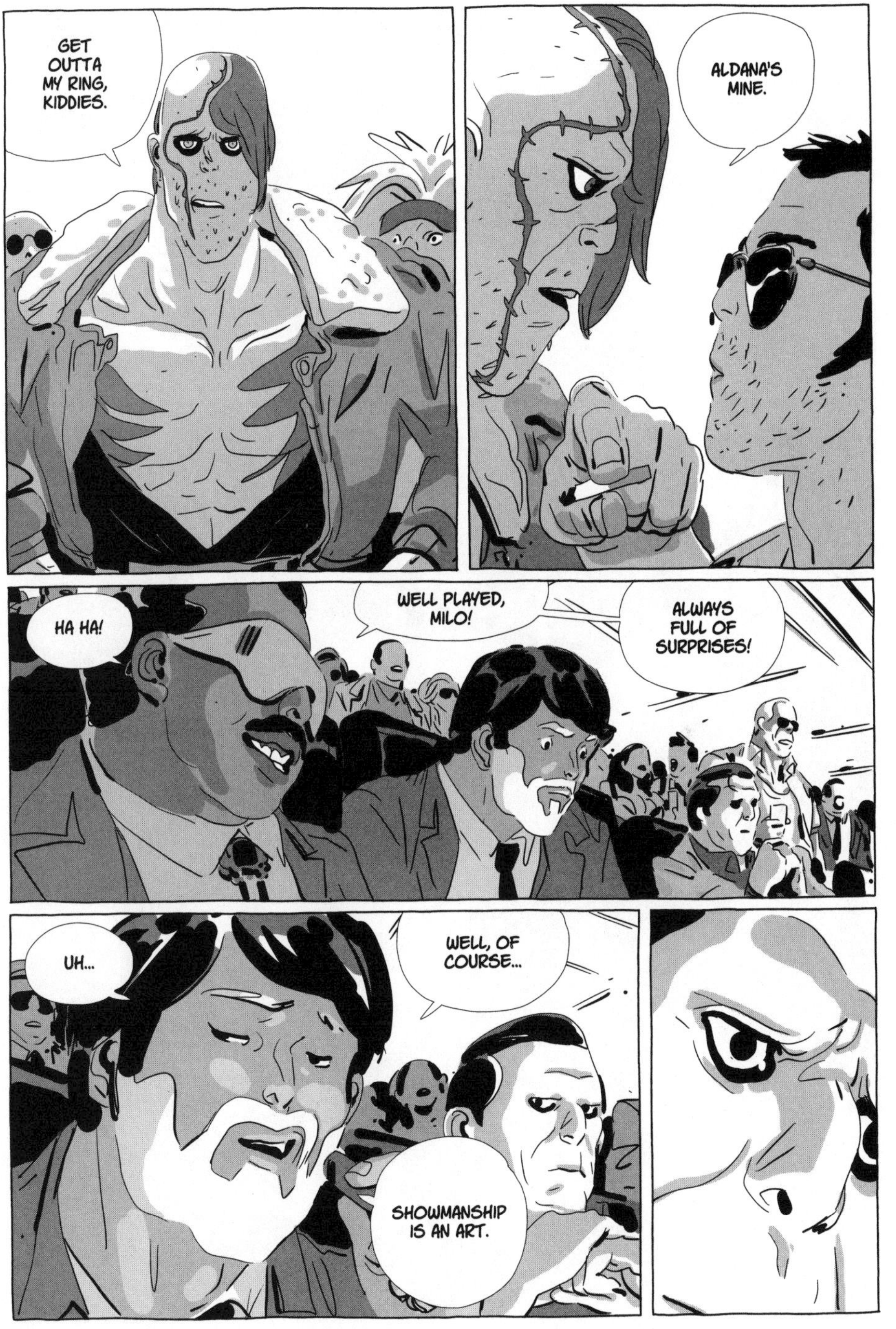
GET OUTTA MY RING, KIDDIES.
ALDANA'S MINE.
HA HA!
WELL PLAYED, MILO!
ALWAYS FULL OF SURPRISES!
UH...
WELL, OF COURSE...
SHOWMANSHIP IS AN ART.

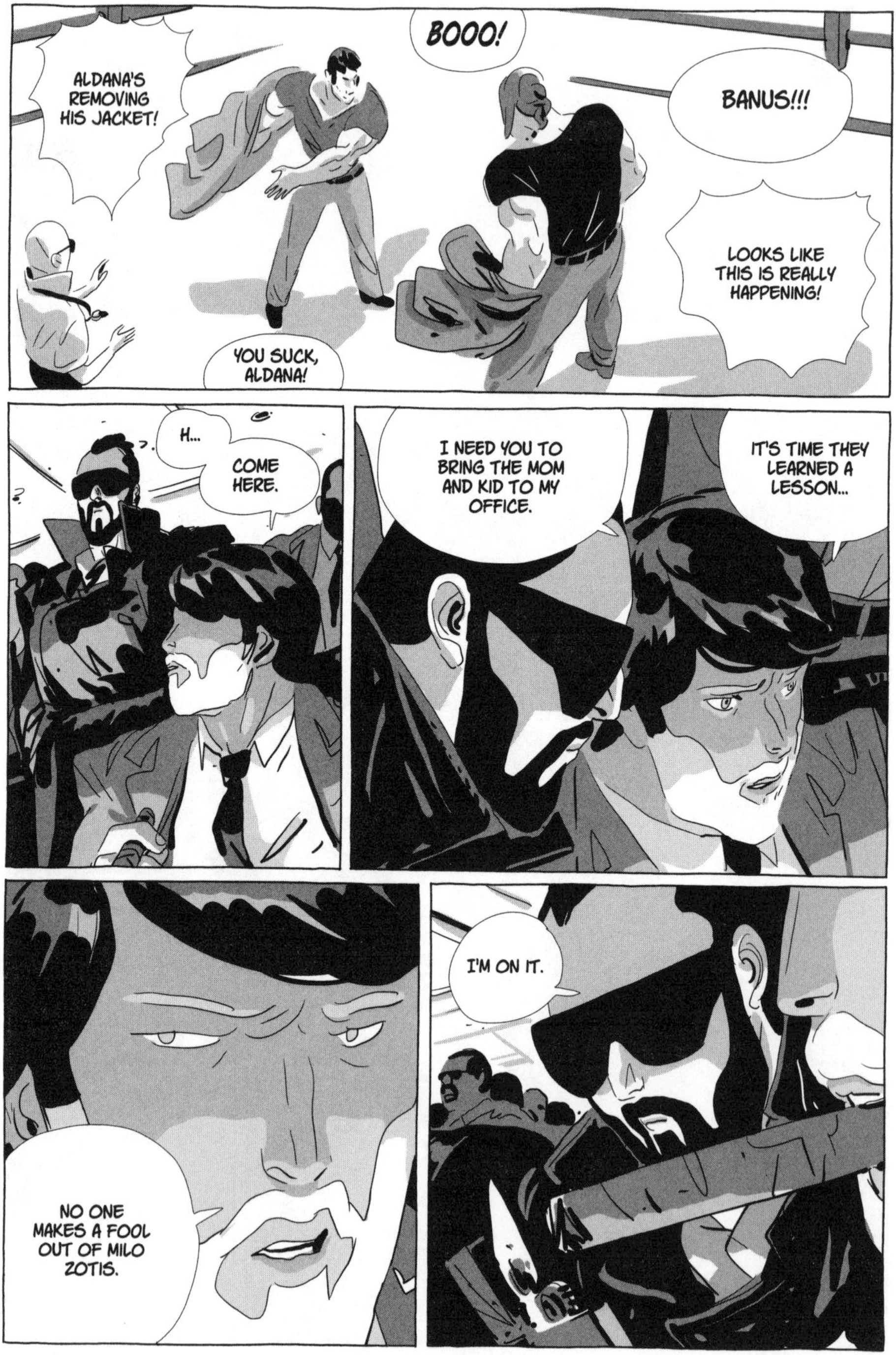

ALDANA'S REMOVING HIS JACKET!
BOOO!
BANUS!!!
LOOKS LIKE THIS IS REALLY HAPPENING!
YOU SUCK, ALDANA!
H...
COME HERE.
I NEED YOU TO BRING THE MOM AND KID TO MY OFFICE.
IT'S TIME THEY LEARNED A LESSON...
NO ONE MAKES A FOOL OUT OF MILO ZOTIS.
I'M ON IT.

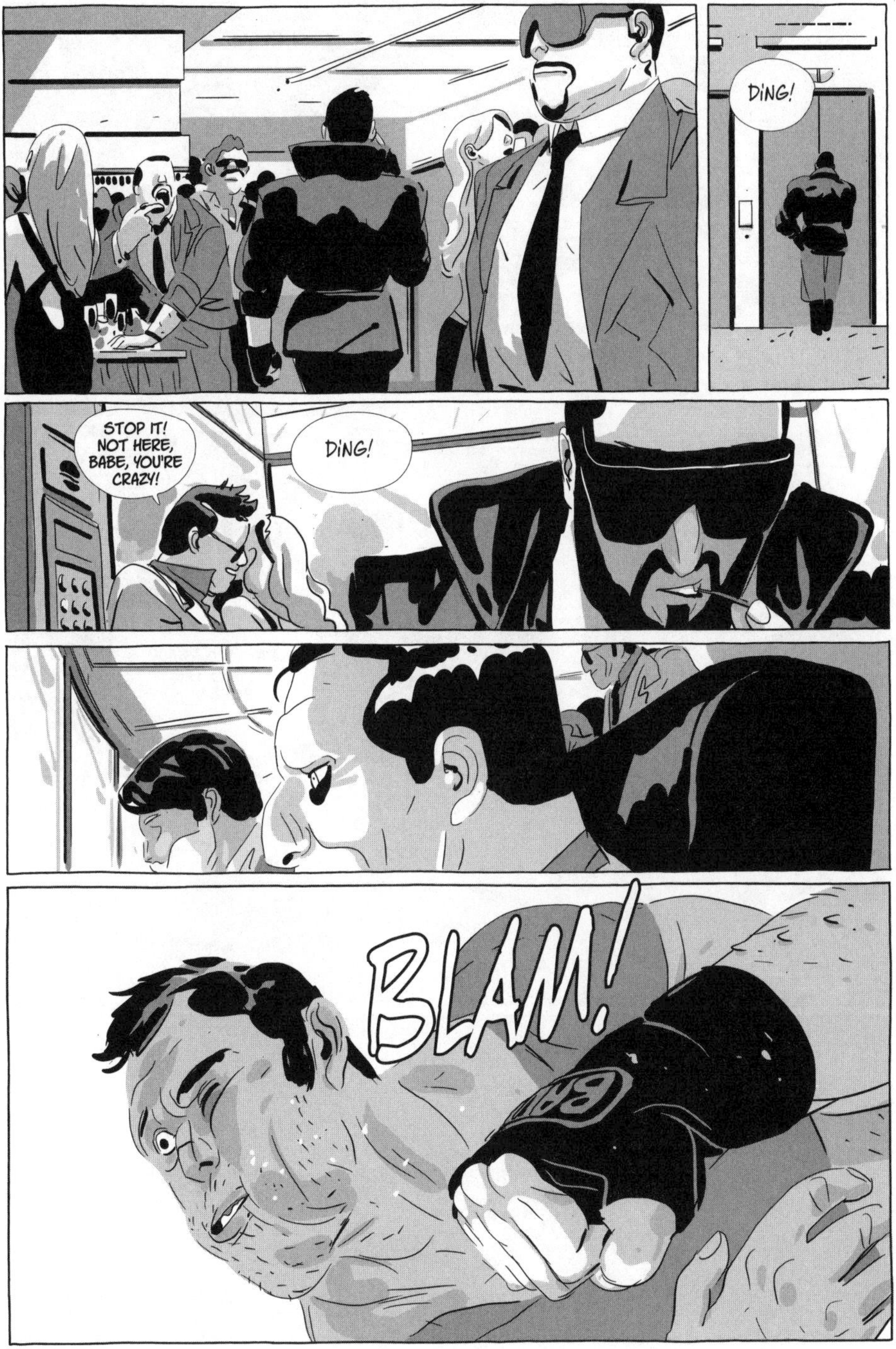
DING!
STOP IT! NOT HERE, BABE, YOU'RE CRAZY!
DING!
BLAM!

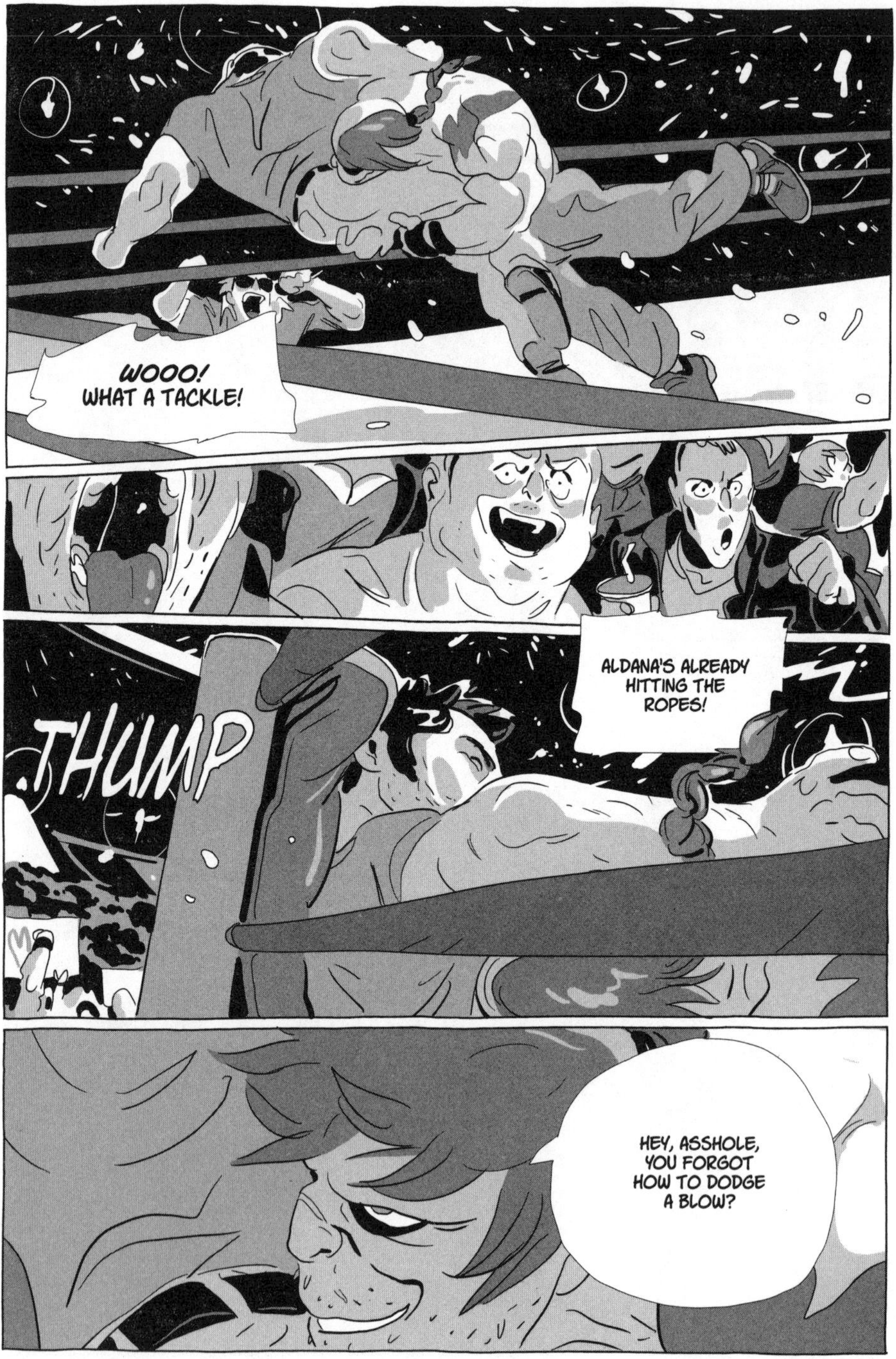
WOOO!
WHAT A TACKLE!
ALDANA'S ALREADY HITTING THE ROPES!
THUMP
HEY, ASSHOLE, YOU FORGOT HOW TO DODGE A BLOW?

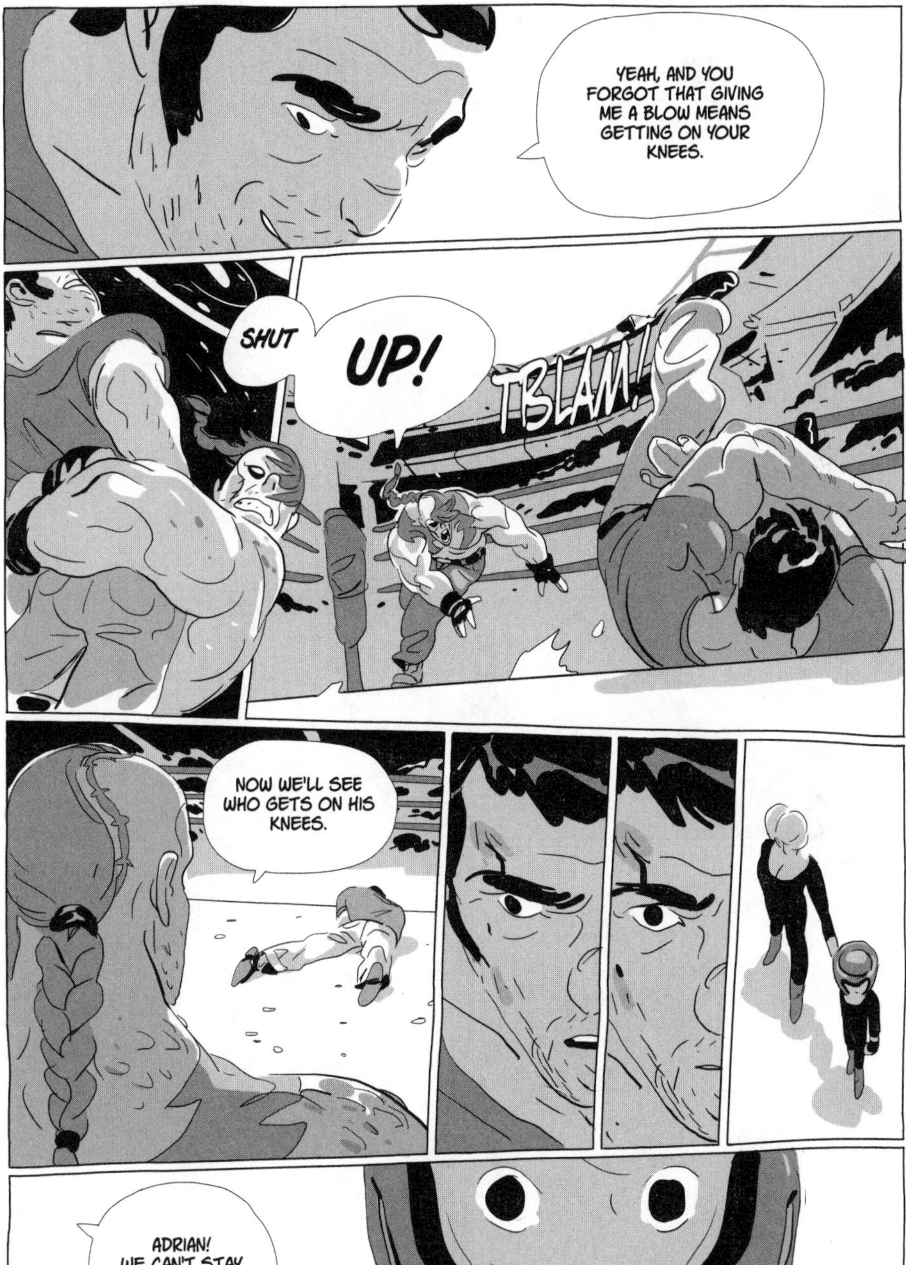
YEAH, AND YOU FORGOT THAT GIVING ME A BLOW MEANS GETTING ON YOUR KNEES.
SHUT
UP!
TBLAM!
NOW WE'LL SEE WHO GETS ON HIS KNEES.
ADRIAN! WE CAN'T STAY HERE!

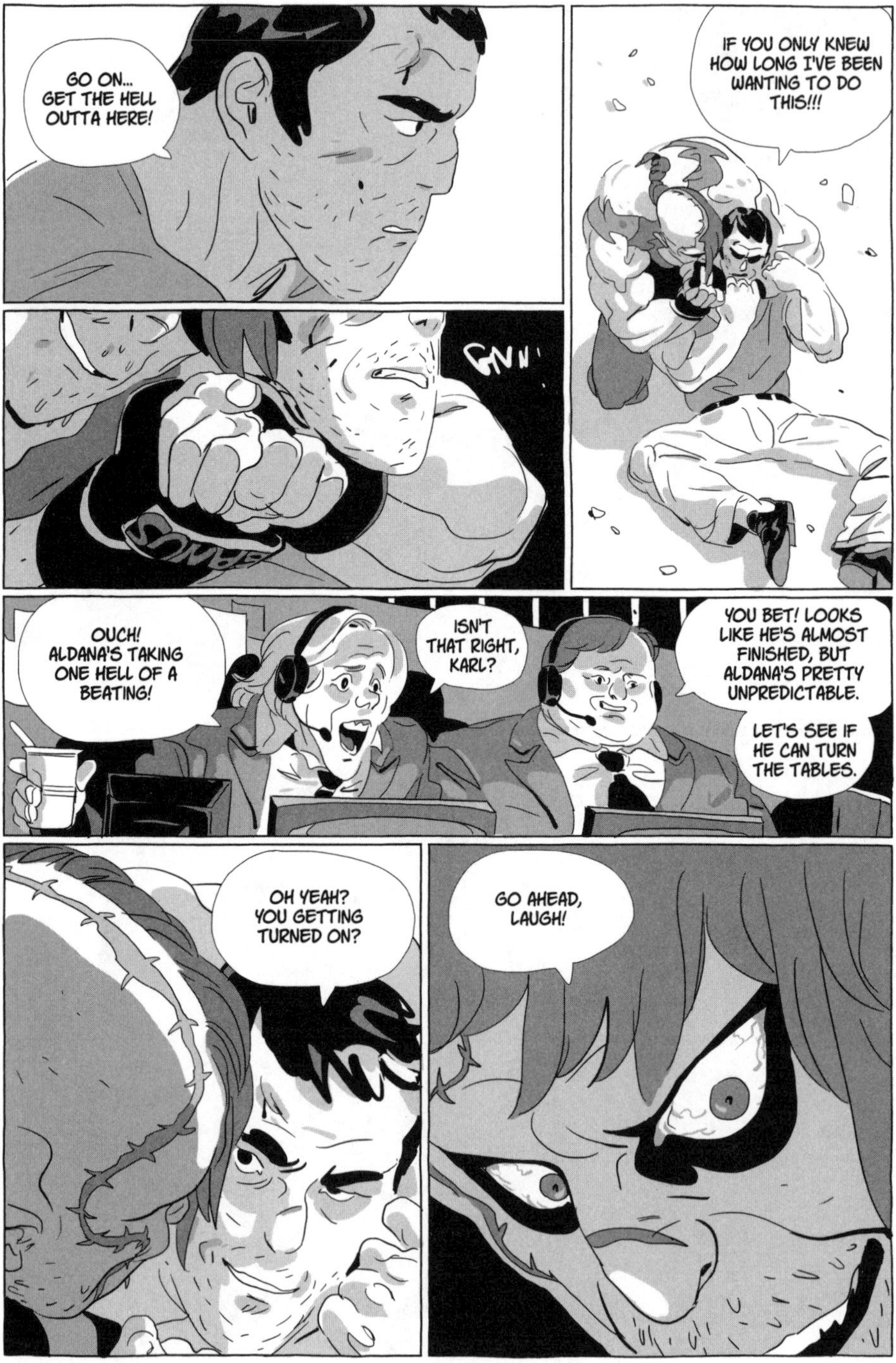
GO ON... GET THE HELL OUTTA HERE!
IF YOU ONLY KNEW HOW LONG I'VE BEEN WANTING TO DO THIS!!!
OUCH! ALDANA'S TAKING ONE HELL OF A BEATING!
ISN'T THAT RIGHT, KARL?
YOU BET! LOOKS LIKE HE'S ALMOST FINISHED, BUT ALDANA'S PRETTY UNPREDICTABLE.
LET'S SEE IF HE CAN TURN THE TABLES.
OH YEAH? YOU GETTING TURNED ON?
GO AHEAD, LAUGH!

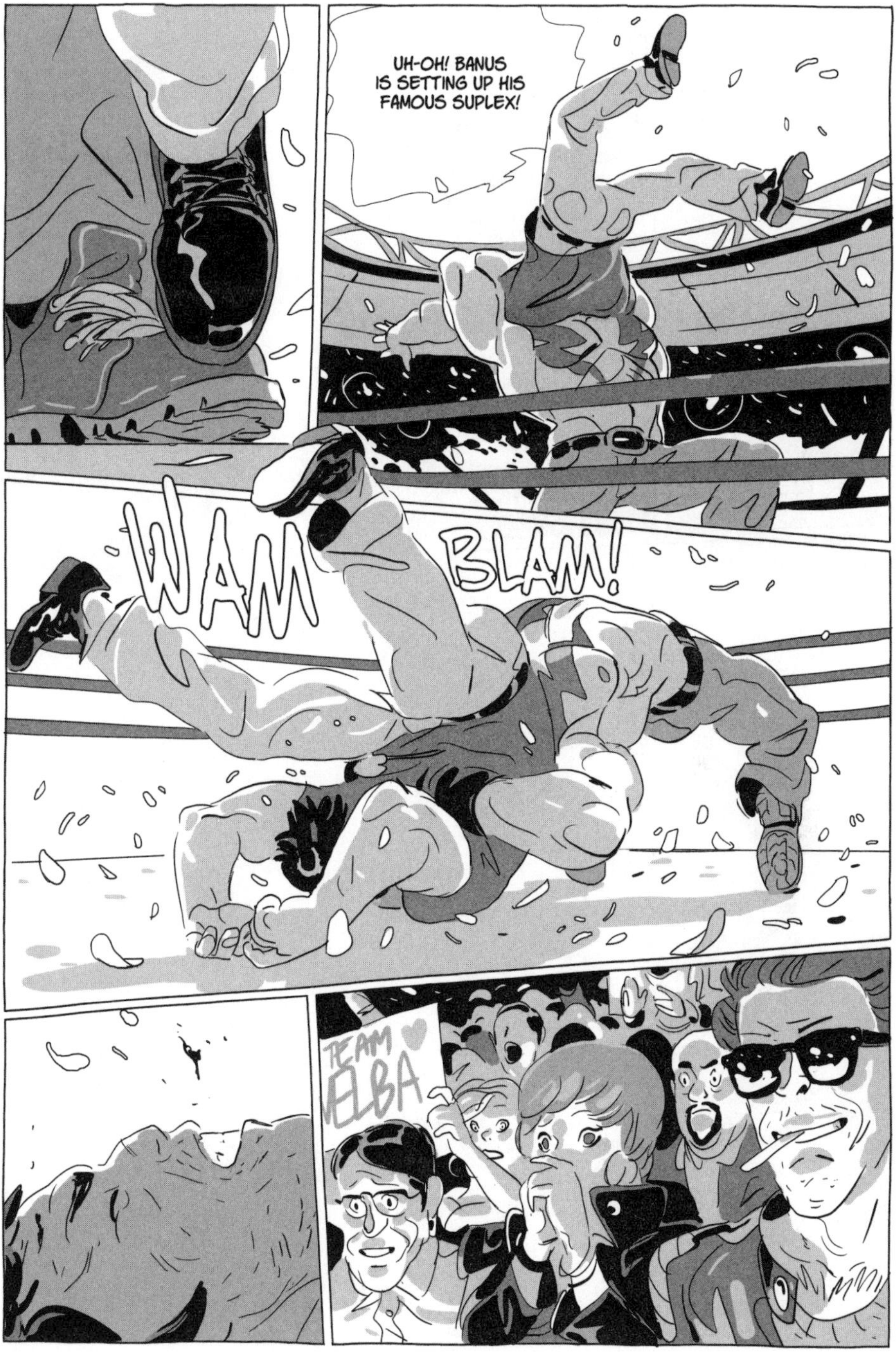
UH-OH! BANUS IS SETTING UP HIS FAMOUS SUPLEX!
WAM
BLAM!
TEAM

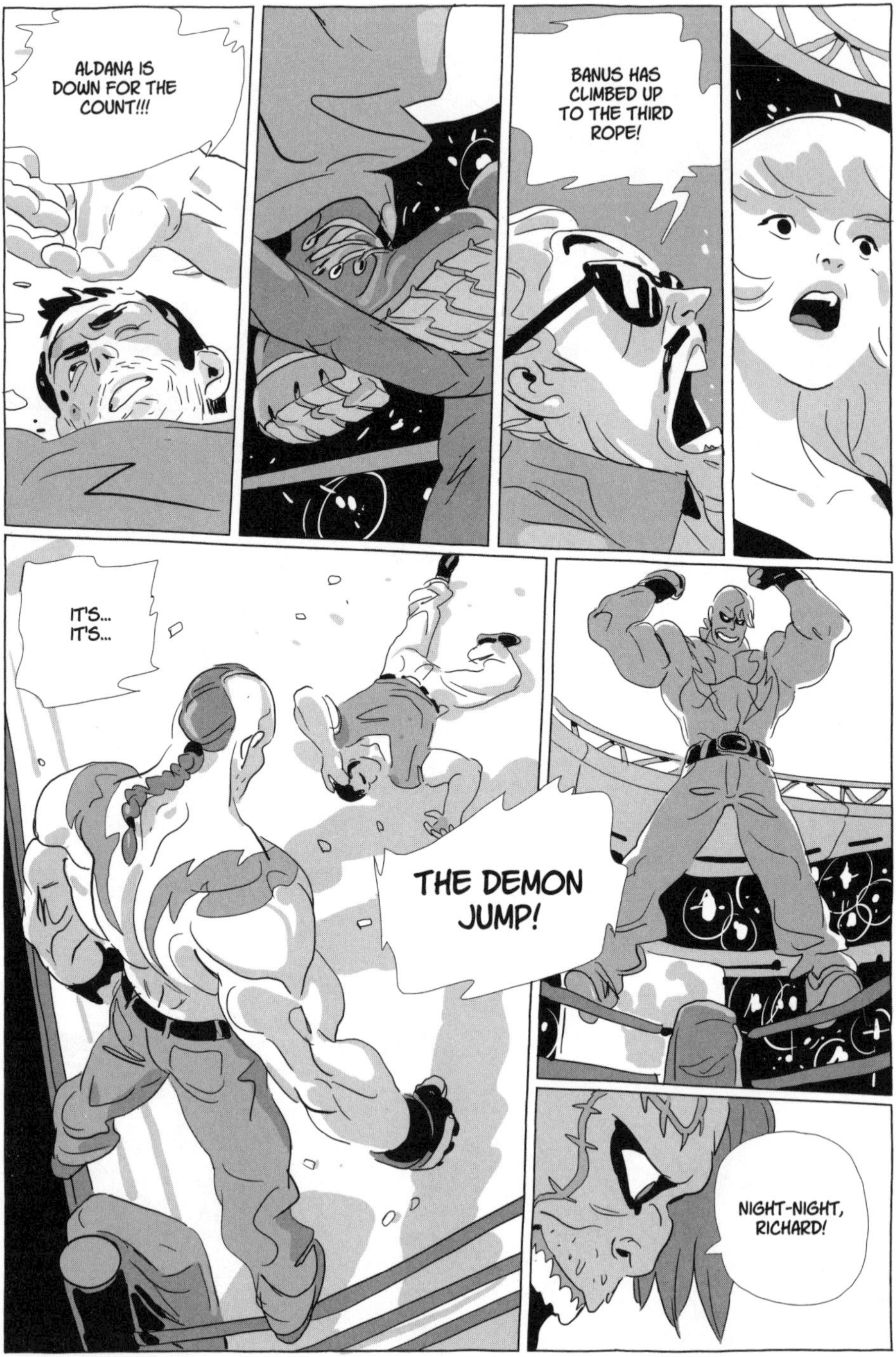
ALDANA IS DOWN FOR THE COUNT!!!
BANUS HAS CLIMBED UP TO THE THIRD ROPE!
IT'S... IT'S...
THE DEMON JUMP!
NIGHT-NIGHT, RICHARD!

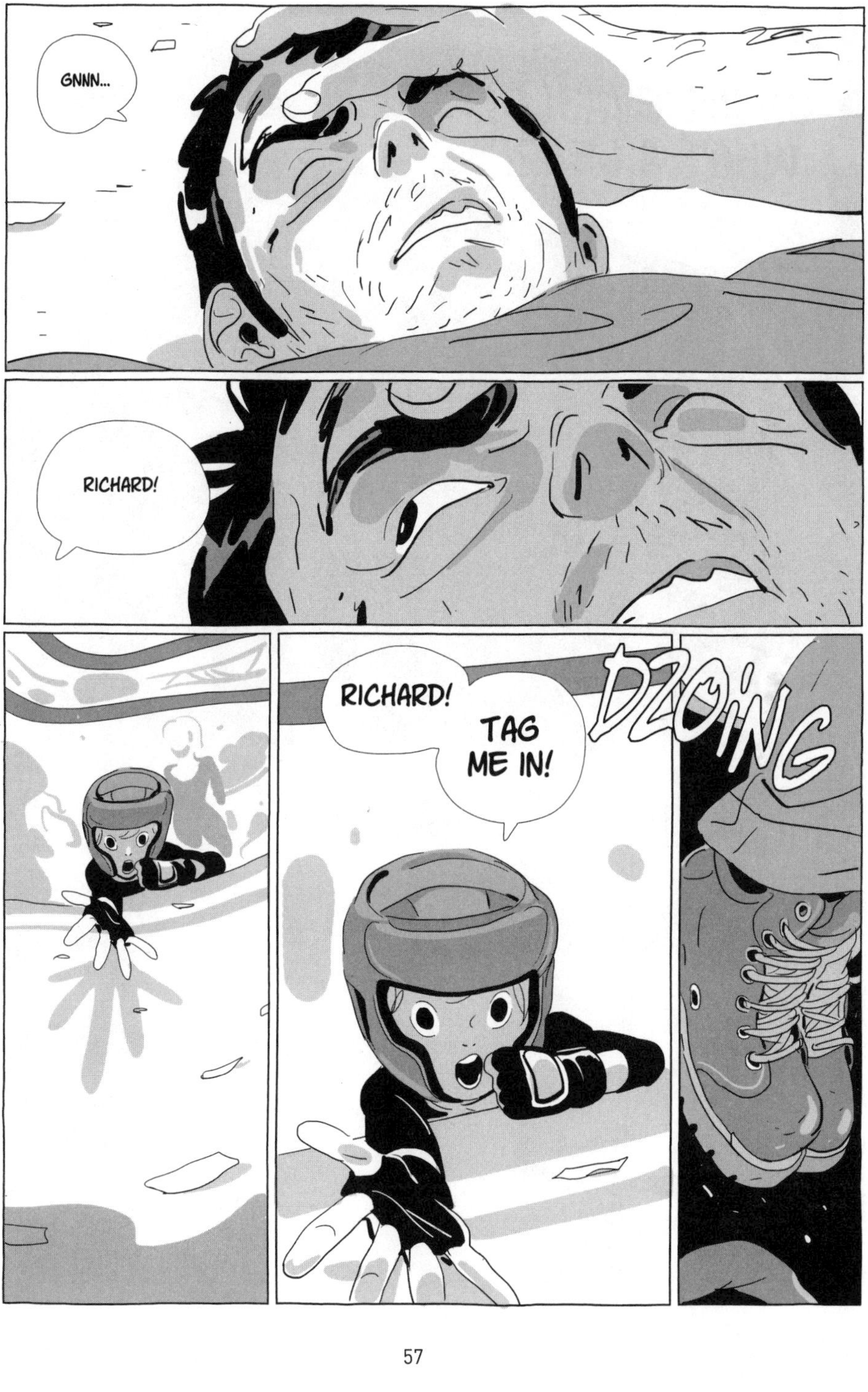
GNNN...
RICHARD!
RICHARD!
TAG ME IN!
DZOING

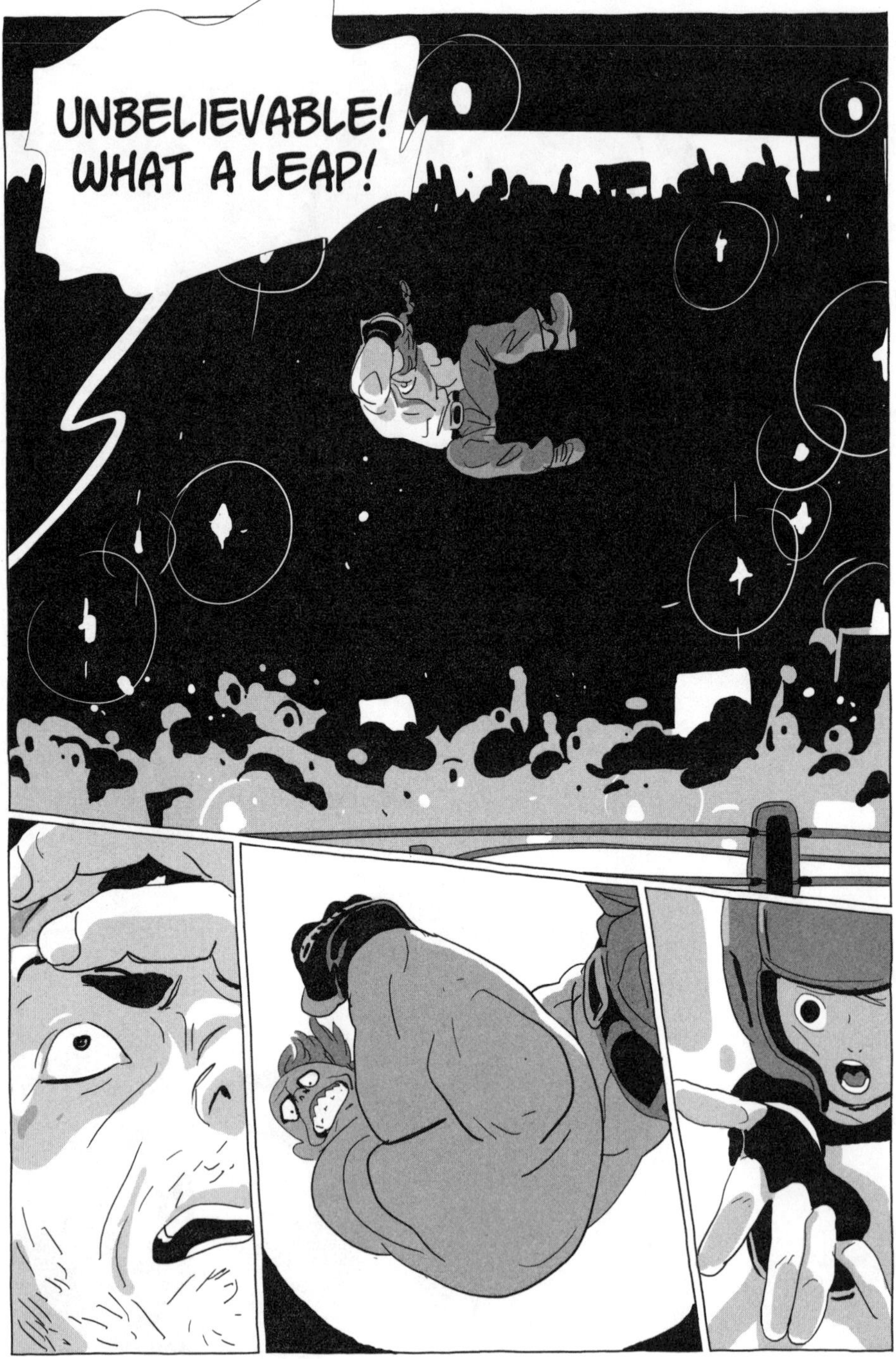
UNBELIEVABLE! WHAT A LEAP!

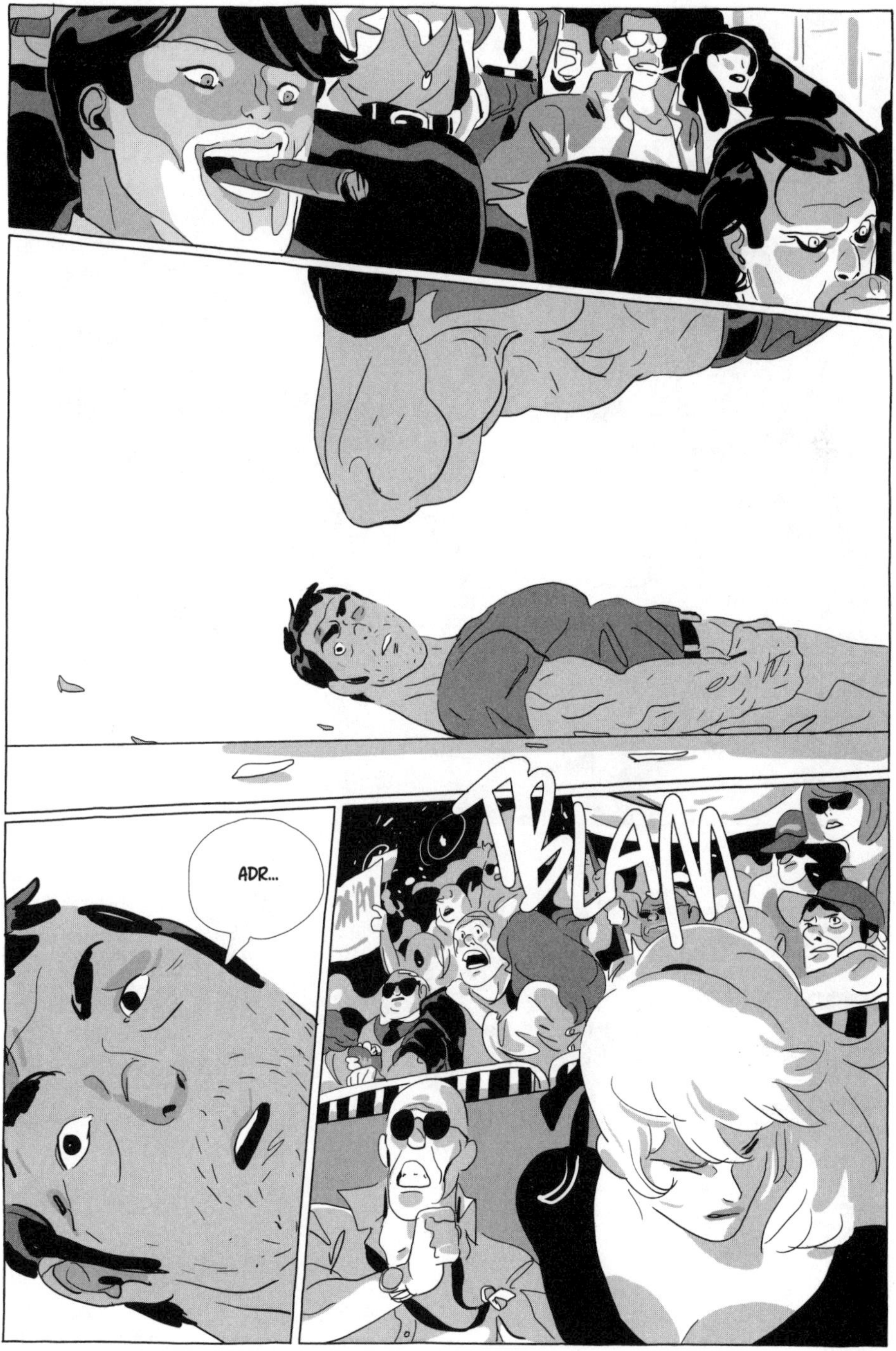
TBLAM
ADR...

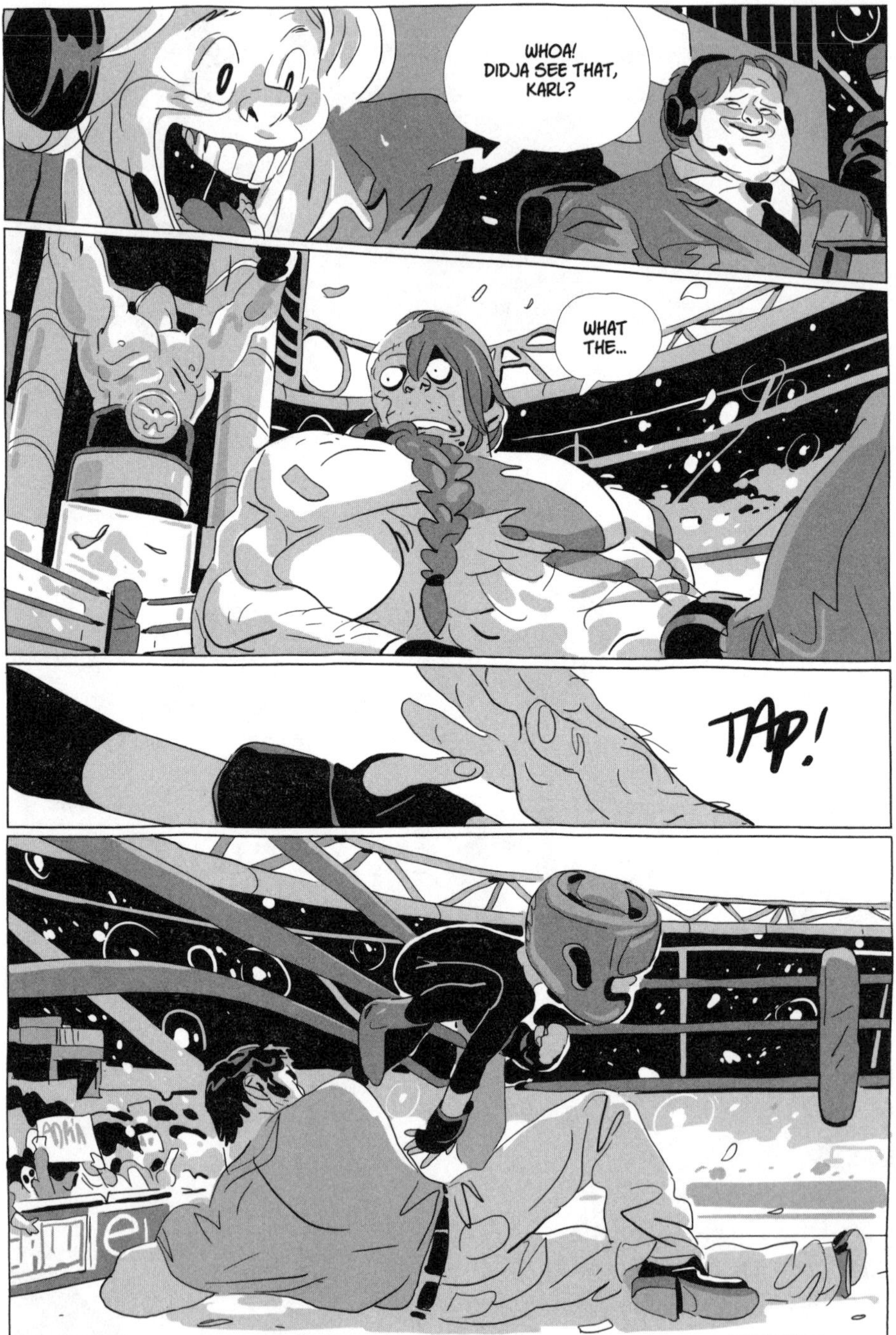
WHOA! DIDJA SEE THAT, KARL?
WHAT THE...
TAP!

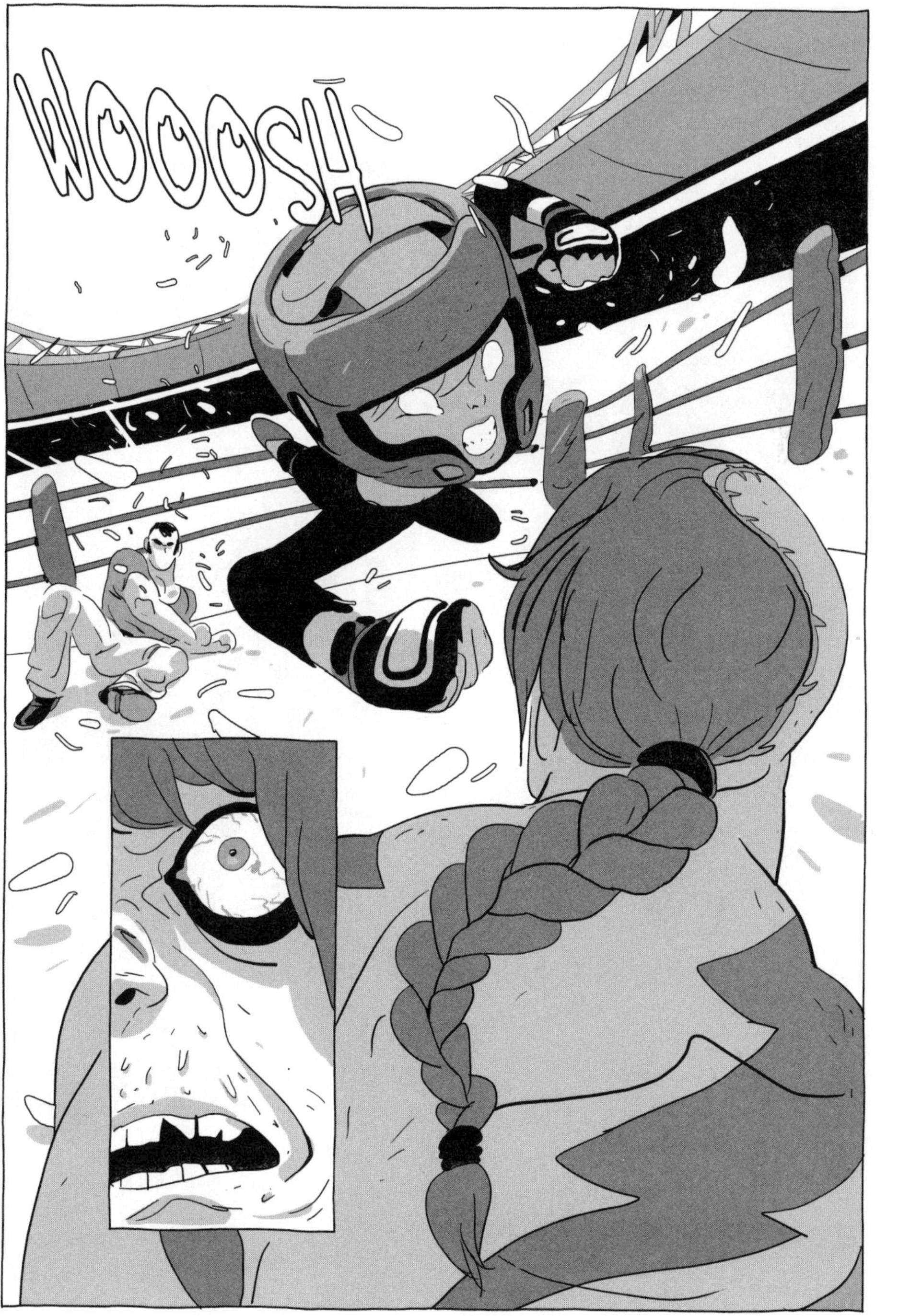
WOOOSH

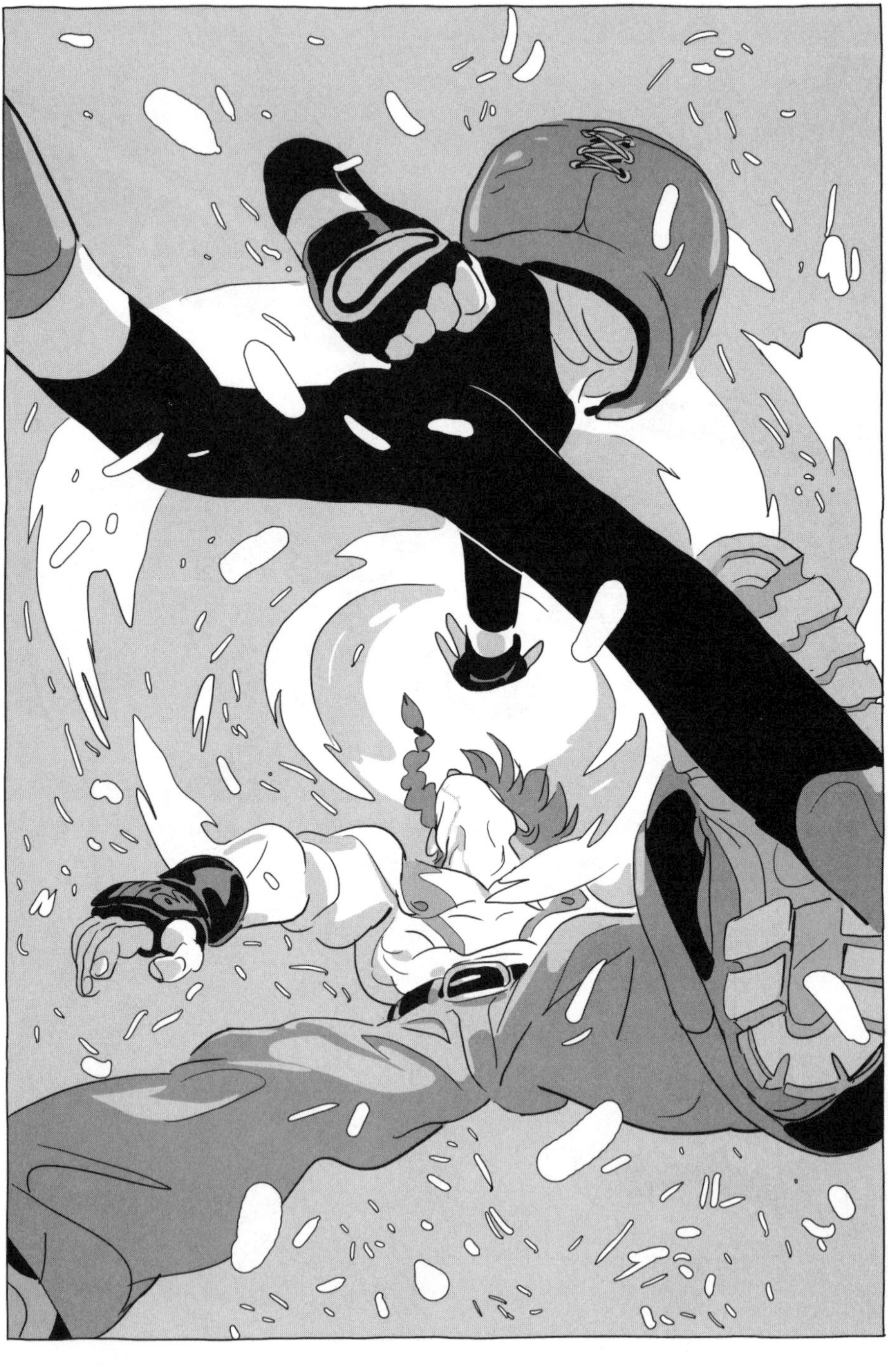

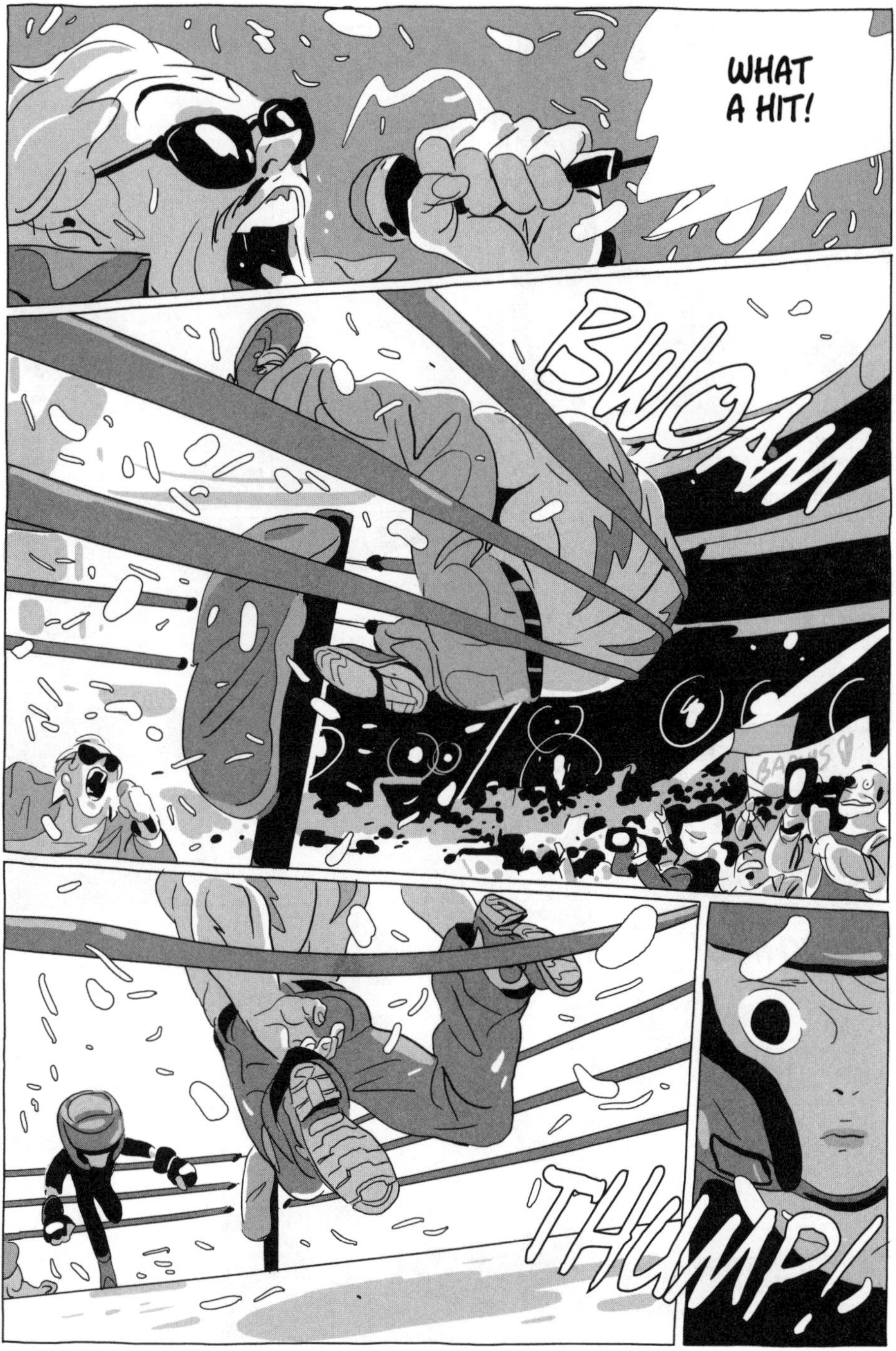
WHAT A HIT!
BWOAM
THUMP!

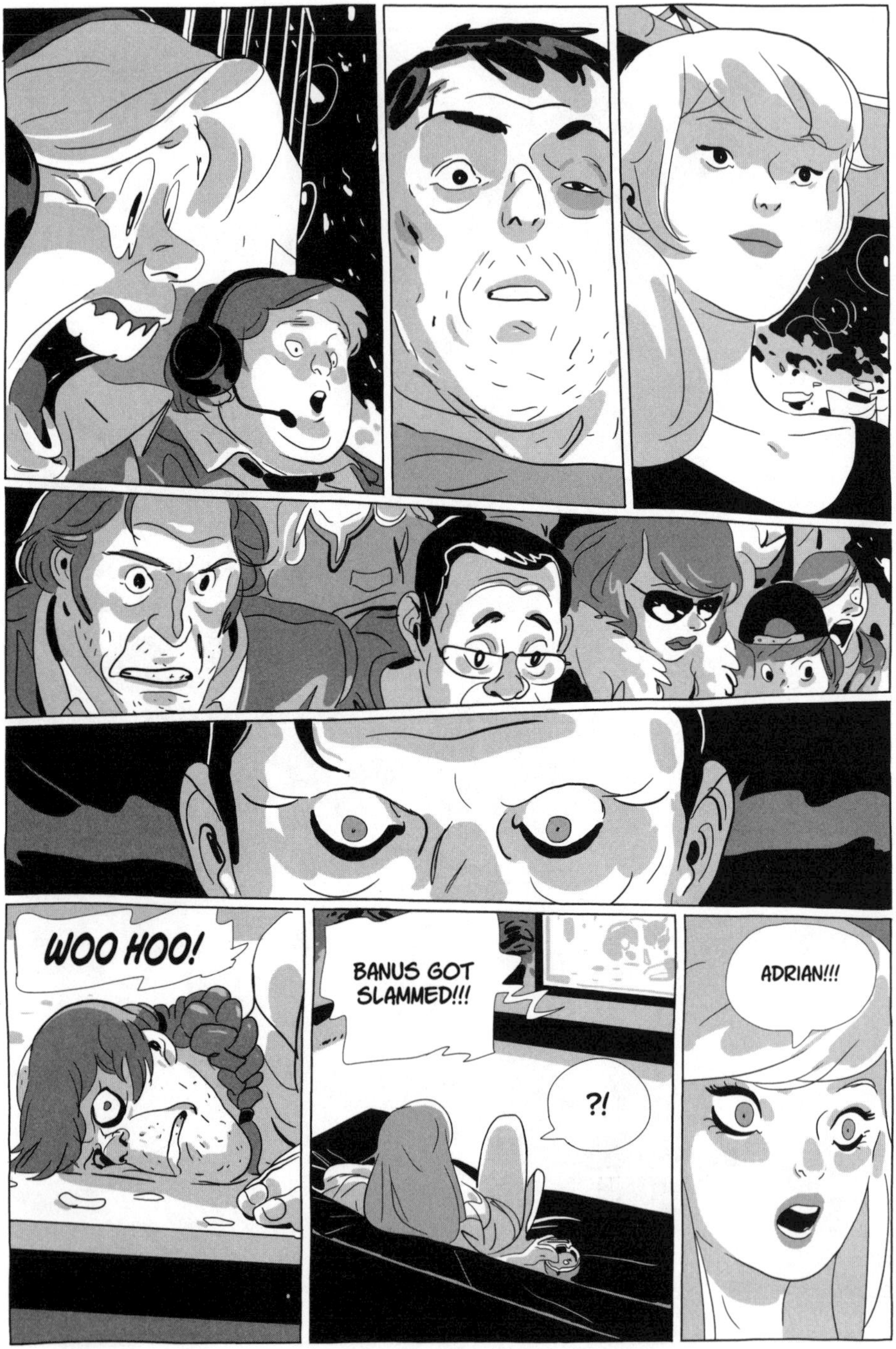
WOO HOO!
BANUS GOT SLAMMED!!!
?!
ADRIAN!!!

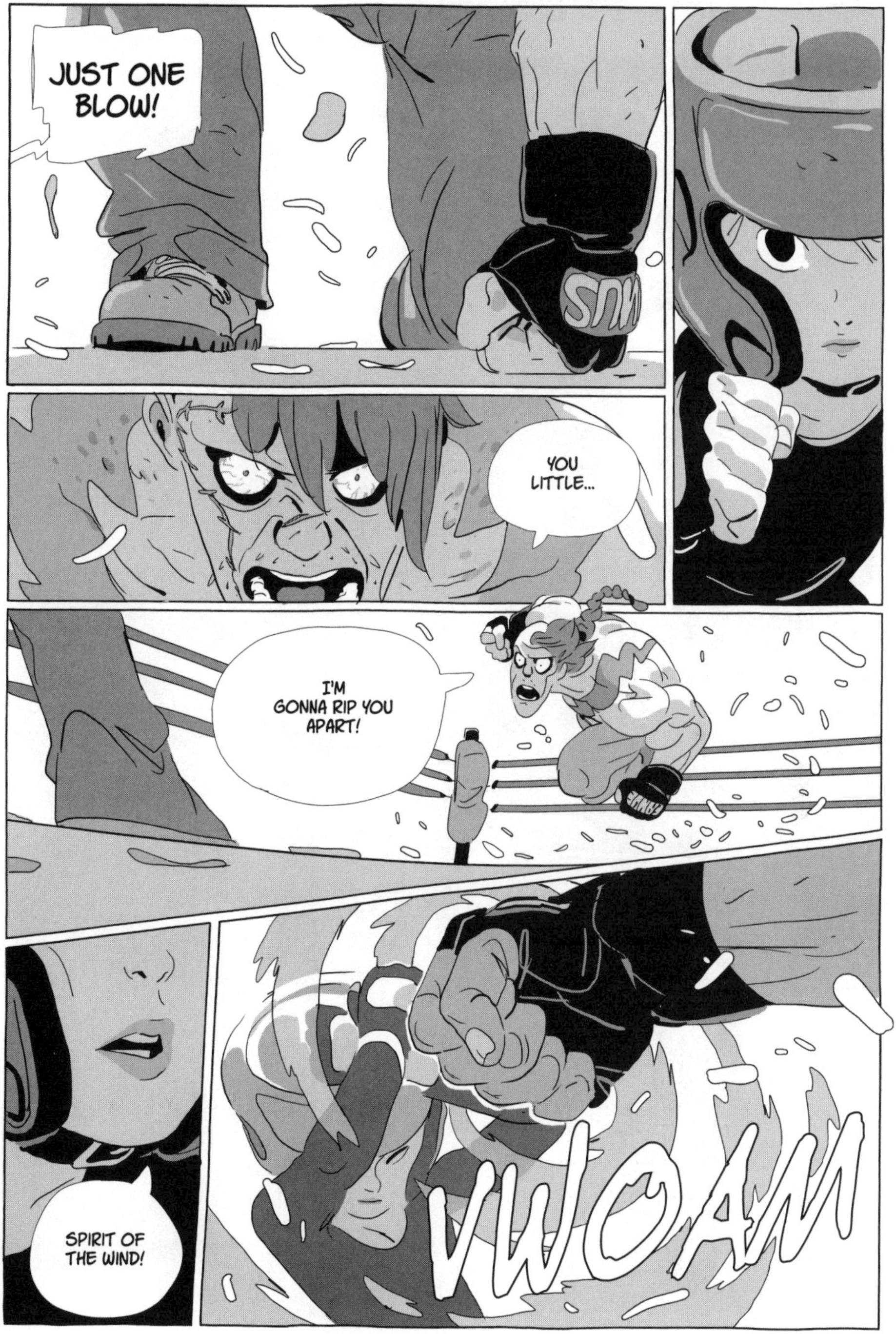
JUST ONE BLOW!
YOU LITTLE...
I'M GONNA RIP YOU APART!
SPIRIT OF THE WIND!
VWOAM

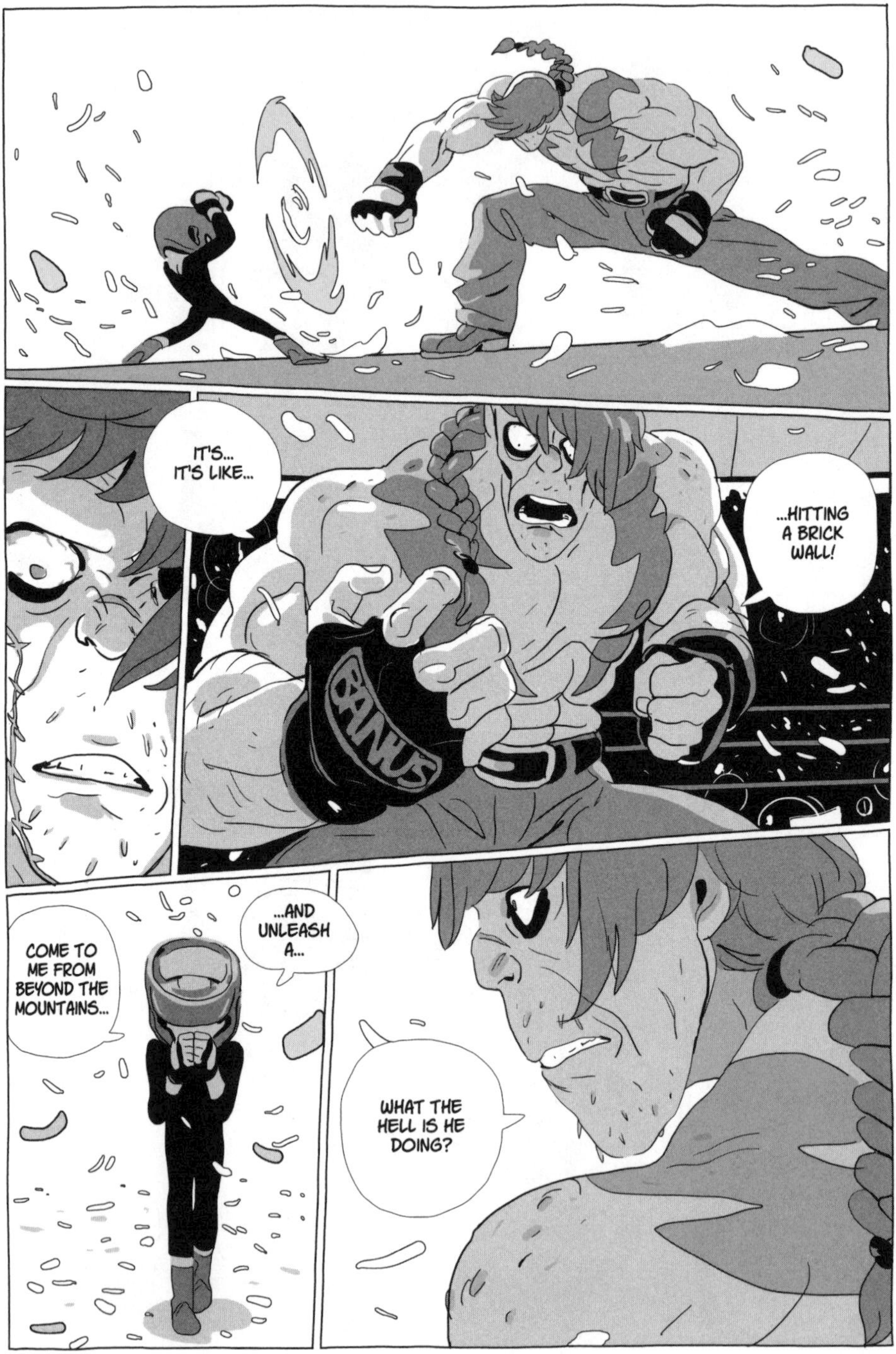
IT'S... IT'S LIKE...
...HITTING A BRICK WALL!
BANHUS
COME TO ME FROM BEYOND THE MOUNTAINS...
...AND UNLEASH A...
WHAT THE HELL IS HE DOING?

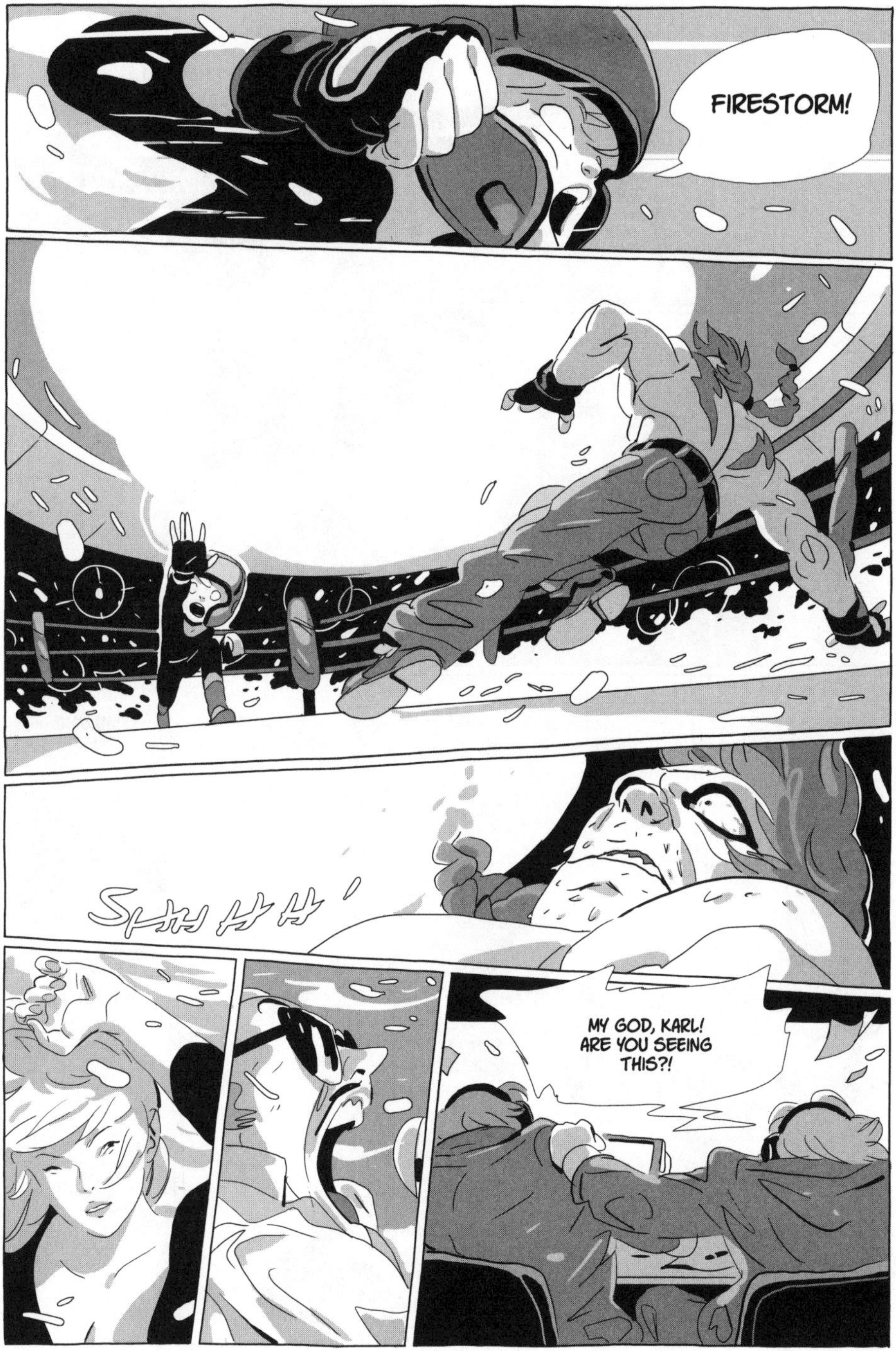
FIRESTORM!
SHHHH
MY GOD, KARL! ARE YOU SEEING THIS?!

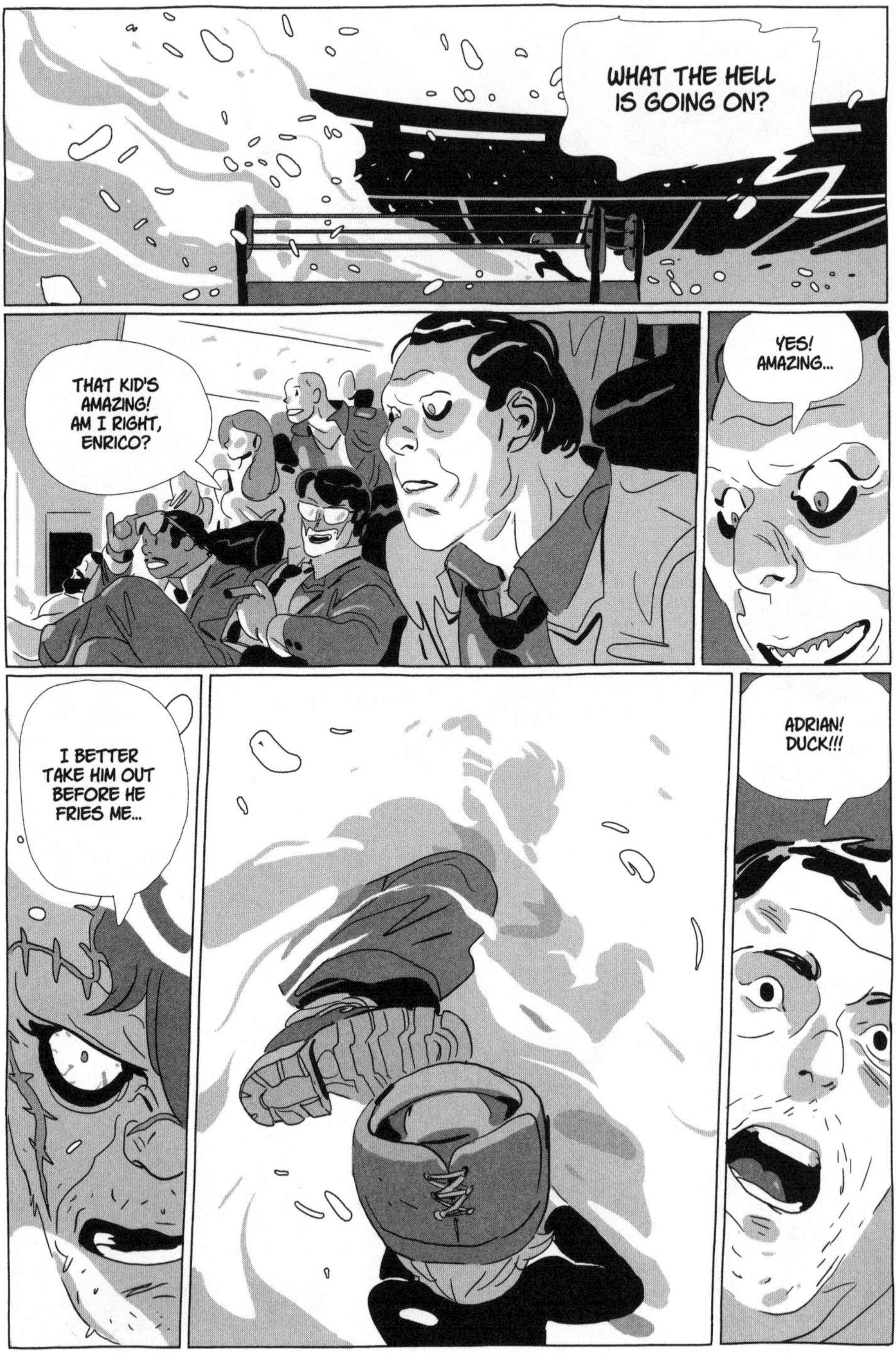
WHAT THE HELL IS GOING ON?
THAT KID'S AMAZING! AM I RIGHT, ENRICO?
YES! AMAZING...
I BETTER TAKE HIM OUT BEFORE HE FRIES ME...
ADRIAN! DUCK!!!

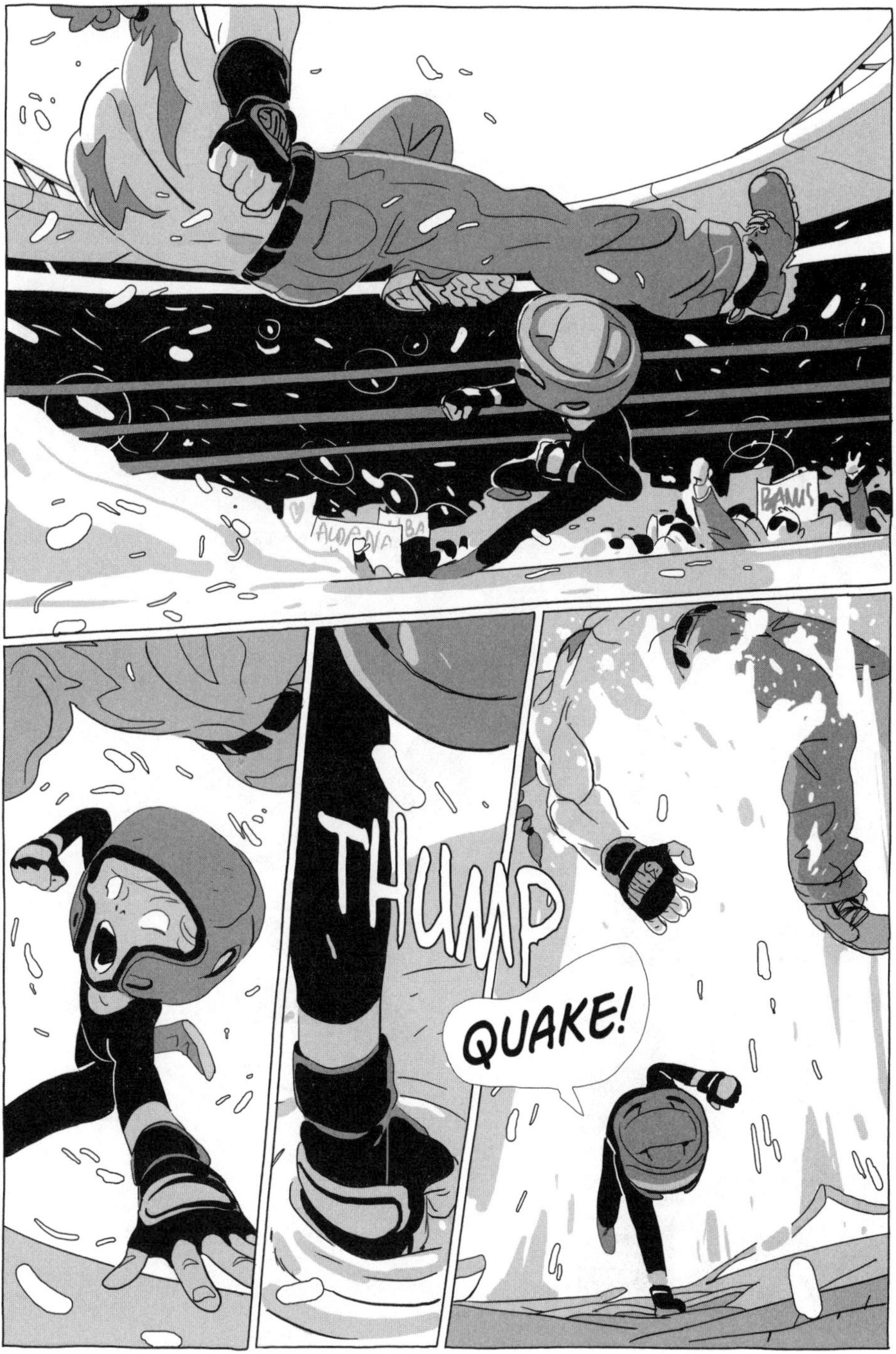

BANUS
THUMP
QUAKE!

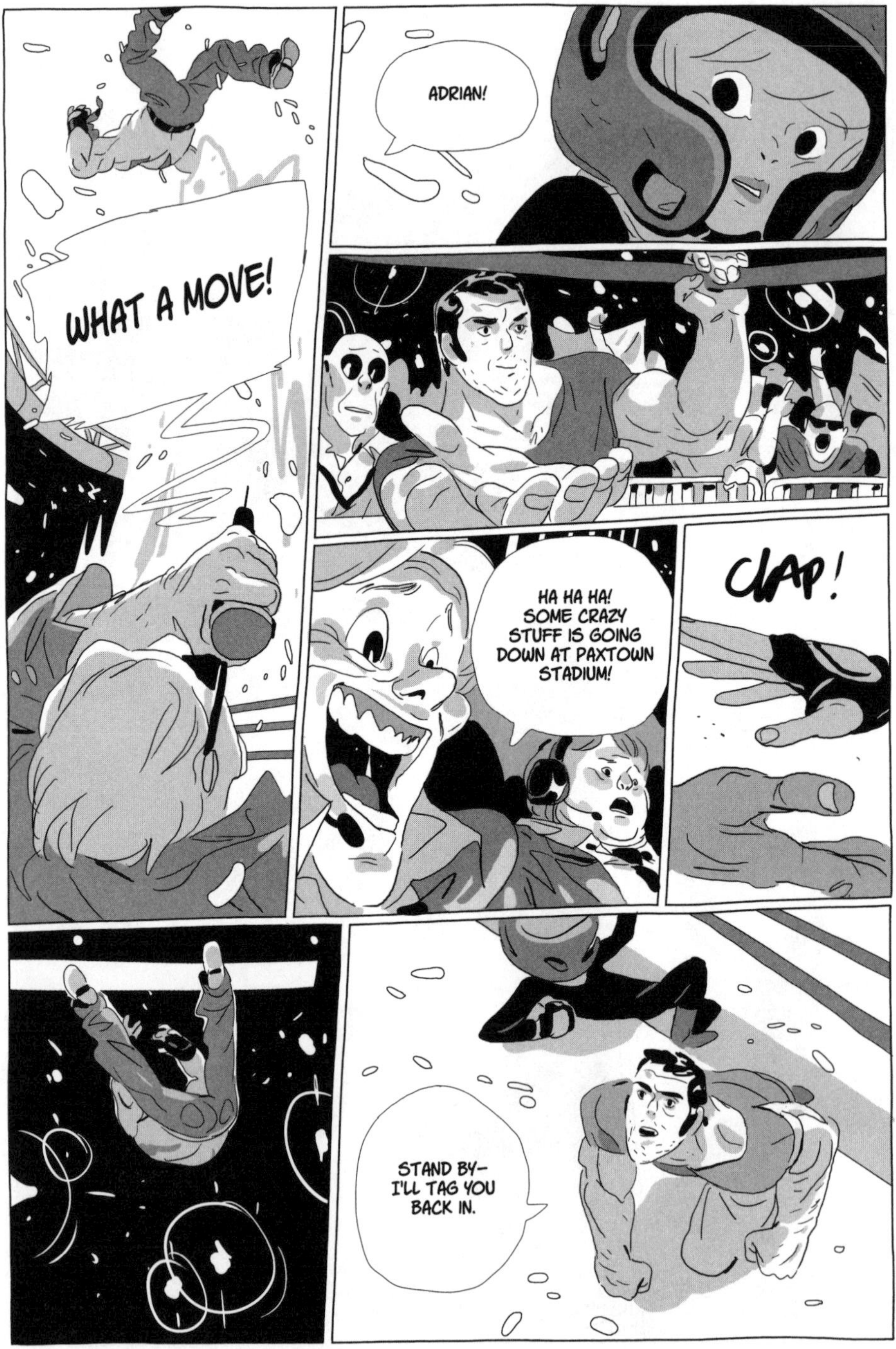
WHAT A MOVE!
ADRIAN!
HA HA HA! SOME CRAZY STUFF IS GOING DOWN AT PAXTOWN STADIUM!
CLAP!
STAND BY— I'LL TAG YOU BACK IN.

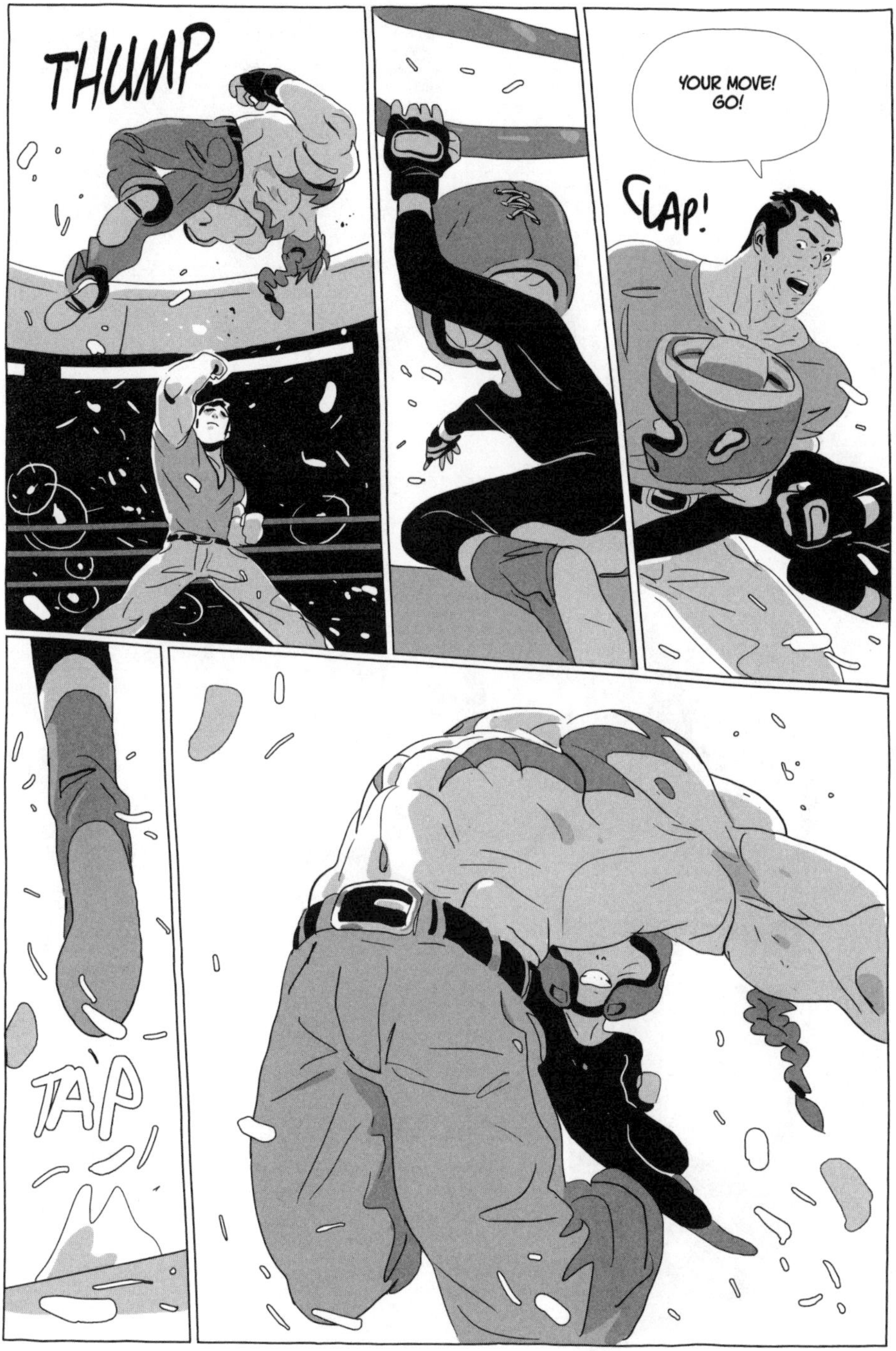
THUMP
CLAP!
YOUR MOVE! GO!
TAP

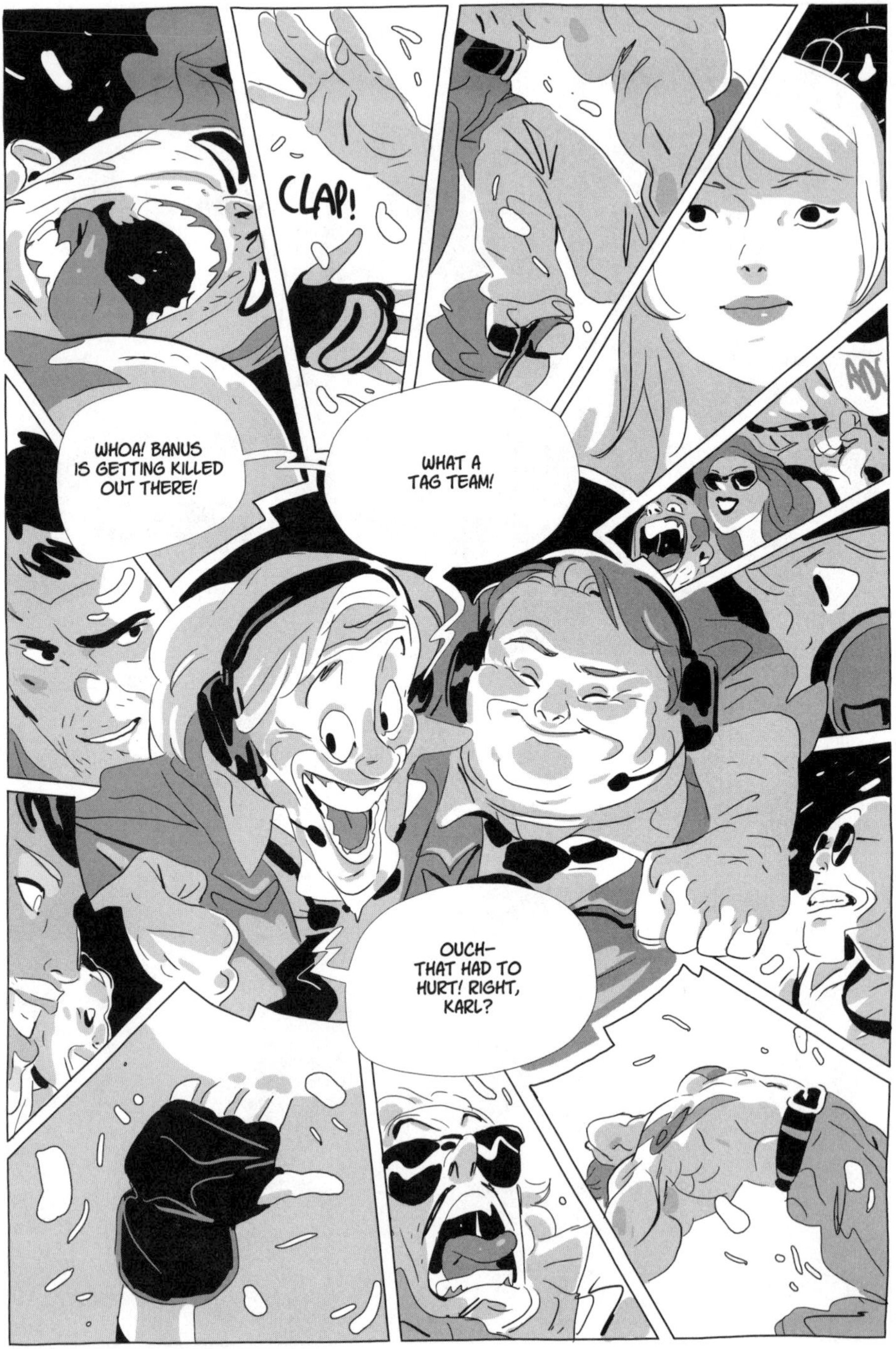
CLAP!
WHOA! BANUS IS GETTING KILLED OUT THERE!
WHAT A TAG TEAM!
OUCH— THAT HAD TO HURT! RIGHT, KARL?

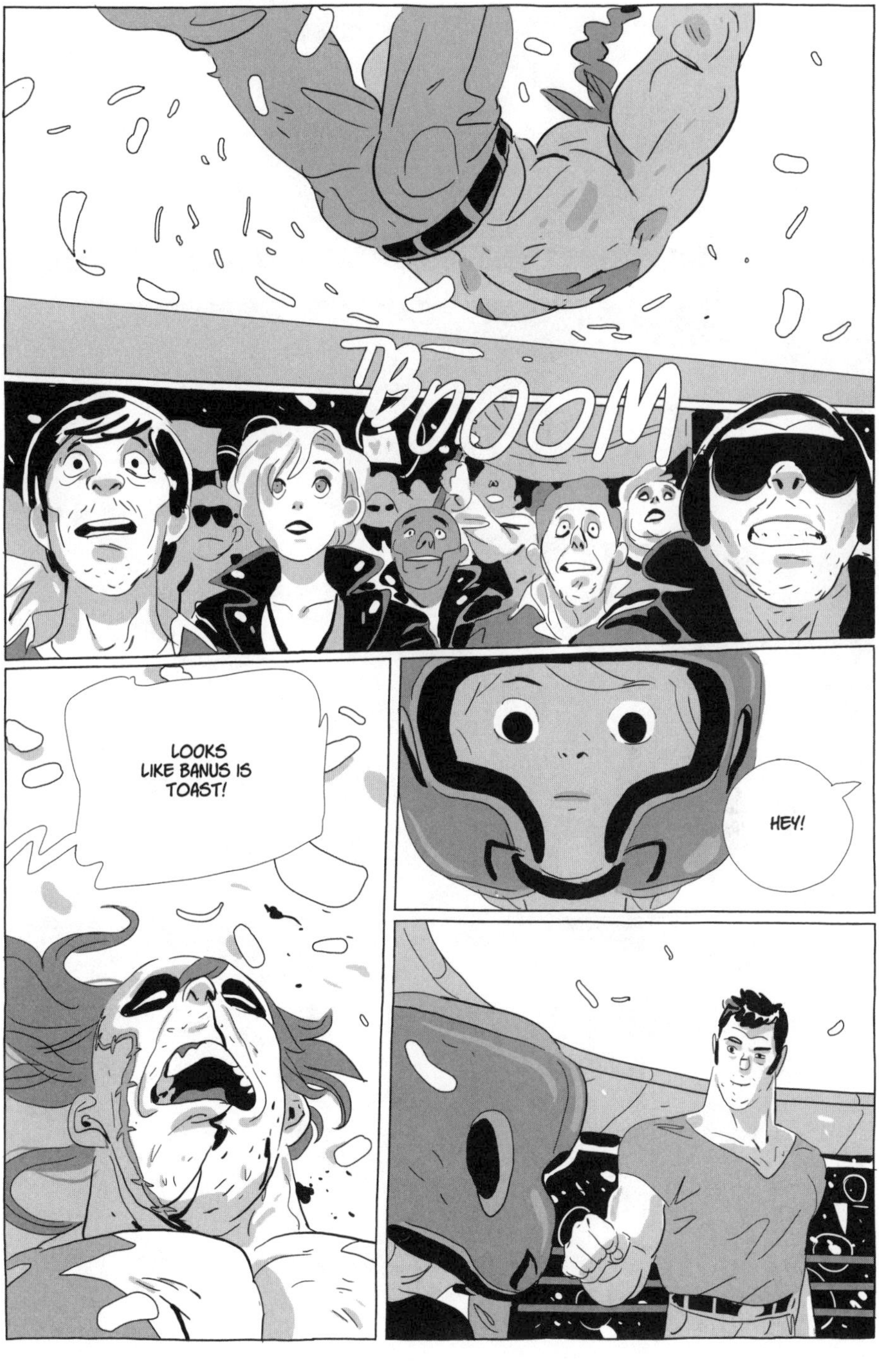
BOOOM
LOOKS LIKE BANUS IS TOAST!
HEY!

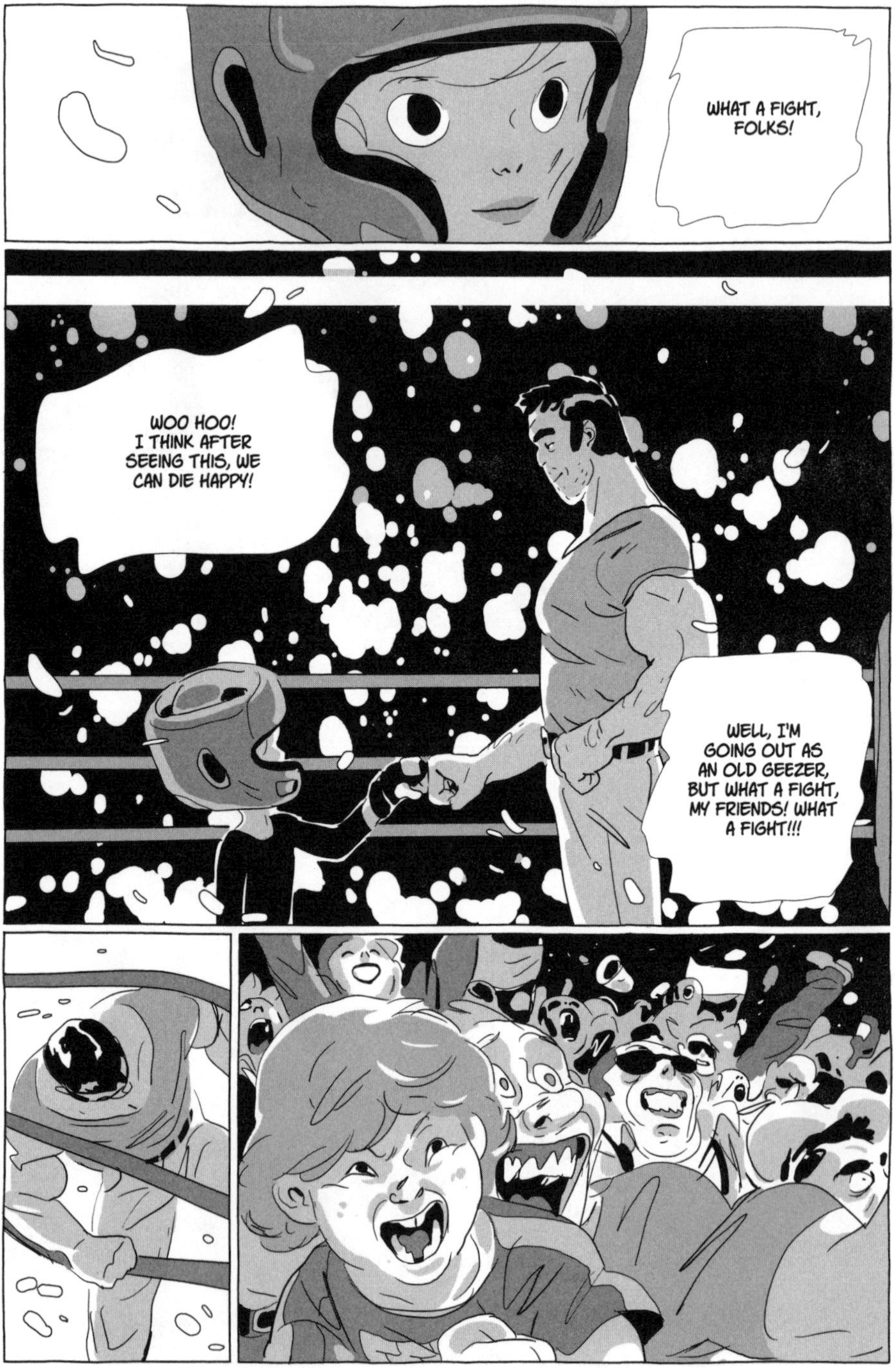
WHAT A FIGHT, FOLKS!
WOO HOO! I THINK AFTER SEEING THIS, WE CAN DIE HAPPY!
WELL, I'M GOING OUT AS AN OLD GEEZER, BUT WHAT A FIGHT, MY FRIENDS! WHAT A FIGHT!!!

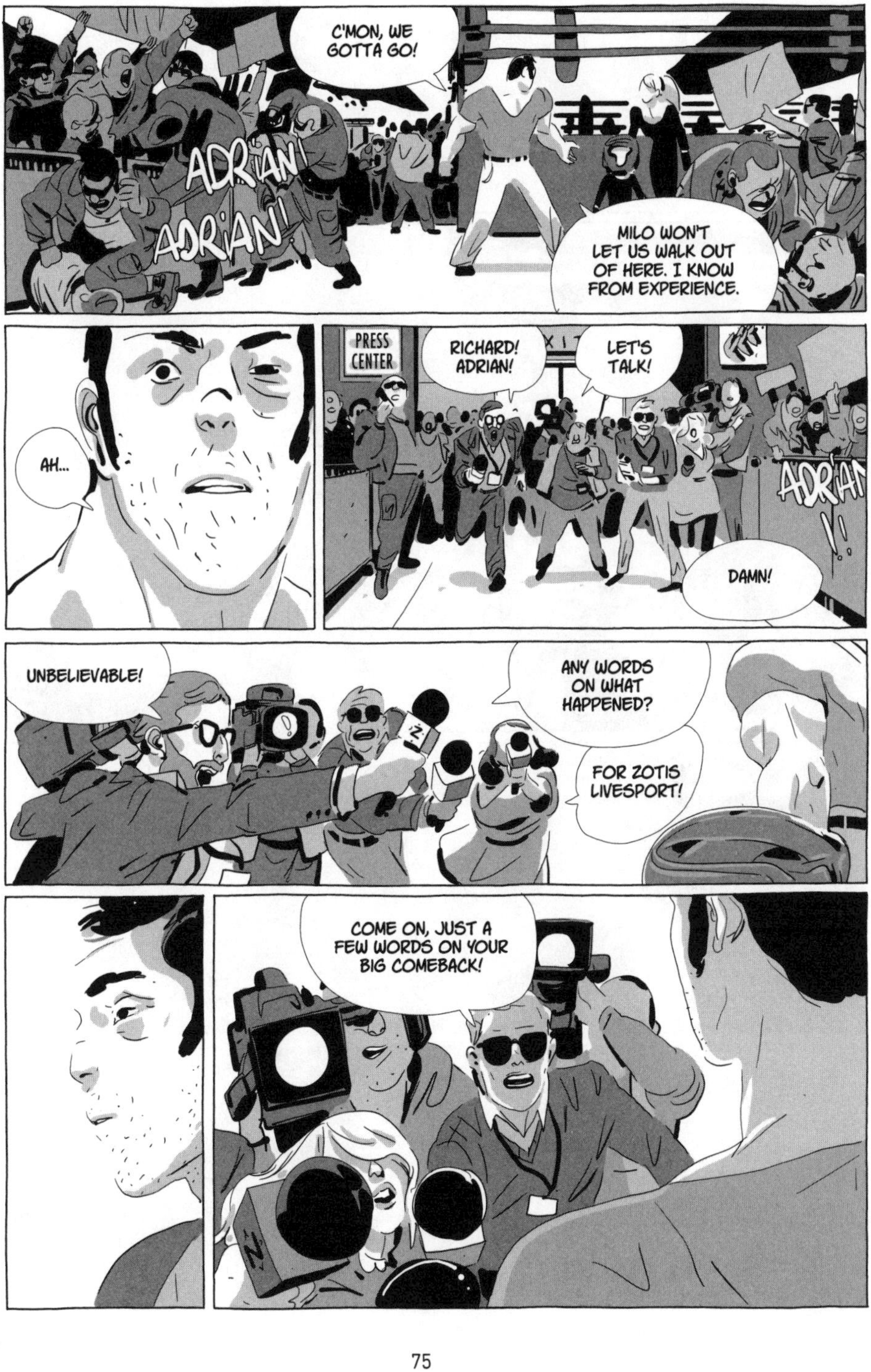
C'MON, WE GOTTA GO!
ADRIAN!
ADRIAN!
MILO WON'T LET US WALK OUT OF HERE. I KNOW FROM EXPERIENCE.
AH...
PRESS CENTER
RICHARD! ADRIAN!
LET'S TALK!
ADRIAN!
DAMN!
UNBELIEVABLE!
ANY WORDS ON WHAT HAPPENED?
FOR ZOTIS LIVESPORT!
COME ON, JUST A FEW WORDS ON YOUR BIG COMEBACK!

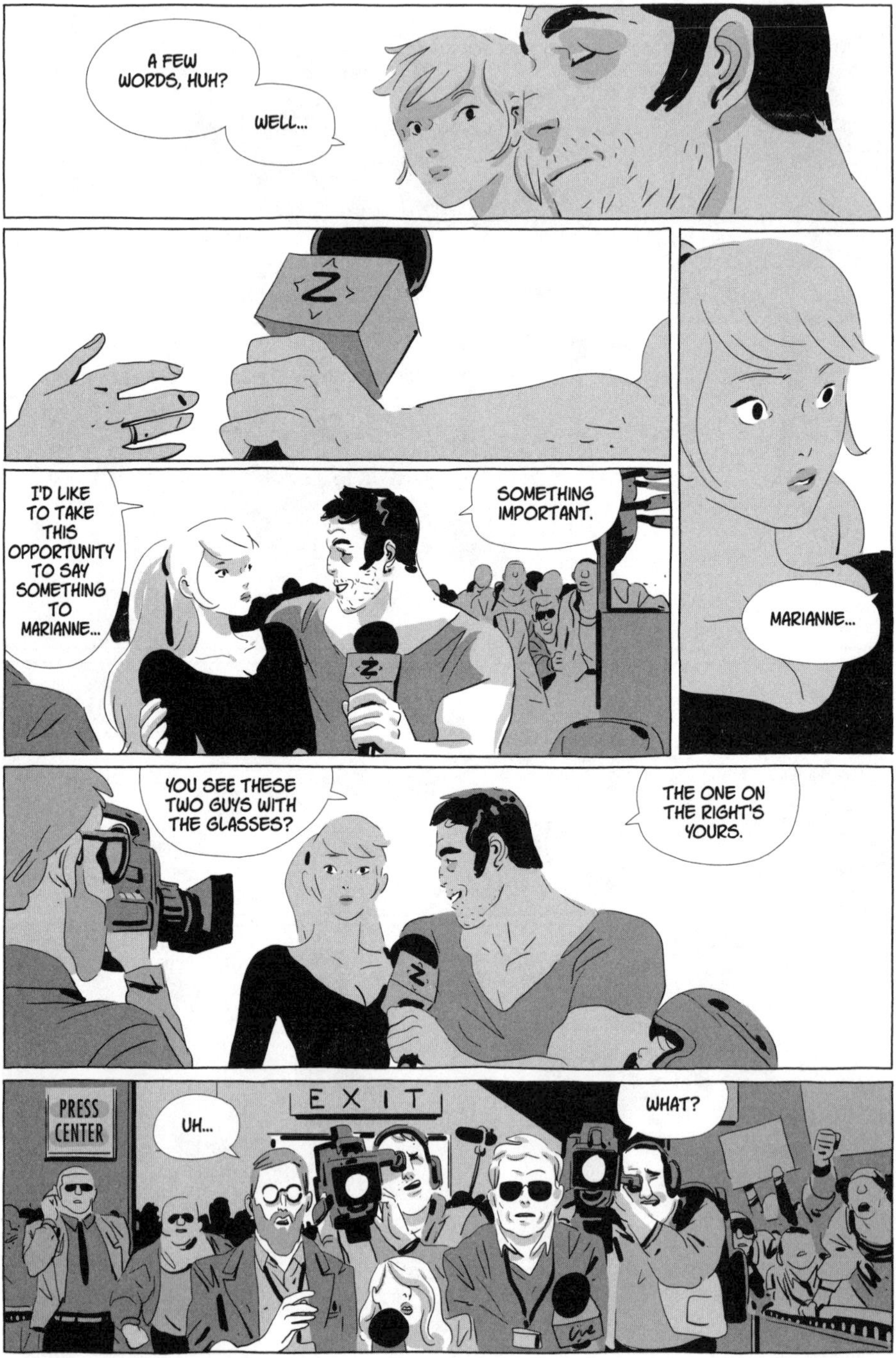
A FEW WORDS, HUH?
WELL...
I'D LIKE TO TAKE THIS OPPORTUNITY TO SAY SOMETHING TO MARIANNE...
SOMETHING IMPORTANT.
MARIANNE...
YOU SEE THESE TWO GUYS WITH THE GLASSES?
THE ONE ON THE RIGHT'S YOURS.
PRESS CENTER
EXIT
UH...
WHAT?

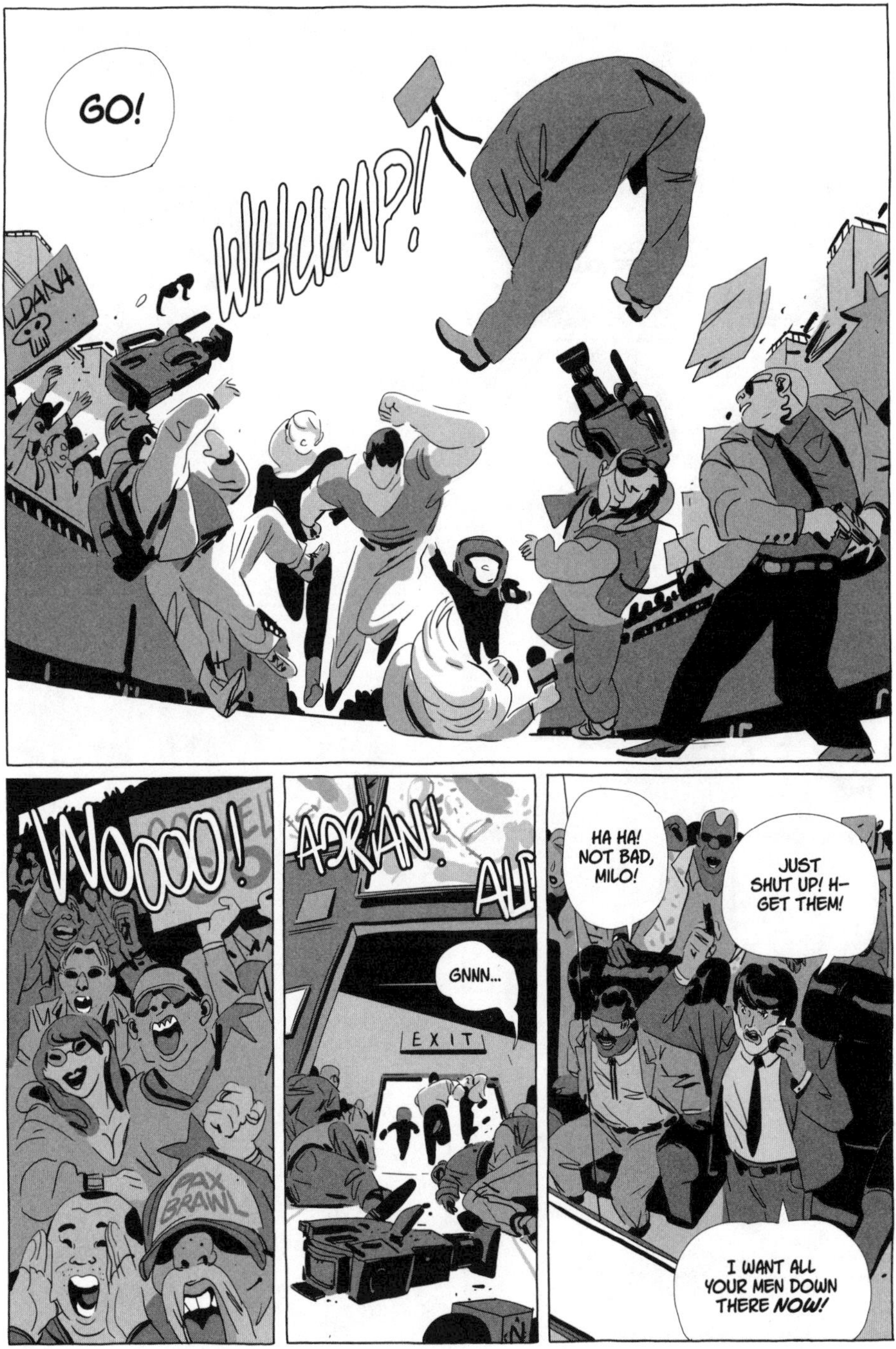
GO!
WHUMP!
WOOOO!
PAX BRAWL
ADRIAN!
GNNN...
EXIT
HA HA! NOT BAD, MILO!
JUST SHUT UP! H- GET THEM!
I WANT ALL YOUR MEN DOWN THERE *NOW!*

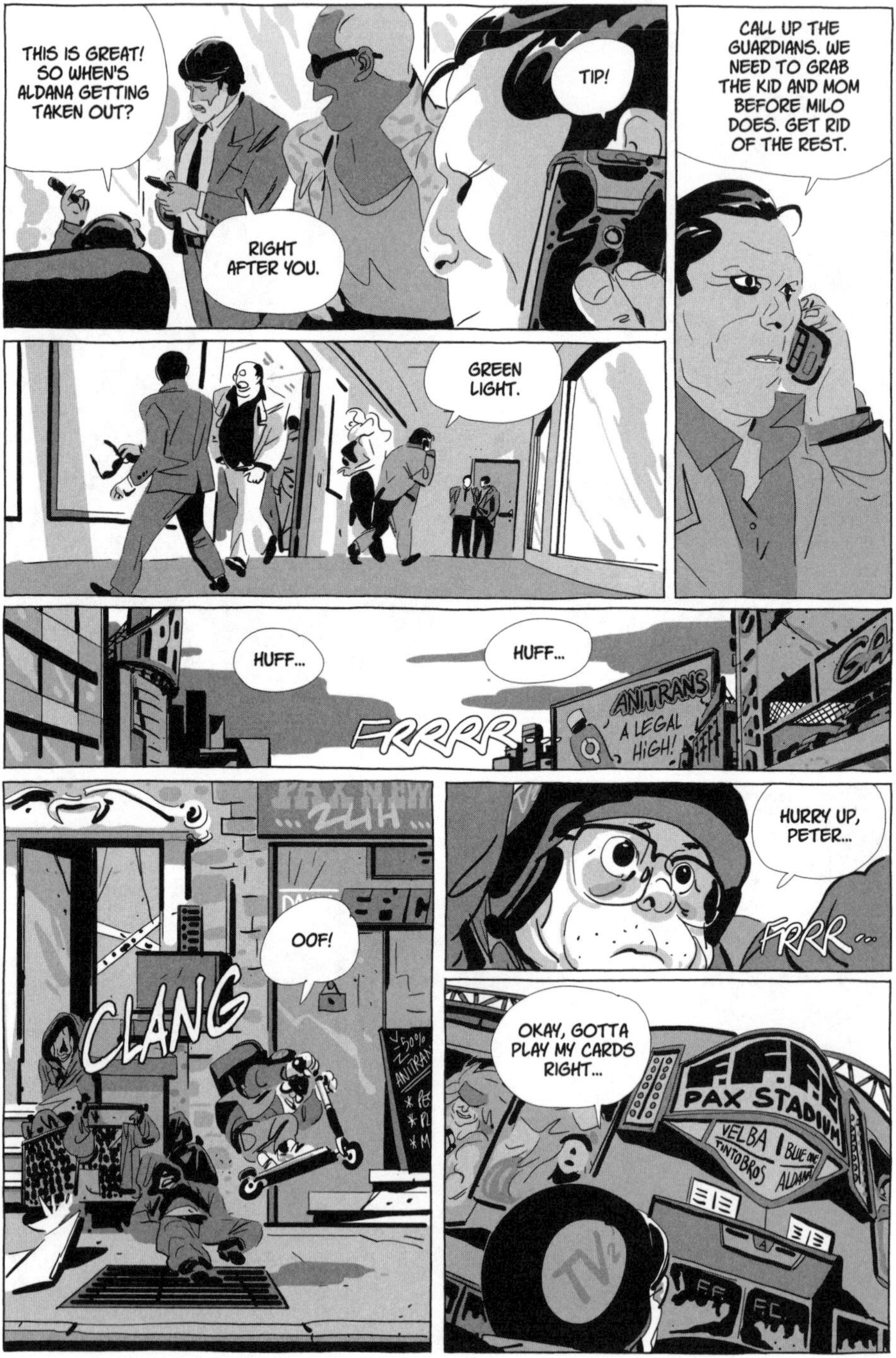
THIS IS GREAT! SO WHEN'S ALDANA GETTING TAKEN OUT?
RIGHT AFTER YOU.
TIP!
CALL UP THE GUARDIANS. WE NEED TO GRAB THE KID AND MOM BEFORE MILO DOES. GET RID OF THE REST.
GREEN LIGHT.
HUFF...
HUFF...
FRRRR
ANITRANS A LEGAL HIGH!
CLANG
OOF!
HURRY UP, PETER...
FRRR...
OKAY, GOTTA PLAY MY CARDS RIGHT...
F.F.F. PAX STADIUM
VELBA
BLUE ONE
TINTOBROS
ALDANA

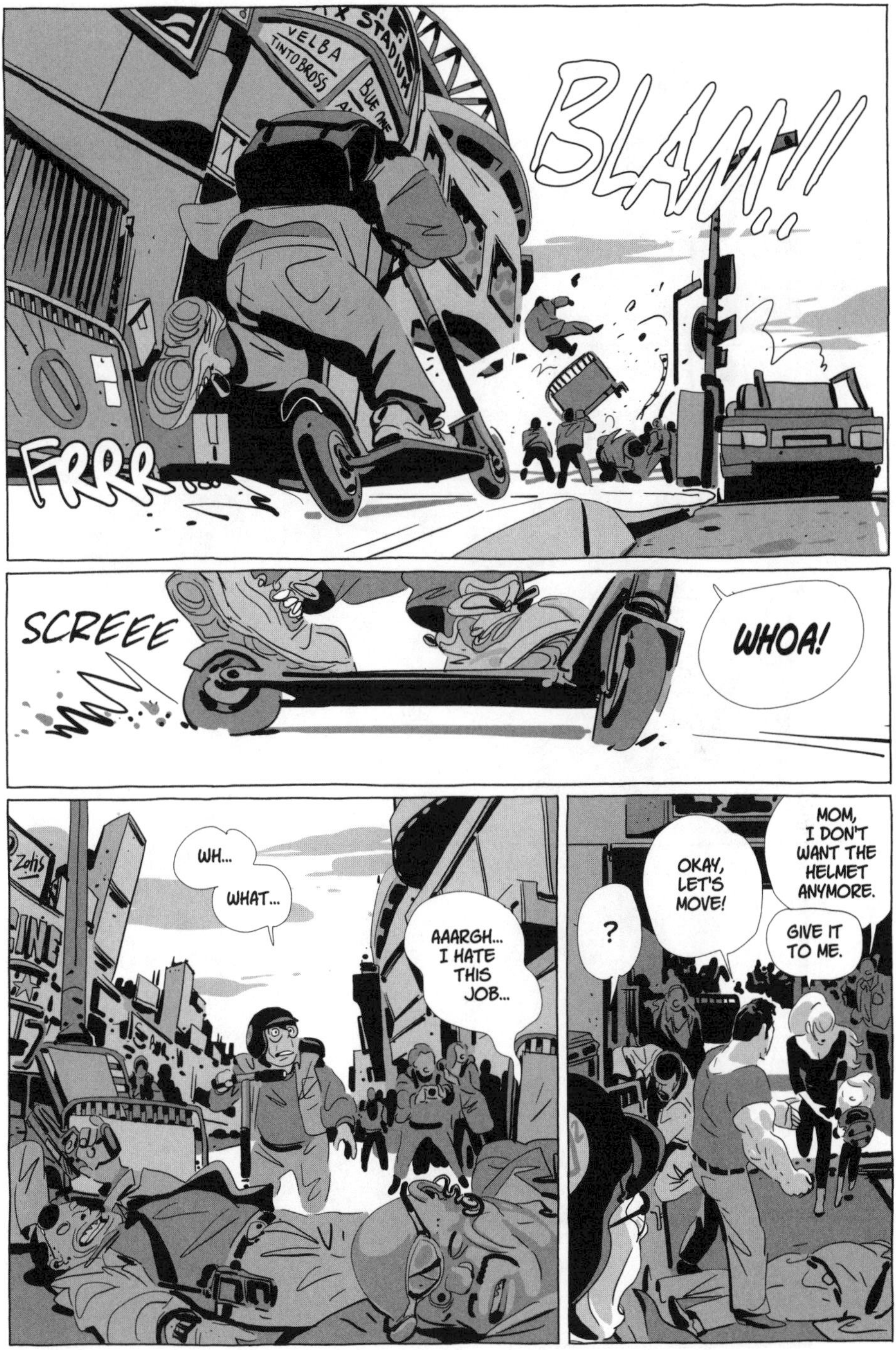
VELBA
TINTO BROSS
BLAM!!
FRRR...
SCREEE
WHOA!
WH...
WHAT...
AAARGH... I HATE THIS JOB...
OKAY, LET'S MOVE!
?
MOM, I DON'T WANT THE HELMET ANYMORE.
GIVE IT TO ME.

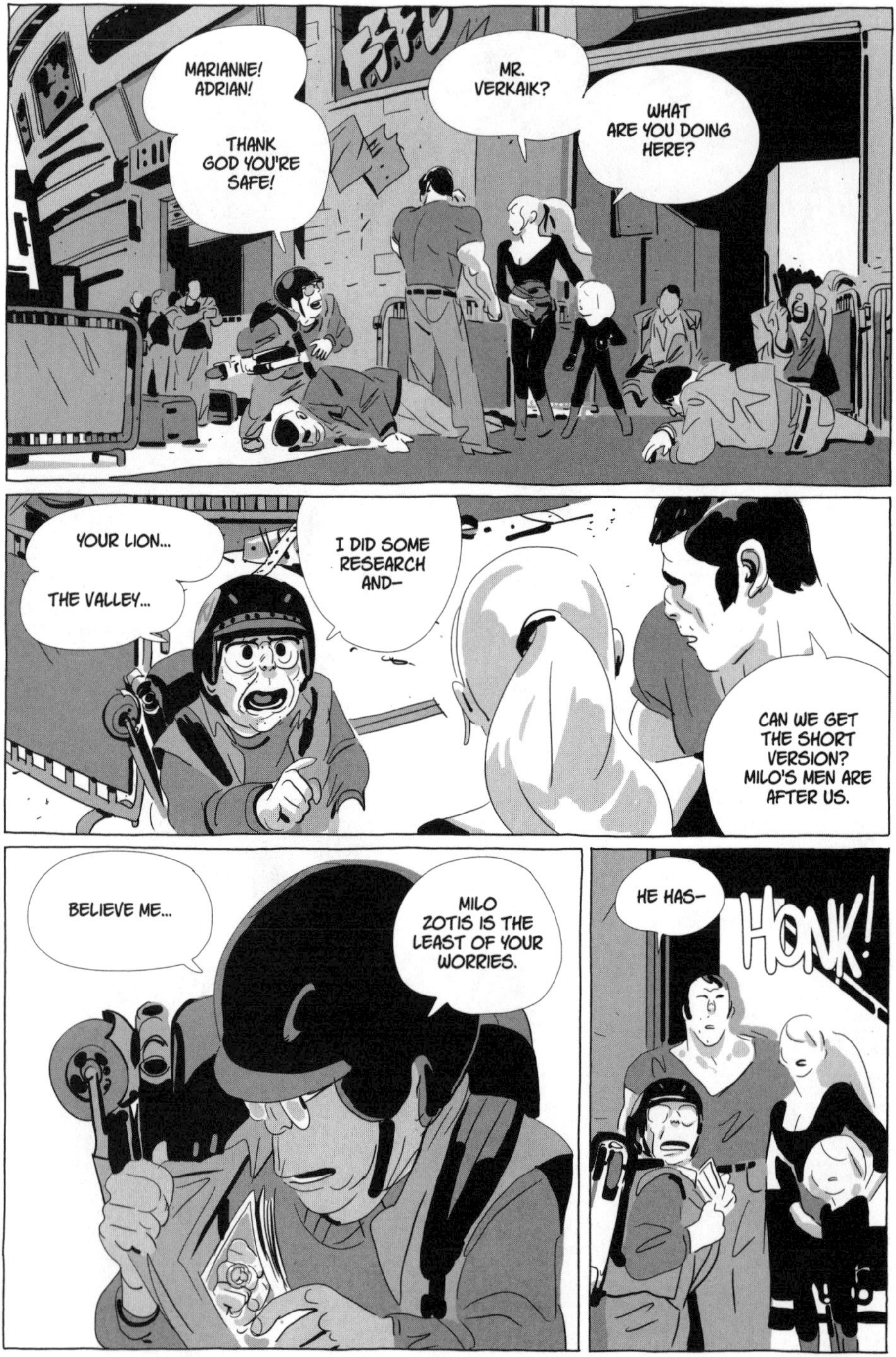
MARIANNE! ADRIAN!
THANK GOD YOU'RE SAFE!
MR. VERKAIK?
WHAT ARE YOU DOING HERE?
YOUR LION...
THE VALLEY...
I DID SOME RESEARCH AND-
CAN WE GET THE SHORT VERSION? MILO'S MEN ARE AFTER US.
BELIEVE ME...
MILO ZOTIS IS THE LEAST OF YOUR WORRIES.
HE HAS-
HONK!

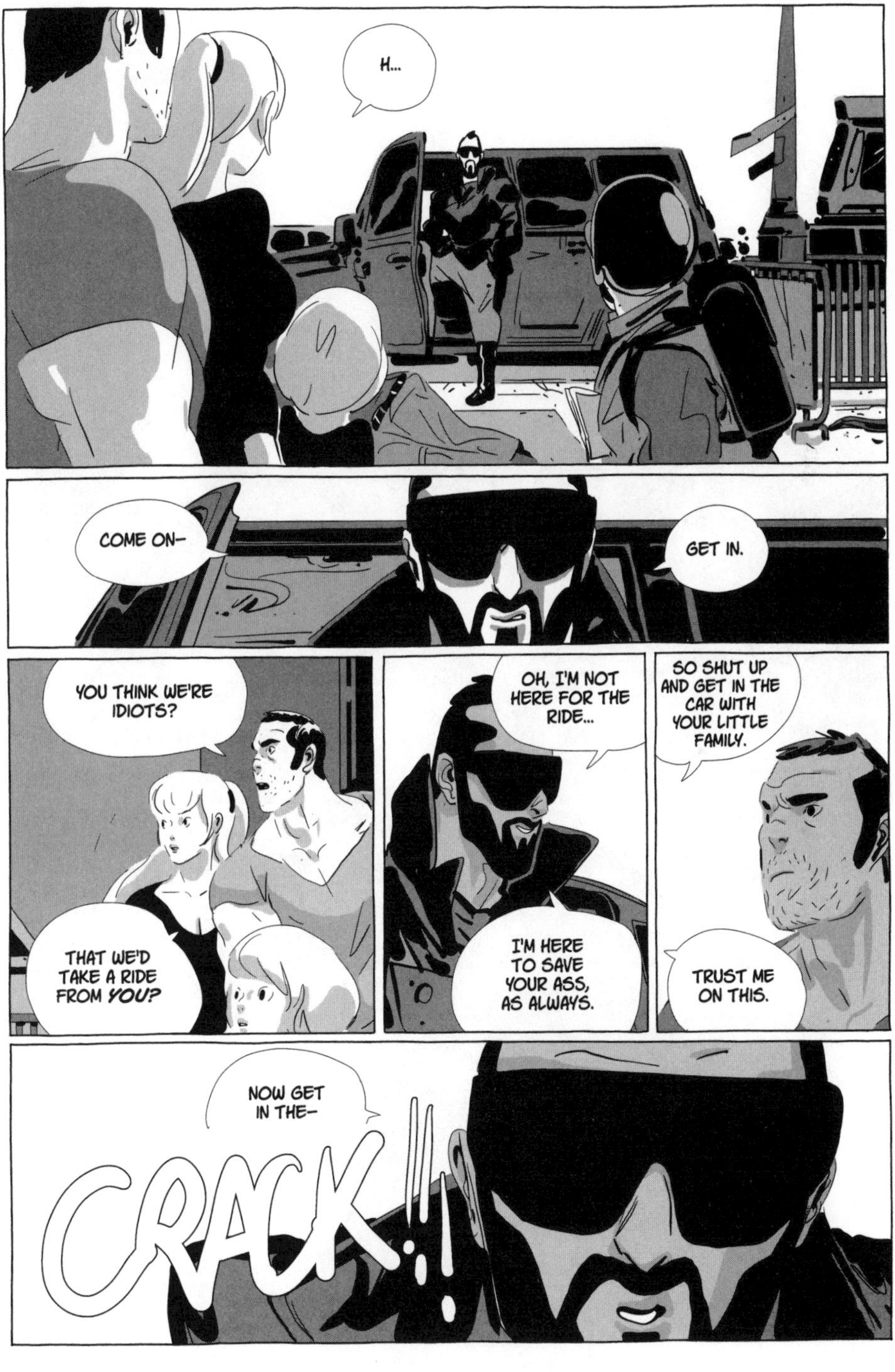
H...
COME ON-
GET IN.
YOU THINK WE'RE IDIOTS?
THAT WE'D TAKE A RIDE FROM *YOU?*
OH, I'M NOT HERE FOR THE RIDE...
I'M HERE TO SAVE YOUR ASS, AS ALWAYS.
SO SHUT UP AND GET IN THE CAR WITH YOUR LITTLE FAMILY.
TRUST ME ON THIS.
NOW GET IN THE-
CRACK!!!

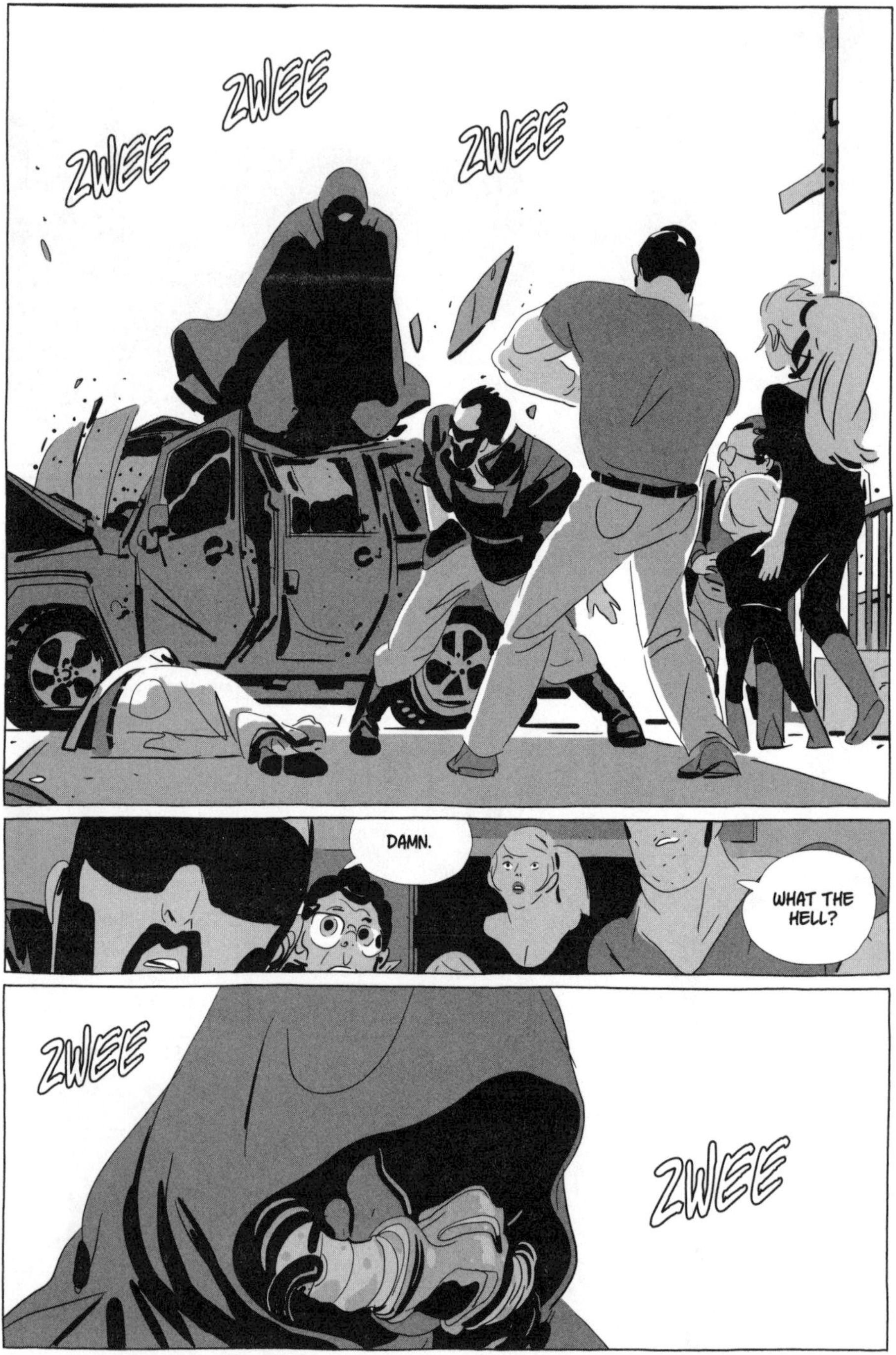
ZWEE
ZWEE
ZWEE
DAMN.
WHAT THE HELL?
ZWEE
ZWEE

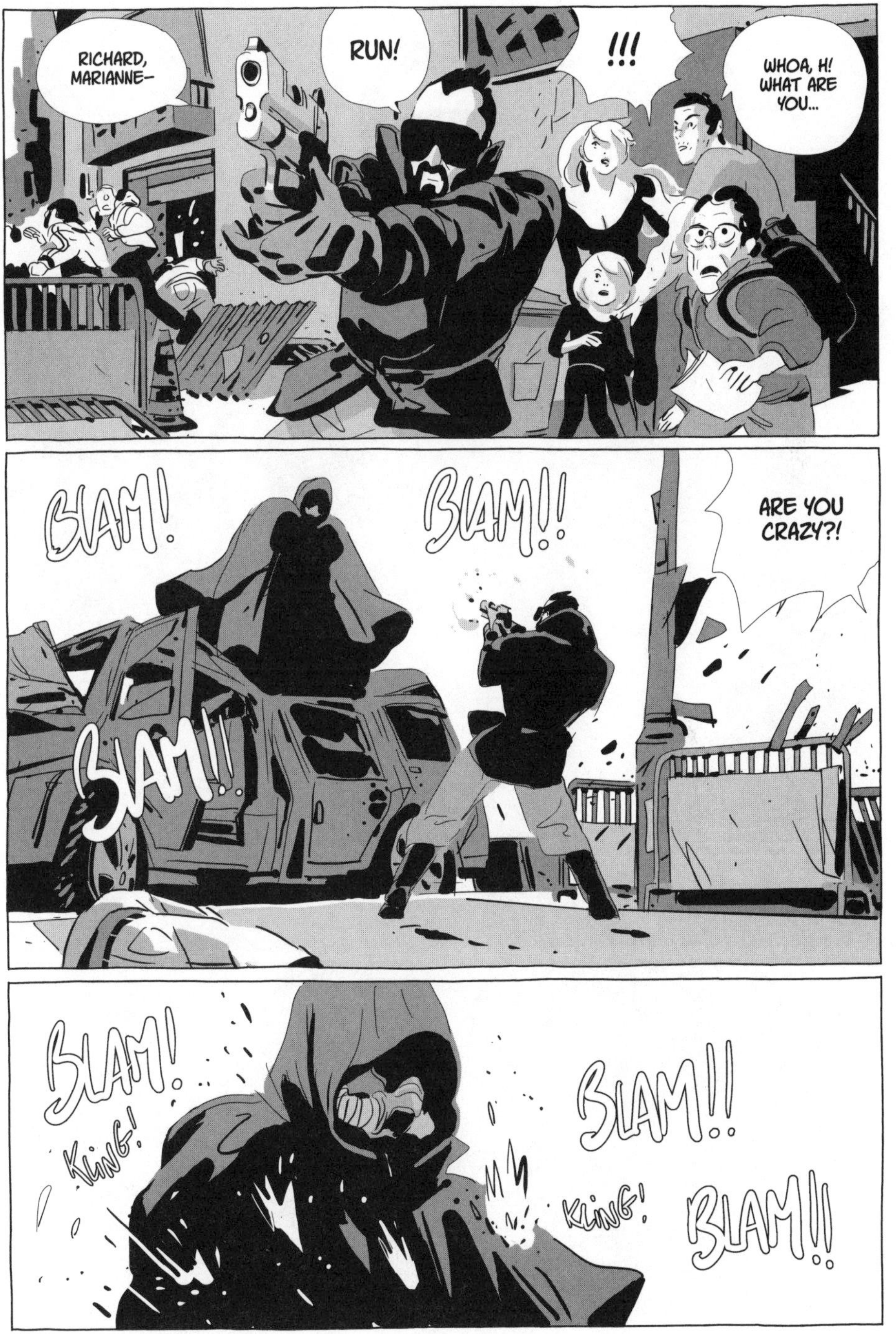
RICHARD, MARIANNE—
RUN!
!!!
WHOA, H! WHAT ARE YOU...
BLAM!
BLAM!!
BLAM!!
ARE YOU CRAZY?!
BLAM!
KLING!
BLAM!!
KLING!
BLAM!!

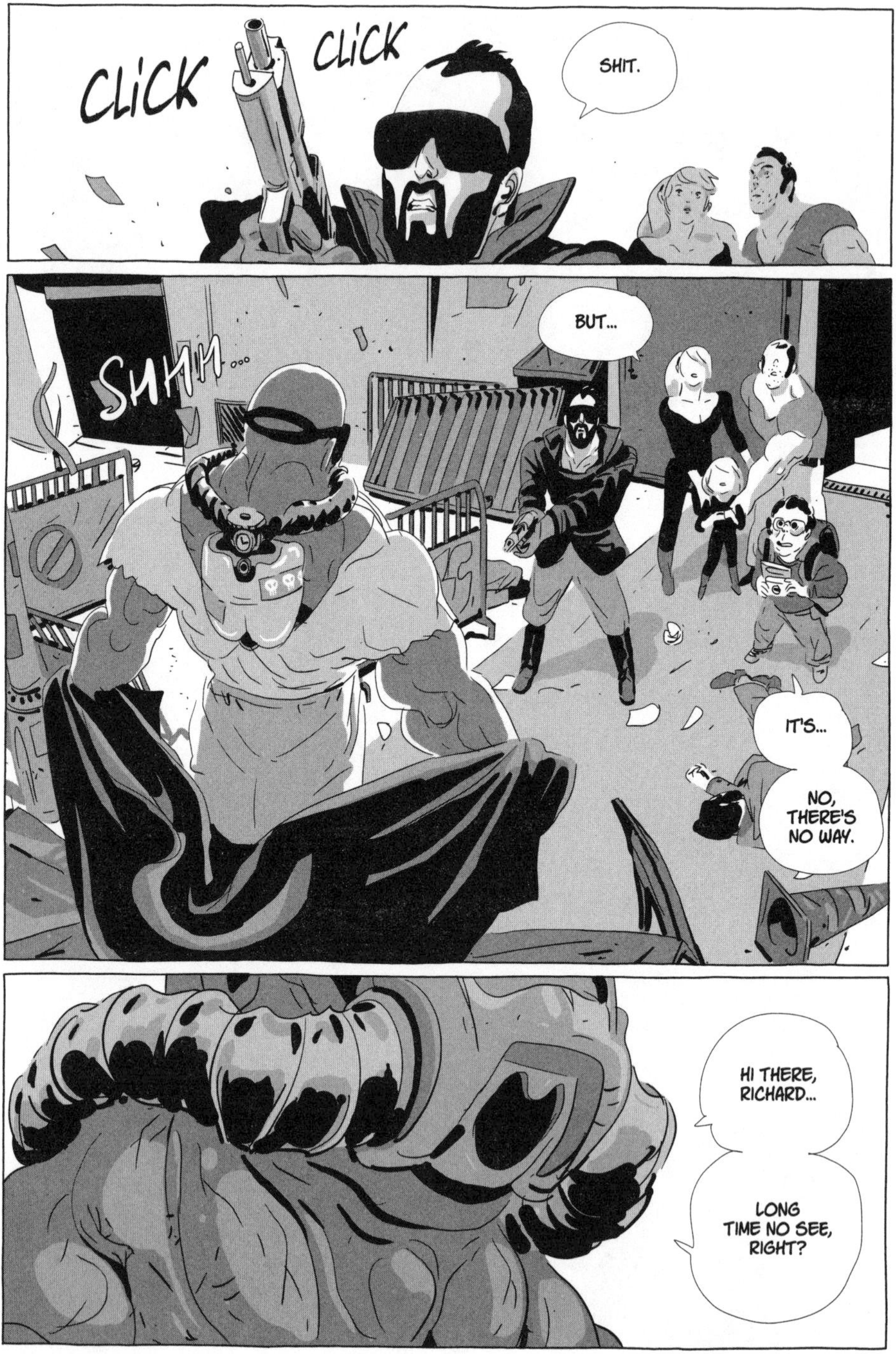
CLICK
CLICK
SHIT.
SHMM...
BUT...
IT'S...
NO, THERE'S NO WAY.
HI THERE, RICHARD...
LONG TIME NO SEE, RIGHT?

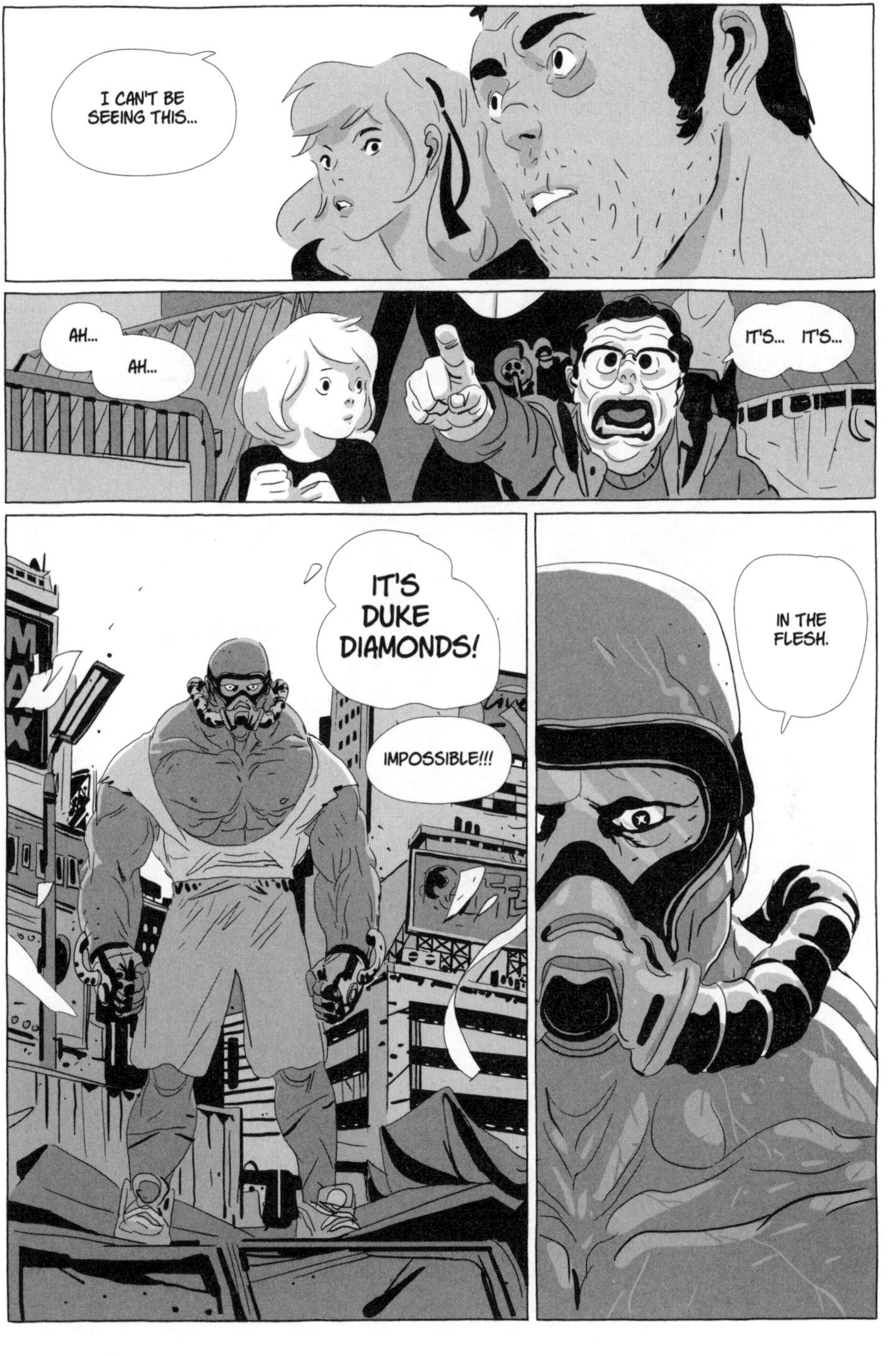
I CAN'T BE SEEING THIS...
AH... AH...
IT'S... IT'S...
IT'S DUKE DIAMONDS!
IMPOSSIBLE!!!
IN THE FLESH.

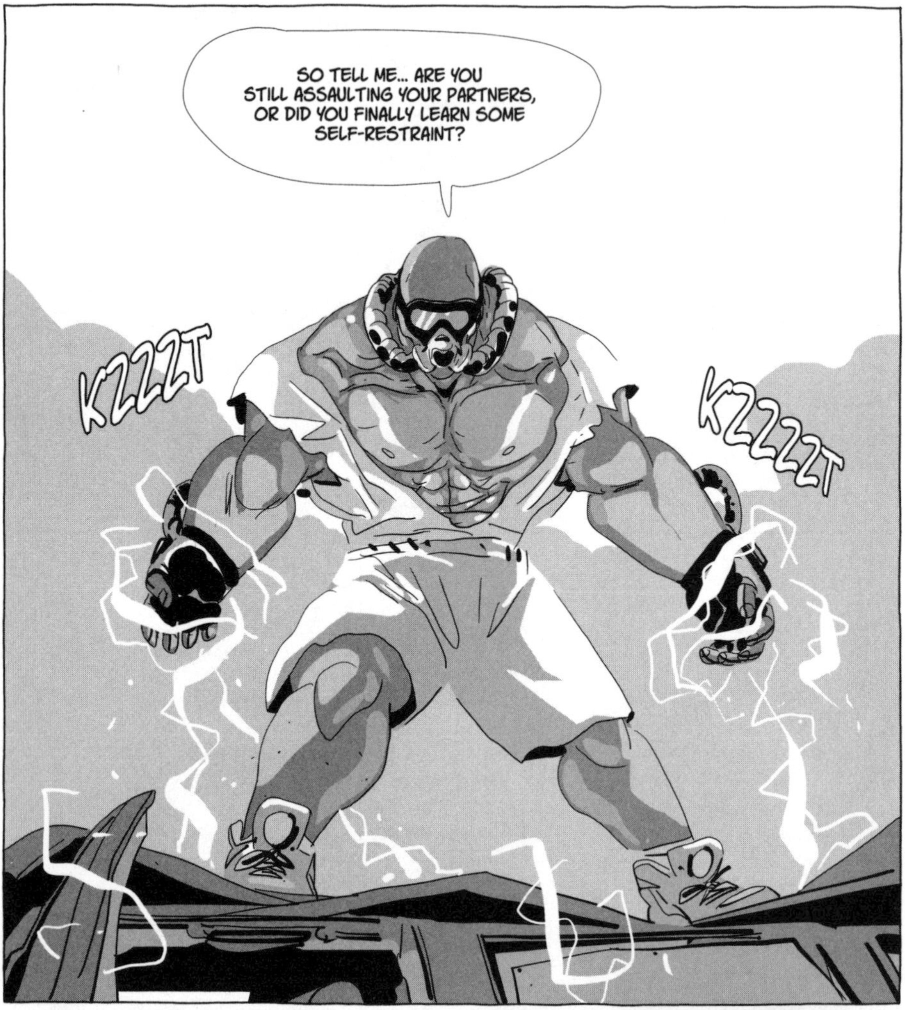
SO TELL ME... ARE YOU STILL ASSAULTING YOUR PARTNERS, OR DID YOU FINALLY LEARN SOME SELF-RESTRAINT?
KZZZT
KZZZZT

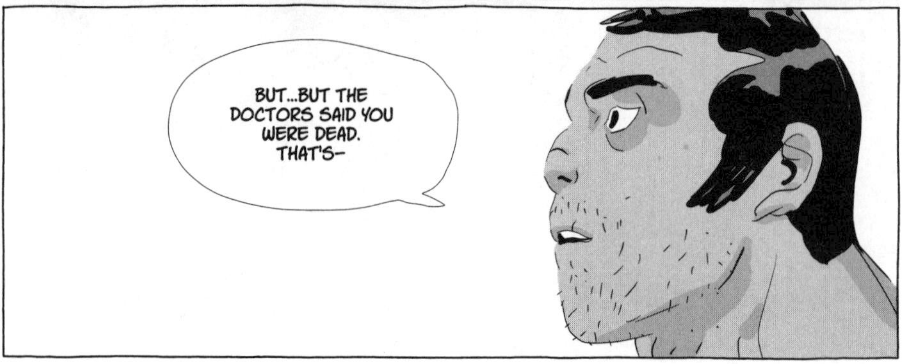
BUT...BUT THE DOCTORS SAID YOU WERE DEAD. THAT'S-

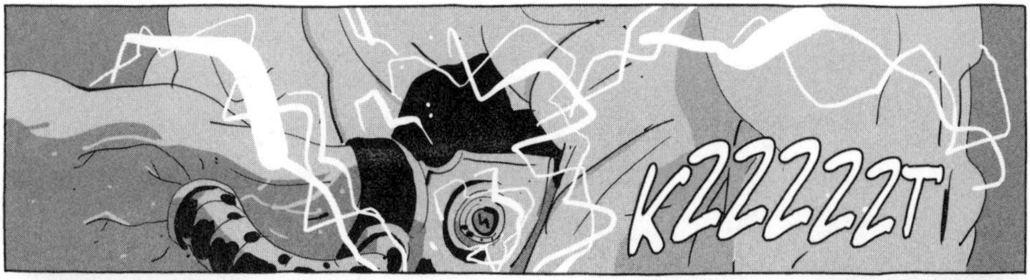
KZZZZZZT

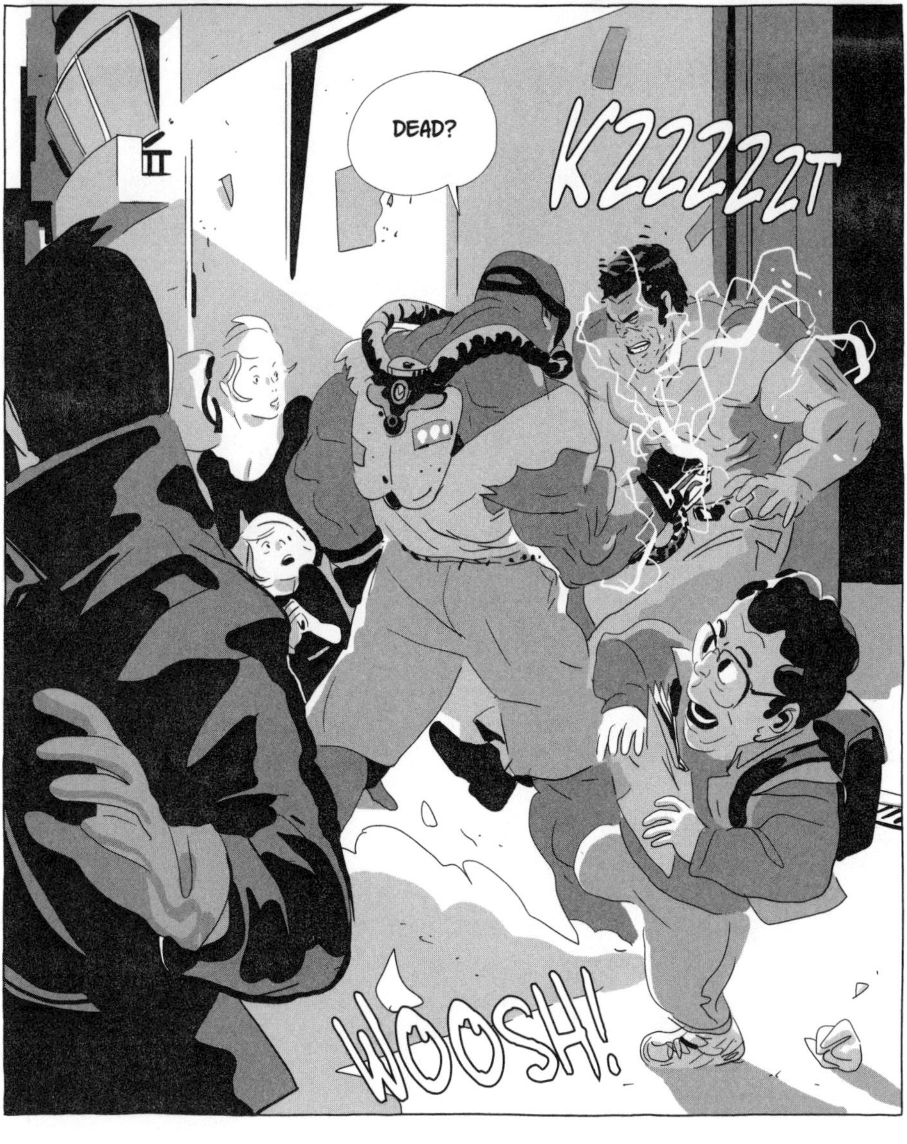
DEAD?
KZZZZZZT
WOOSH!

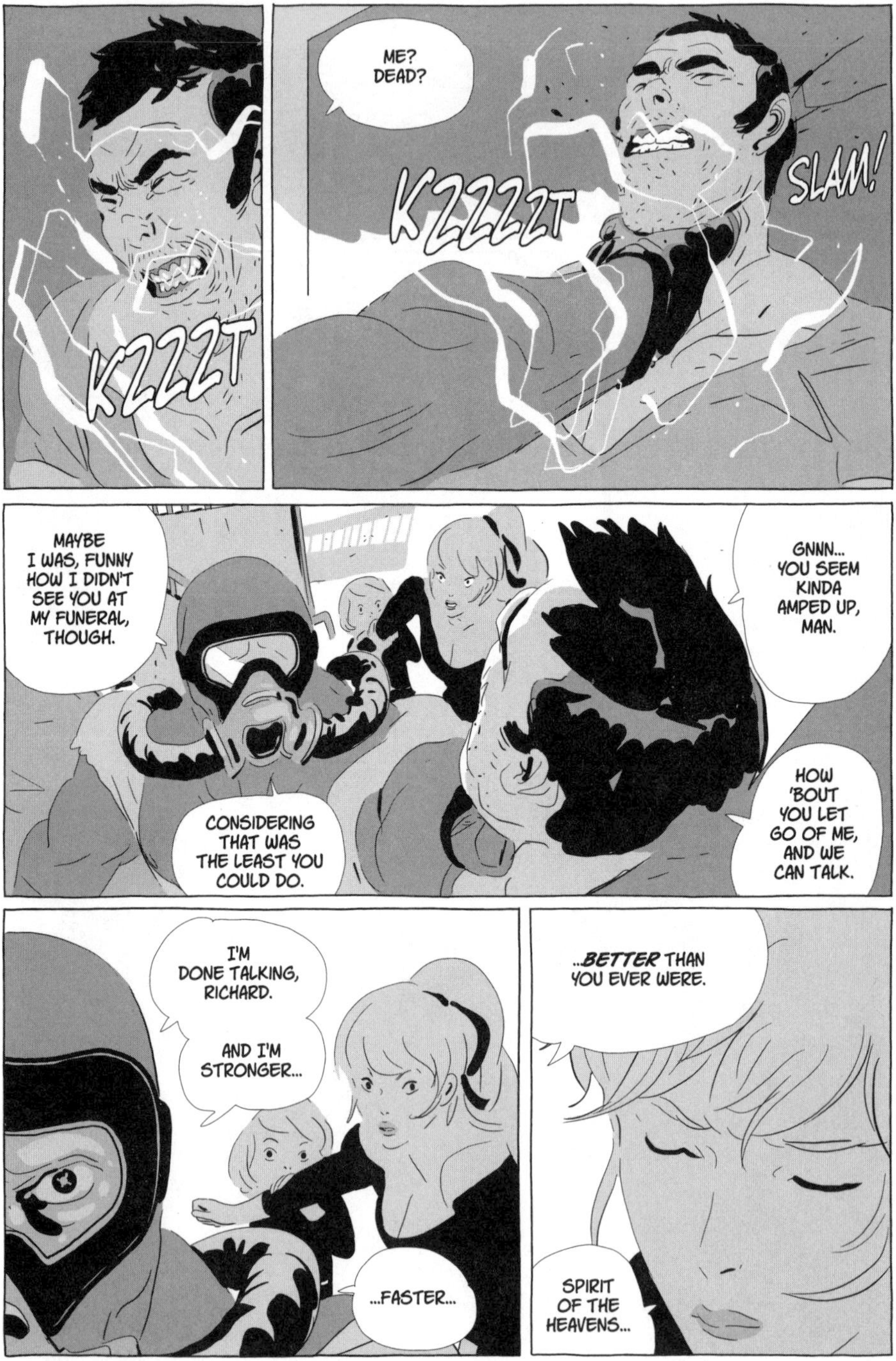
KZZZT
ME? DEAD?
KZZZZZT
SLAM!
MAYBE I WAS, FUNNY HOW I DIDN'T SEE YOU AT MY FUNERAL, THOUGH.
CONSIDERING THAT WAS THE LEAST YOU COULD DO.
GNNN... YOU SEEM KINDA AMPED UP, MAN.
HOW 'BOUT YOU LET GO OF ME, AND WE CAN TALK.
I'M DONE TALKING, RICHARD.
AND I'M STRONGER...
...FASTER...
...**BETTER** THAN YOU EVER WERE.
SPIRIT OF THE HEAVENS...

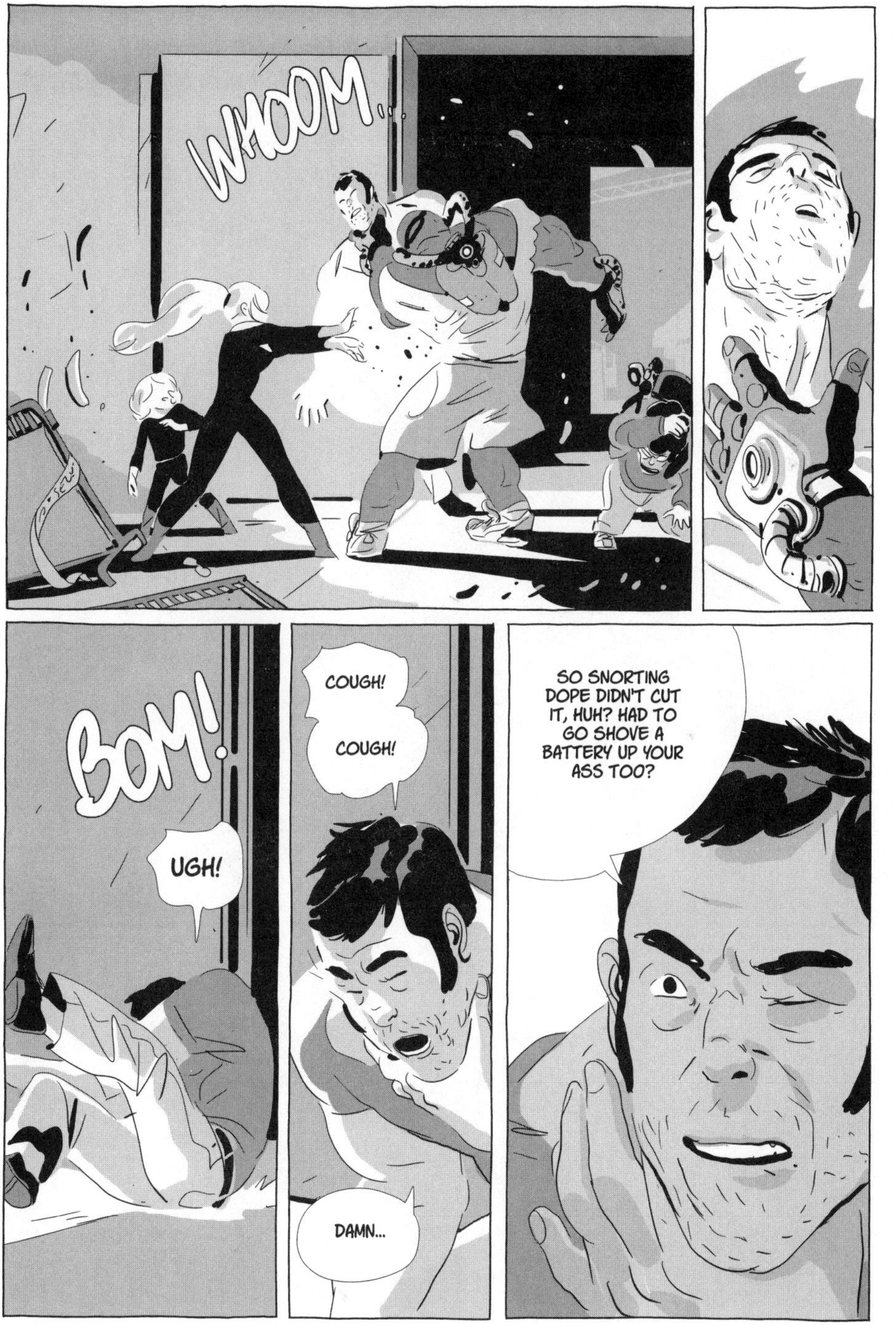
WHOOM...
BOM!
UGH!
COUGH!
COUGH!
DAMN...
SO SNORTING DOPE DIDN'T CUT IT, HUH? HAD TO GO SHOVE A BATTERY UP YOUR ASS TOO?

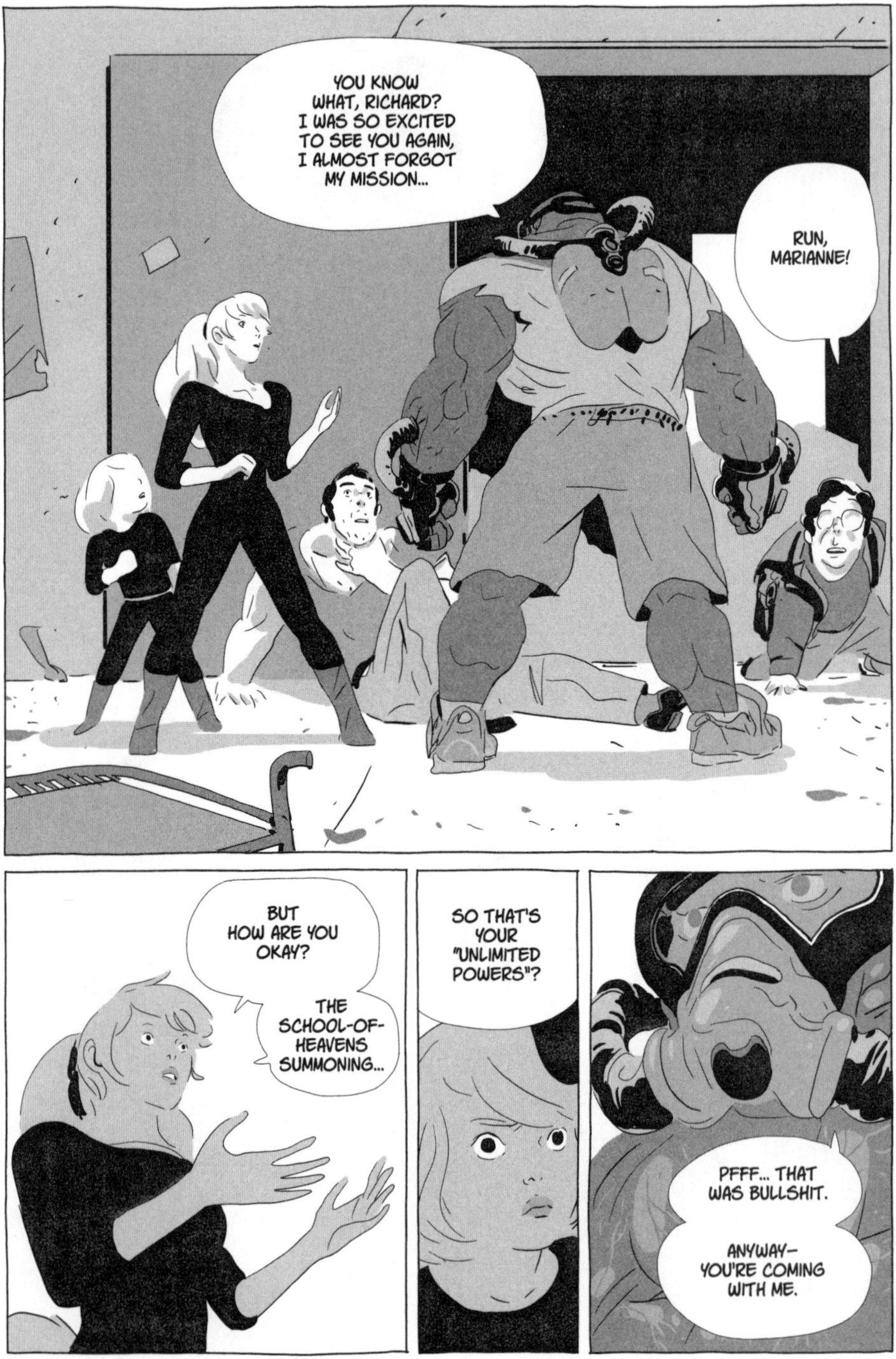
YOU KNOW WHAT, RICHARD? I WAS SO EXCITED TO SEE YOU AGAIN, I ALMOST FORGOT MY MISSION...
RUN, MARIANNE!
BUT HOW ARE YOU OKAY?
THE SCHOOL-OF-HEAVENS SUMMONING...
SO THAT'S YOUR "UNLIMITED POWERS"?
PFFF... THAT WAS BULLSHIT.
ANYWAY— YOU'RE COMING WITH ME.

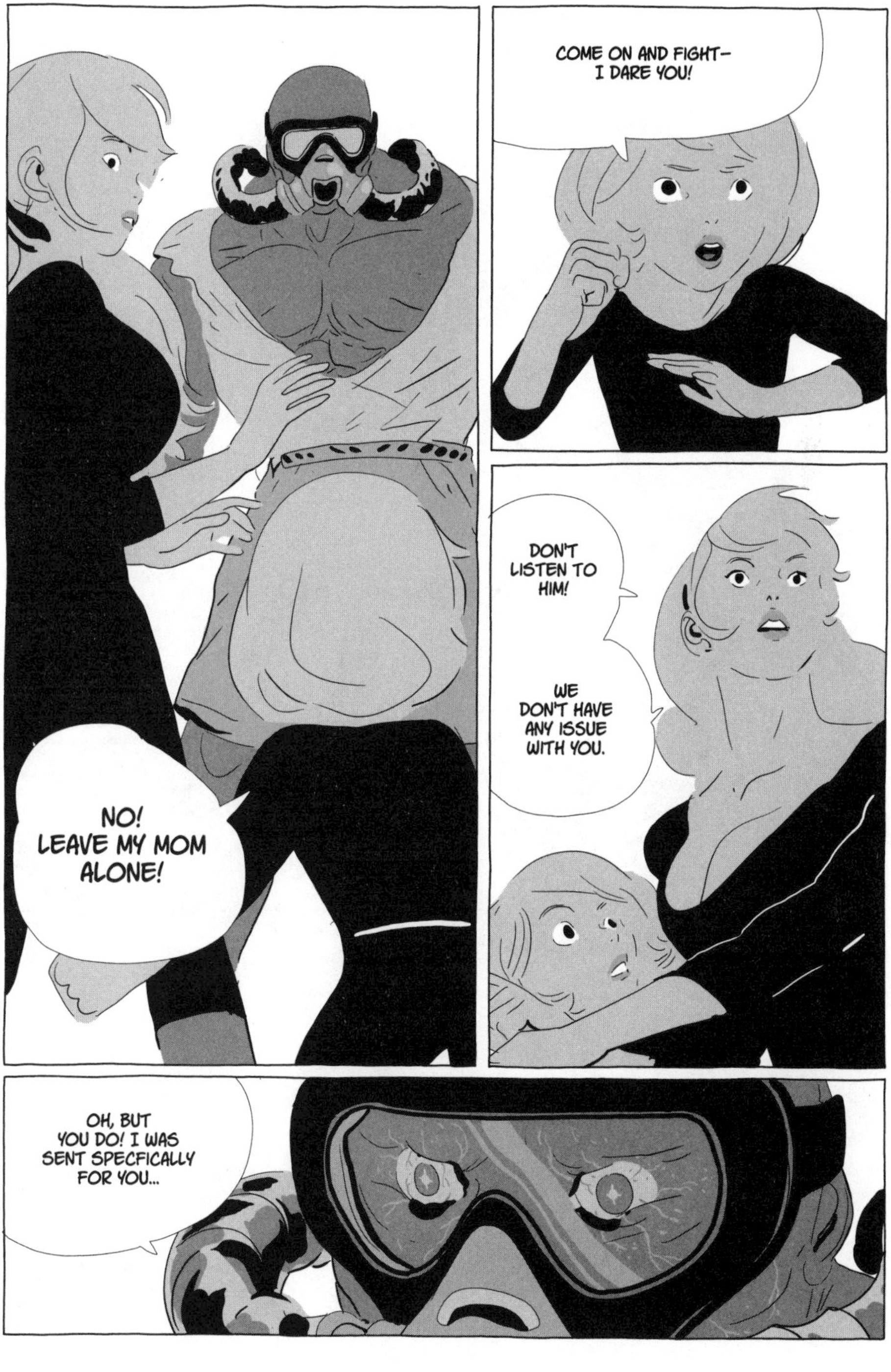
NO! LEAVE MY MOM ALONE!
COME ON AND FIGHT— I DARE YOU!
DON'T LISTEN TO HIM!
WE DON'T HAVE ANY ISSUE WITH YOU.
OH, BUT YOU DO! I WAS SENT SPECFICALLY FOR YOU...

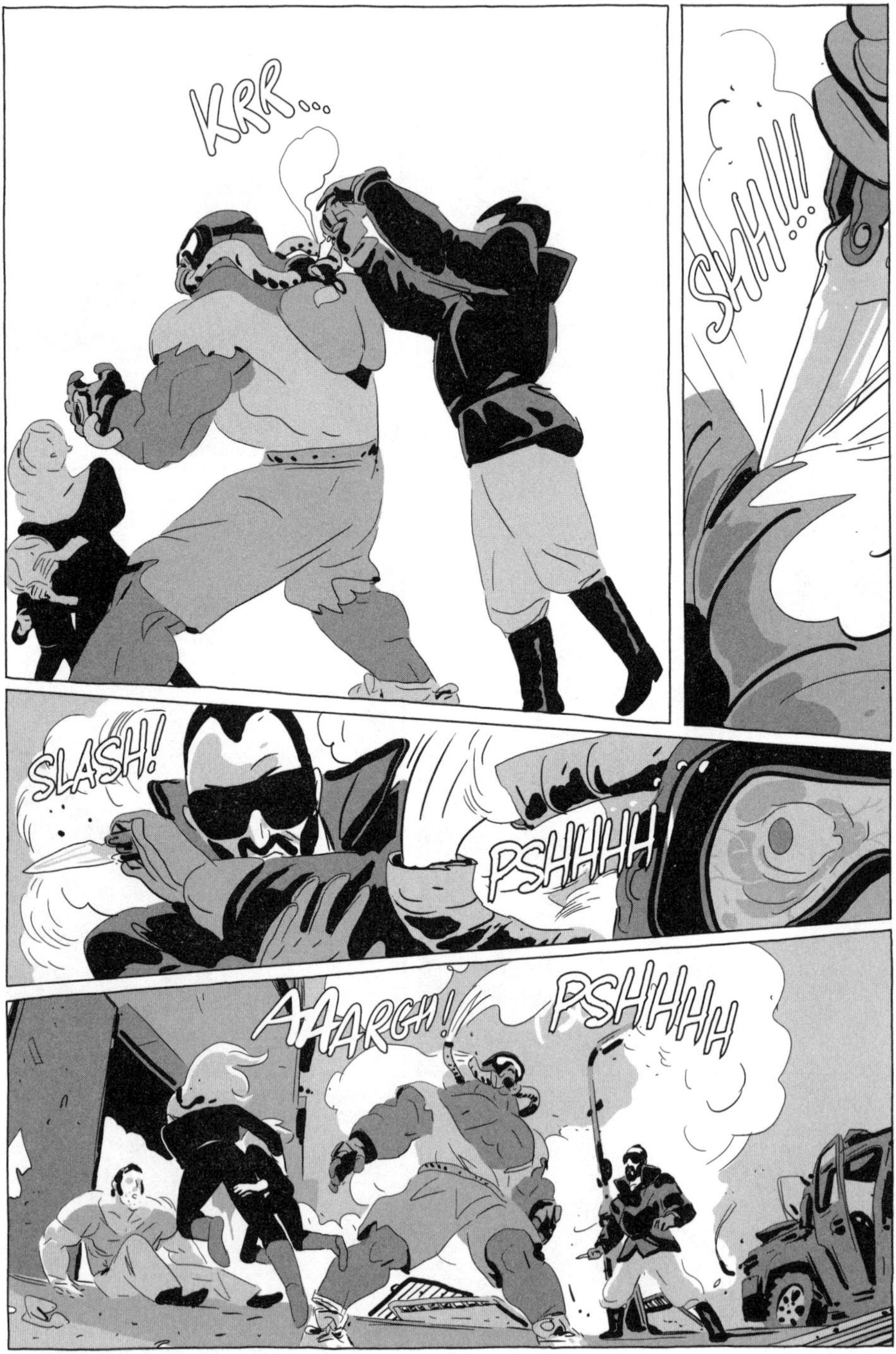
KRR...
SHH!!!...
SLASH!
PSHHHH
AAARGH!!
PSHHHH

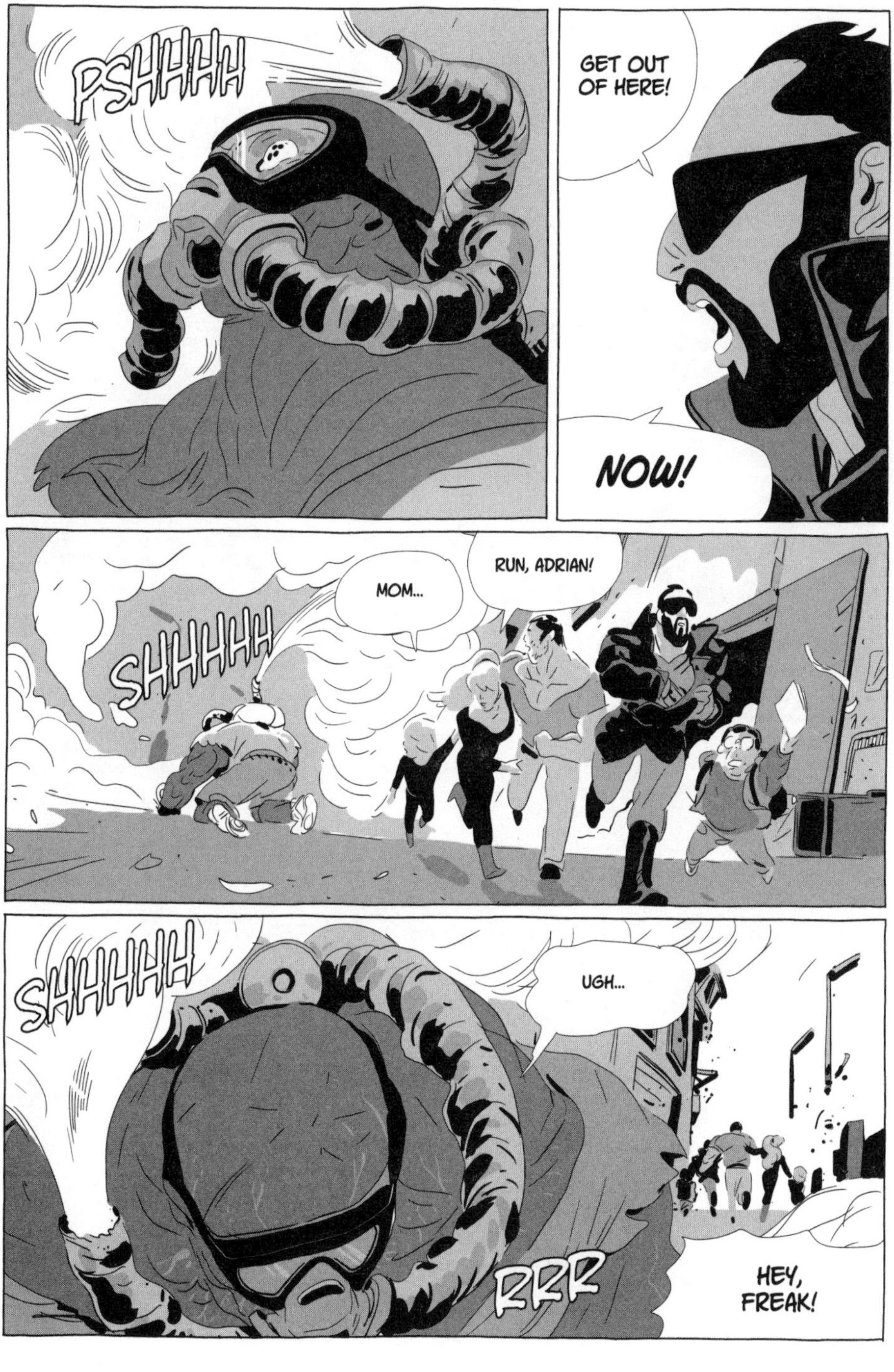
PSHHHH
GET OUT OF HERE!
NOW!
SHHHHH
MOM...
RUN, ADRIAN!
SHHHHH
UGH...
RRR
HEY, FREAK!

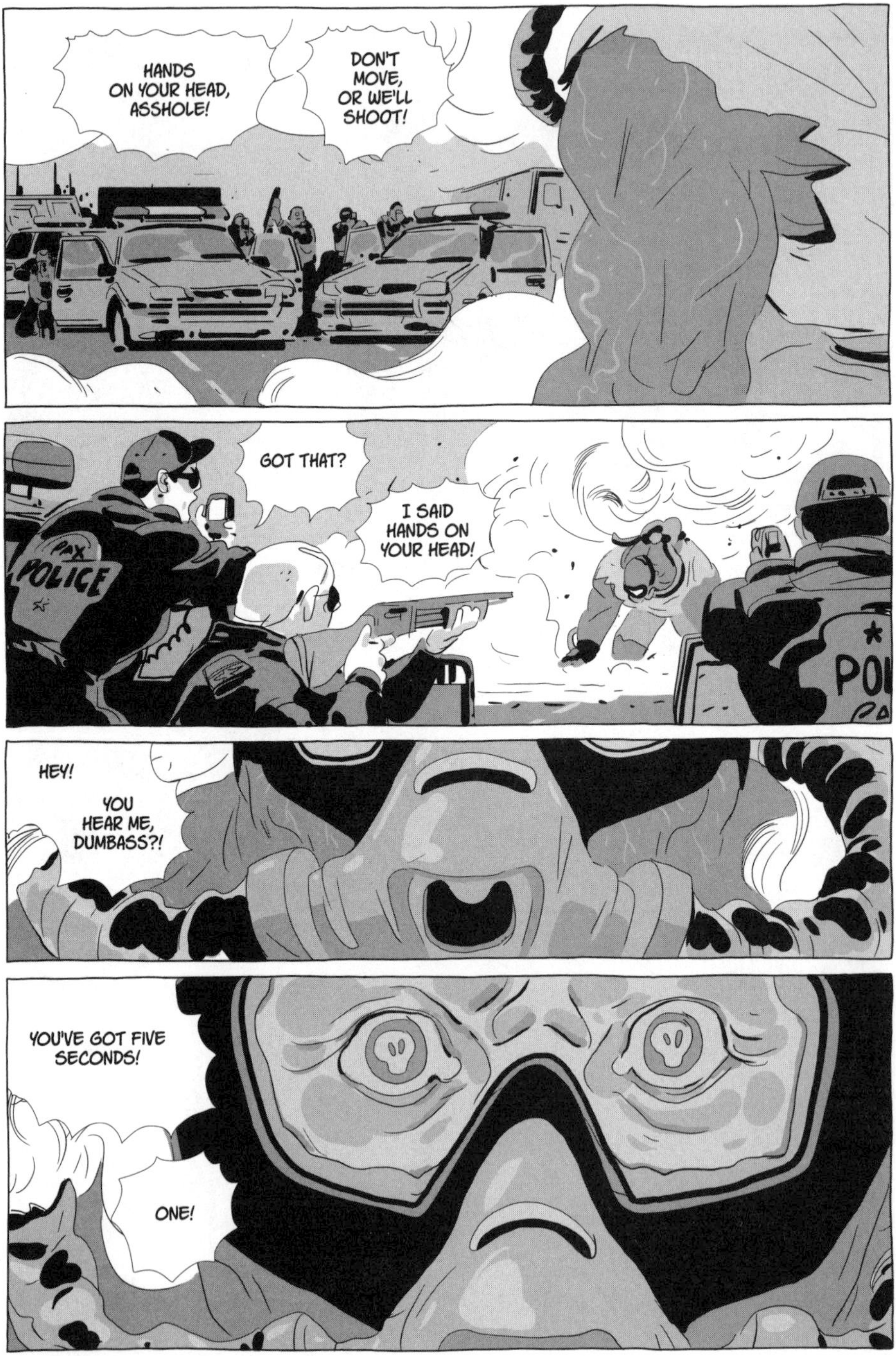
HANDS ON YOUR HEAD, ASSHOLE!
DON'T MOVE, OR WE'LL SHOOT!
GOT THAT?
I SAID HANDS ON YOUR HEAD!
PAX POLICE
POL PA
HEY!
YOU HEAR ME, DUMBASS?!
YOU'VE GOT FIVE SECONDS!
ONE!

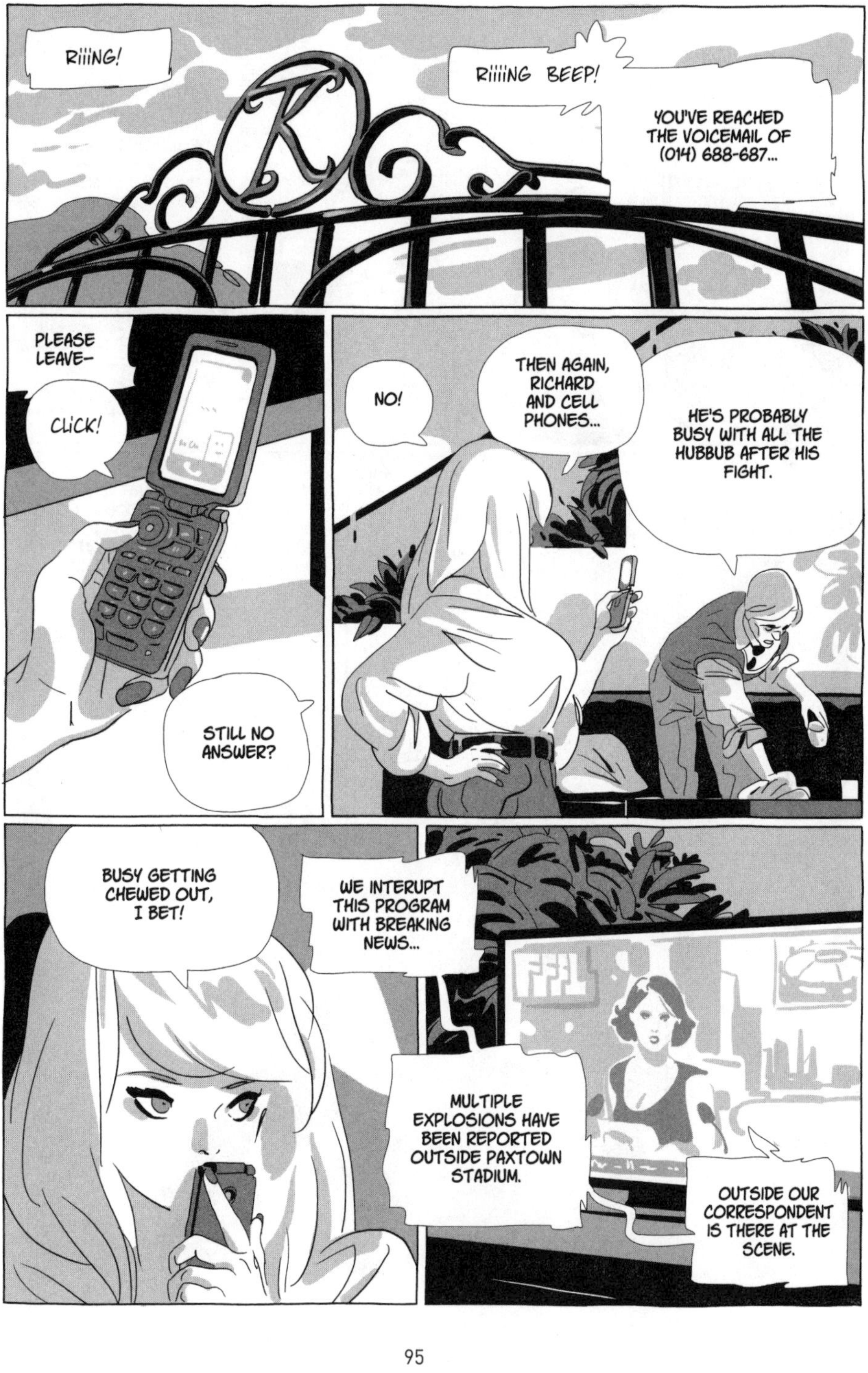
RiiiNG!
RiiiNG BEEP!
YOU'VE REACHED THE VOICEMAIL OF (014) 688-687...
PLEASE LEAVE-
CLiCK!
STILL NO ANSWER?
NO!
THEN AGAIN, RICHARD AND CELL PHONES...
HE'S PROBABLY BUSY WITH ALL THE HUBBUB AFTER HIS FIGHT.
BUSY GETTING CHEWED OUT, I BET!
WE INTERUPT THIS PROGRAM WITH BREAKING NEWS...
MULTIPLE EXPLOSIONS HAVE BEEN REPORTED OUTSIDE PAXTOWN STADIUM.
OUTSIDE OUR CORRESPONDENT IS THERE AT THE SCENE.

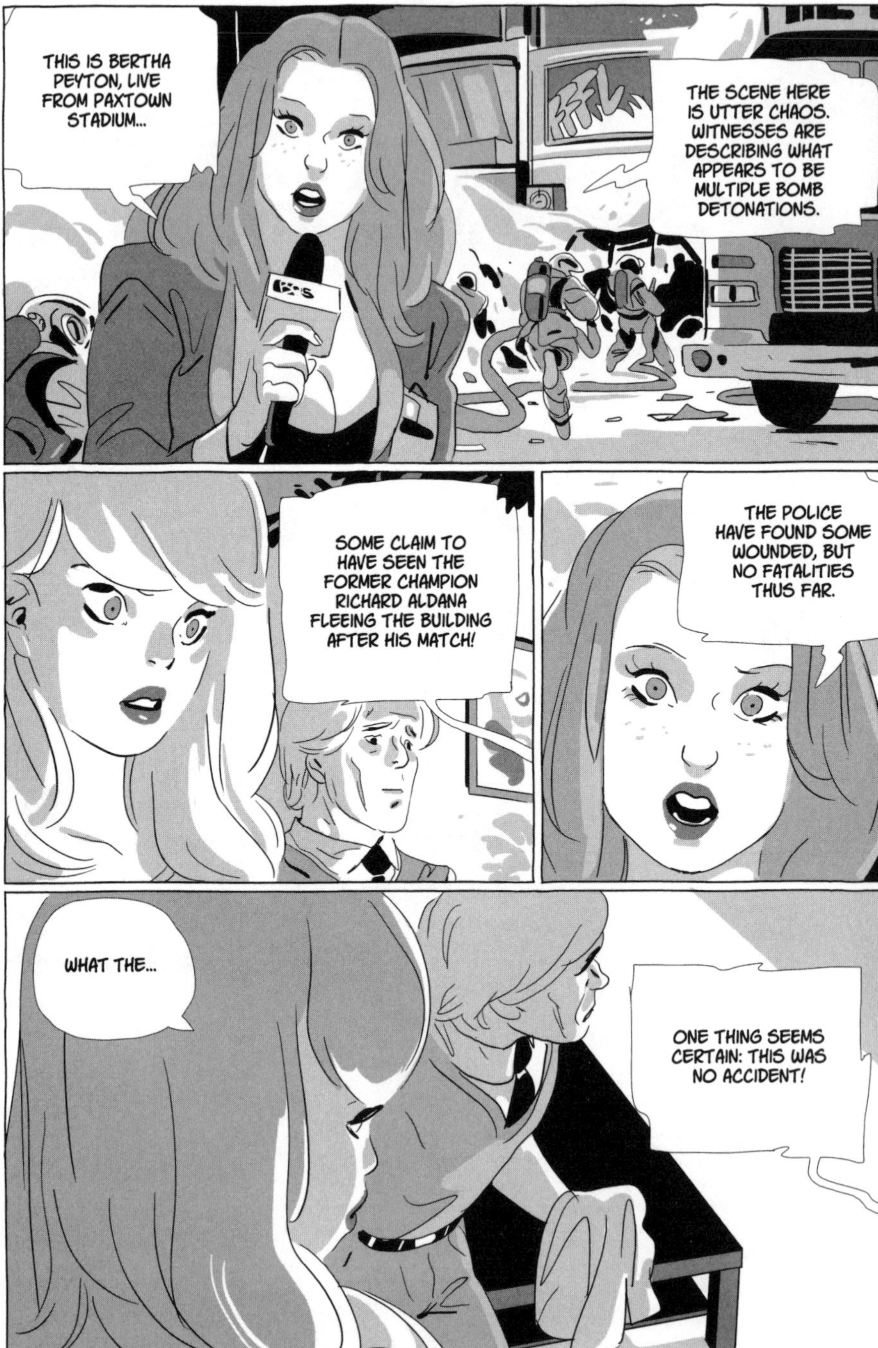
THIS IS BERTHA PEYTON, LIVE FROM PAXTOWN STADIUM...
THE SCENE HERE IS UTTER CHAOS. WITNESSES ARE DESCRIBING WHAT APPEARS TO BE MULTIPLE BOMB DETONATIONS.
SOME CLAIM TO HAVE SEEN THE FORMER CHAMPION RICHARD ALDANA FLEEING THE BUILDING AFTER HIS MATCH!
THE POLICE HAVE FOUND SOME WOUNDED, BUT NO FATALITIES THUS FAR.
WHAT THE...
ONE THING SEEMS CERTAIN: THIS WAS NO ACCIDENT!

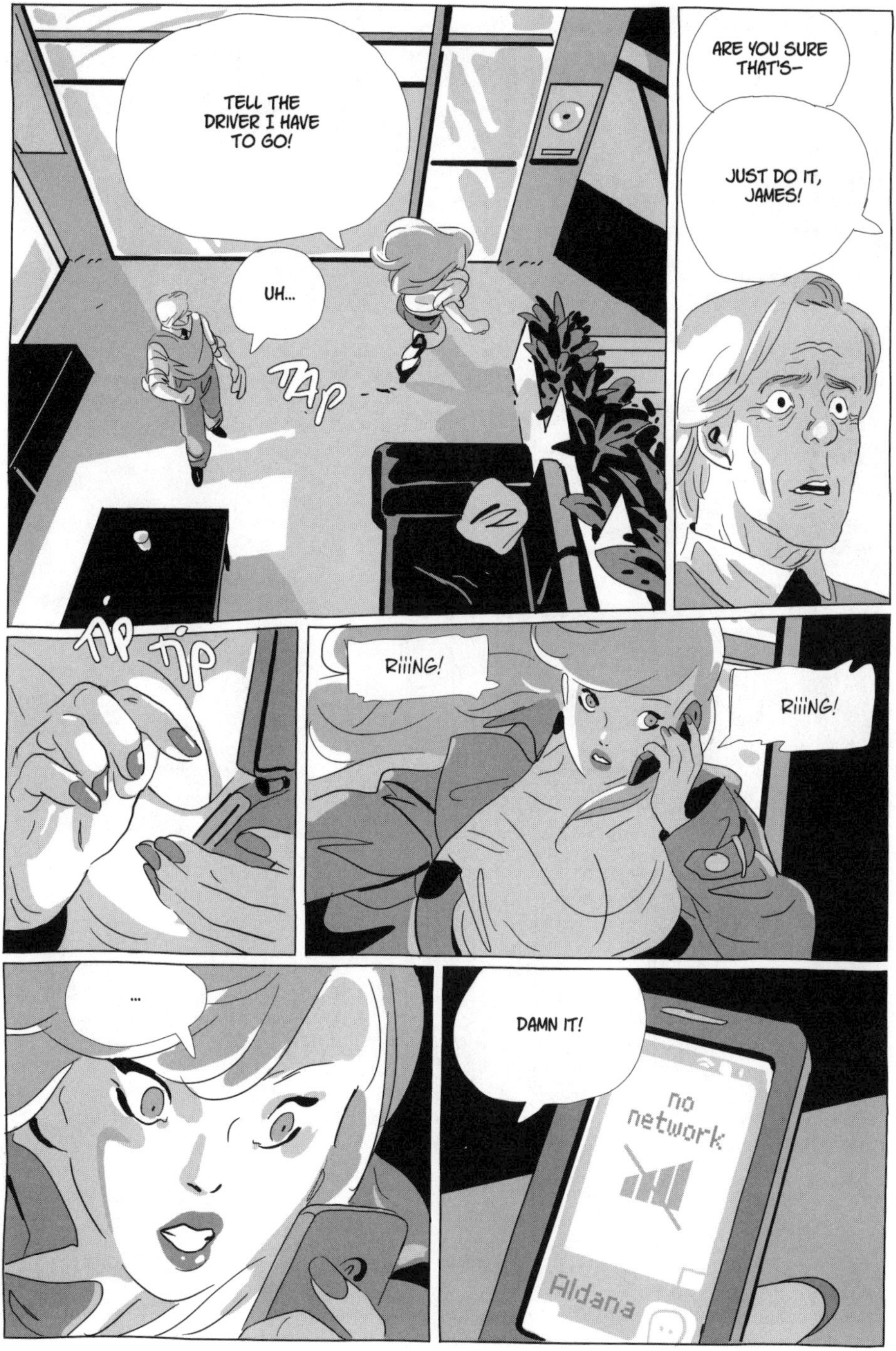
TELL THE DRIVER I HAVE TO GO!
UH...
TAP
ARE YOU SURE THAT'S—
JUST DO IT, JAMES!
TAP TIP
RiiiNG!
RiiiNG!
...
DAMN IT!
no network
Aldana

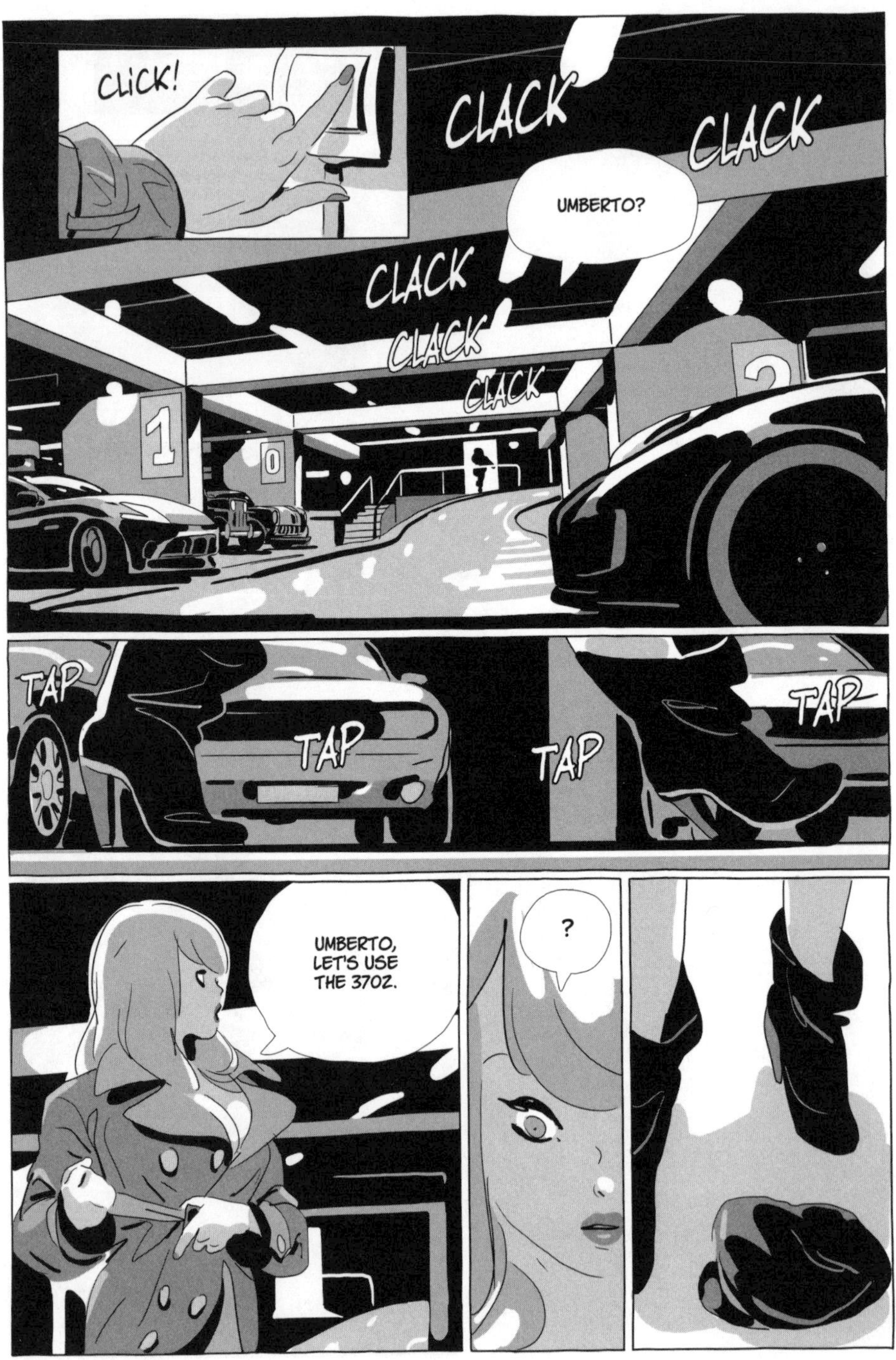
CLiCK!
CLACK
CLACK
UMBERTO?
CLACK
CLACK
CLACK
TAP
TAP
TAP
TAP
UMBERTO, LET'S USE THE 370Z.
?

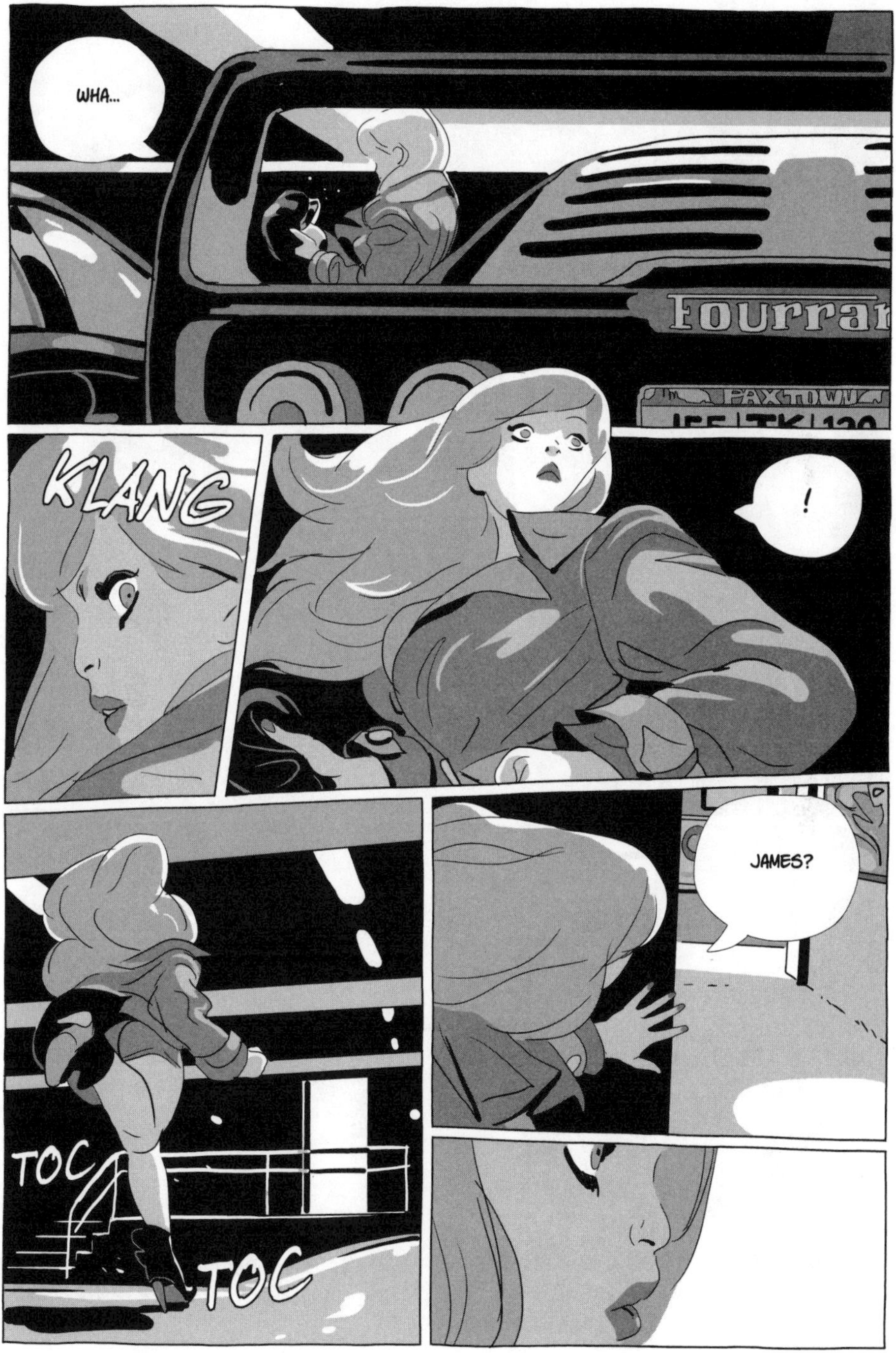
WHA...
Fourrar
PAXTOWN
KLANG
!
TOC
TOC
JAMES?

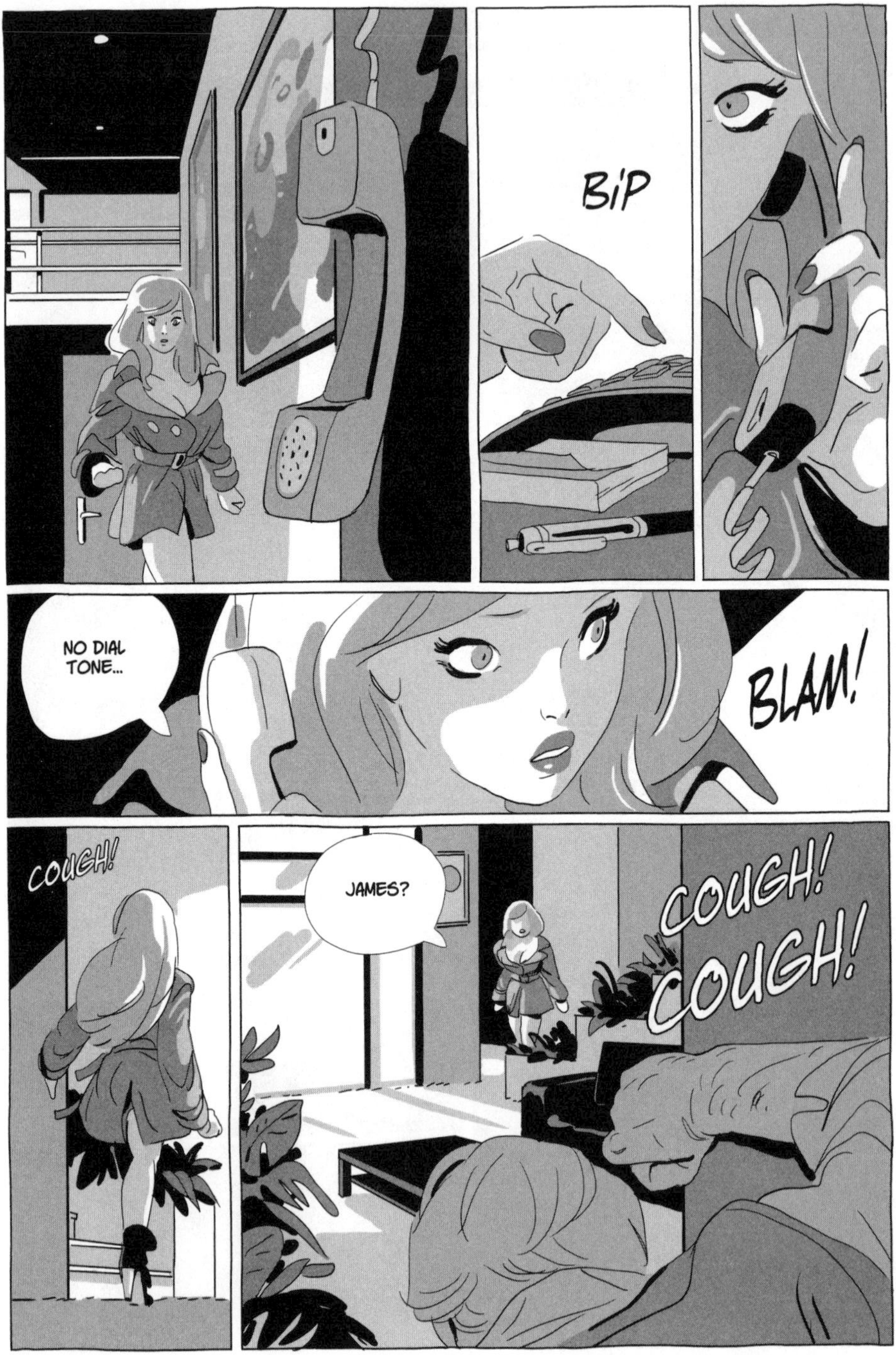
BiP
NO DIAL TONE...
BLAM!
COUGH!
JAMES?
COUGH! COUGH!

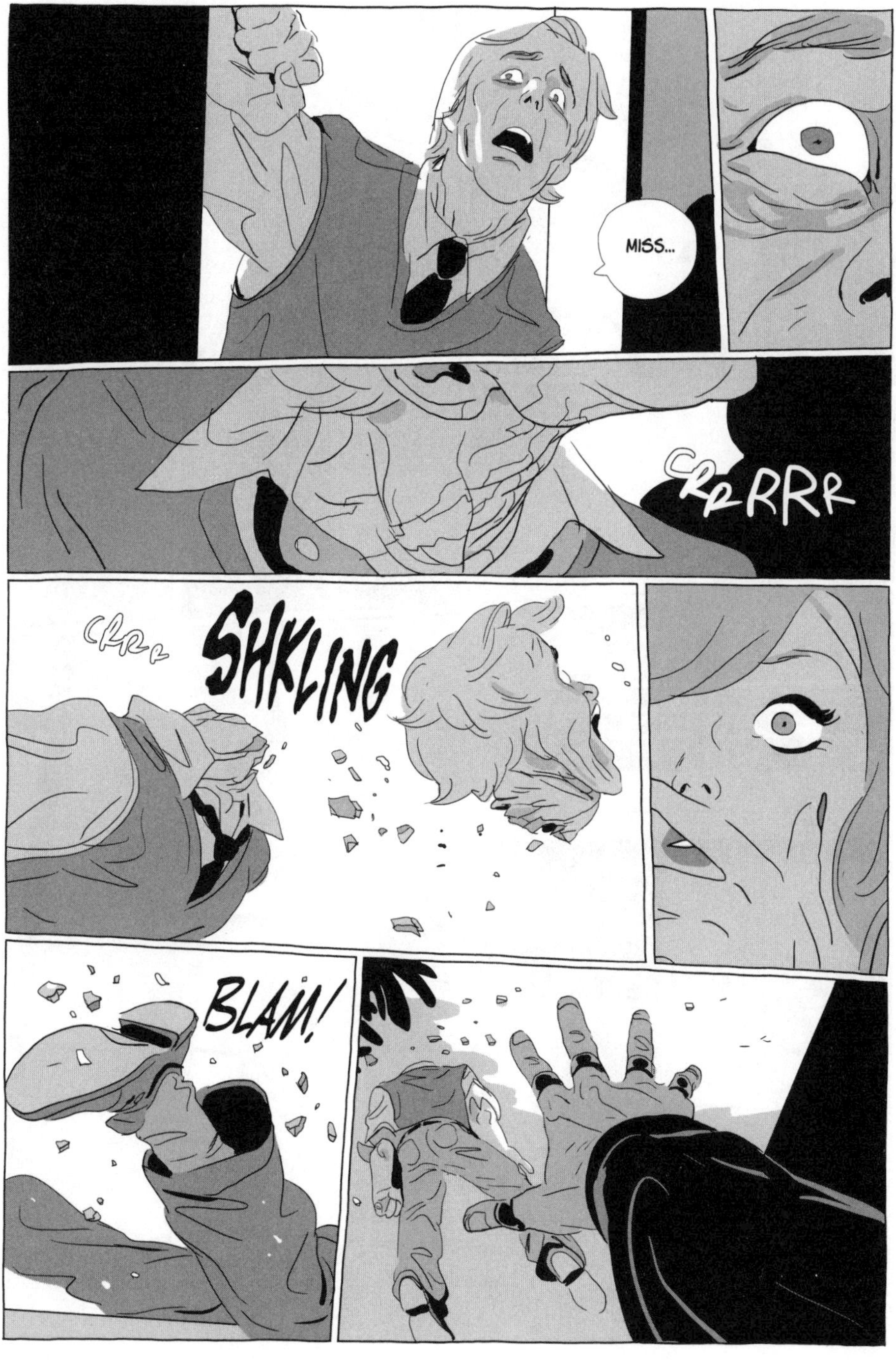
MISS...
CRRRRR
CRRR
SHKLING
BLAM!

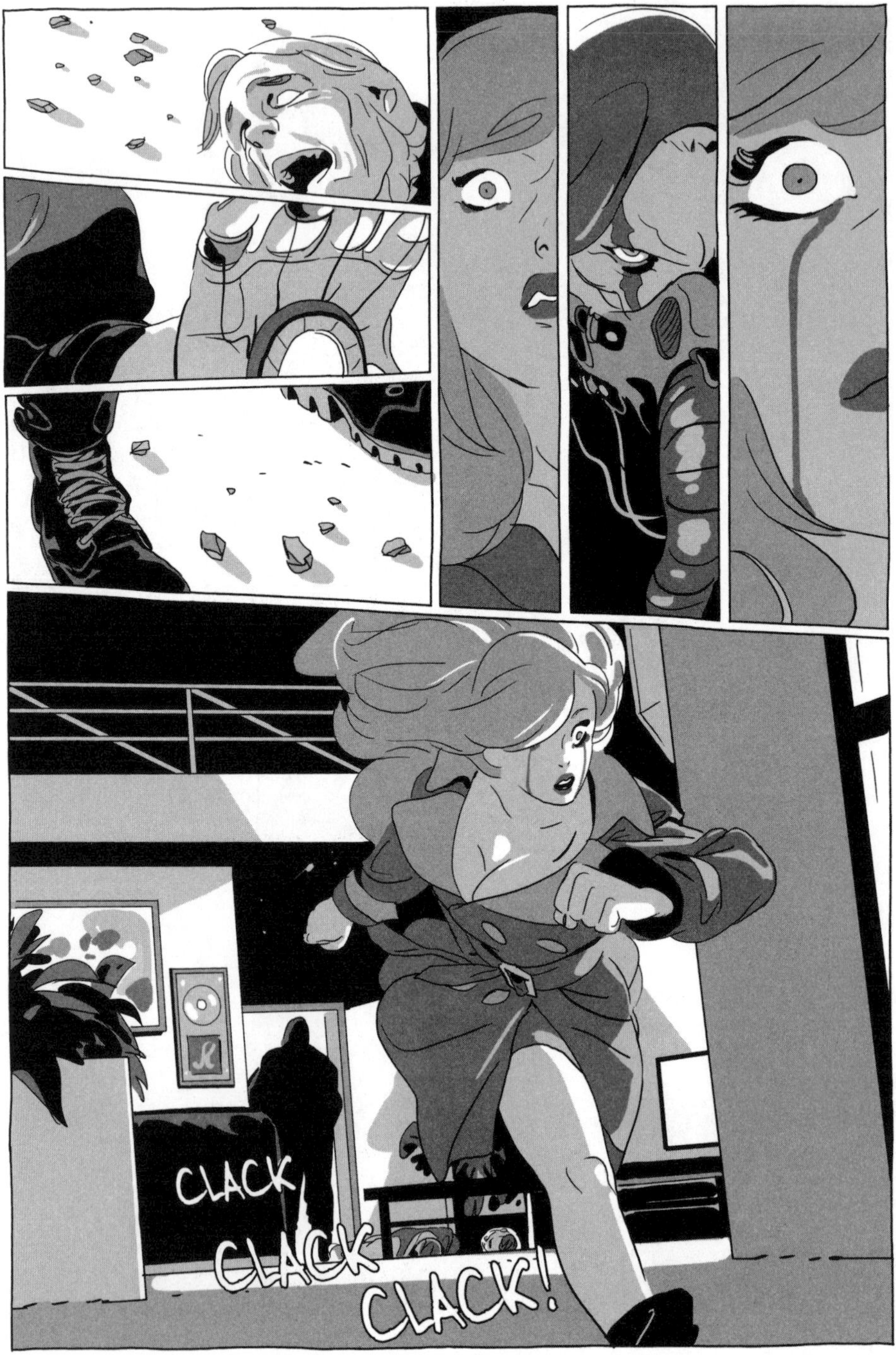
CLACK
CLACK
CLACK!

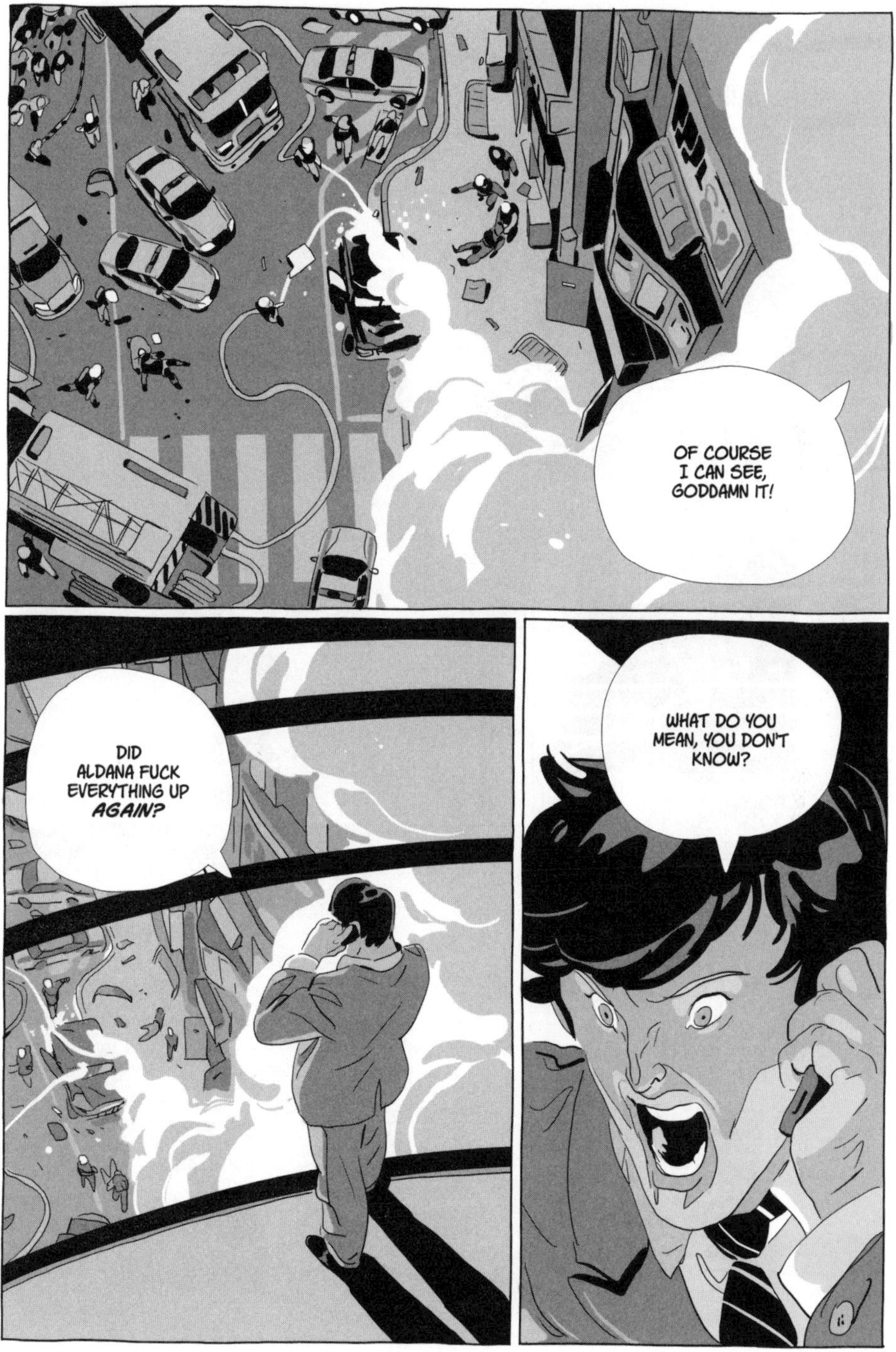
OF COURSE I CAN SEE, GODDAMN IT!
DID ALDANA FUCK EVERYTHING UP *AGAIN?*
WHAT DO YOU MEAN, YOU DON'T KNOW?

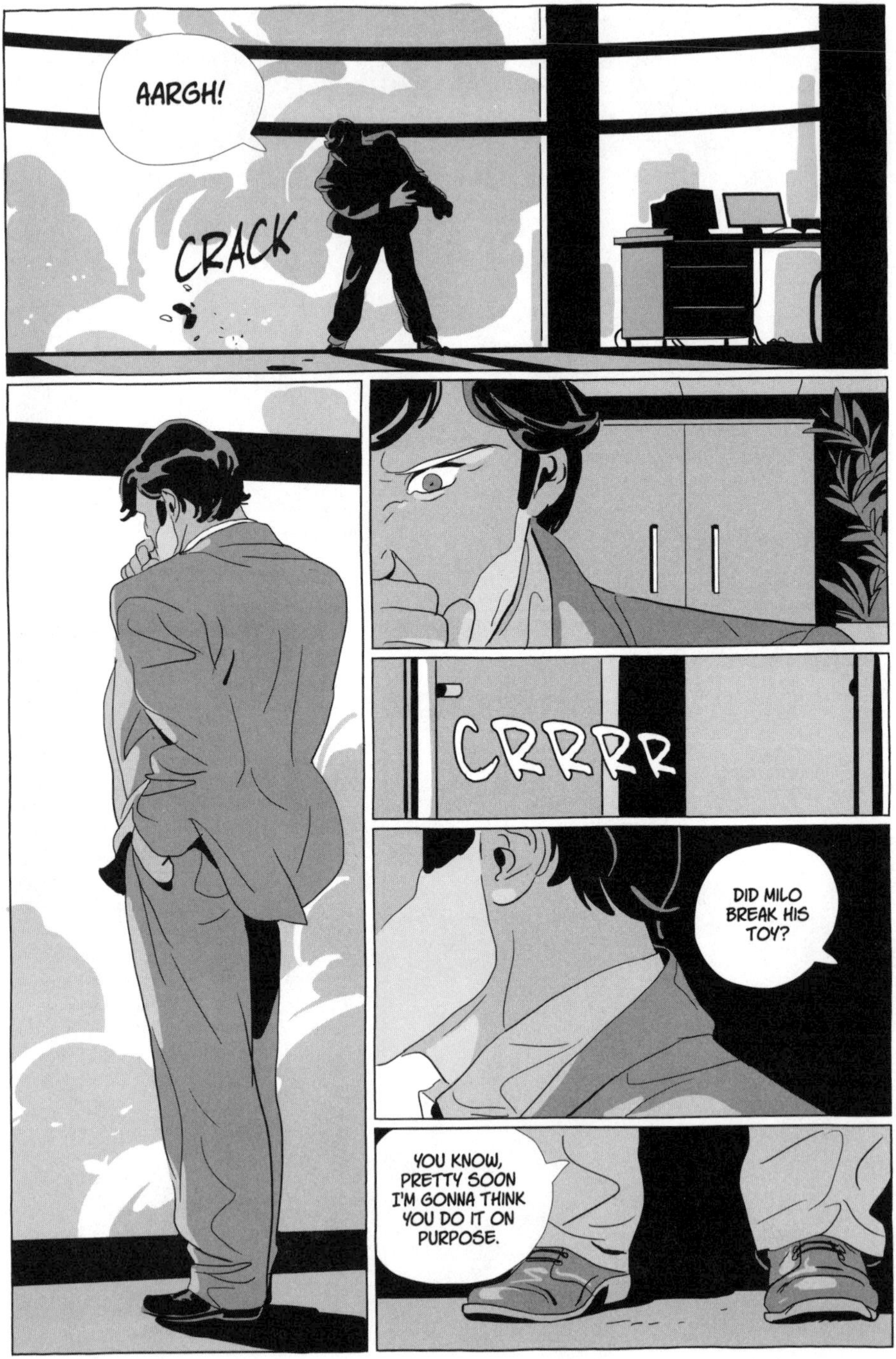
AARGH!
CRACK
CRRRR
DID MILO BREAK HIS TOY?
YOU KNOW, PRETTY SOON I'M GONNA THINK YOU DO IT ON PURPOSE.

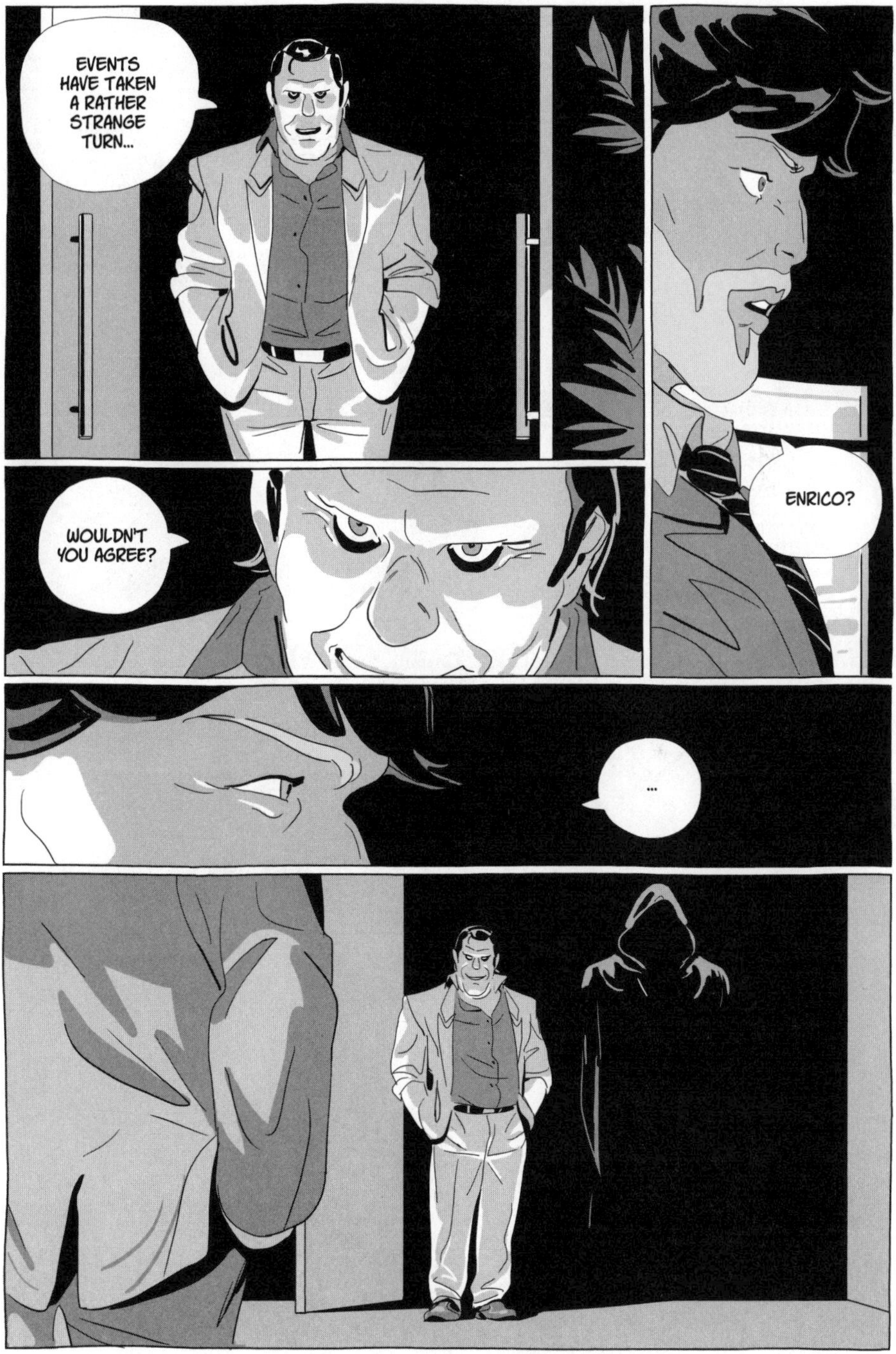
EVENTS HAVE TAKEN A RATHER STRANGE TURN...
ENRICO?
WOULDN'T YOU AGREE?
...

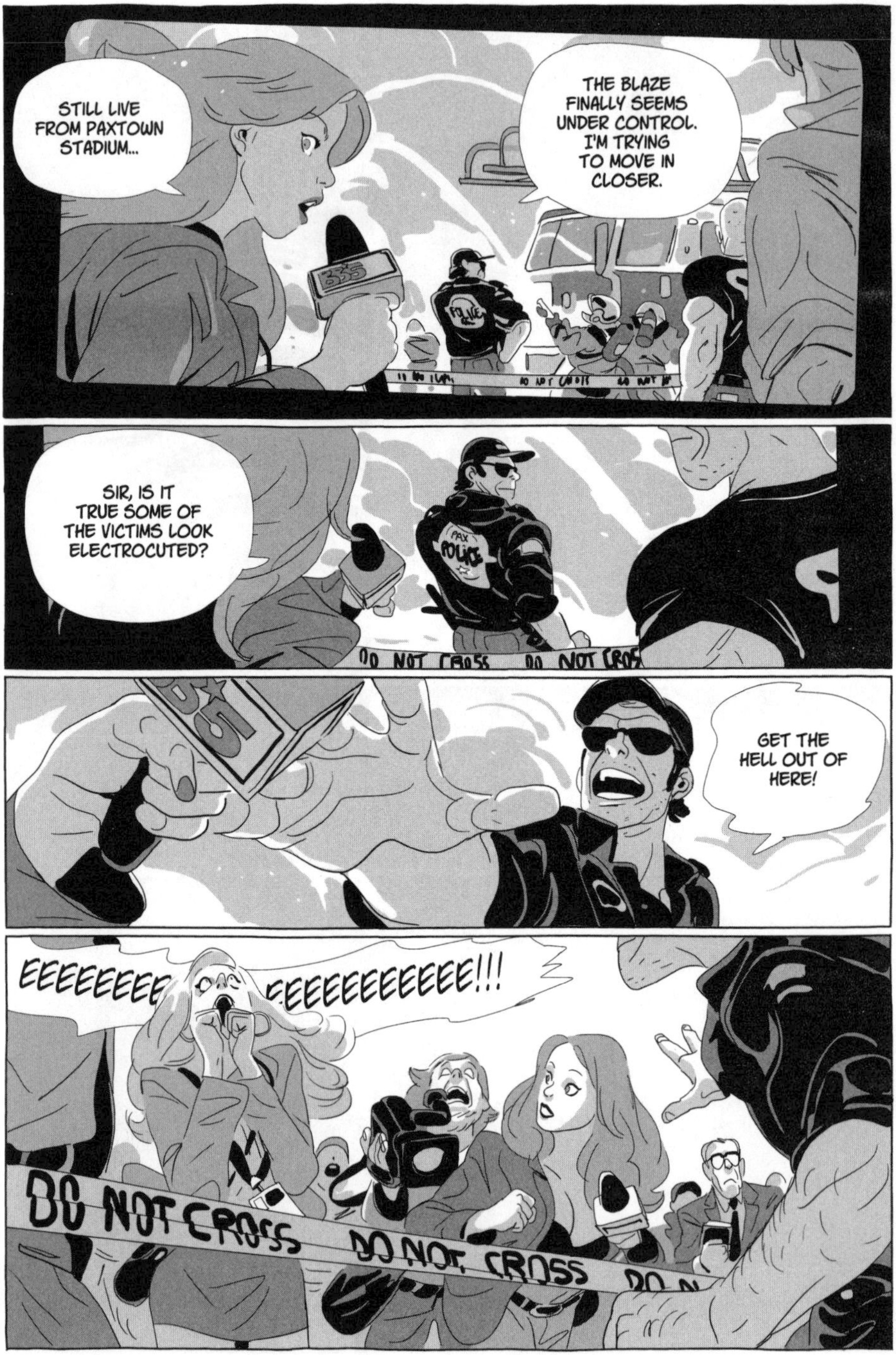
STILL LIVE FROM PAXTOWN STADIUM...
THE BLAZE FINALLY SEEMS UNDER CONTROL. I'M TRYING TO MOVE IN CLOSER.
DO NOT CROSS
SIR, IS IT TRUE SOME OF THE VICTIMS LOOK ELECTROCUTED?
PAX POLICE
DO NOT CROSS DO NOT CROS
GET THE HELL OUT OF HERE!
EEEEEEEE EEEEEEEEEEE!!!
DO NOT CROSS DO NOT CROSS

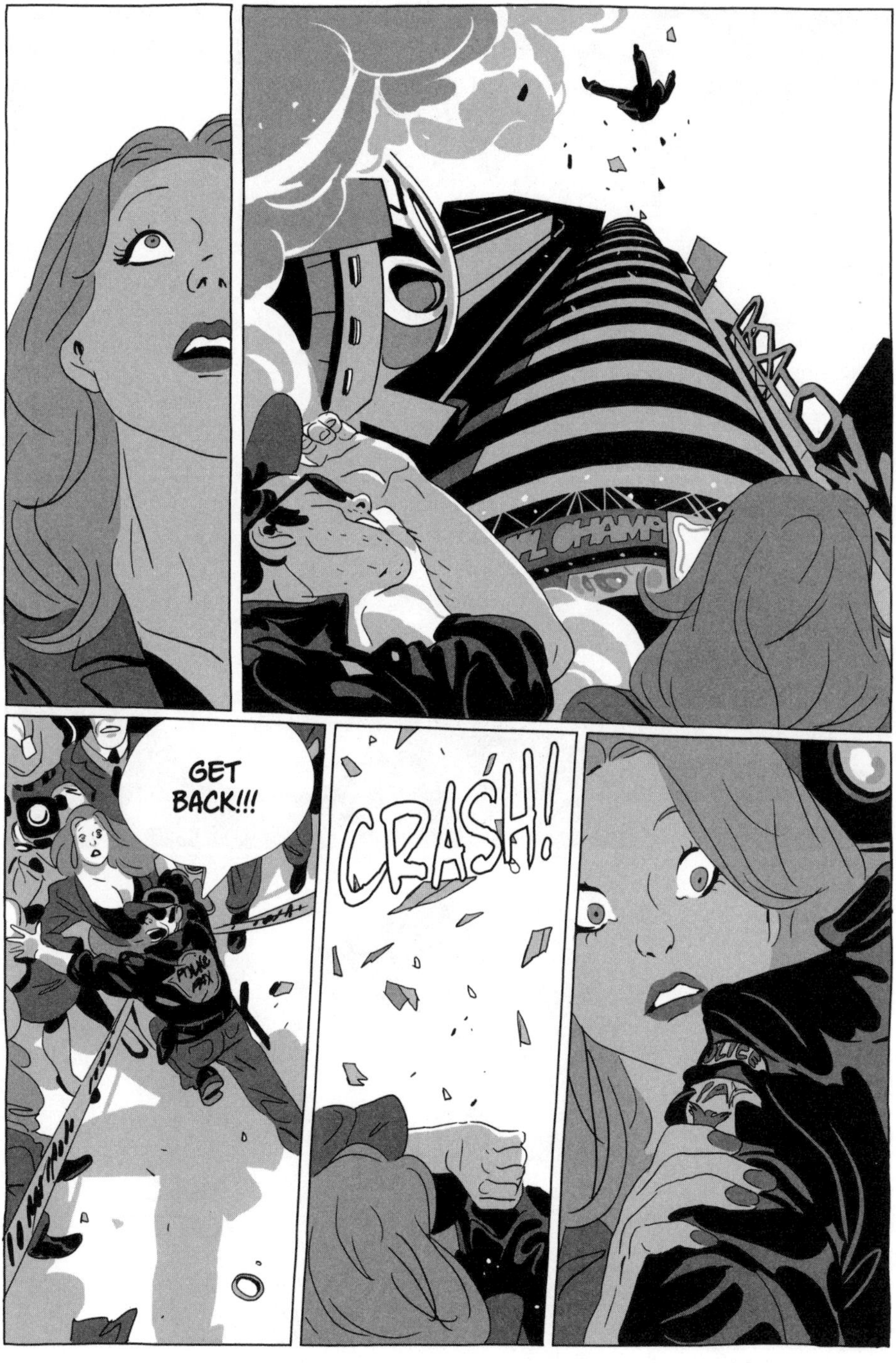
GET BACK!!!
CRASH!

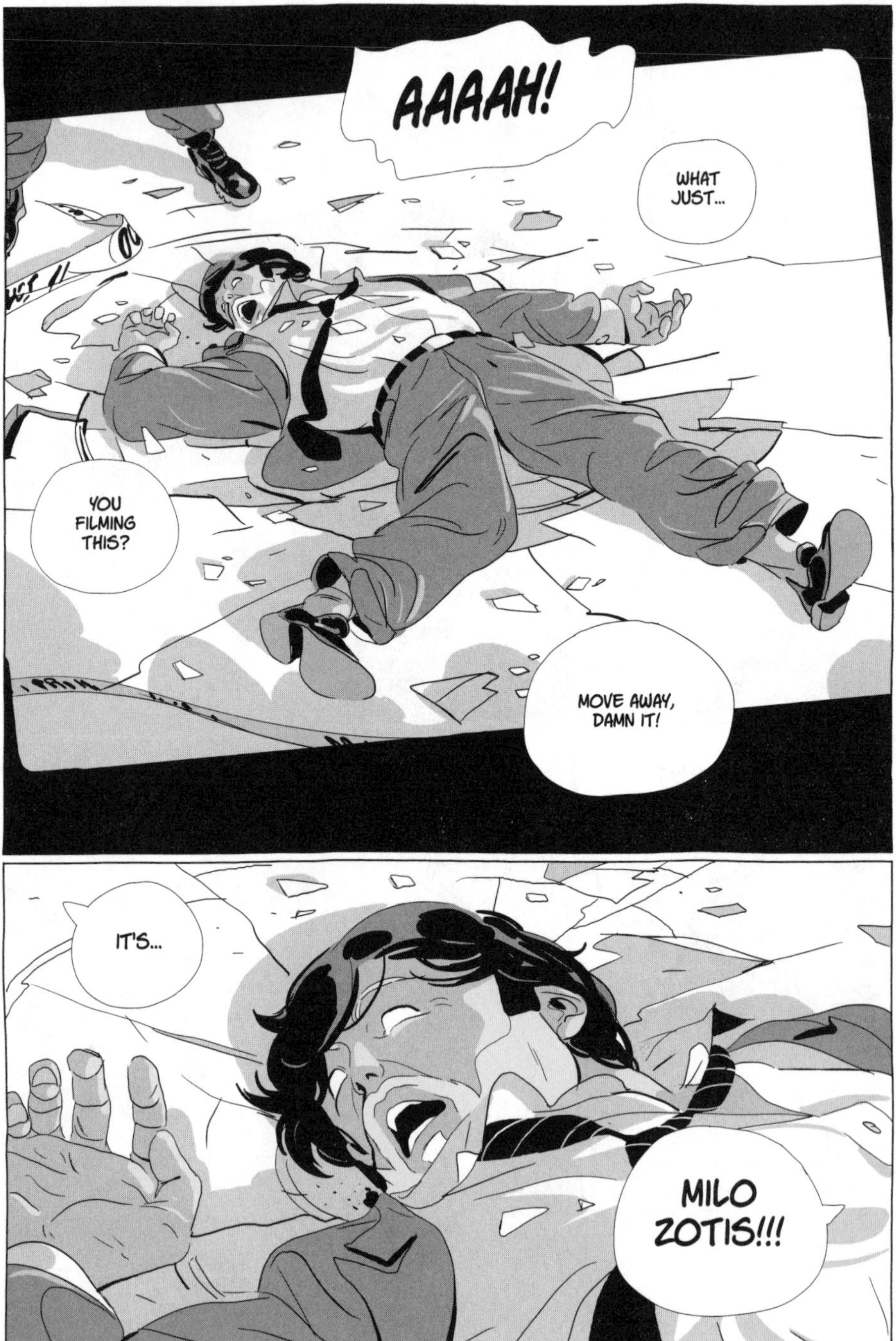
AAAAH!
WHAT JUST...
YOU FILMING THIS?
MOVE AWAY, DAMN IT!
IT'S...
MILO ZOTIS!!!

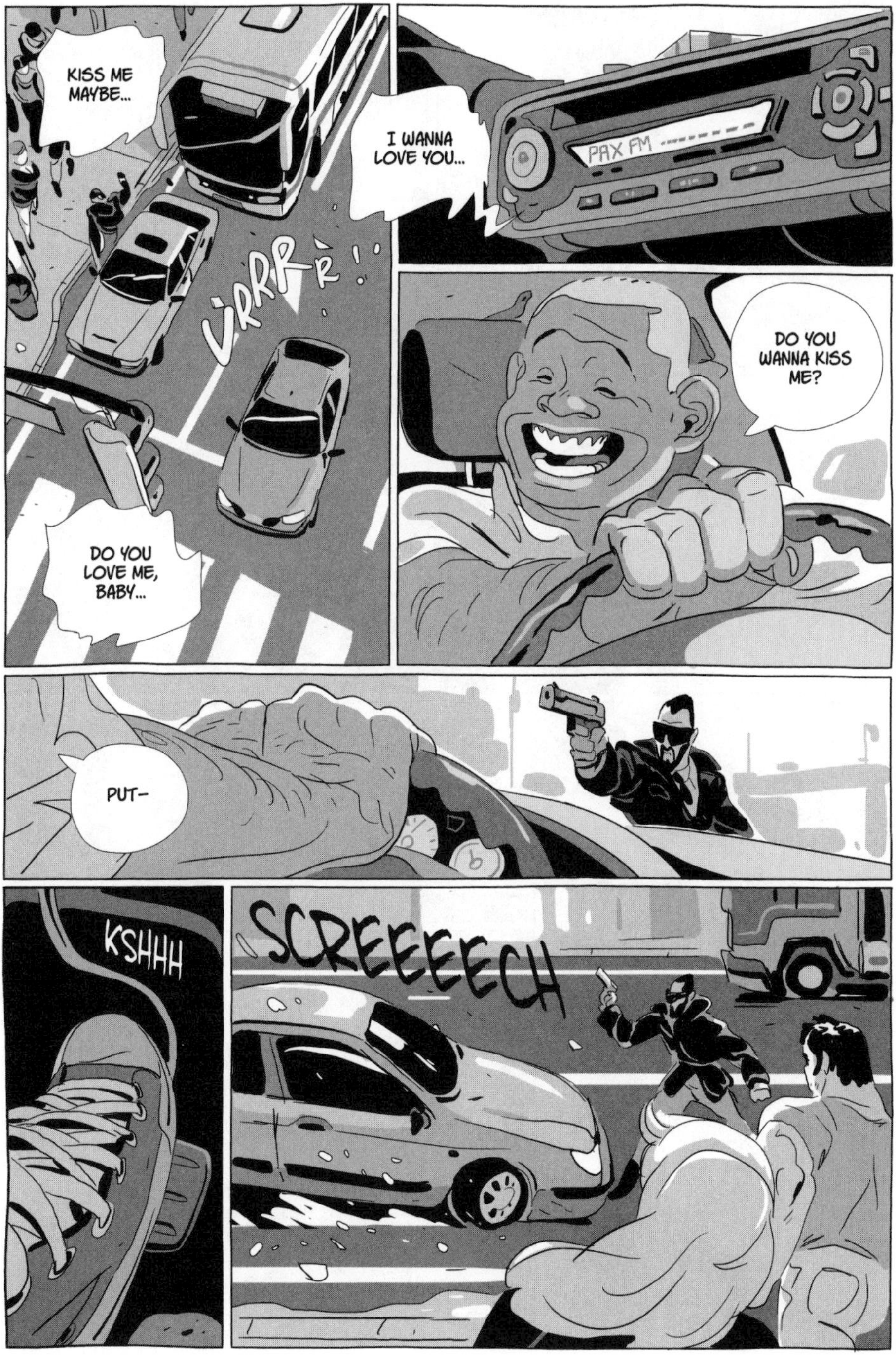
KISS ME MAYBE...
VRRRR!
I WANNA LOVE YOU...
PAX FM
DO YOU LOVE ME, BABY...
DO YOU WANNA KISS ME?
PUT-
KSHHH
SCREEEECH

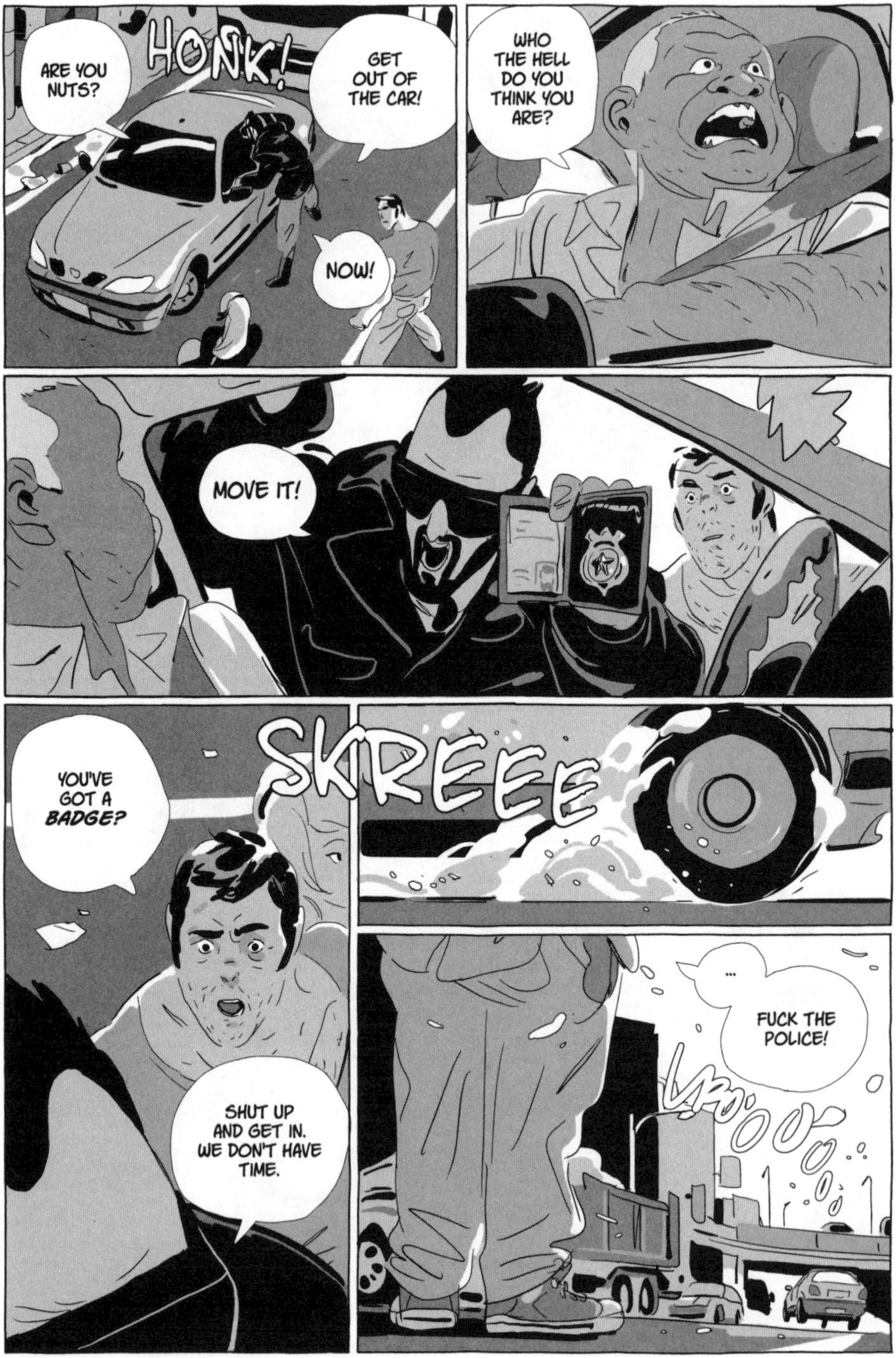
ARE YOU NUTS?
HONK!
GET OUT OF THE CAR!
NOW!
WHO THE HELL DO YOU THINK YOU ARE?
MOVE IT!
YOU'VE GOT A *BADGE?*
SHUT UP AND GET IN. WE DON'T HAVE TIME.
SKREEE
...
FUCK THE POLICE!
VROOOOOOO

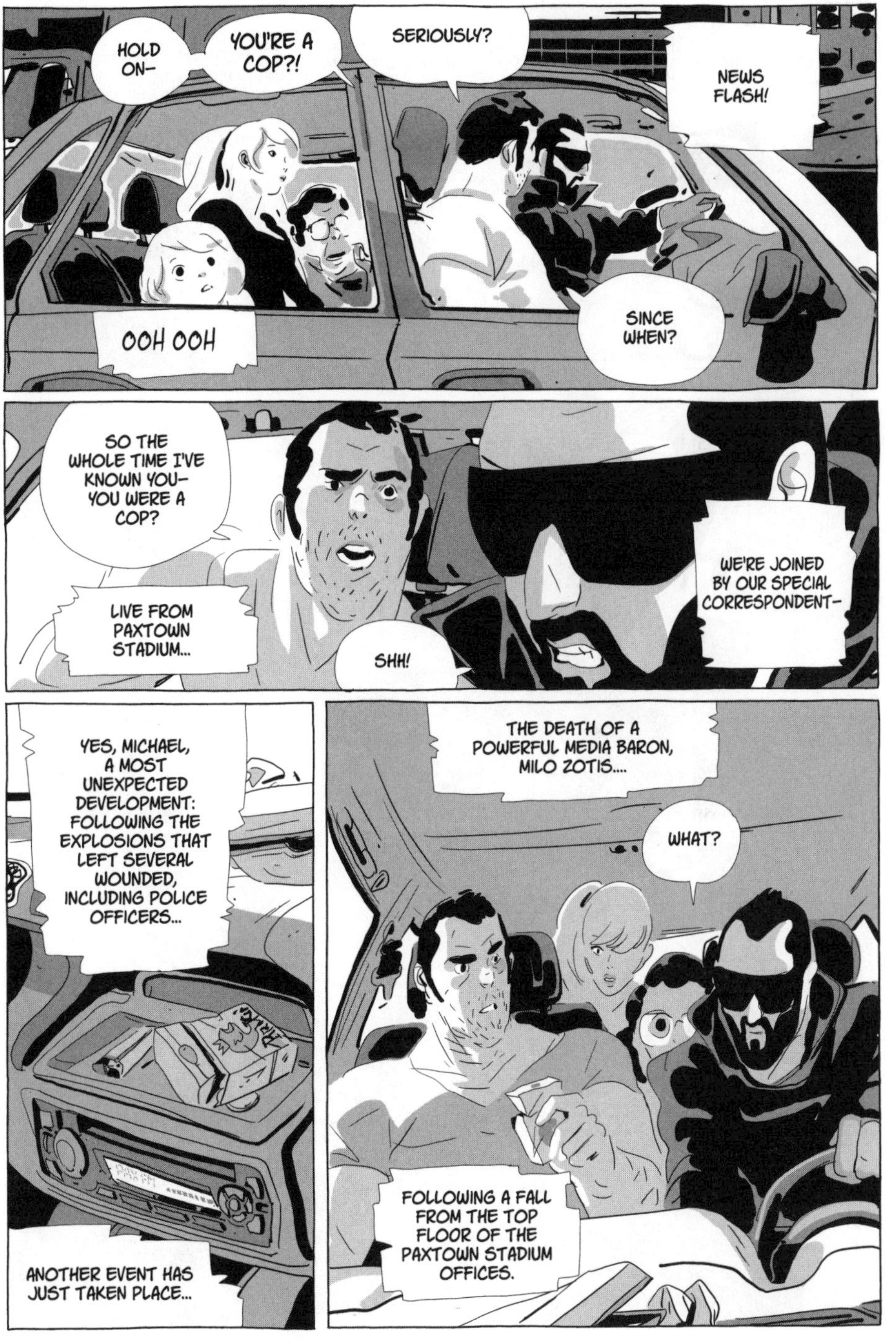
HOLD ON-
YOU'RE A COP?!
SERIOUSLY?
NEWS FLASH!
OOH OOH
SINCE WHEN?
SO THE WHOLE TIME I'VE KNOWN YOU- YOU WERE A COP?
LIVE FROM PAXTOWN STADIUM...
SHH!
WE'RE JOINED BY OUR SPECIAL CORRESPONDENT-
YES, MICHAEL, A MOST UNEXPECTED DEVELOPMENT: FOLLOWING THE EXPLOSIONS THAT LEFT SEVERAL WOUNDED, INCLUDING POLICE OFFICERS...
ANOTHER EVENT HAS JUST TAKEN PLACE...
THE DEATH OF A POWERFUL MEDIA BARON, MILO ZOTIS....
WHAT?
FOLLOWING A FALL FROM THE TOP FLOOR OF THE PAXTOWN STADIUM OFFICES.

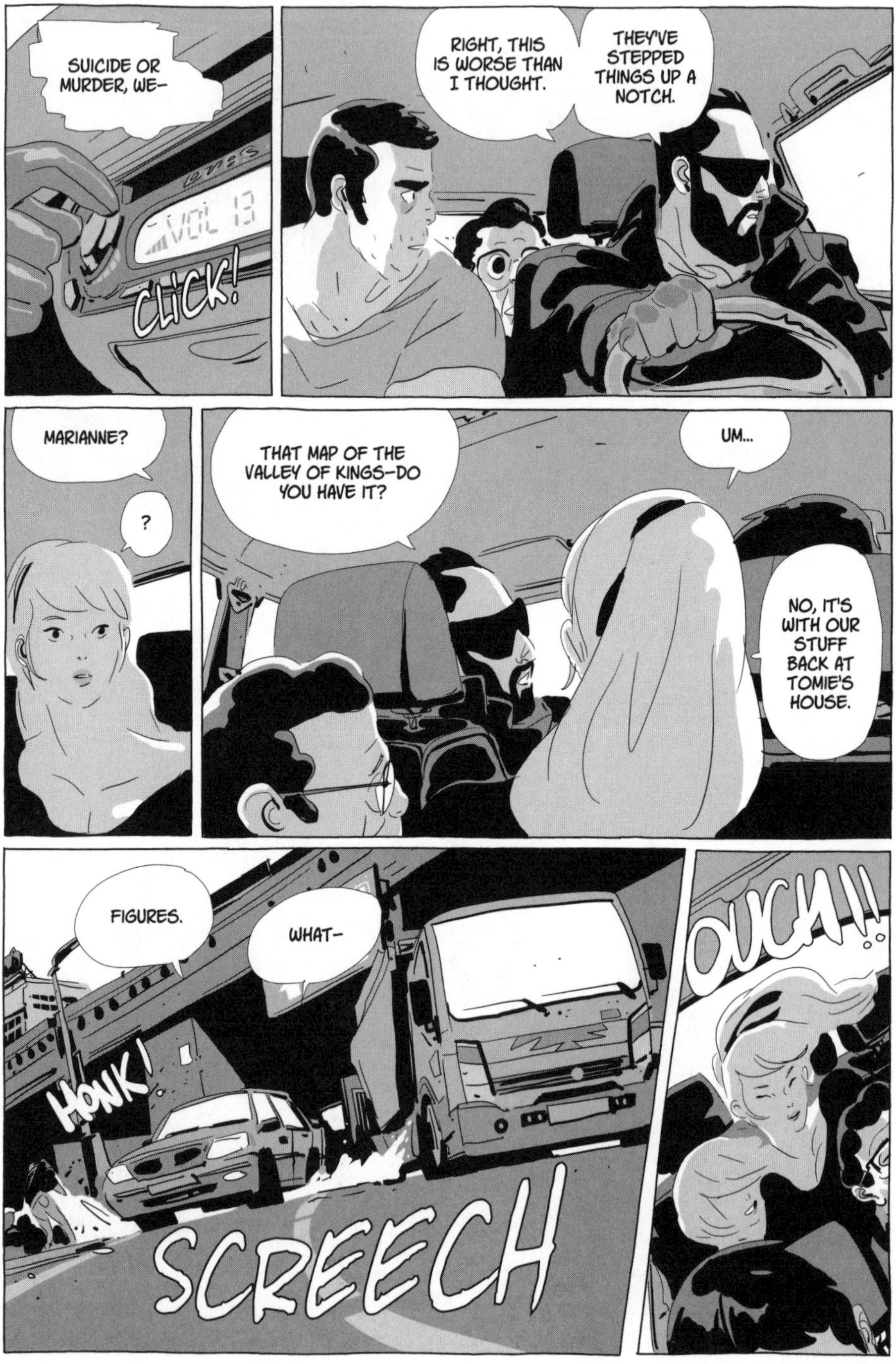
SUICIDE OR MURDER, WE-
CLICK!
RIGHT, THIS IS WORSE THAN I THOUGHT.
THEY'VE STEPPED THINGS UP A NOTCH.
MARIANNE?
?
THAT MAP OF THE VALLEY OF KINGS—DO YOU HAVE IT?
UM...
NO, IT'S WITH OUR STUFF BACK AT TOMIE'S HOUSE.
FIGURES.
WHAT-
HONK!
SCREECH
OUCH!!

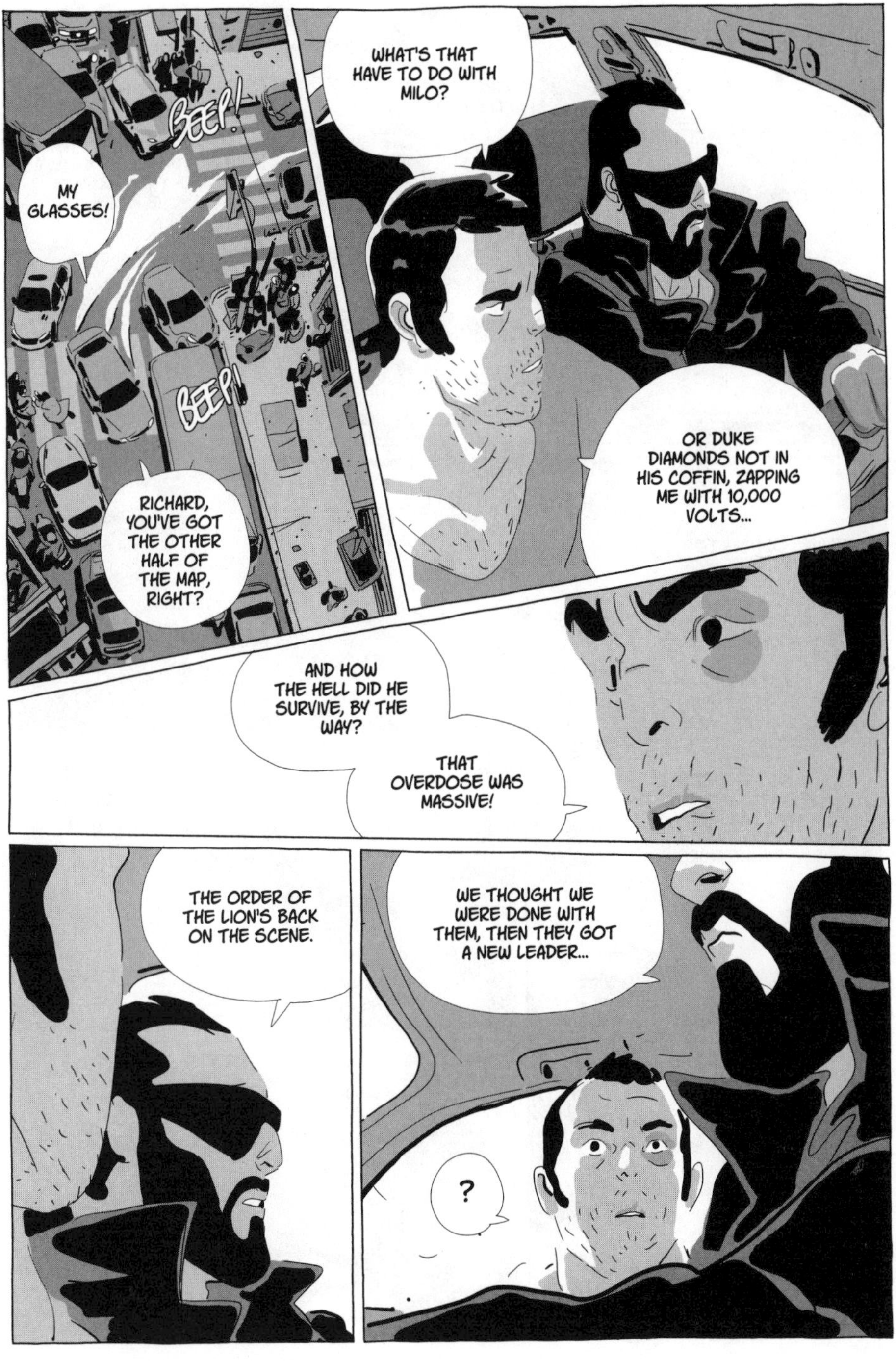
BEEP!
MY GLASSES!
BEEP!
RICHARD, YOU'VE GOT THE OTHER HALF OF THE MAP, RIGHT?
WHAT'S THAT HAVE TO DO WITH MILO?
OR DUKE DIAMONDS NOT IN HIS COFFIN, ZAPPING ME WITH 10,000 VOLTS...
AND HOW THE HELL DID HE SURVIVE, BY THE WAY?
THAT OVERDOSE WAS MASSIVE!
THE ORDER OF THE LION'S BACK ON THE SCENE.
WE THOUGHT WE WERE DONE WITH THEM, THEN THEY GOT A NEW LEADER...
?

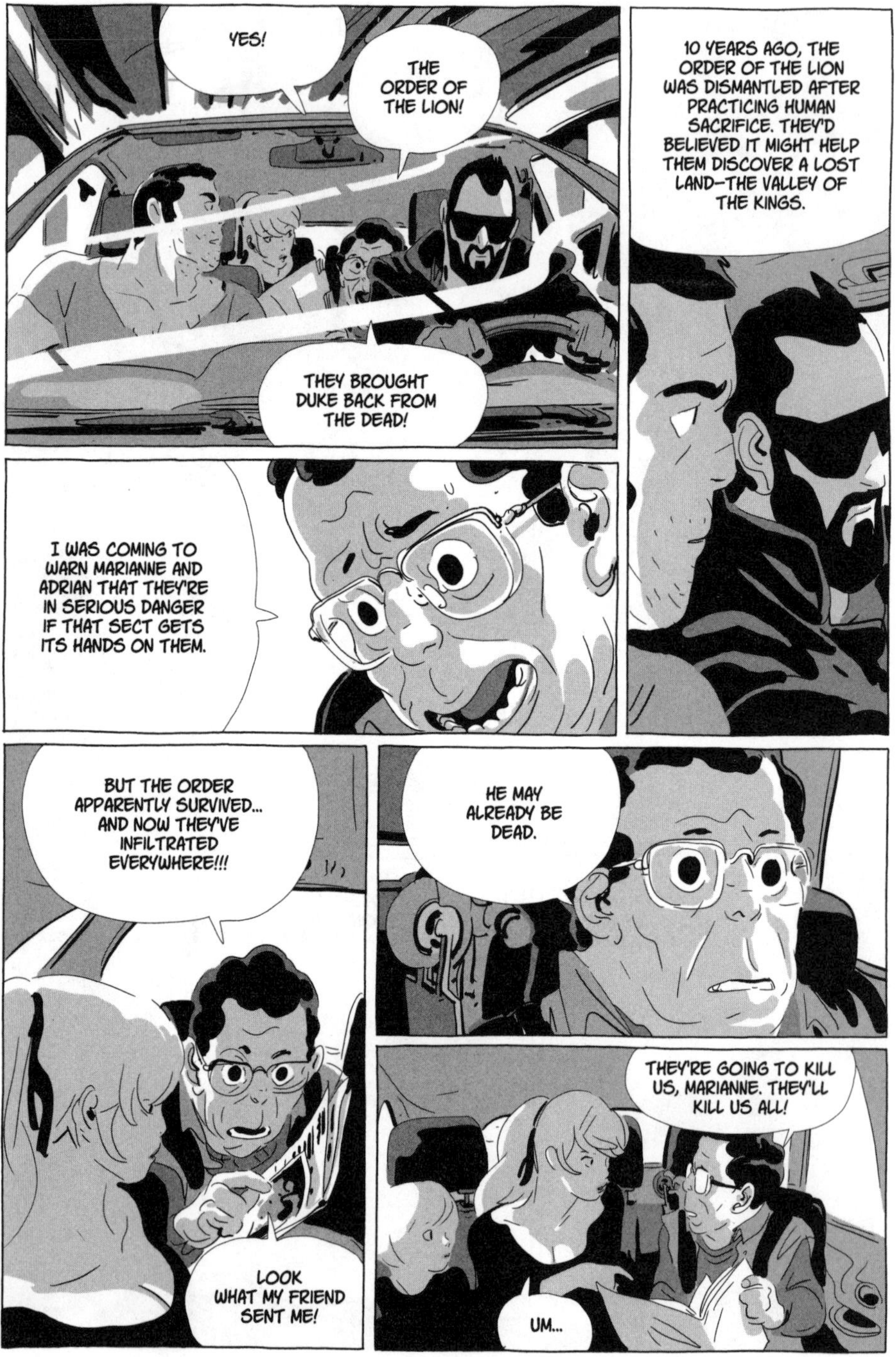
YES!
THE ORDER OF THE LION!
THEY BROUGHT DUKE BACK FROM THE DEAD!
I WAS COMING TO WARN MARIANNE AND ADRIAN THAT THEY'RE IN SERIOUS DANGER IF THAT SECT GETS ITS HANDS ON THEM.
10 YEARS AGO, THE ORDER OF THE LION WAS DISMANTLED AFTER PRACTICING HUMAN SACRIFICE. THEY'D BELIEVED IT MIGHT HELP THEM DISCOVER A LOST LAND—THE VALLEY OF THE KINGS.
BUT THE ORDER APPARENTLY SURVIVED... AND NOW THEY'VE INFILTRATED EVERYWHERE!!!
LOOK WHAT MY FRIEND SENT ME!
HE MAY ALREADY BE DEAD.
THEY'RE GOING TO KILL US, MARIANNE. THEY'LL KILL US ALL!
UM...

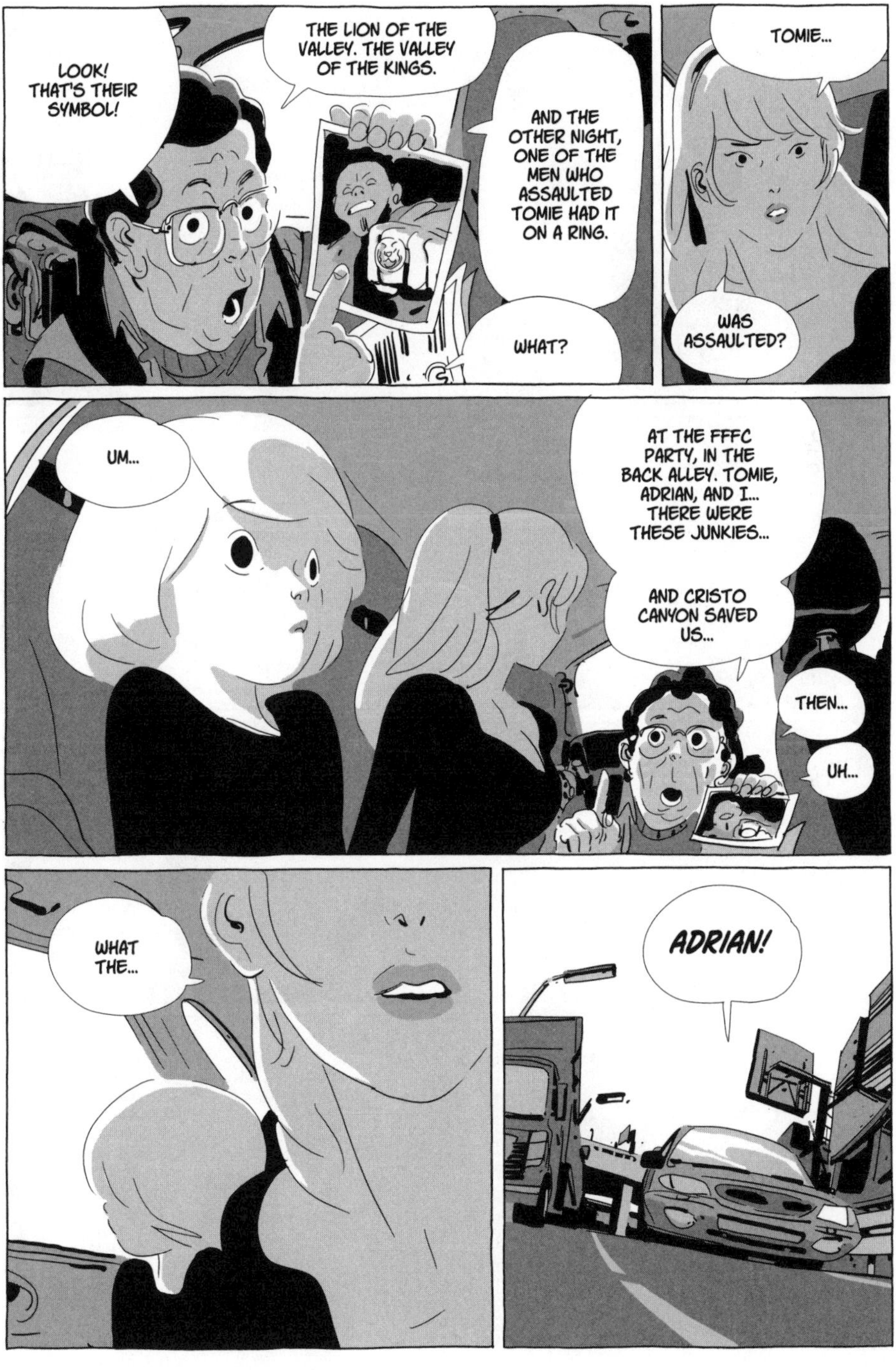
LOOK! THAT'S THEIR SYMBOL!
THE LION OF THE VALLEY. THE VALLEY OF THE KINGS.
AND THE OTHER NIGHT, ONE OF THE MEN WHO ASSAULTED TOMIE HAD IT ON A RING.
WHAT?
TOMIE...
WAS ASSAULTED?
UM...
AT THE FFFC PARTY, IN THE BACK ALLEY. TOMIE, ADRIAN, AND I... THERE WERE THESE JUNKIES...
AND CRISTO CANYON SAVED US...
THEN...
UH...
WHAT THE...
ADRIAN!

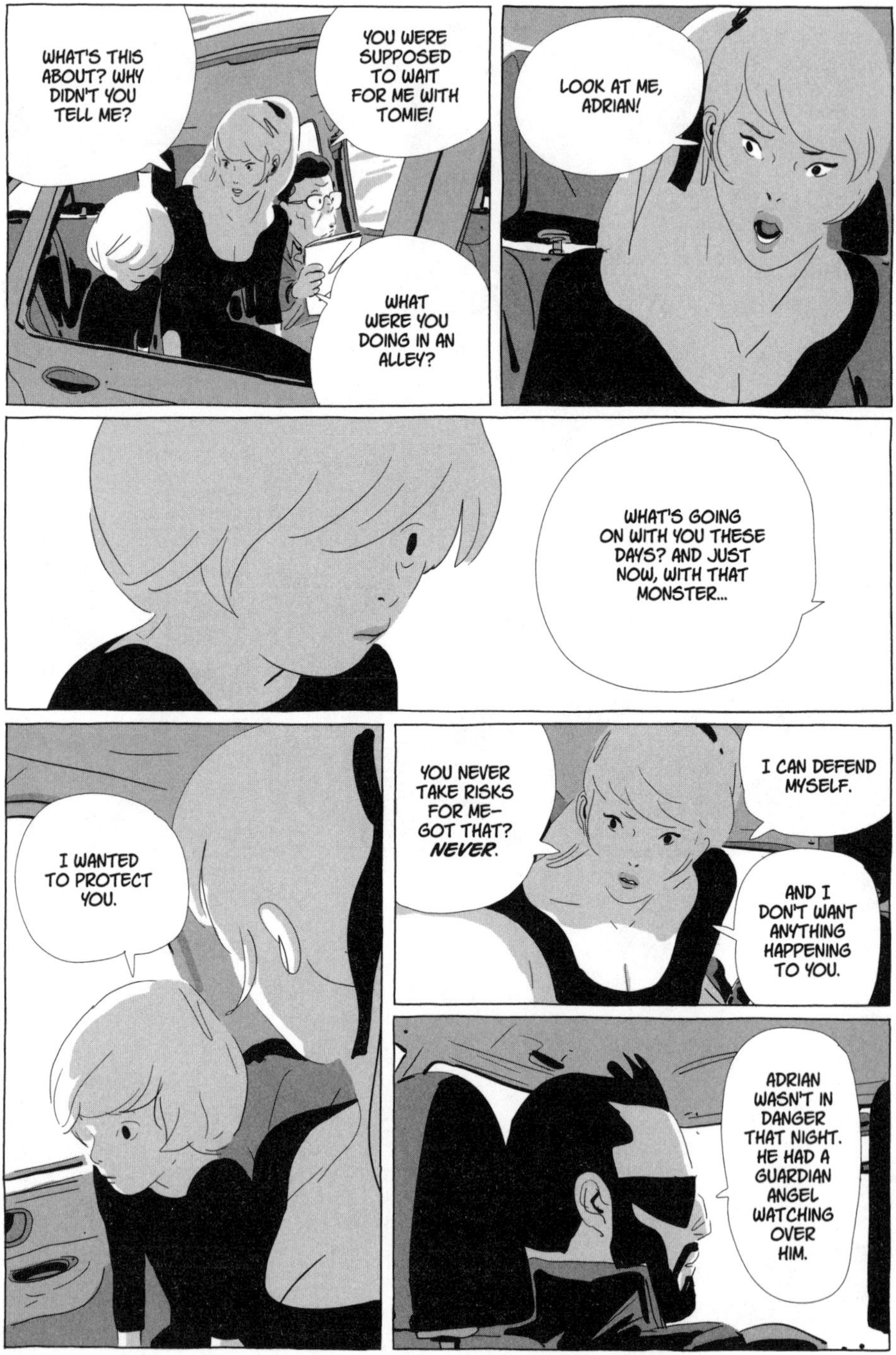
WHAT'S THIS ABOUT? WHY DIDN'T YOU TELL ME?
YOU WERE SUPPOSED TO WAIT FOR ME WITH TOMIE!
WHAT WERE YOU DOING IN AN ALLEY?
LOOK AT ME, ADRIAN!
WHAT'S GOING ON WITH YOU THESE DAYS? AND JUST NOW, WITH THAT MONSTER...
I WANTED TO PROTECT YOU.
YOU NEVER TAKE RISKS FOR ME–GOT THAT? NEVER.
I CAN DEFEND MYSELF.
AND I DON'T WANT ANYTHING HAPPENING TO YOU.
ADRIAN WASN'T IN DANGER THAT NIGHT. HE HAD A GUARDIAN ANGEL WATCHING OVER HIM.

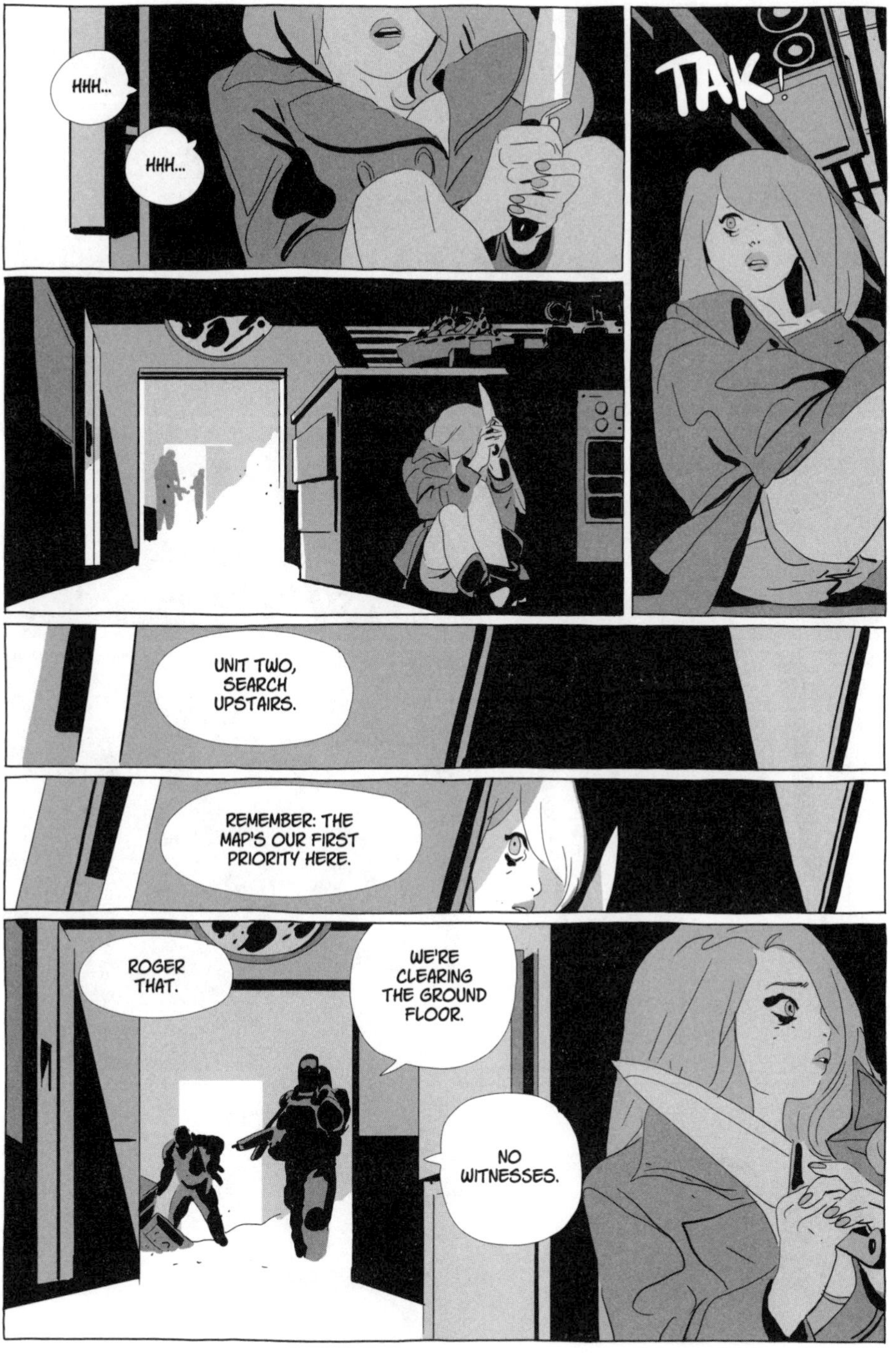
HHH...
HHH...
TAK!
UNIT TWO, SEARCH UPSTAIRS.
REMEMBER: THE MAP'S OUR FIRST PRIORITY HERE.
ROGER THAT.
WE'RE CLEARING THE GROUND FLOOR.
NO WITNESSES.

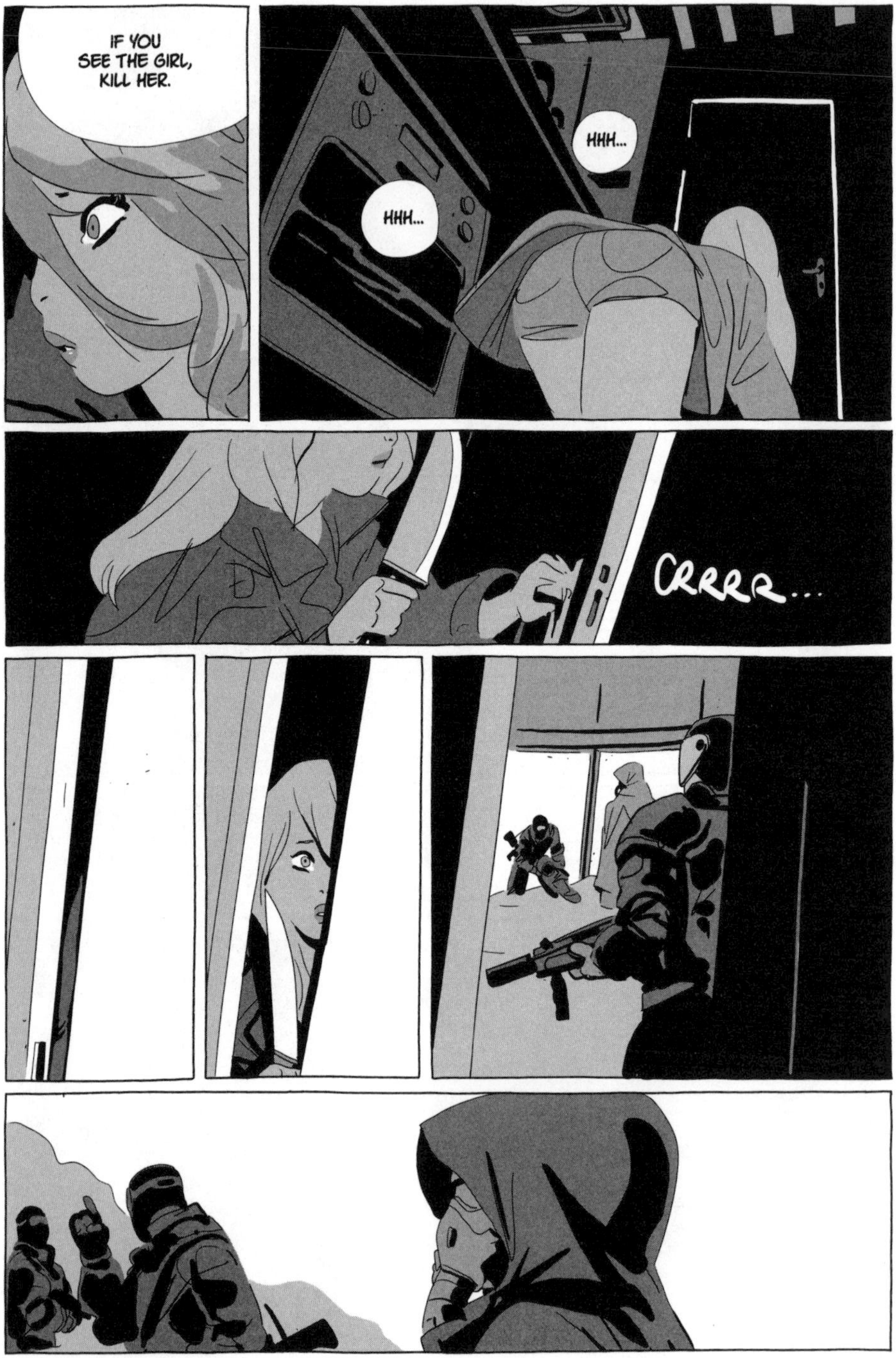
IF YOU SEE THE GIRL, KILL HER.
HHH...
HHH...
CRRRR...

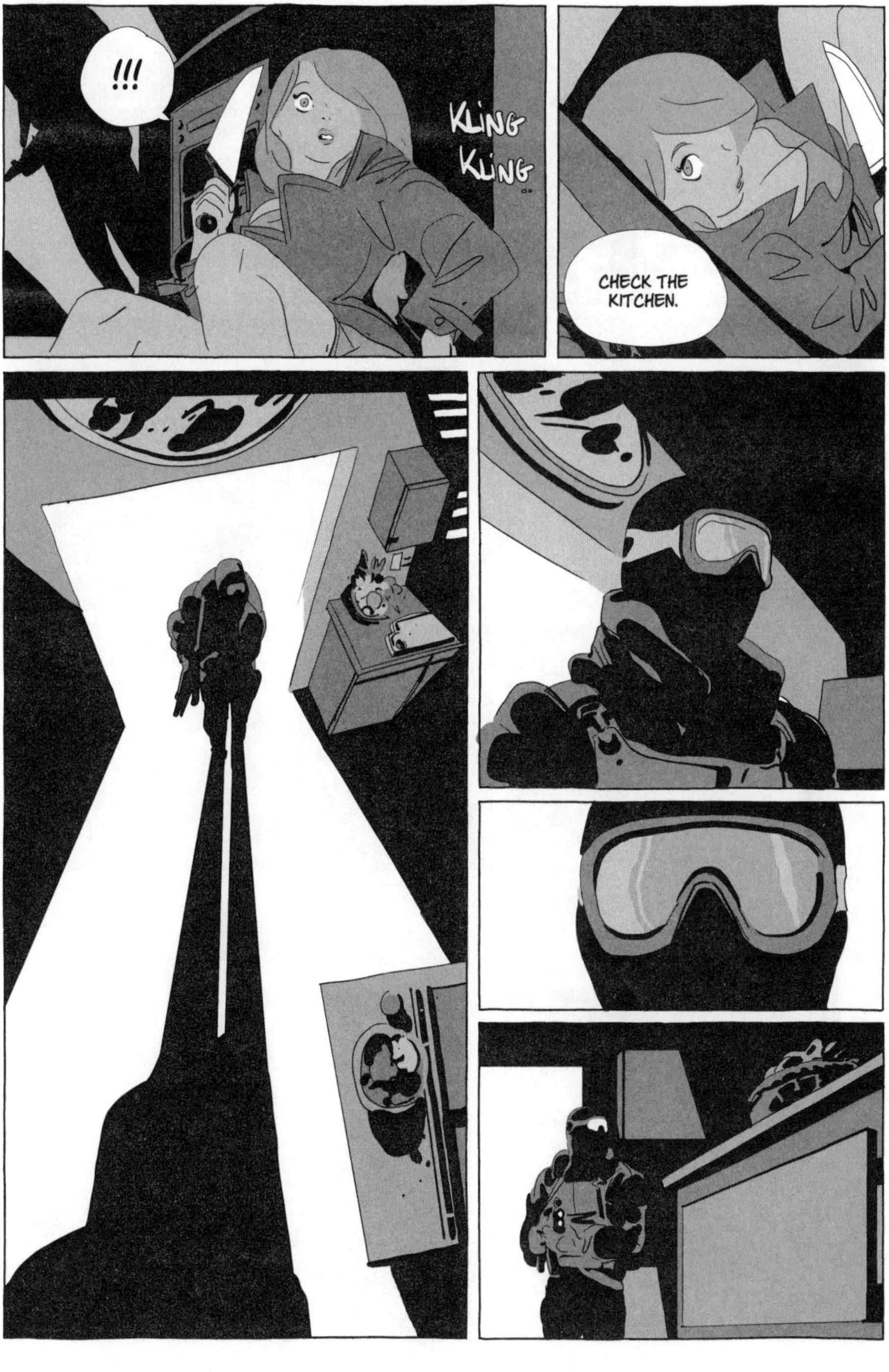
!!!
KLING KLING
CHECK THE KITCHEN.

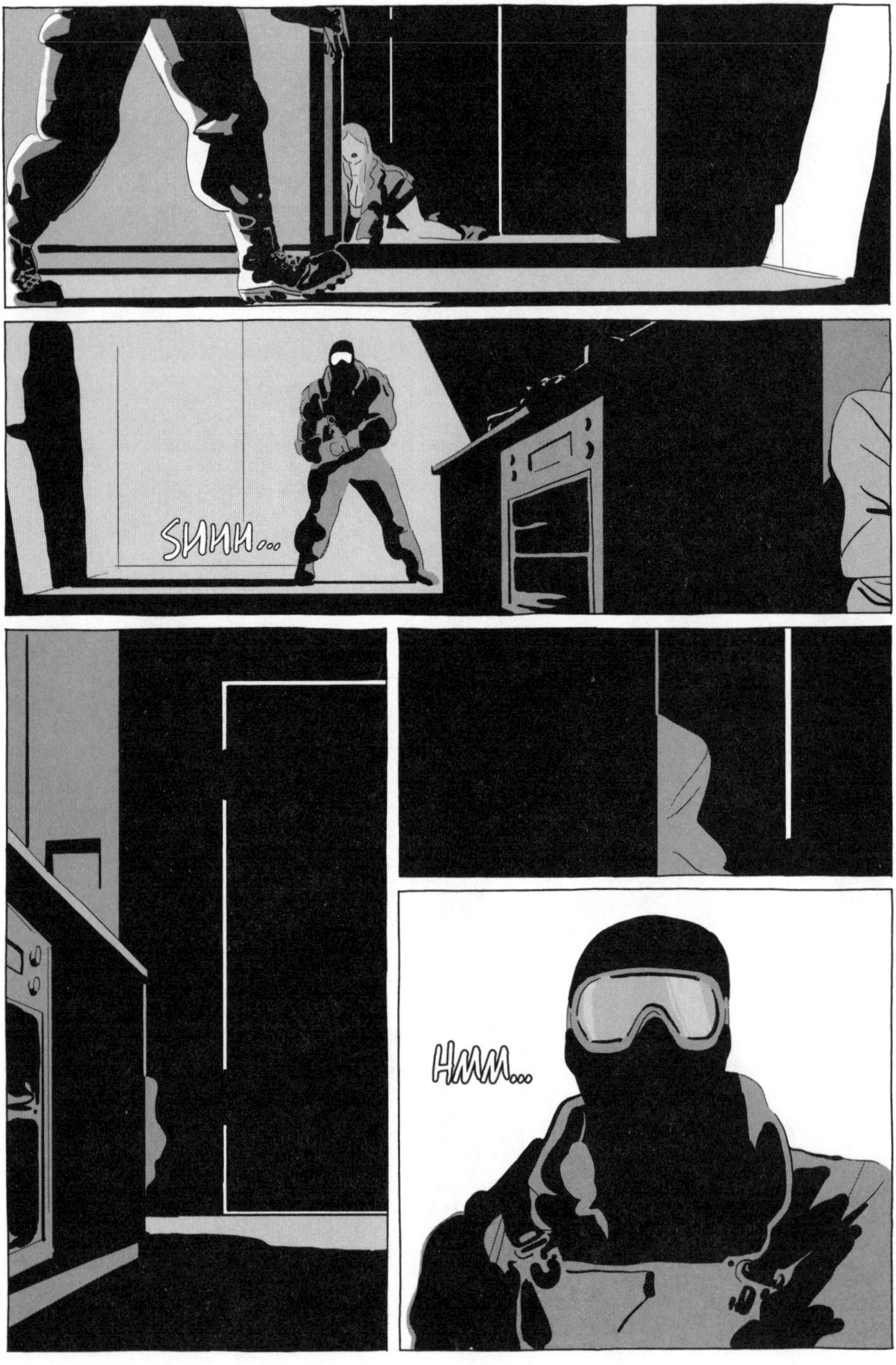
SHHH...
HMM...

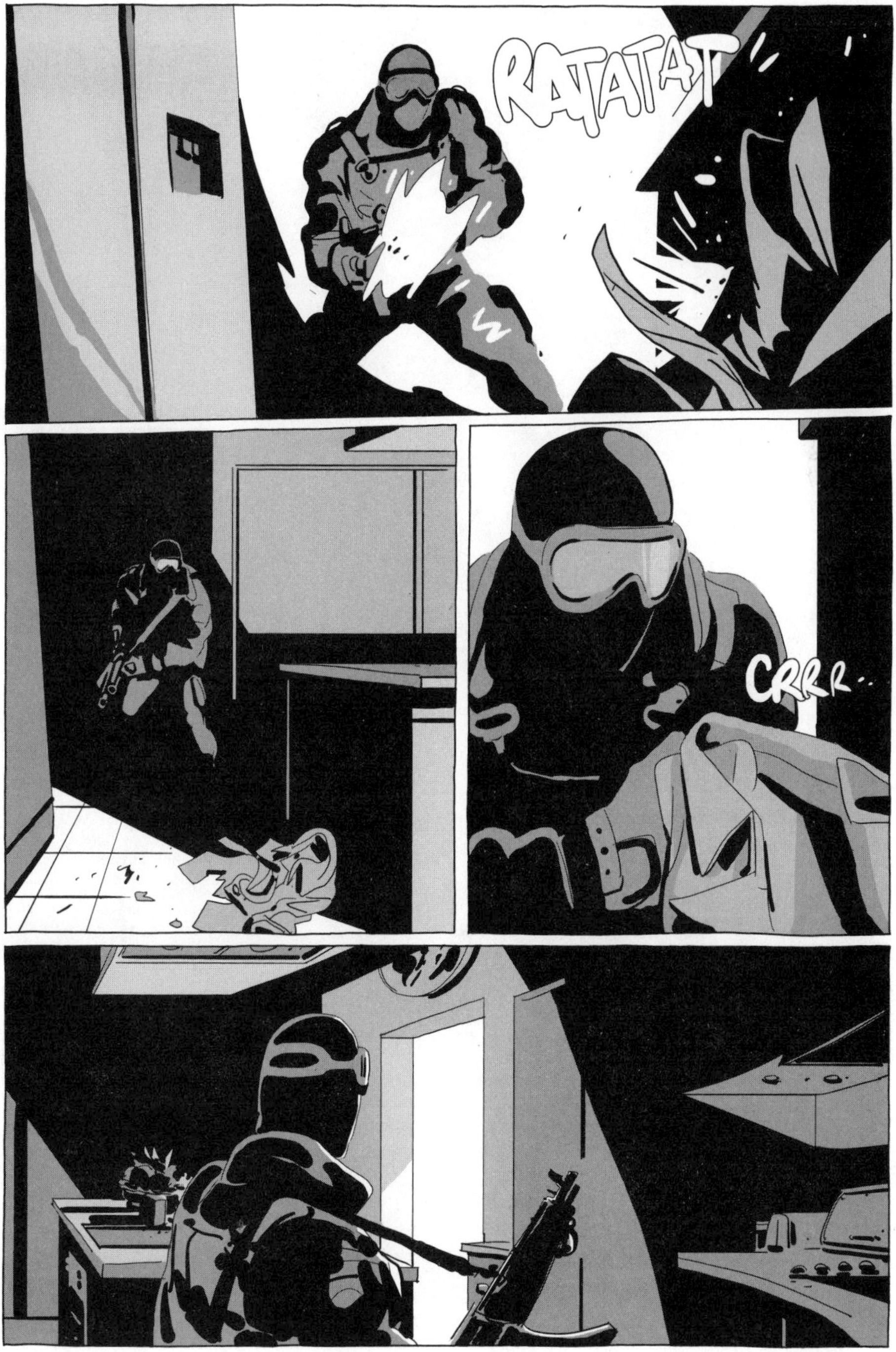
RATATAT
CRRR...

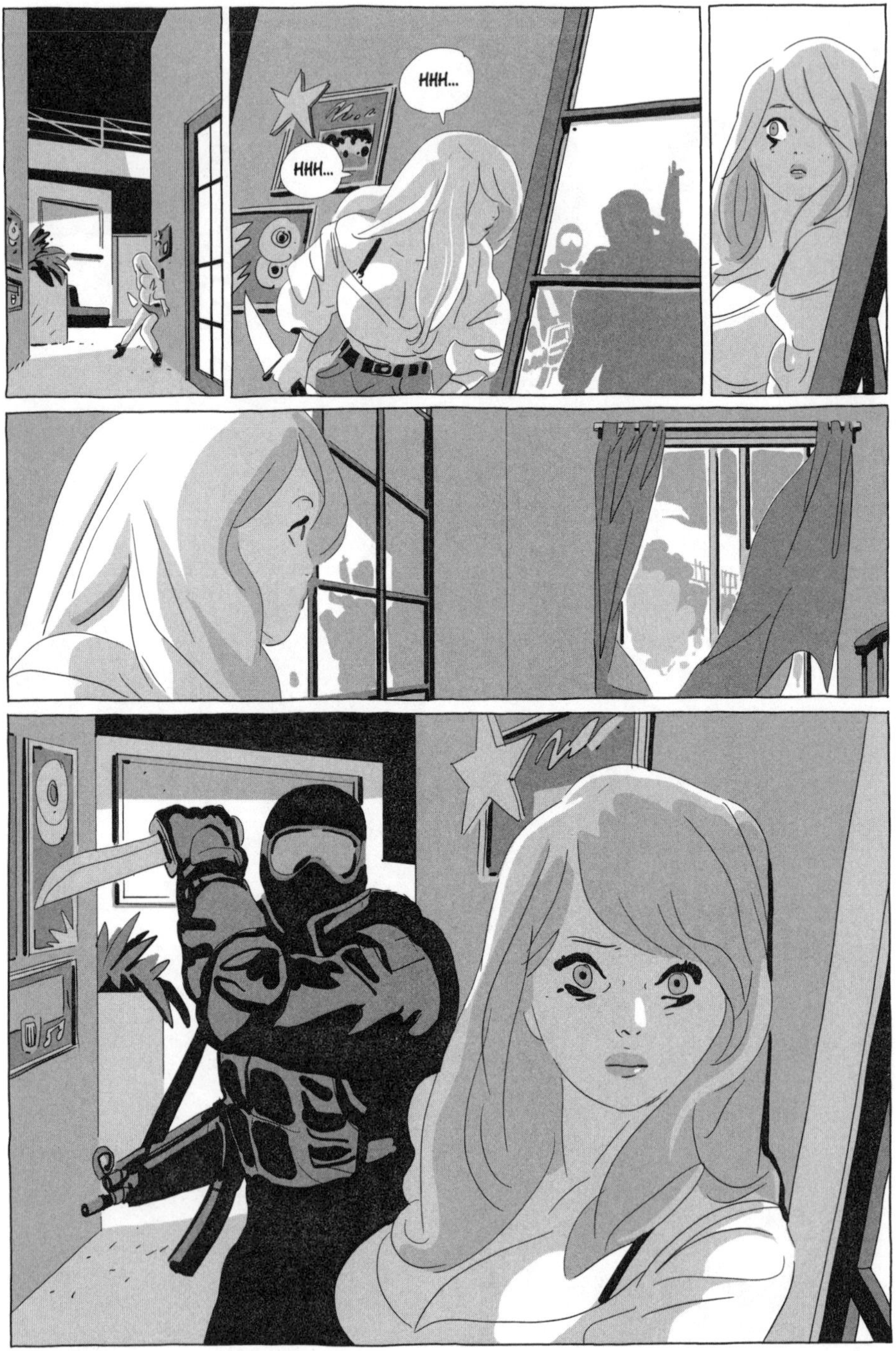
HHH...
HHH...

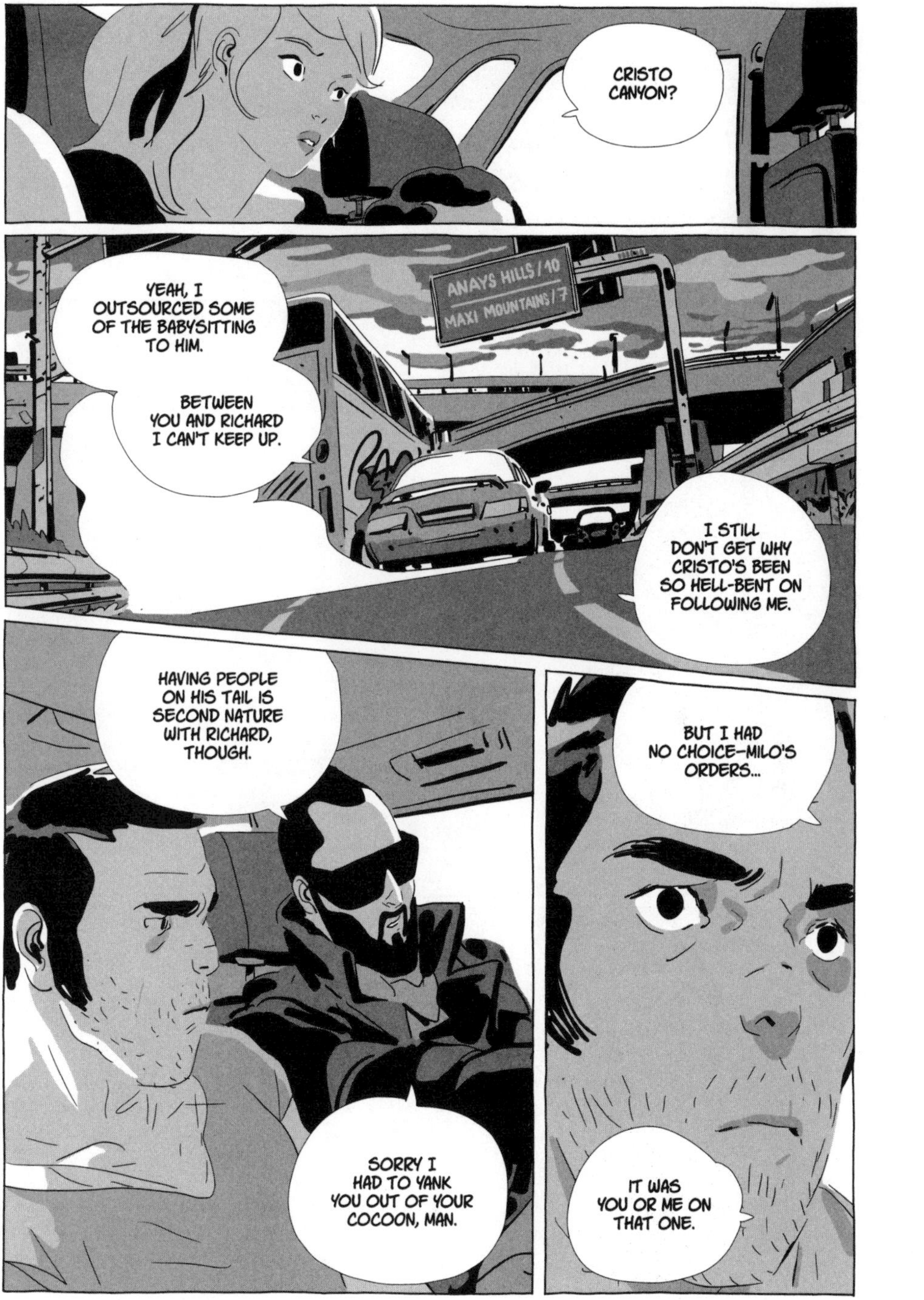
CRISTO CANYON?
ANAYS HILLS / 10
MAXI MOUNTAINS / 7
YEAH, I OUTSOURCED SOME OF THE BABYSITTING TO HIM.
BETWEEN YOU AND RICHARD I CAN'T KEEP UP.
I STILL DON'T GET WHY CRISTO'S BEEN SO HELL-BENT ON FOLLOWING ME.
HAVING PEOPLE ON HIS TAIL IS SECOND NATURE WITH RICHARD, THOUGH.
SORRY I HAD TO YANK YOU OUT OF YOUR COCOON, MAN.
BUT I HAD NO CHOICE—MILO'S ORDERS...
IT WAS YOU OR ME ON THAT ONE.

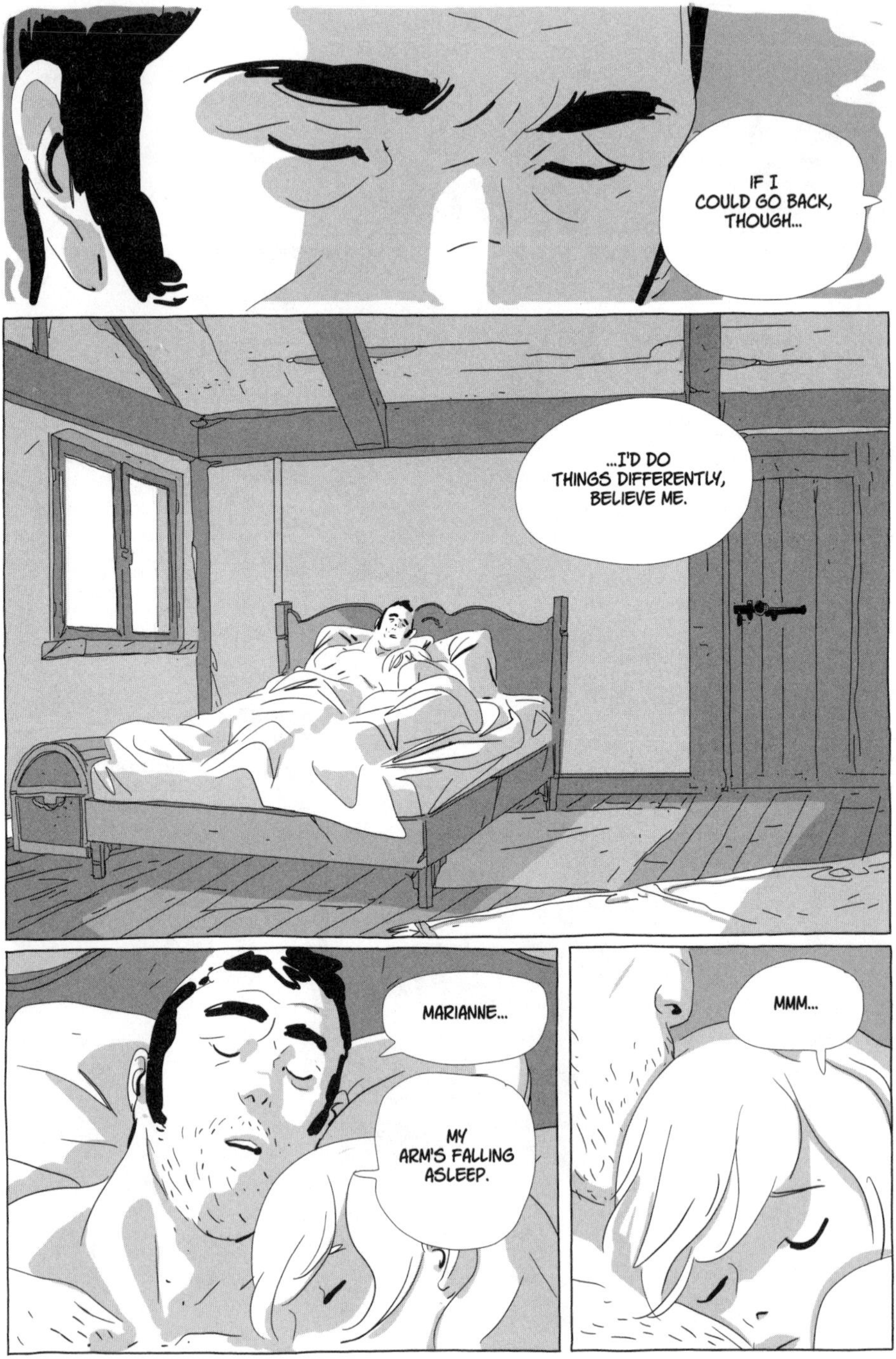
IF I COULD GO BACK, THOUGH...
...I'D DO THINGS DIFFERENTLY, BELIEVE ME.
MARIANNE...
MY ARM'S FALLING ASLEEP.
MMM...

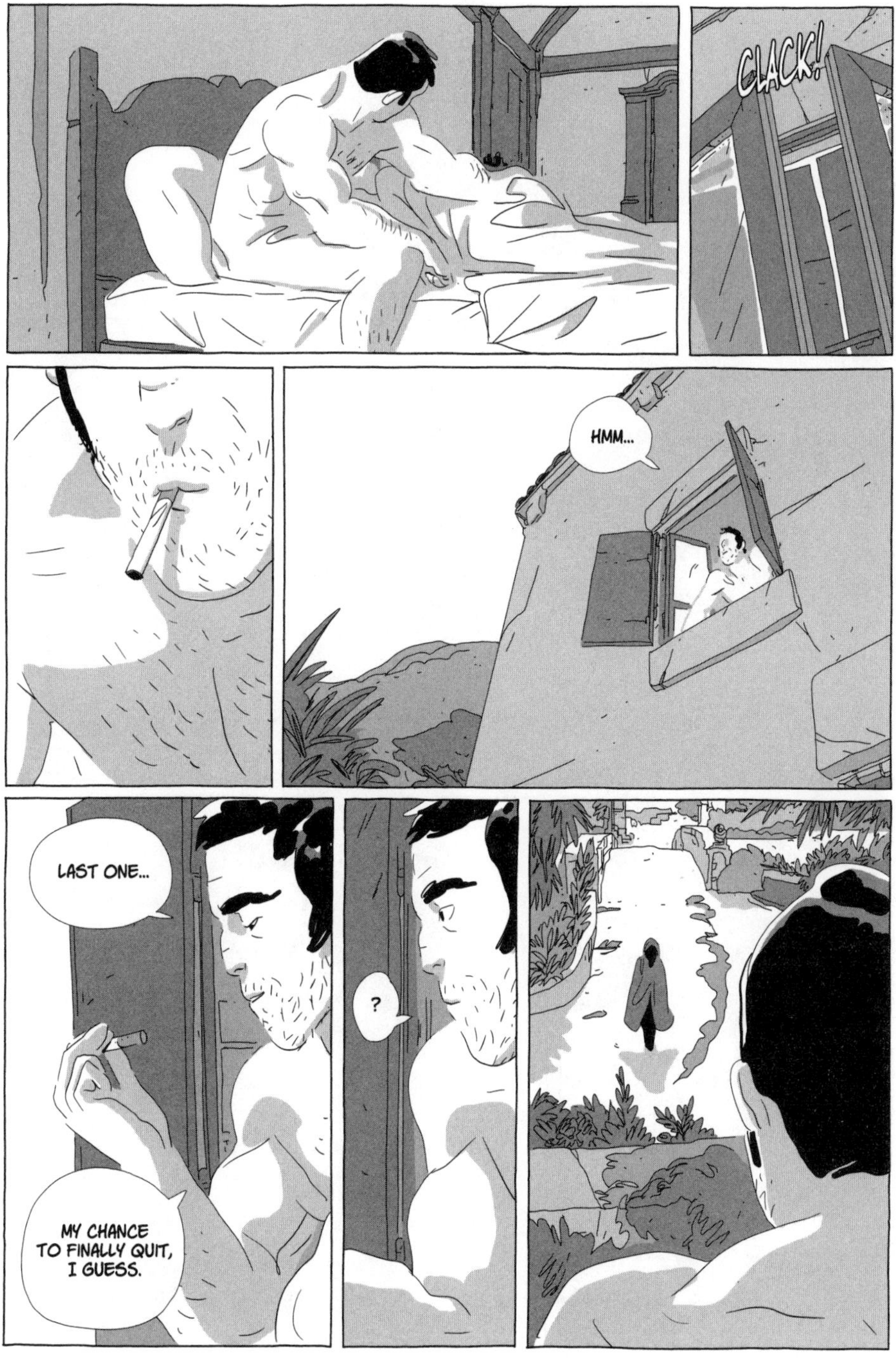
CLACK!
HMM...
LAST ONE...
MY CHANCE TO FINALLY QUIT, I GUESS.
?

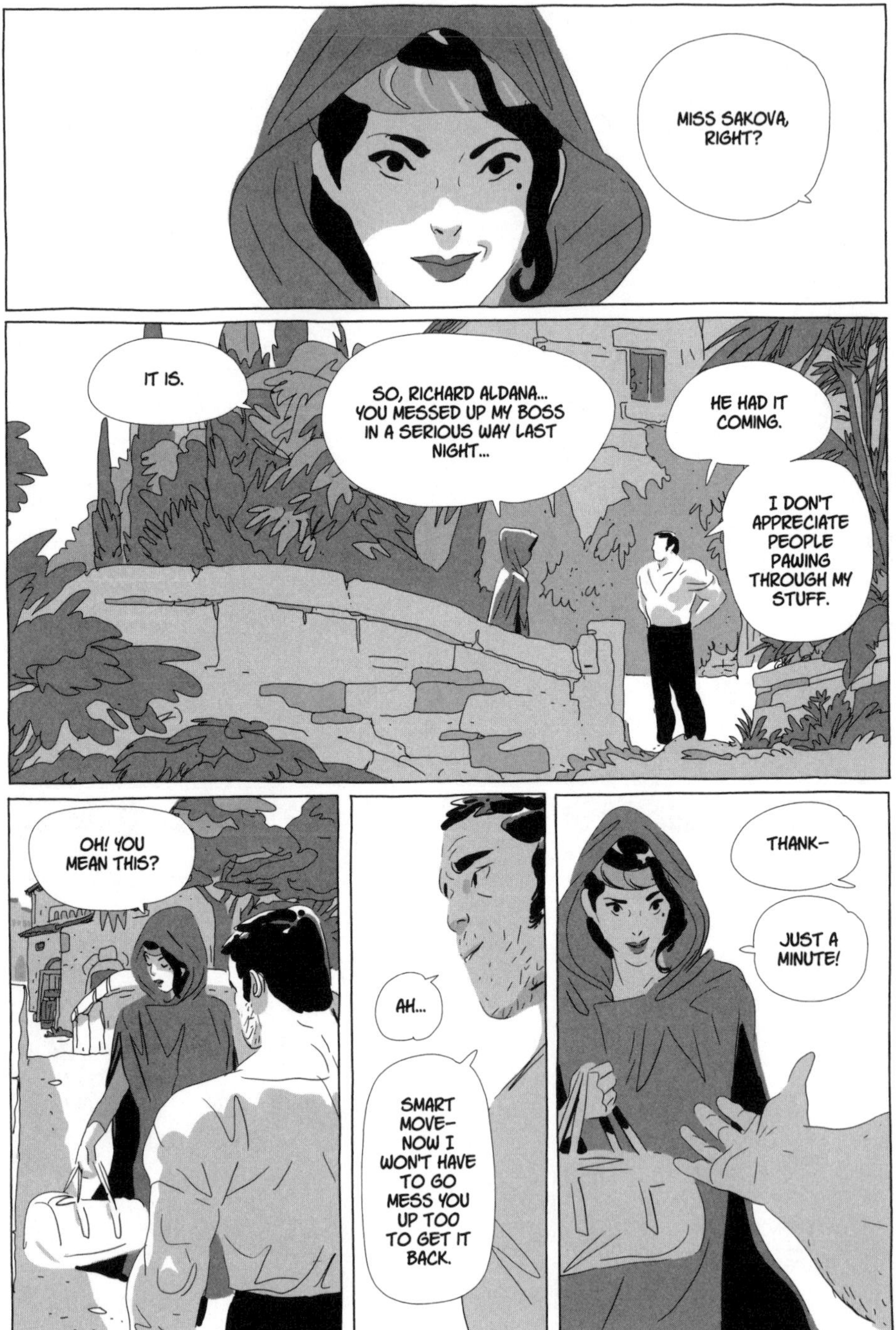
MISS SAKOVA, RIGHT?
IT IS.
SO, RICHARD ALDANA... YOU MESSED UP MY BOSS IN A SERIOUS WAY LAST NIGHT...
HE HAD IT COMING.
I DON'T APPRECIATE PEOPLE PAWING THROUGH MY STUFF.
OH! YOU MEAN THIS?
AH...
SMART MOVE– NOW I WON'T HAVE TO GO MESS YOU UP TOO TO GET IT BACK.
THANK–
JUST A MINUTE!

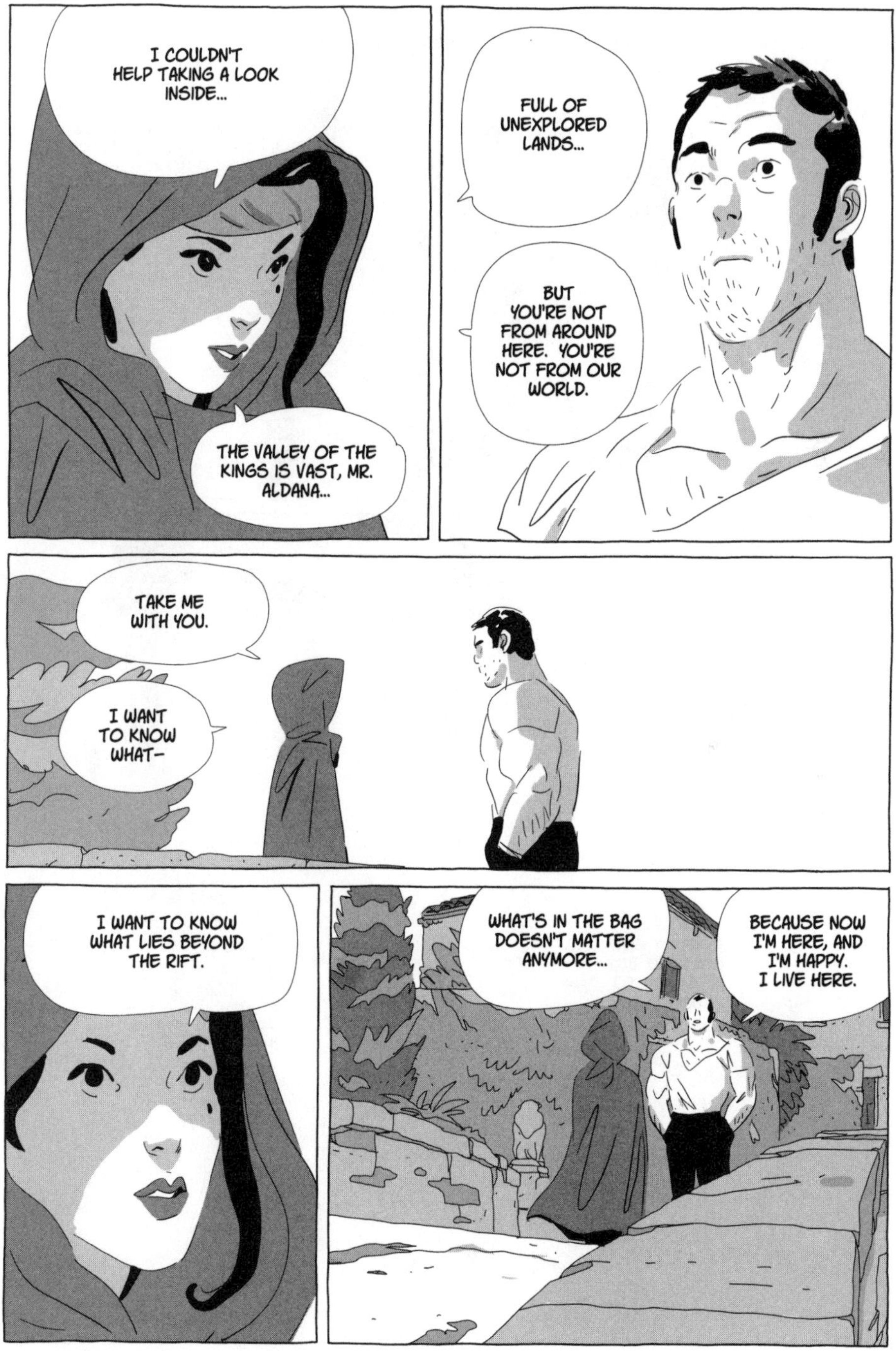
I COULDN'T HELP TAKING A LOOK INSIDE...
THE VALLEY OF THE KINGS IS VAST, MR. ALDANA...
FULL OF UNEXPLORED LANDS...
BUT YOU'RE NOT FROM AROUND HERE. YOU'RE NOT FROM OUR WORLD.
TAKE ME WITH YOU.
I WANT TO KNOW WHAT-
I WANT TO KNOW WHAT LIES BEYOND THE RIFT.
WHAT'S IN THE BAG DOESN'T MATTER ANYMORE...
BECAUSE NOW I'M HERE, AND I'M HAPPY. I LIVE HERE.

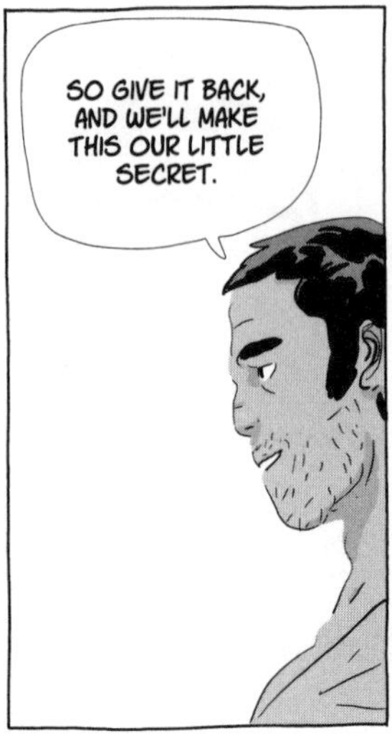
SO GIVE IT BACK, AND WE'LL MAKE THIS OUR LITTLE SECRET.
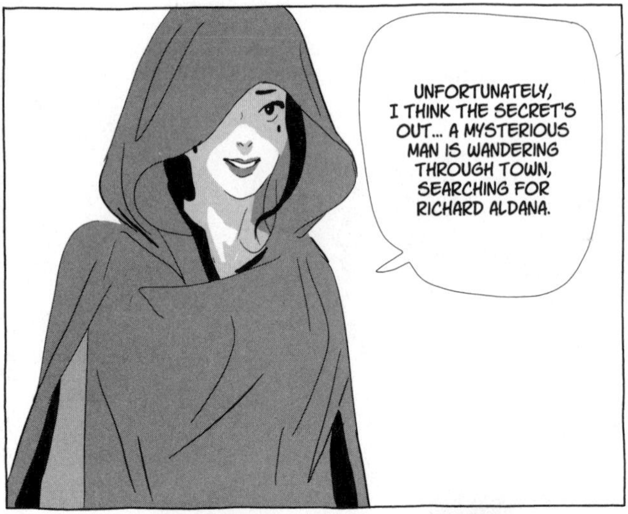
UNFORTUNATELY, I THINK THE SECRET'S OUT... A MYSTERIOUS MAN IS WANDERING THROUGH TOWN, SEARCHING FOR RICHARD ALDANA.
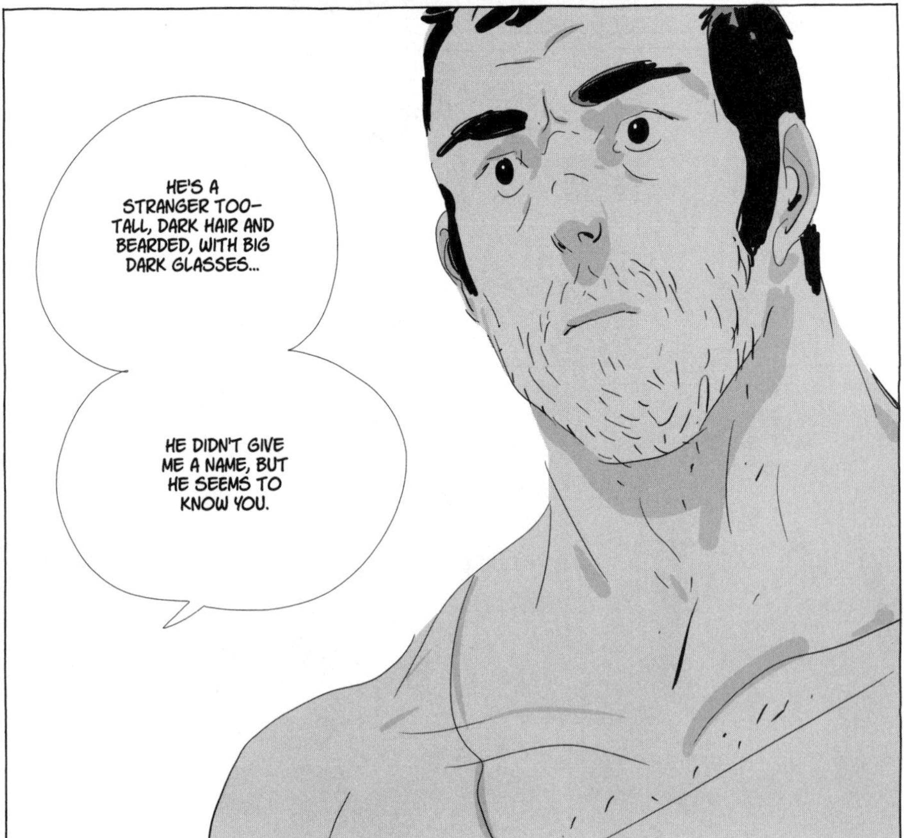
HE'S A STRANGER TOO–TALL, DARK HAIR AND BEARDED, WITH BIG DARK GLASSES...
HE DIDN'T GIVE ME A NAME, BUT HE SEEMS TO KNOW YOU.

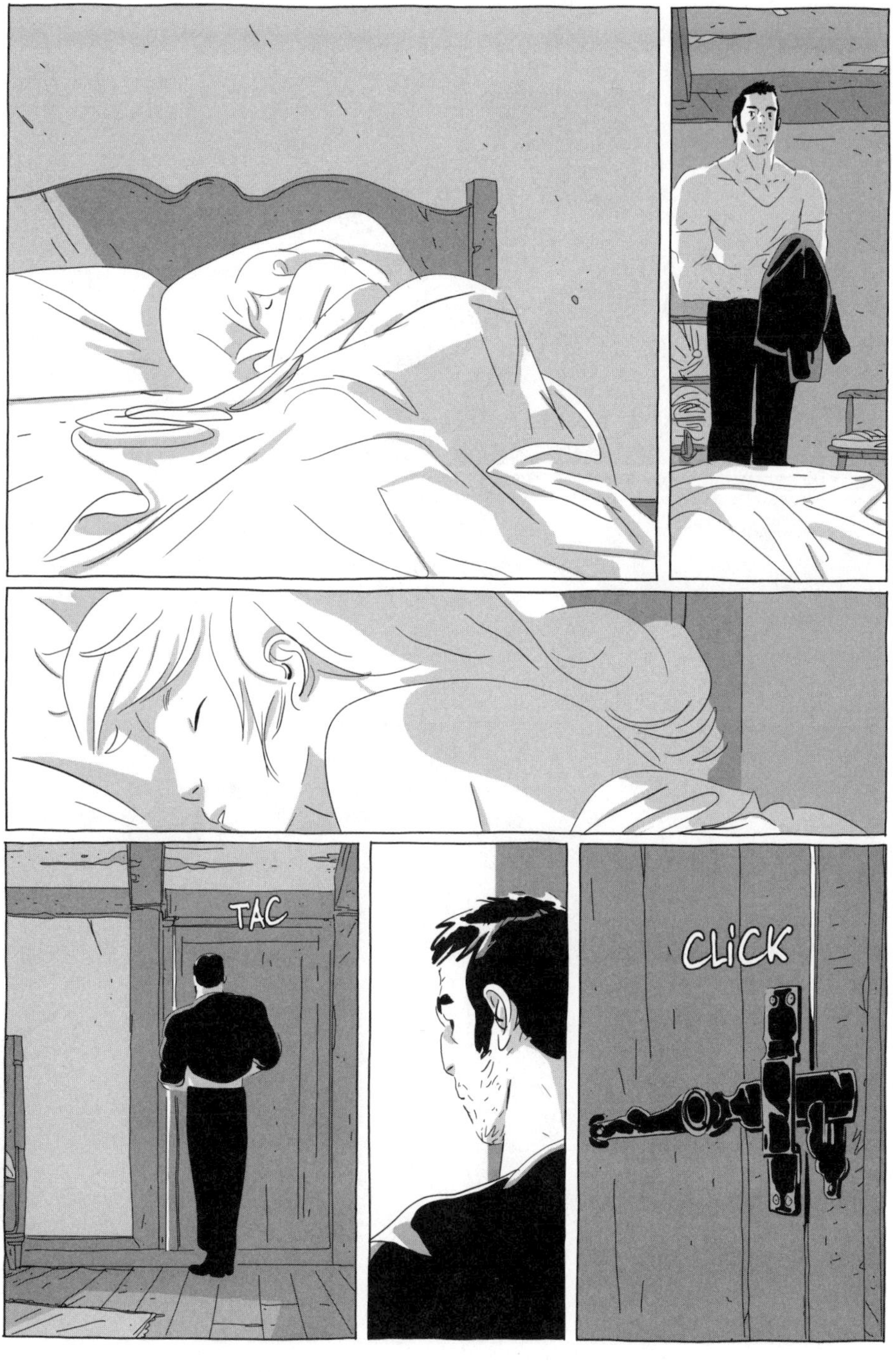
TAC
CLiCK

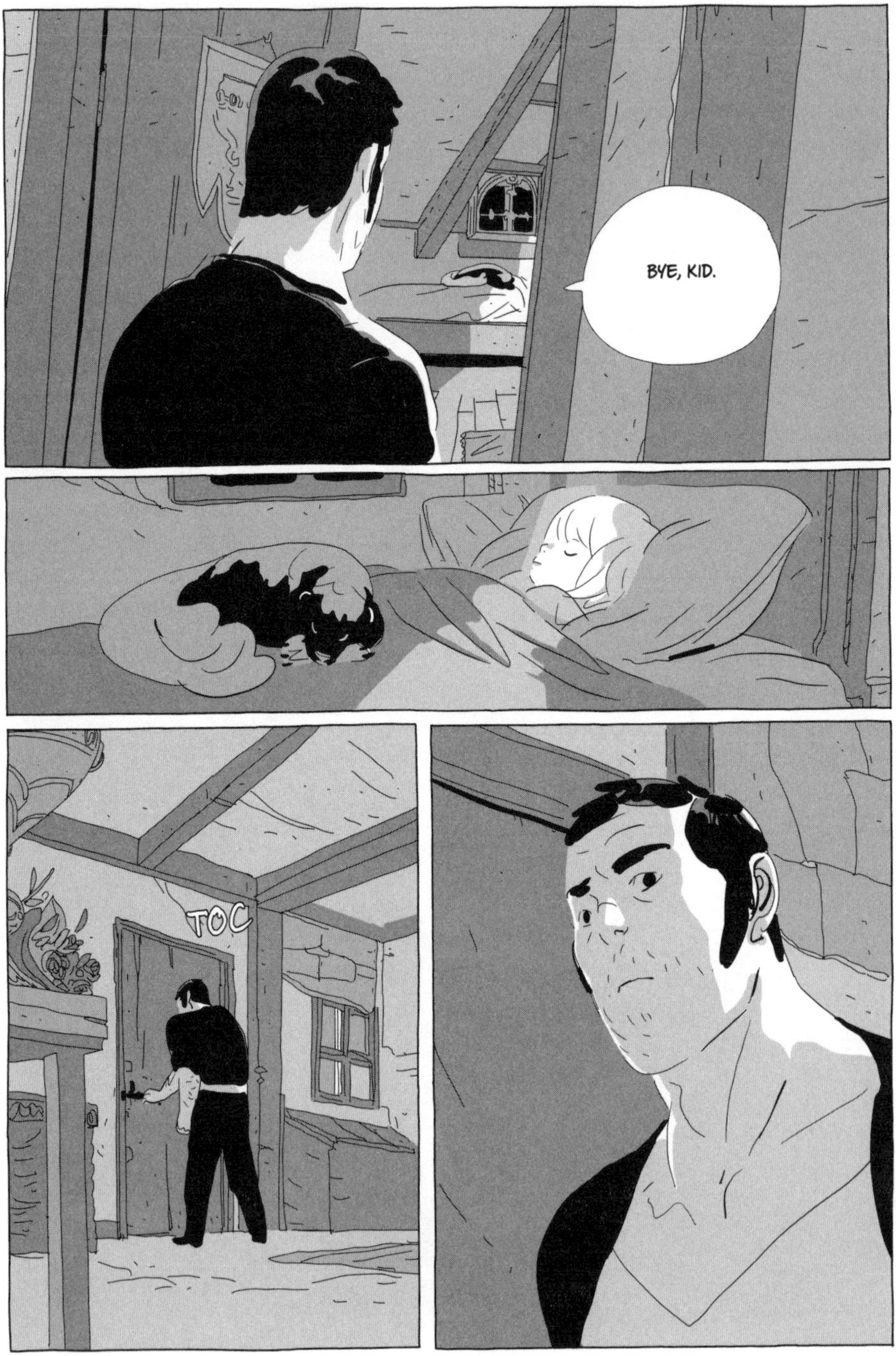
BYE, KID.
TOC

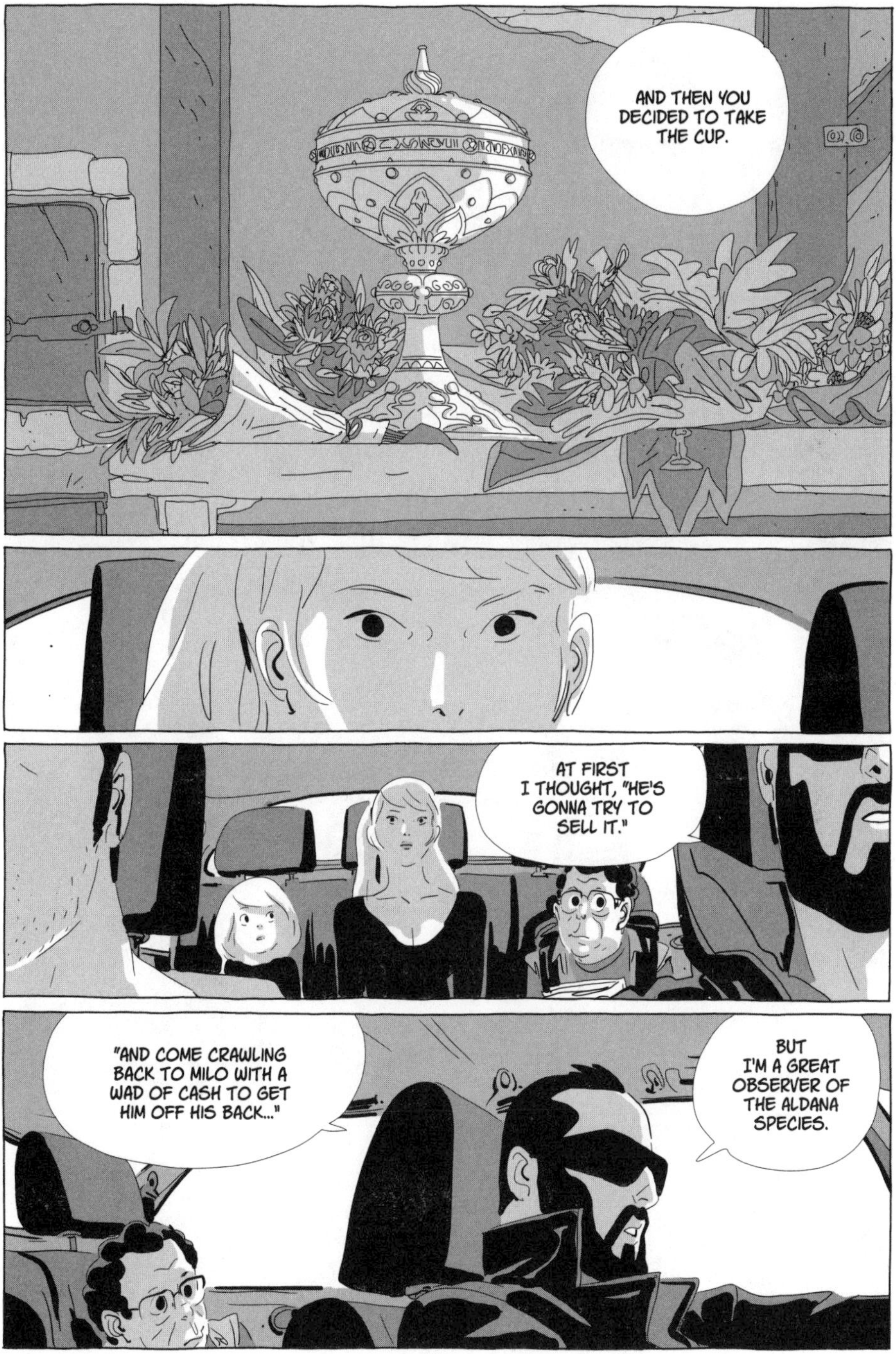
AND THEN YOU DECIDED TO TAKE THE CUP.
AT FIRST I THOUGHT, "HE'S GONNA TRY TO SELL IT."
"AND COME CRAWLING BACK TO MILO WITH A WAD OF CASH TO GET HIM OFF HIS BACK..."
BUT I'M A GREAT OBSERVER OF THE ALDANA SPECIES.

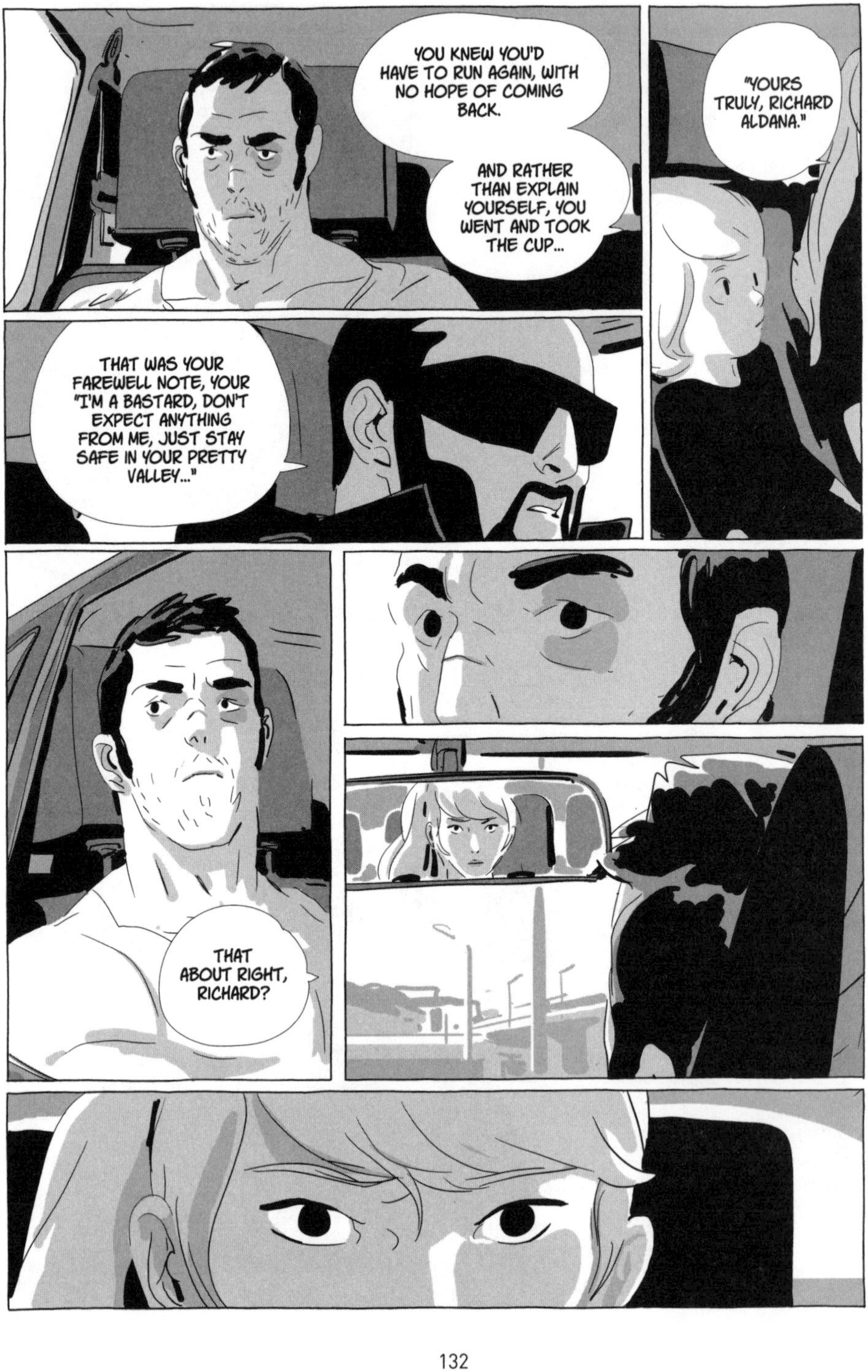
YOU KNEW YOU'D HAVE TO RUN AGAIN, WITH NO HOPE OF COMING BACK.
AND RATHER THAN EXPLAIN YOURSELF, YOU WENT AND TOOK THE CUP...
"YOURS TRULY, RICHARD ALDANA."
THAT WAS YOUR FAREWELL NOTE, YOUR "I'M A BASTARD, DON'T EXPECT ANYTHING FROM ME, JUST STAY SAFE IN YOUR PRETTY VALLEY..."
THAT ABOUT RIGHT, RICHARD?

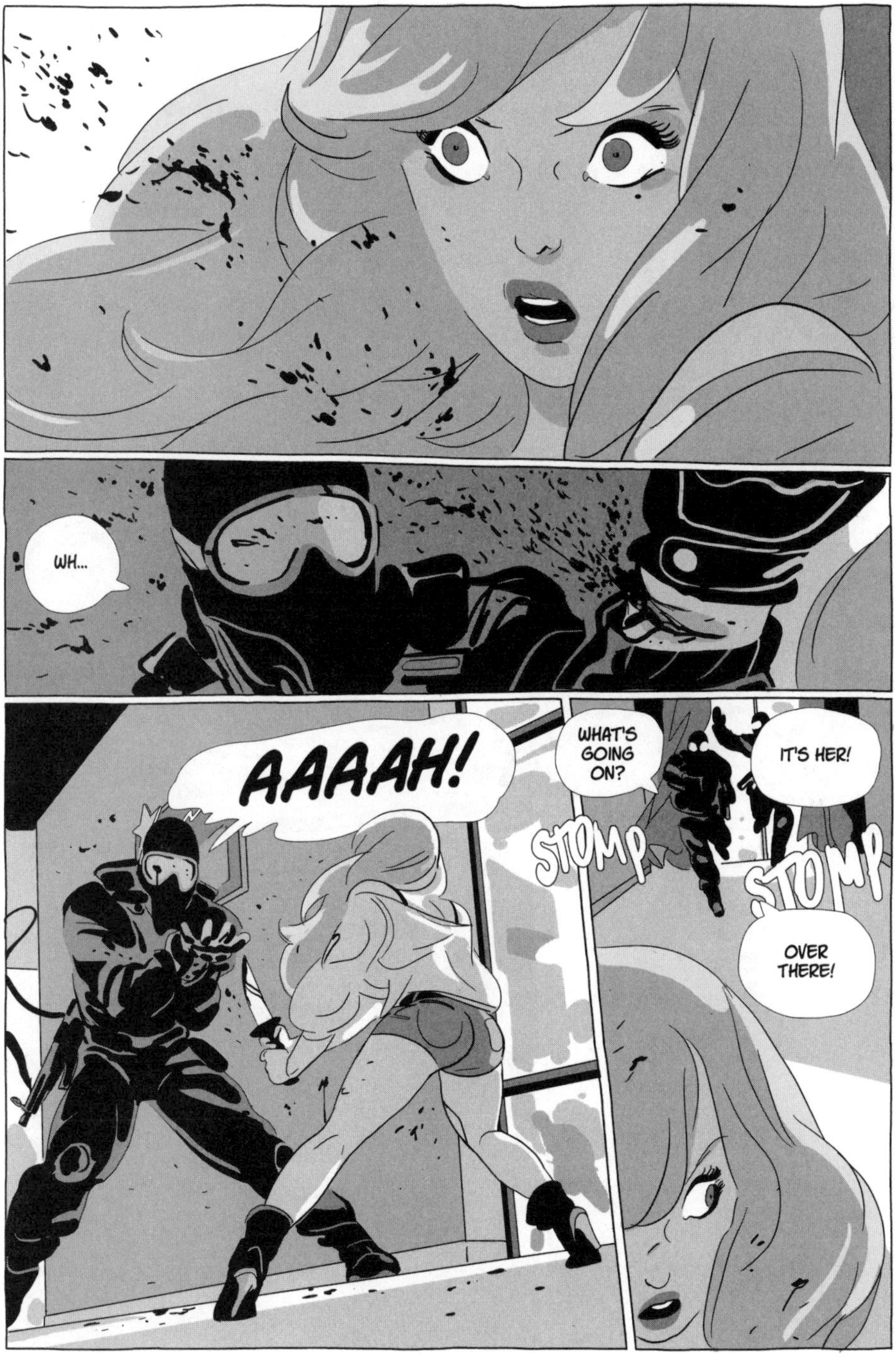
WH...
AAAAH!
WHAT'S GOING ON?
STOMP
IT'S HER!
STOMP
OVER THERE!

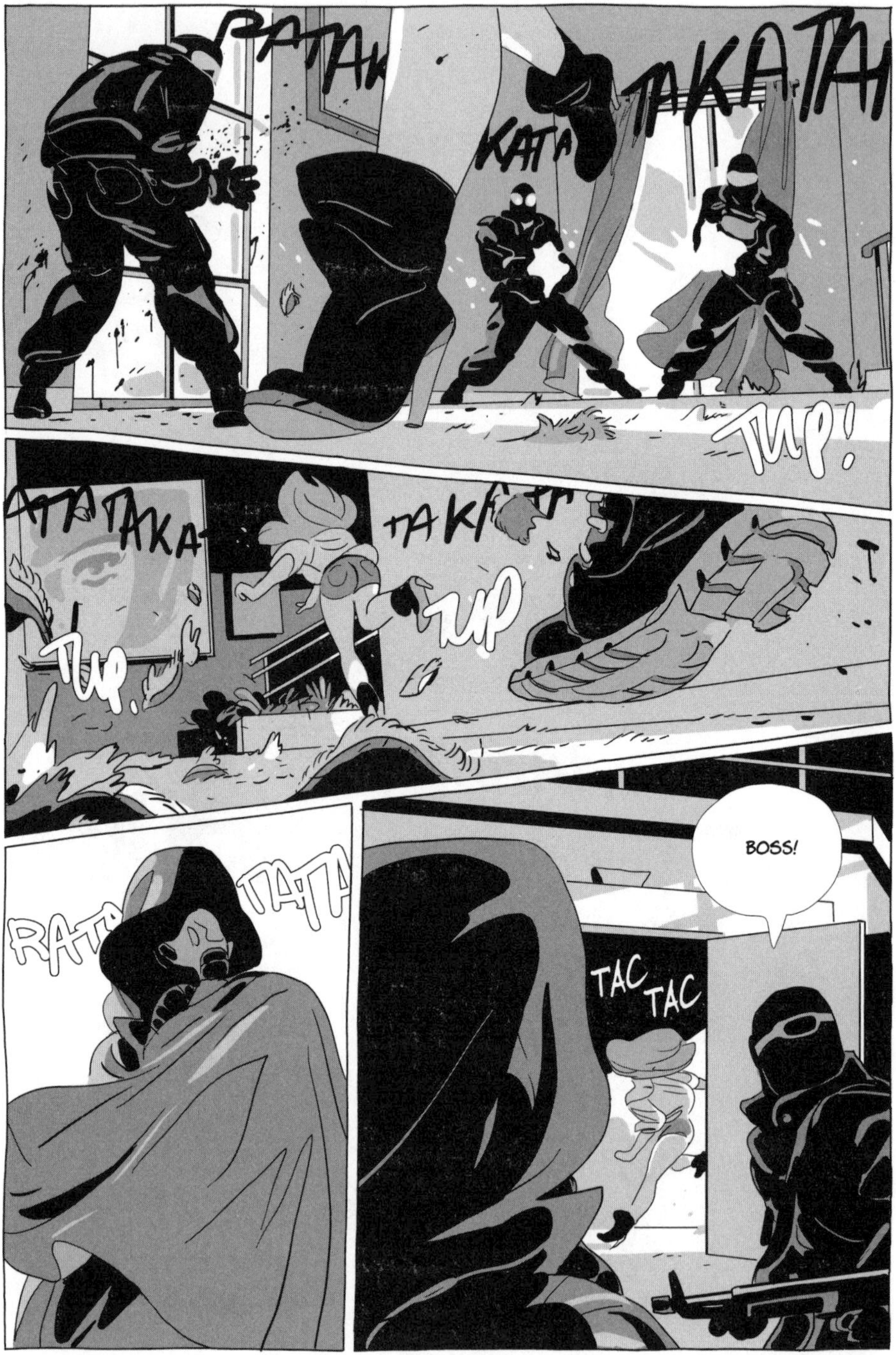
KATA
TUP!
TAKA
TUP
TUP.
RATA
BOSS!
TAC TAC

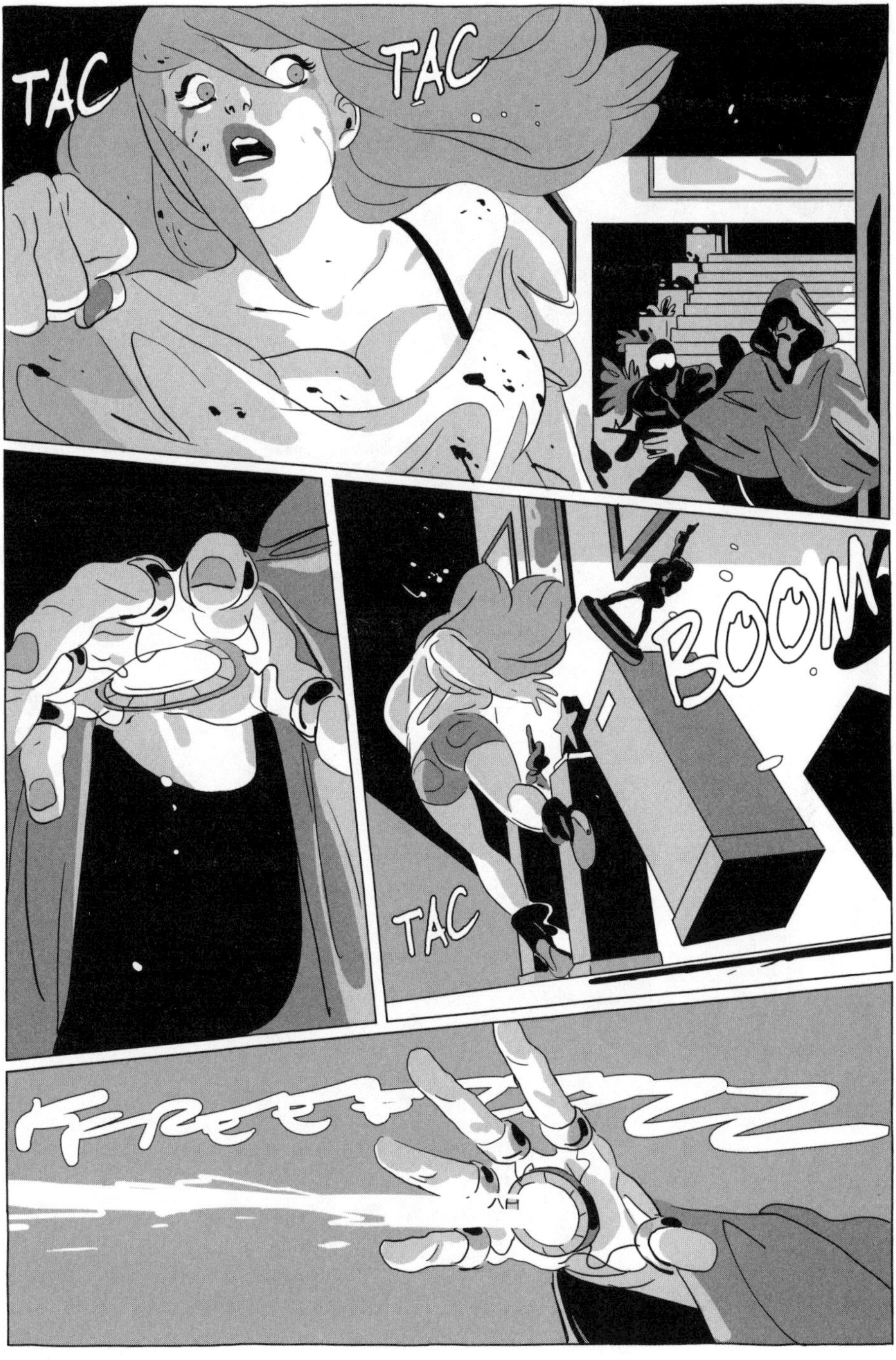
TAC
TAC
BOOM
TAC

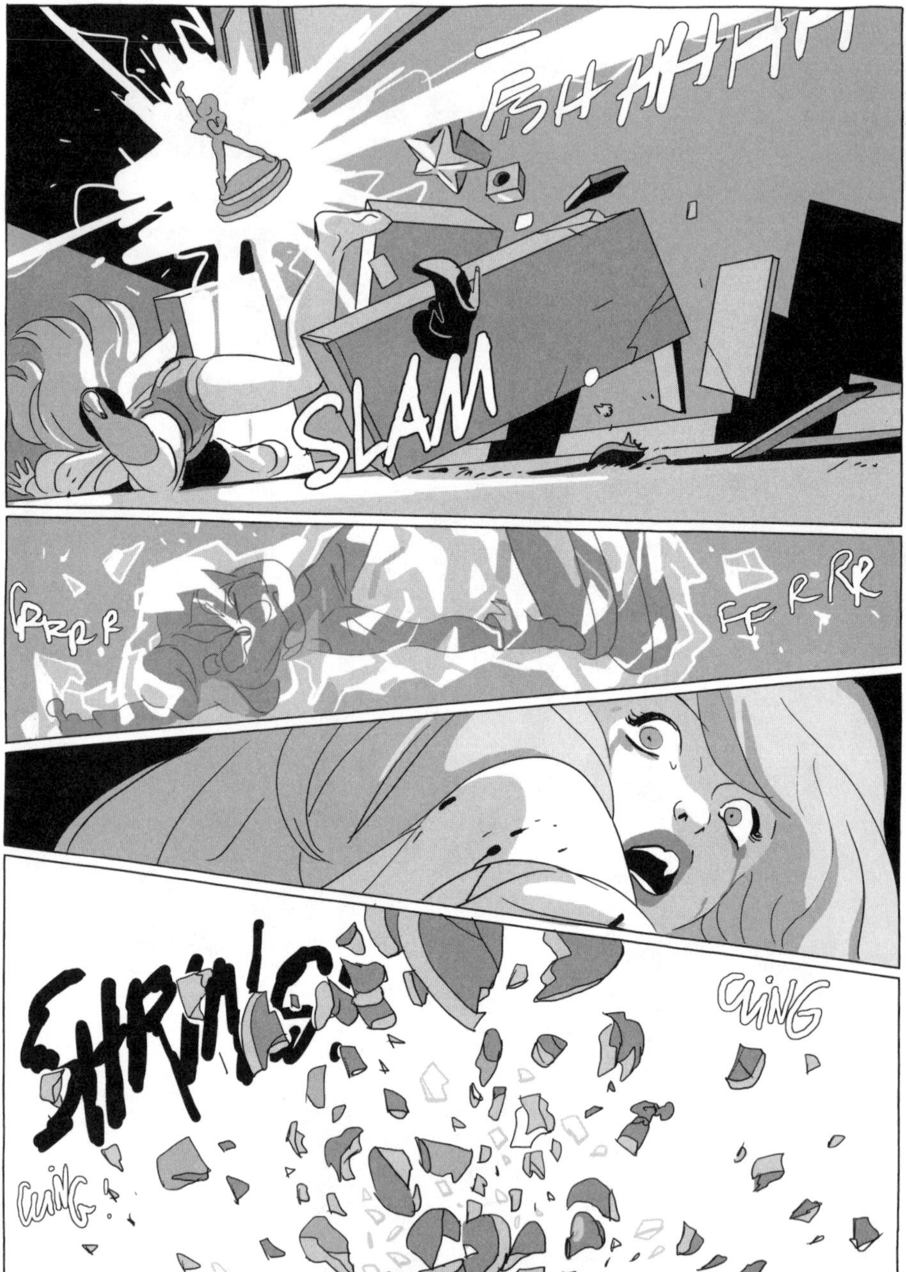
FSHHHHHHH
SLAM
GRRRR
FFRRRR
SHRING
CLING
CLING
CLING
CLING

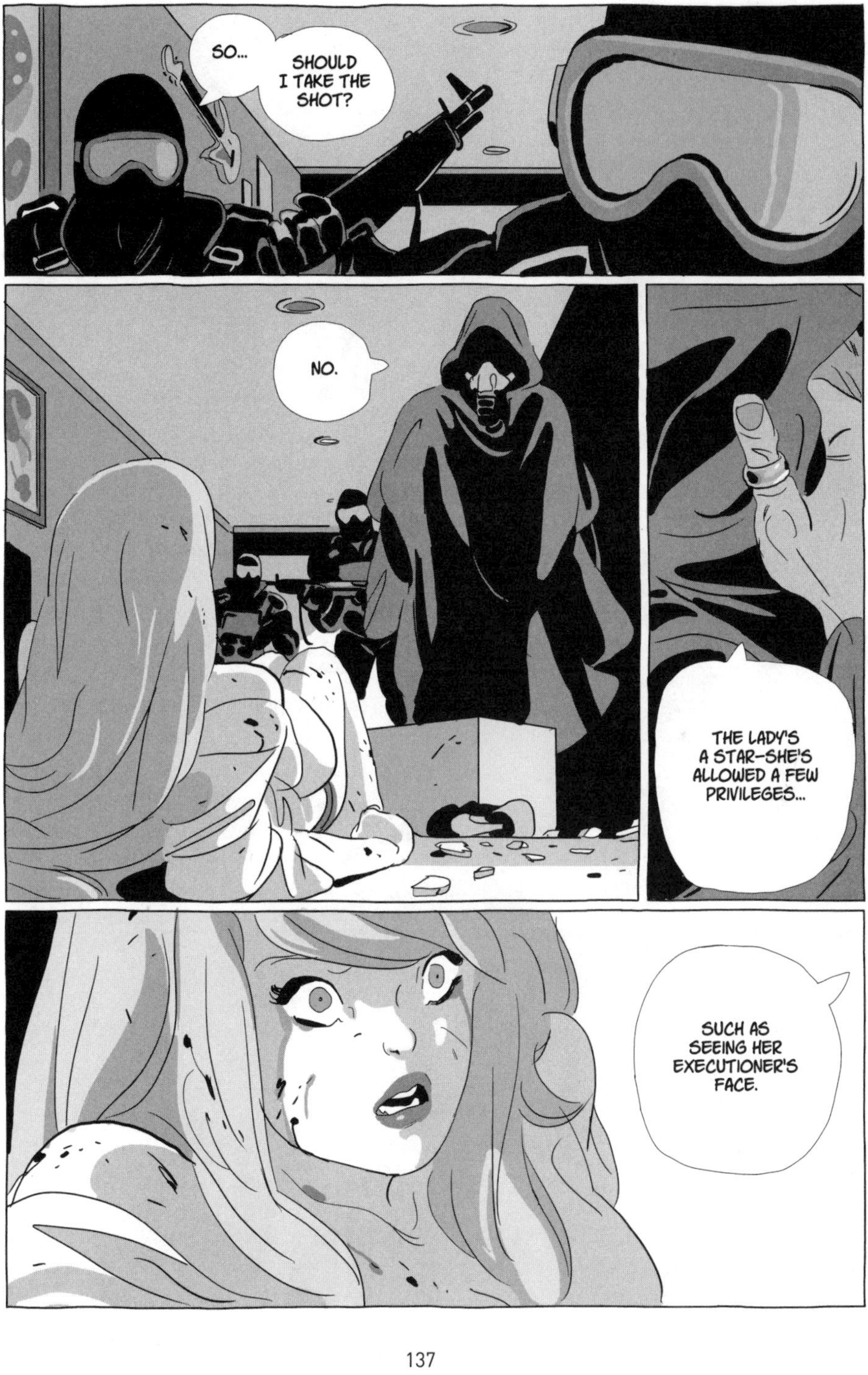
SO...
SHOULD I TAKE THE SHOT?
NO.
THE LADY'S A STAR–SHE'S ALLOWED A FEW PRIVILEGES...
SUCH AS SEEING HER EXECUTIONER'S FACE.

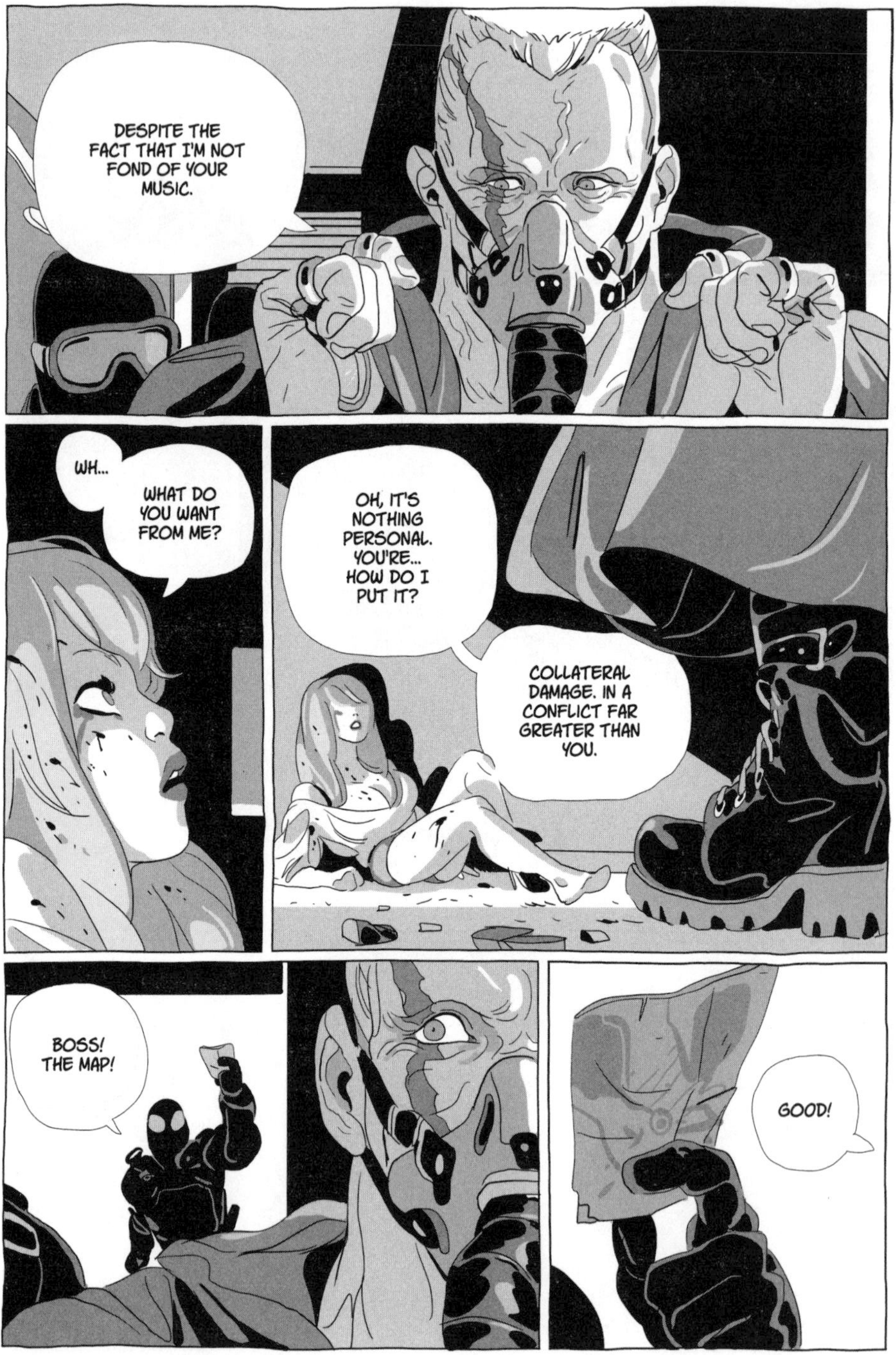
DESPITE THE FACT THAT I'M NOT FOND OF YOUR MUSIC.
WH...
WHAT DO YOU WANT FROM ME?
OH, IT'S NOTHING PERSONAL. YOU'RE... HOW DO I PUT IT?
COLLATERAL DAMAGE. IN A CONFLICT FAR GREATER THAN YOU.
BOSS! THE MAP!
GOOD!

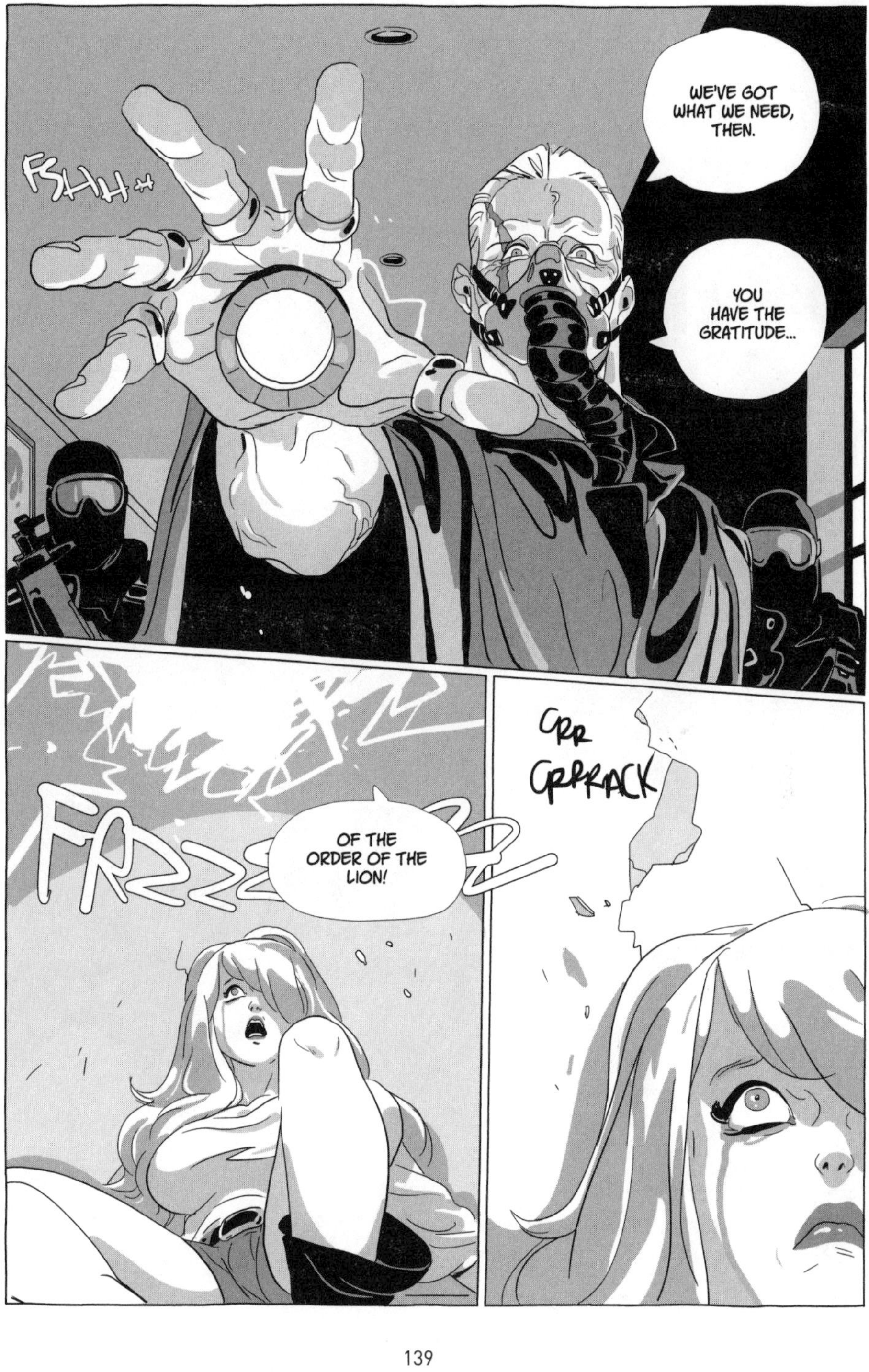
FSHH
WE'VE GOT WHAT WE NEED, THEN.
YOU HAVE THE GRATITUDE...
FRZZZ
OF THE ORDER OF THE LION!
CRR CRRRACK

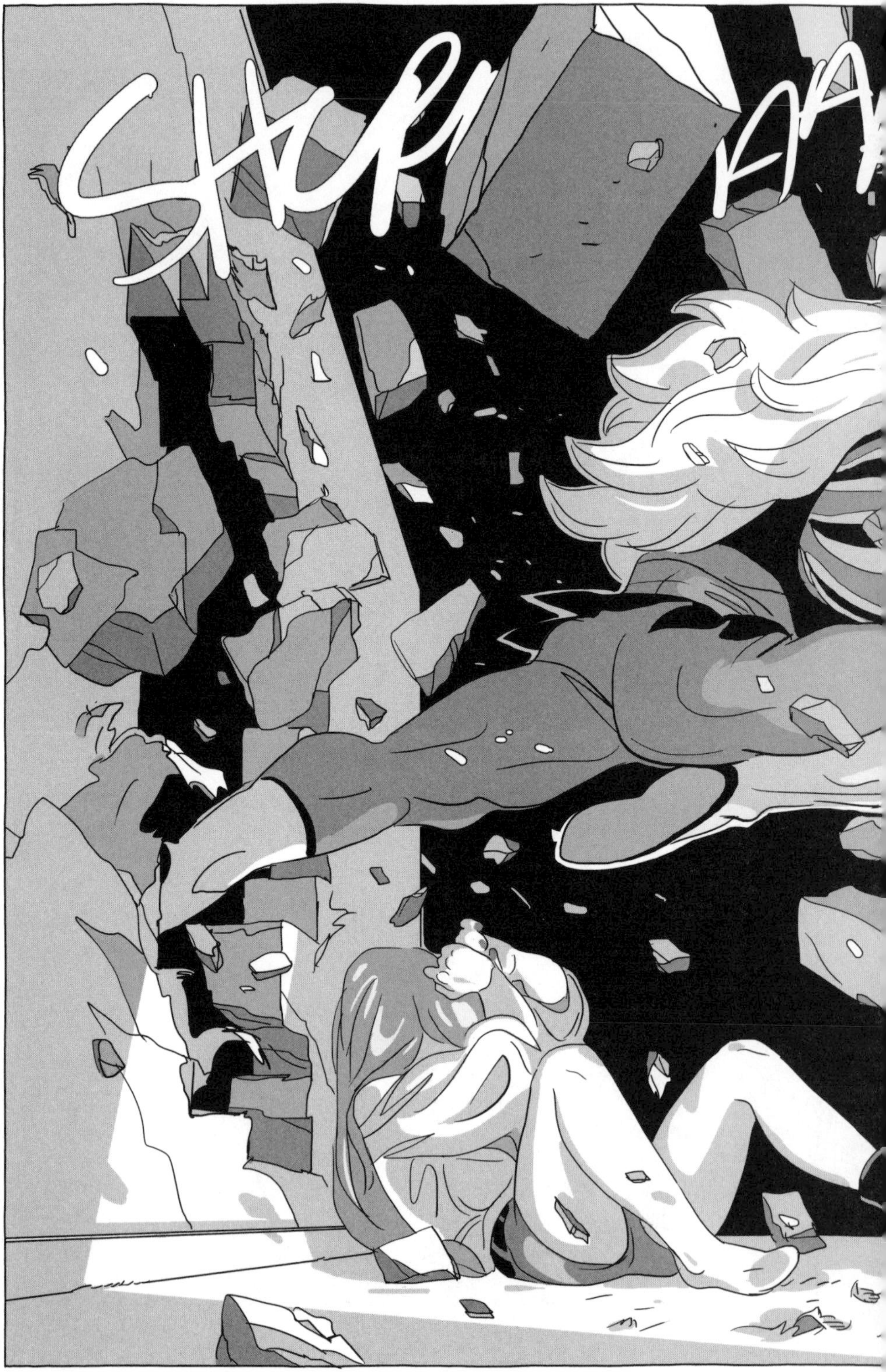

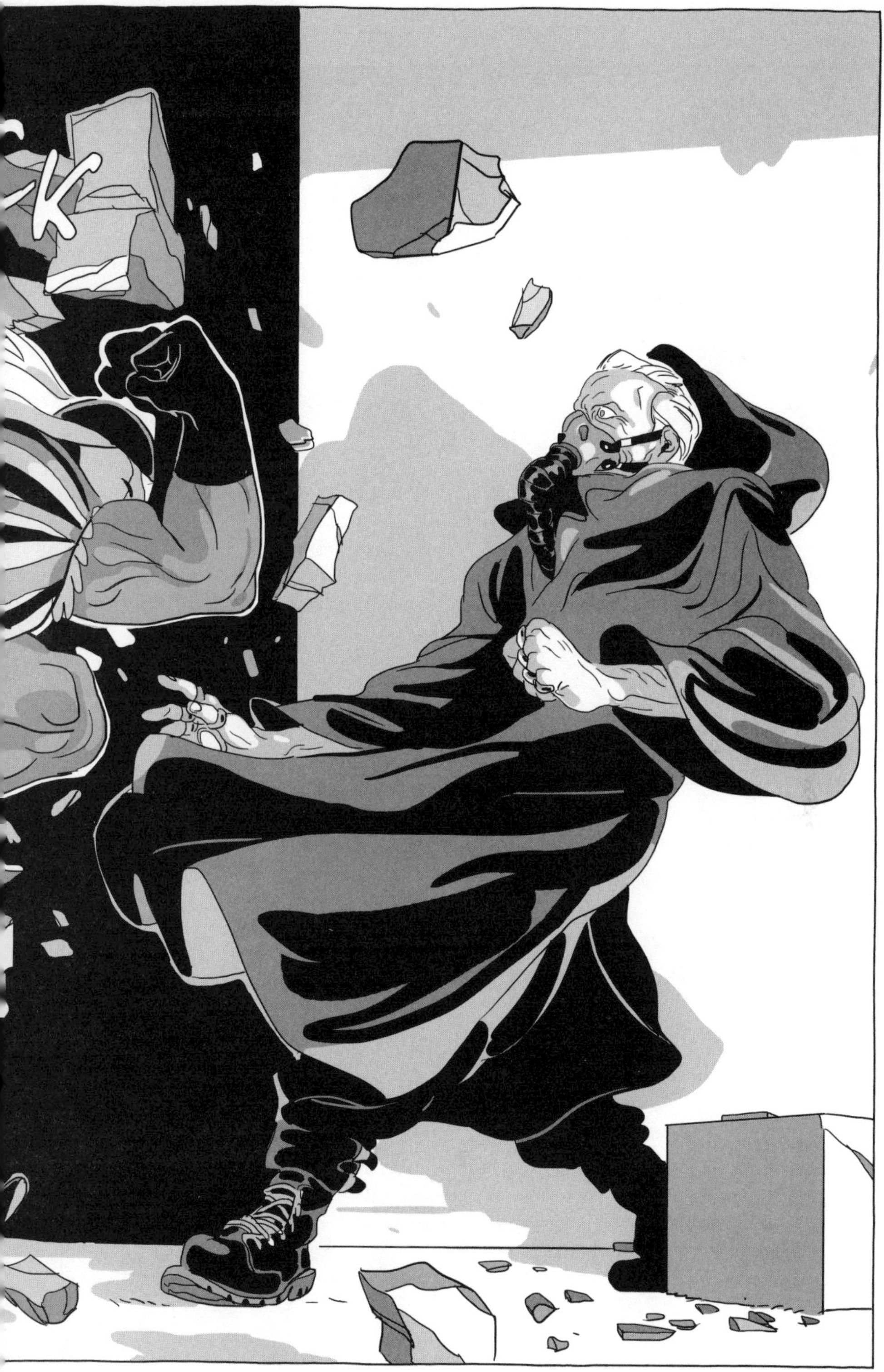

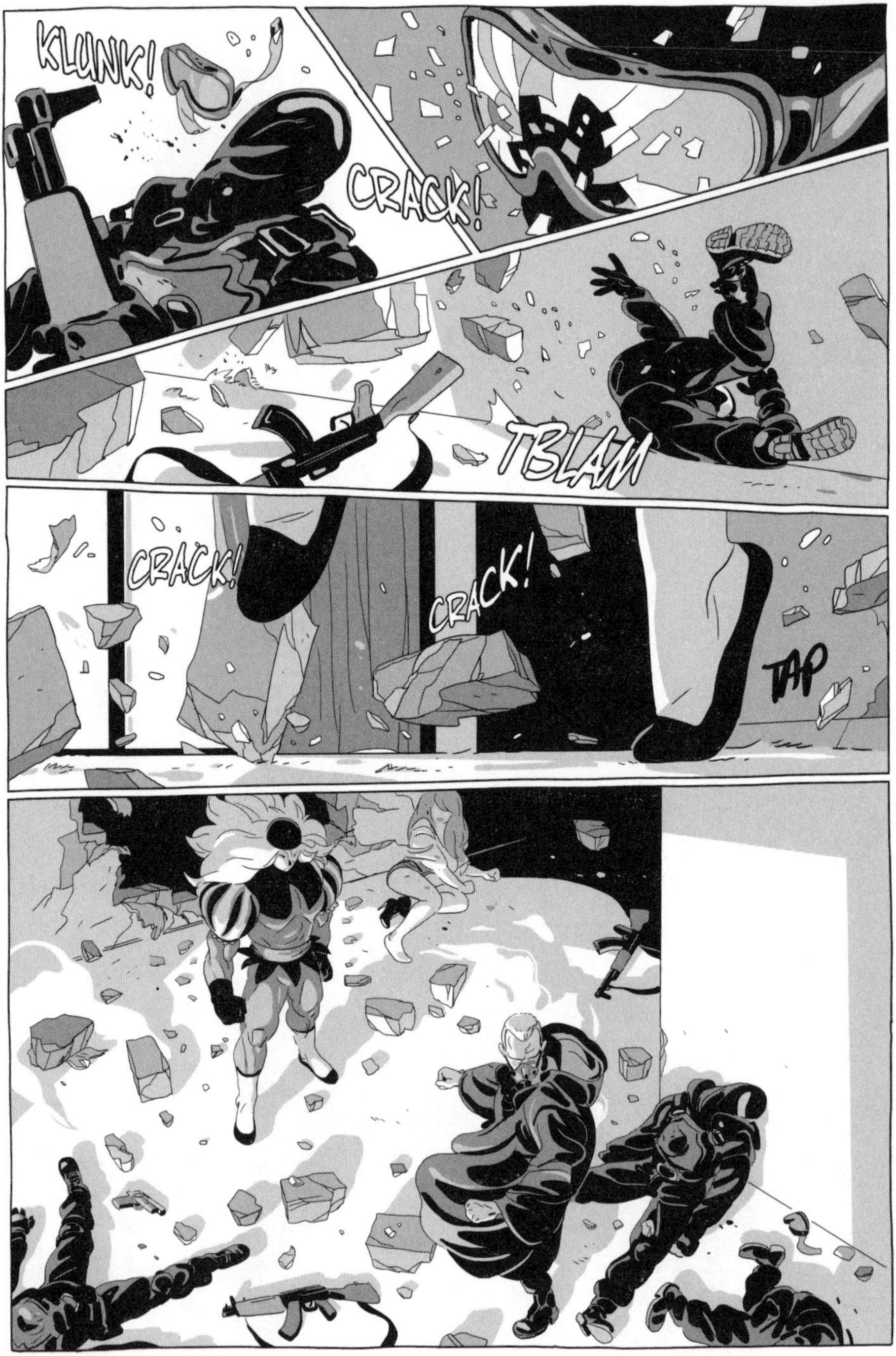
KLUNK!
CRACK!
TBLAM
CRACK!
CRACK!
TAP

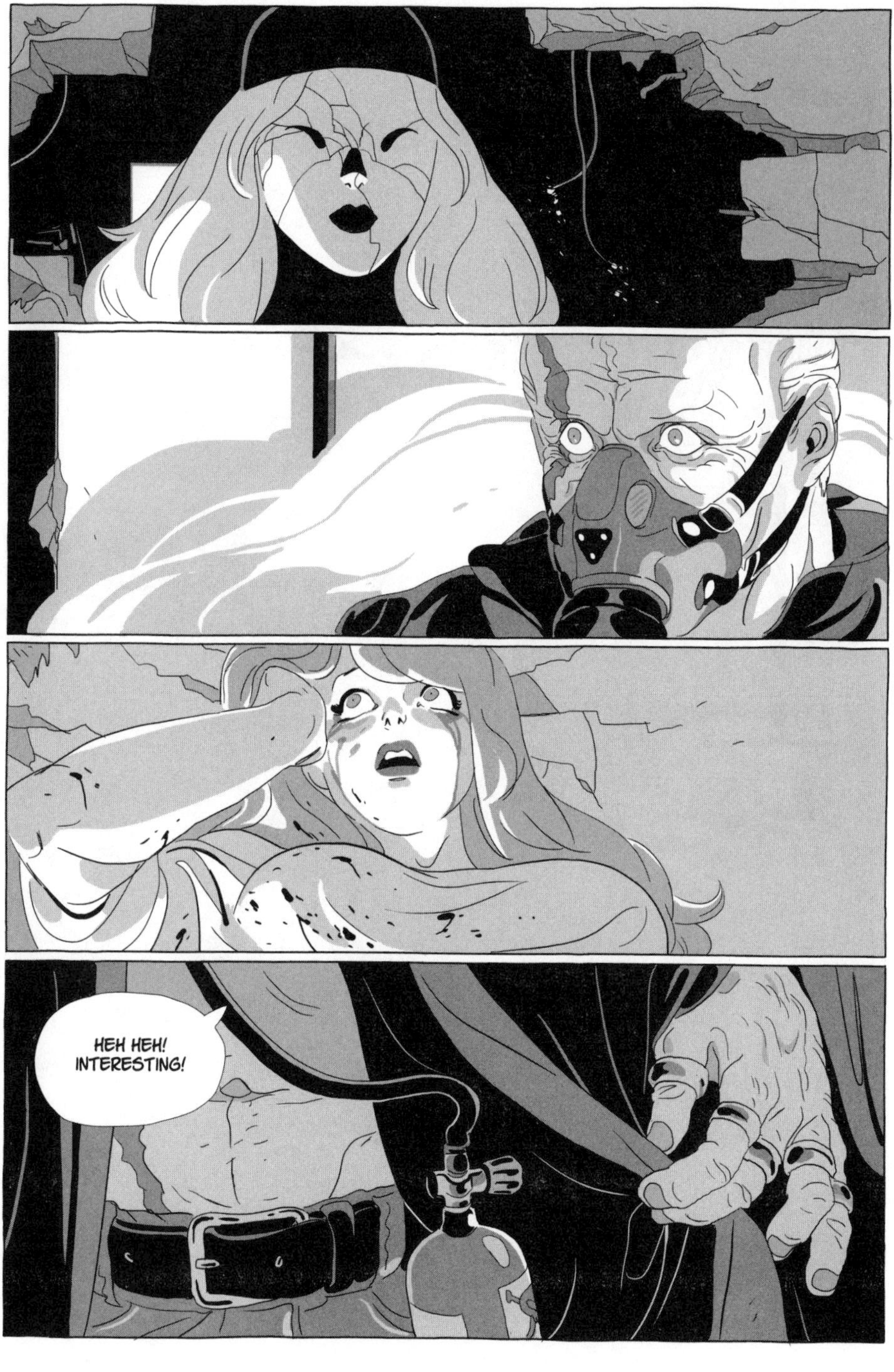
HEH HEH!
INTERESTING!

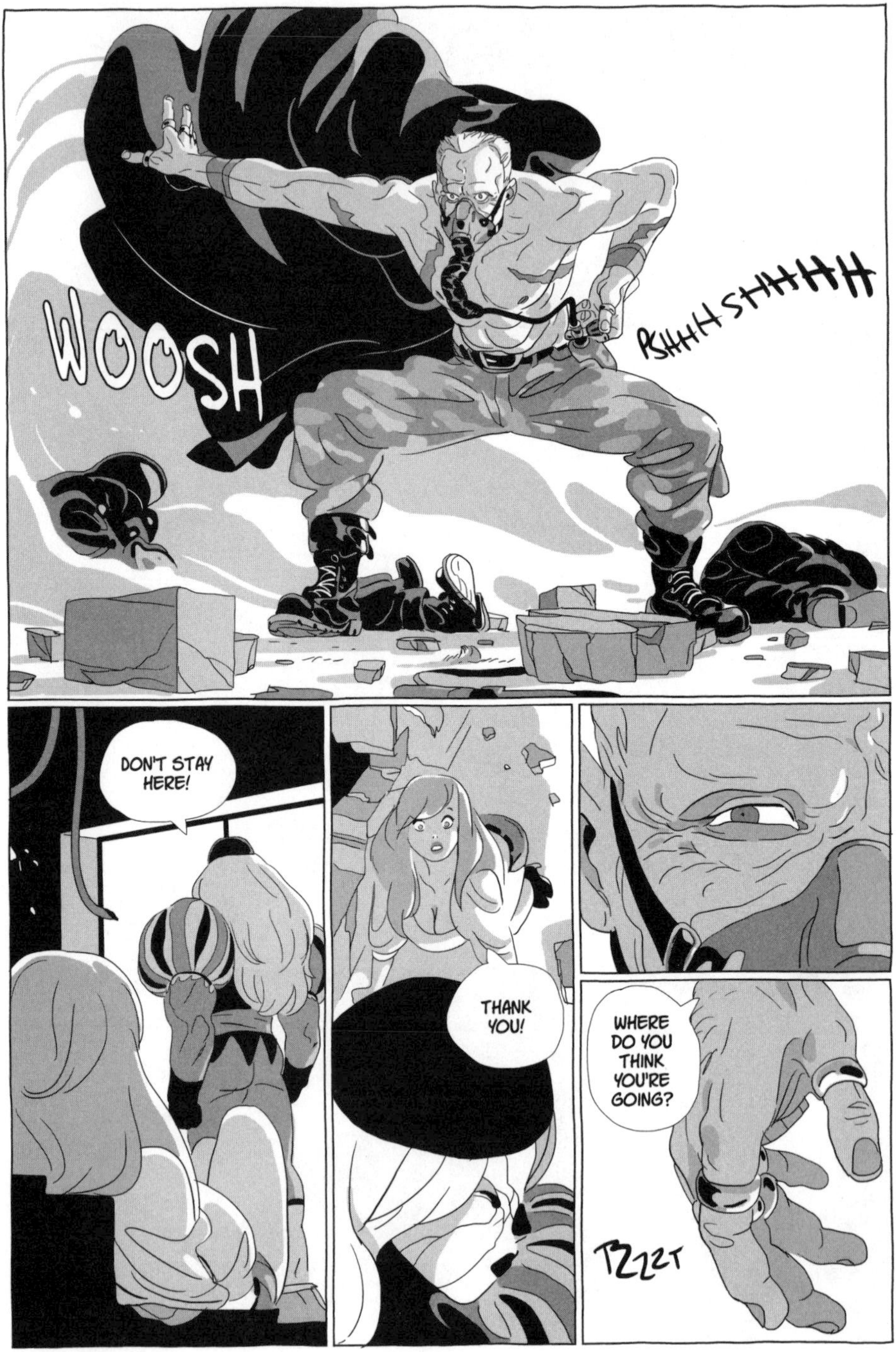
WOOSH
PSHHHSHHHHH
DON'T STAY HERE!
THANK YOU!
WHERE DO YOU THINK YOU'RE GOING?
TZZZT

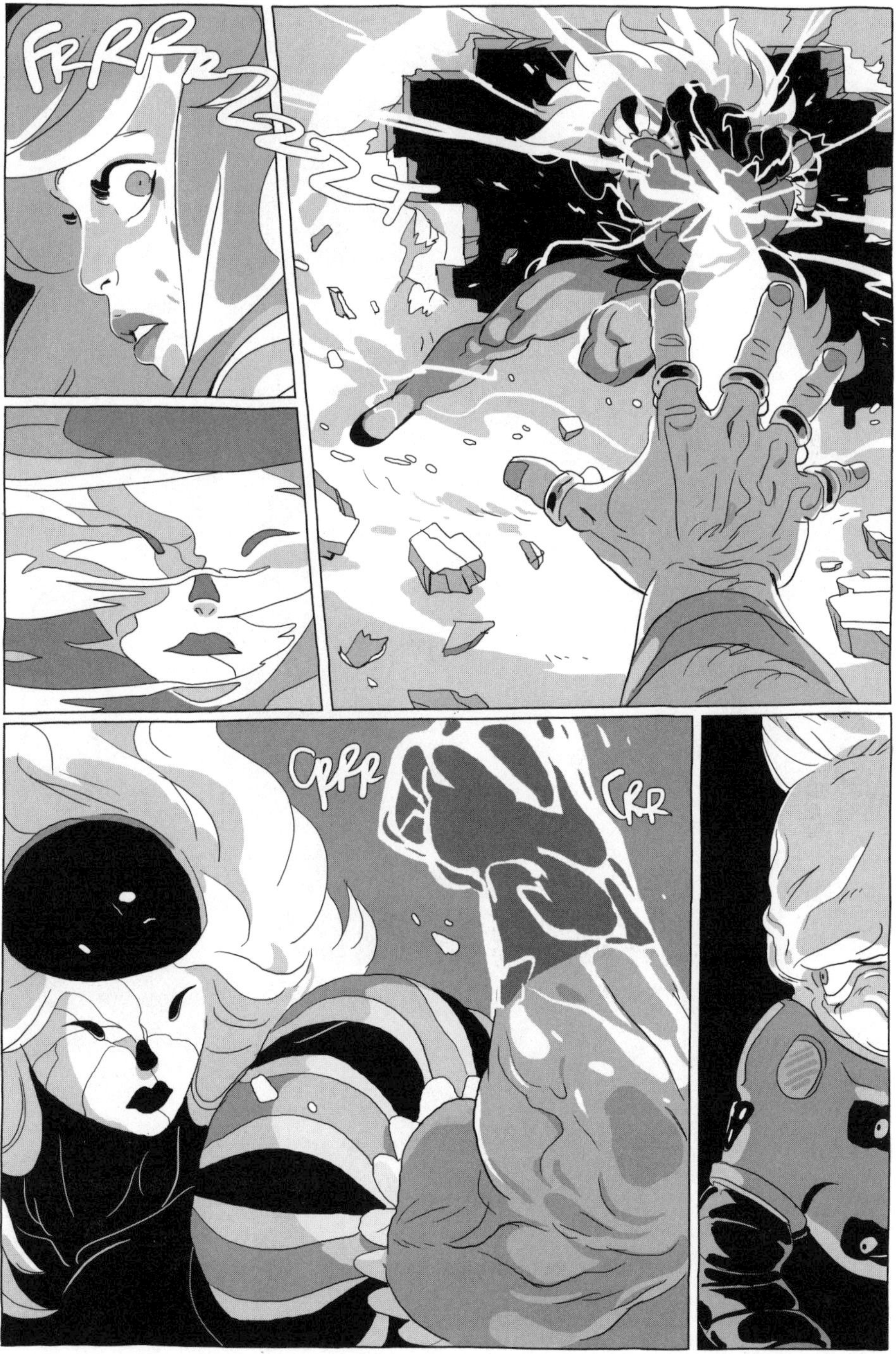
FRRRRZZZT
CRRR
CRR

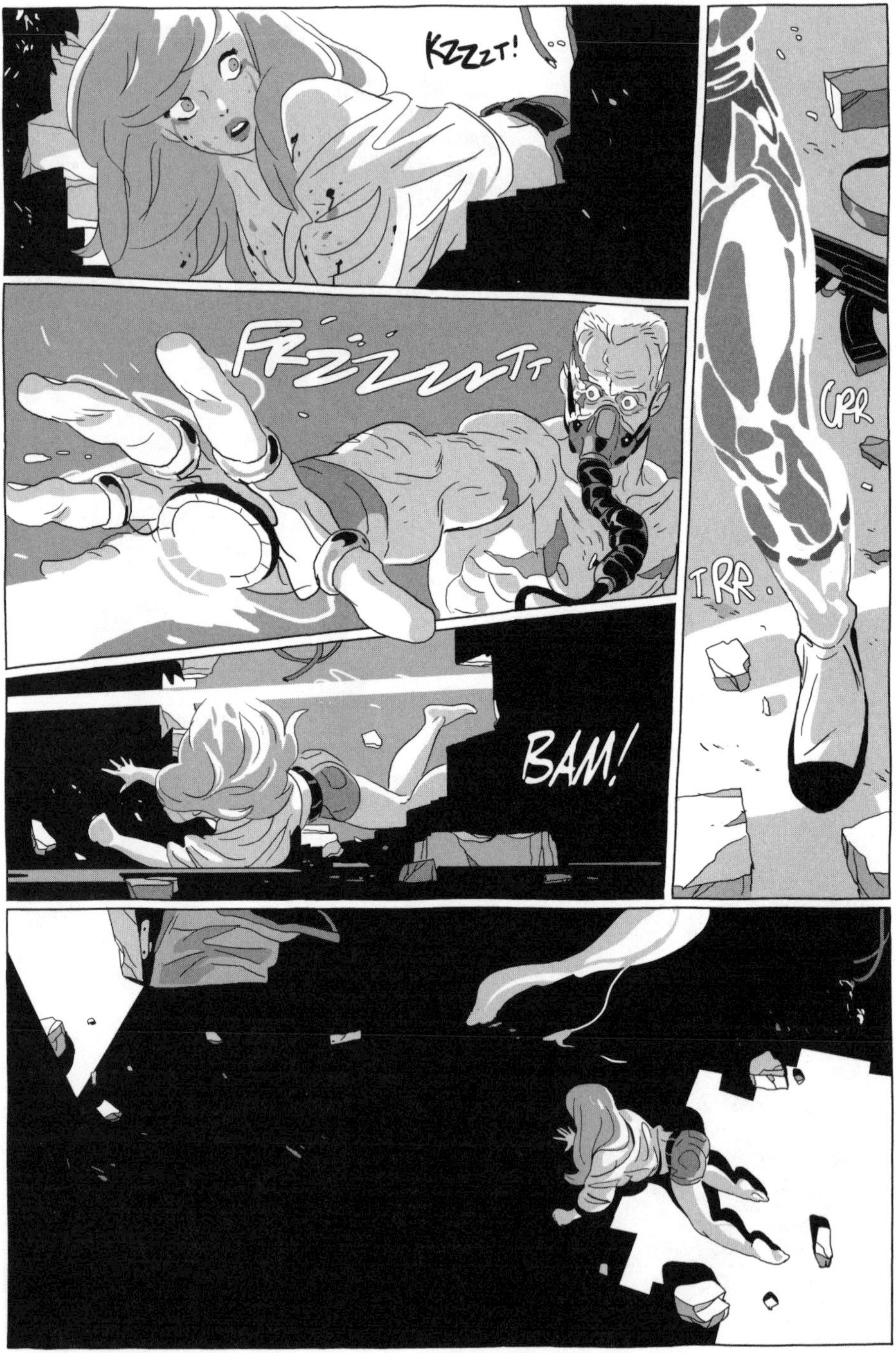
KZZZT!
FRZZZZZTT
CRR
TRR
BAM!

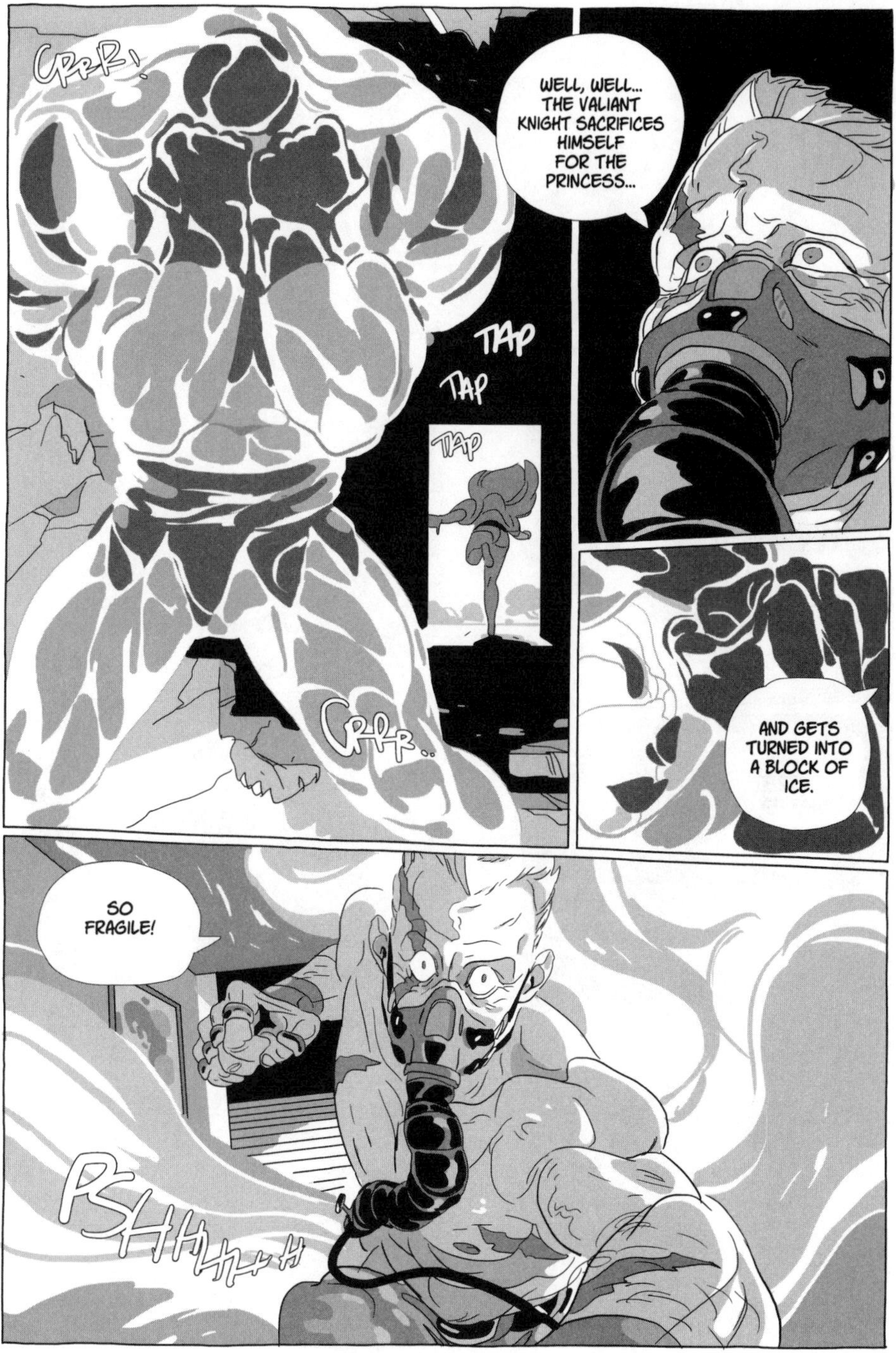
GRRR!
TAP
TAP
TAP
GRRR..
WELL, WELL... THE VALIANT KNIGHT SACRIFICES HIMSELF FOR THE PRINCESS...
AND GETS TURNED INTO A BLOCK OF ICE.
SO FRAGILE!
PSHHHHHHH

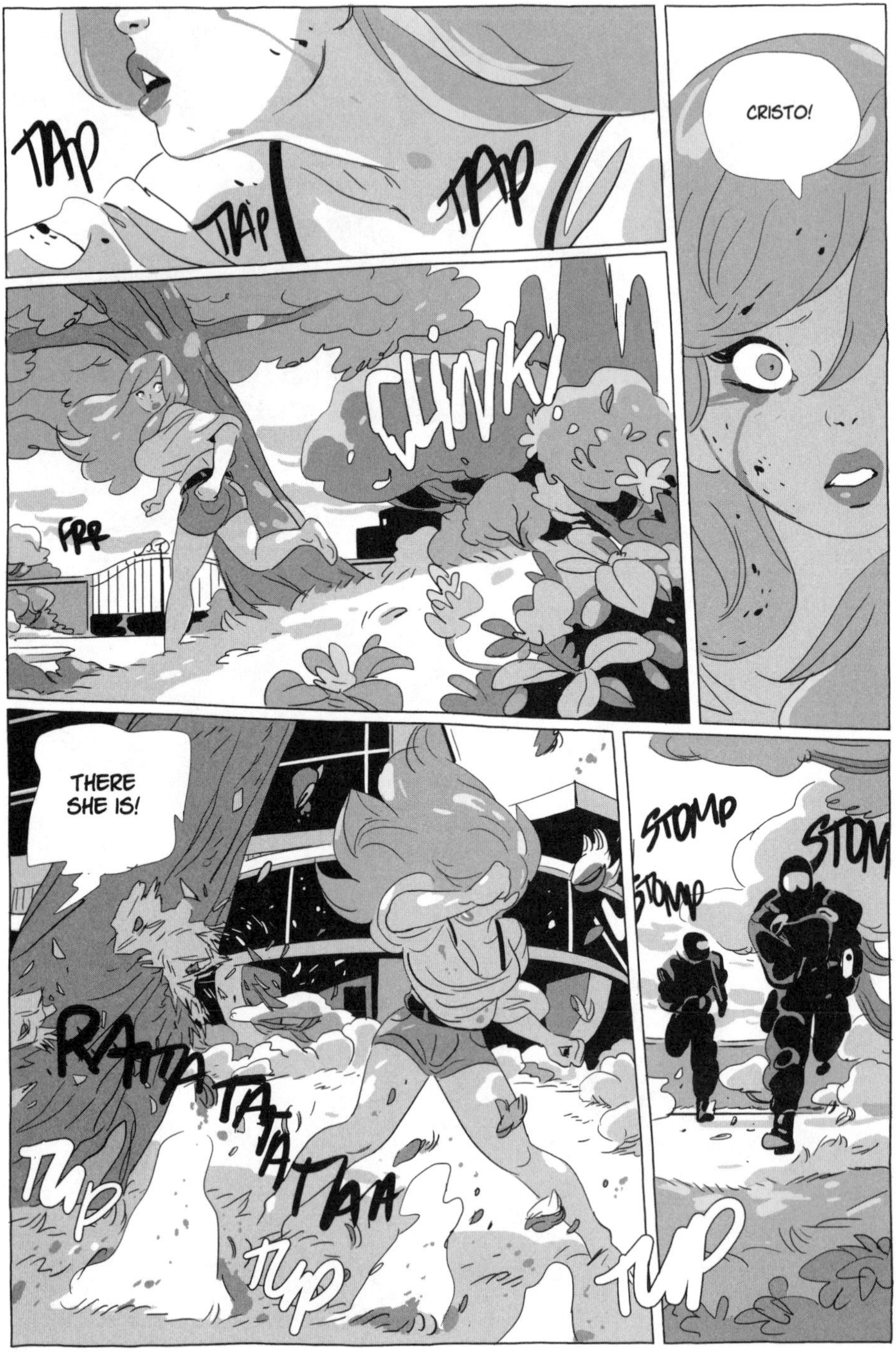
TAP
TAP
TAP
CLINK!
FRR
CRISTO!
THERE SHE IS!
RATATATATAA
TUP
TUP
TUP
STOMP
STOMP
STOMP

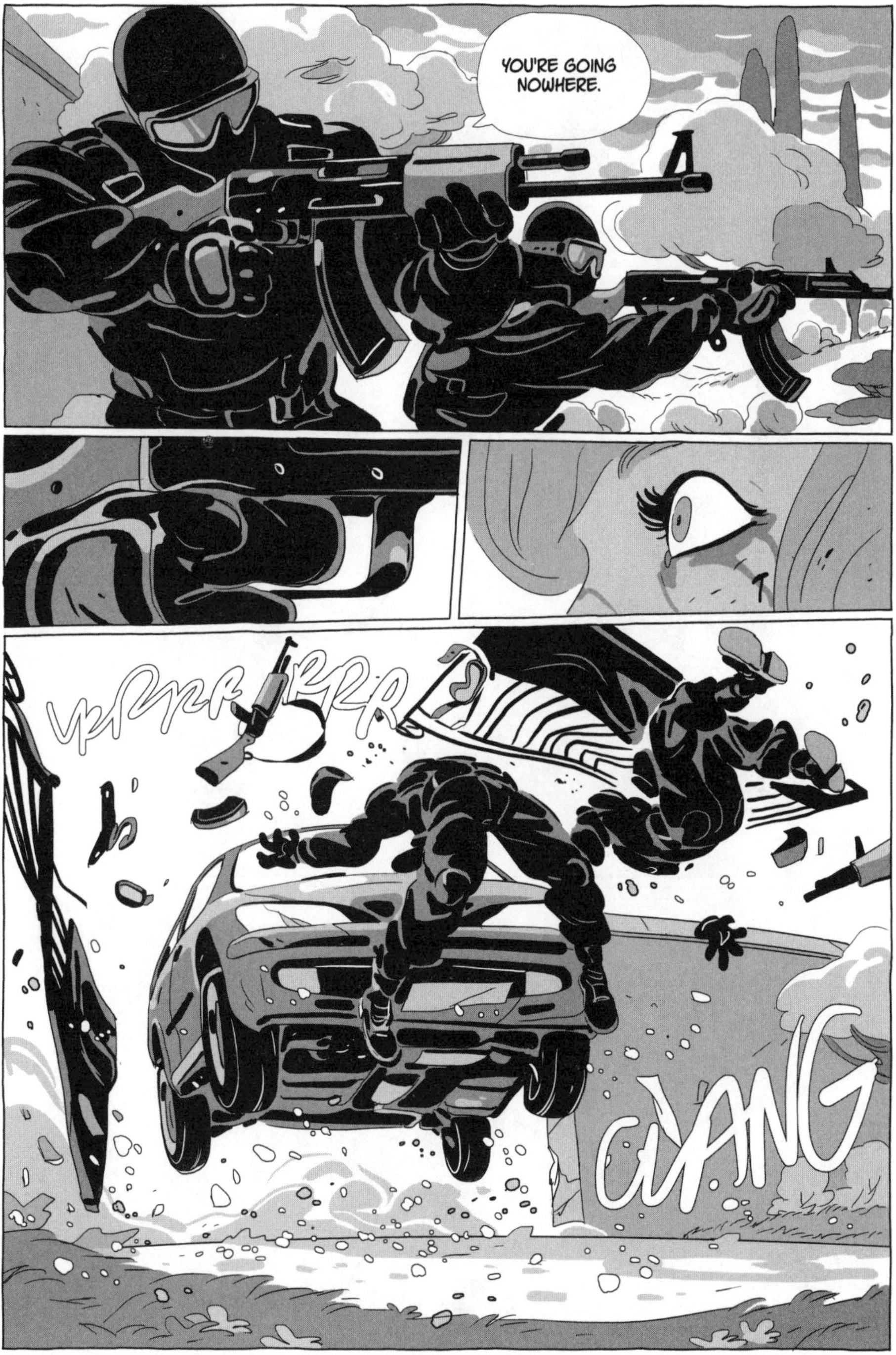
YOU'RE GOING NOWHERE.
VRRRRRR
CLANG

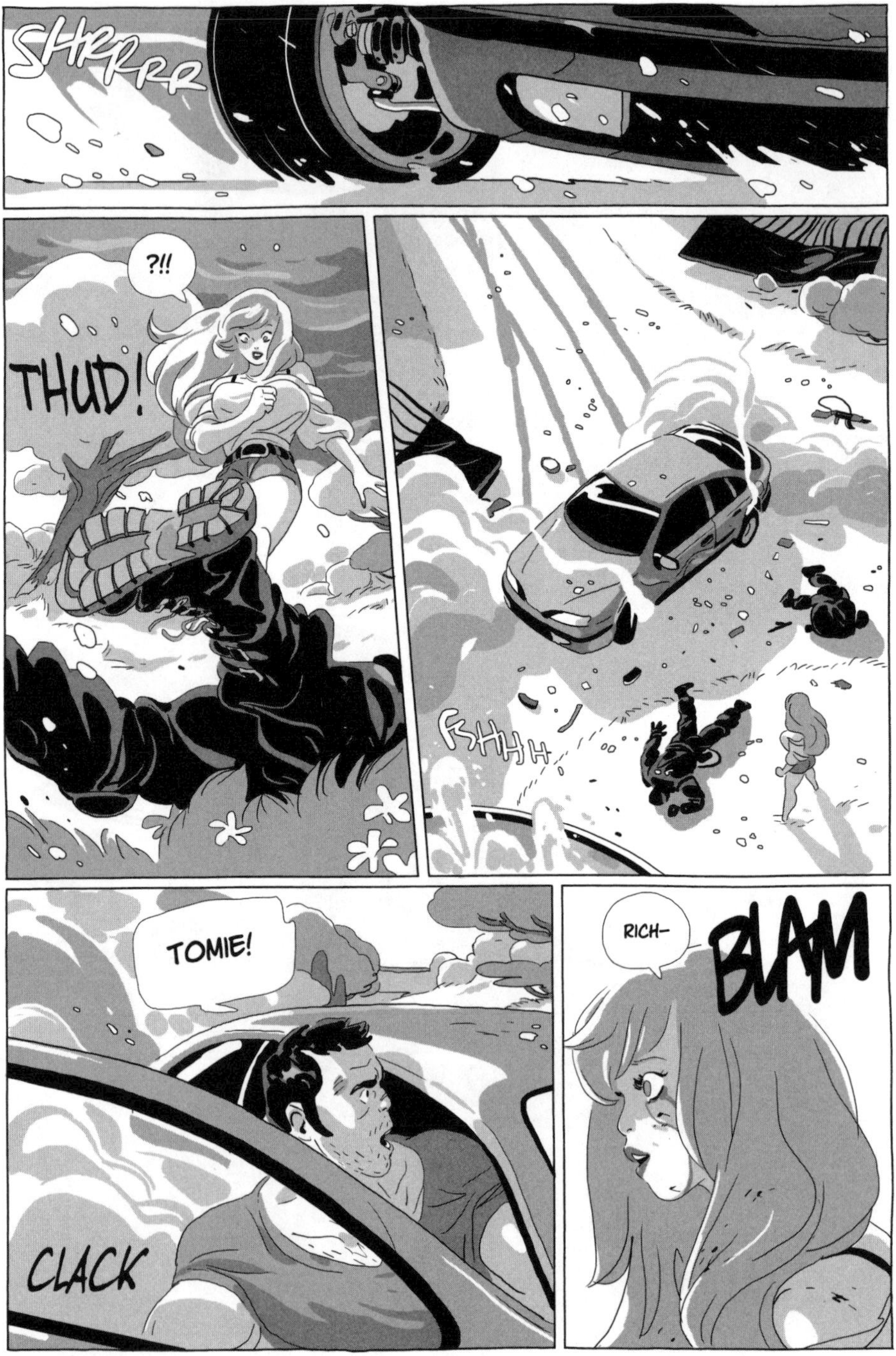
SHRRRR
?!!
THUD!
FSHHHH
TOMIE!
CLACK
RICH–
BLAM

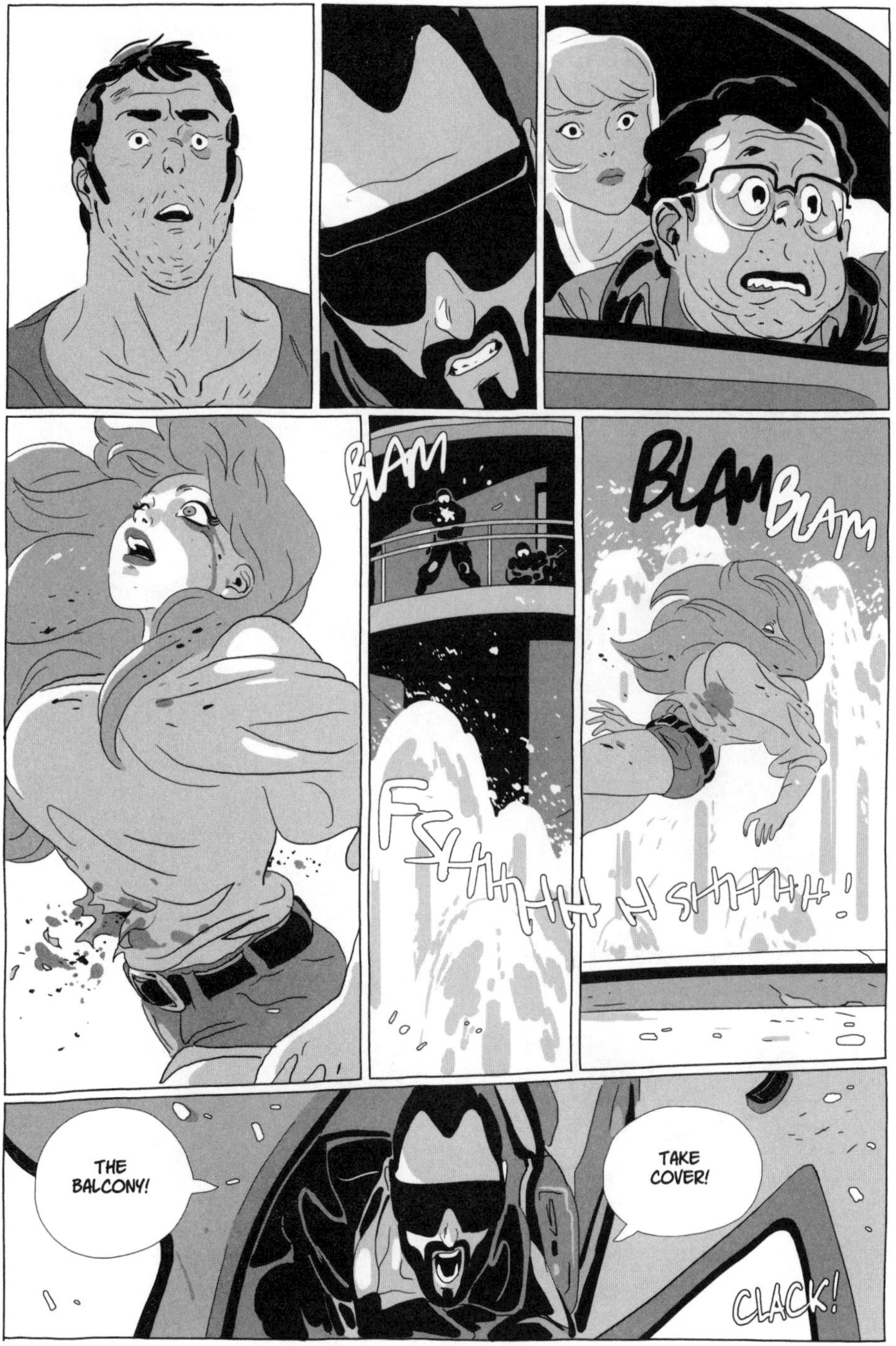
BLAM
BLAM BLAM
FSHHHHH H SHHHHH!
THE BALCONY!
TAKE COVER!
CLACK!

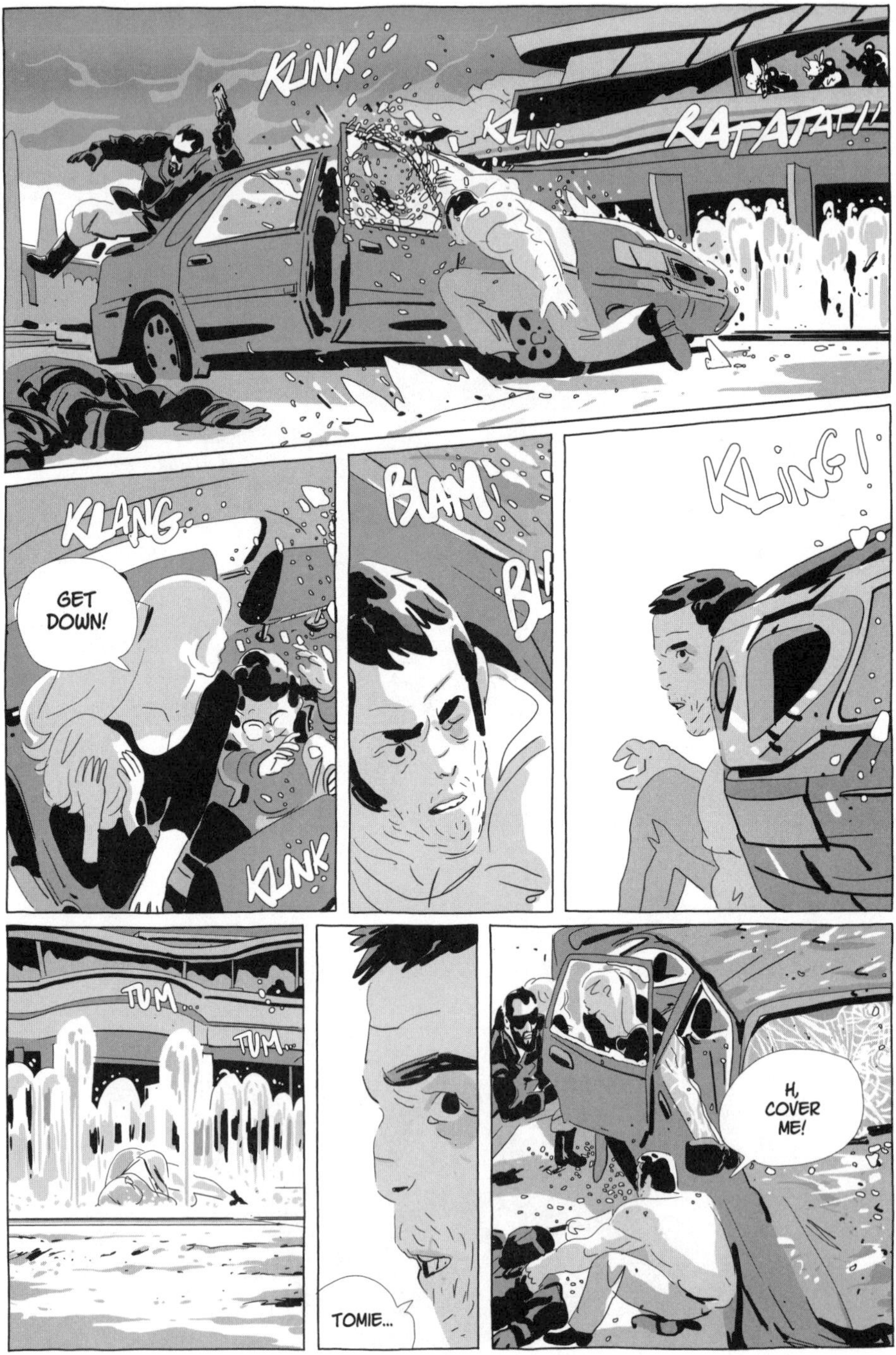
KLINK
KLIN.
RATATAT!!
KLANG
GET DOWN!
KLINK
BLAM
BL
KLING!
TUM
TUM...
TOMIE...
H, COVER ME!

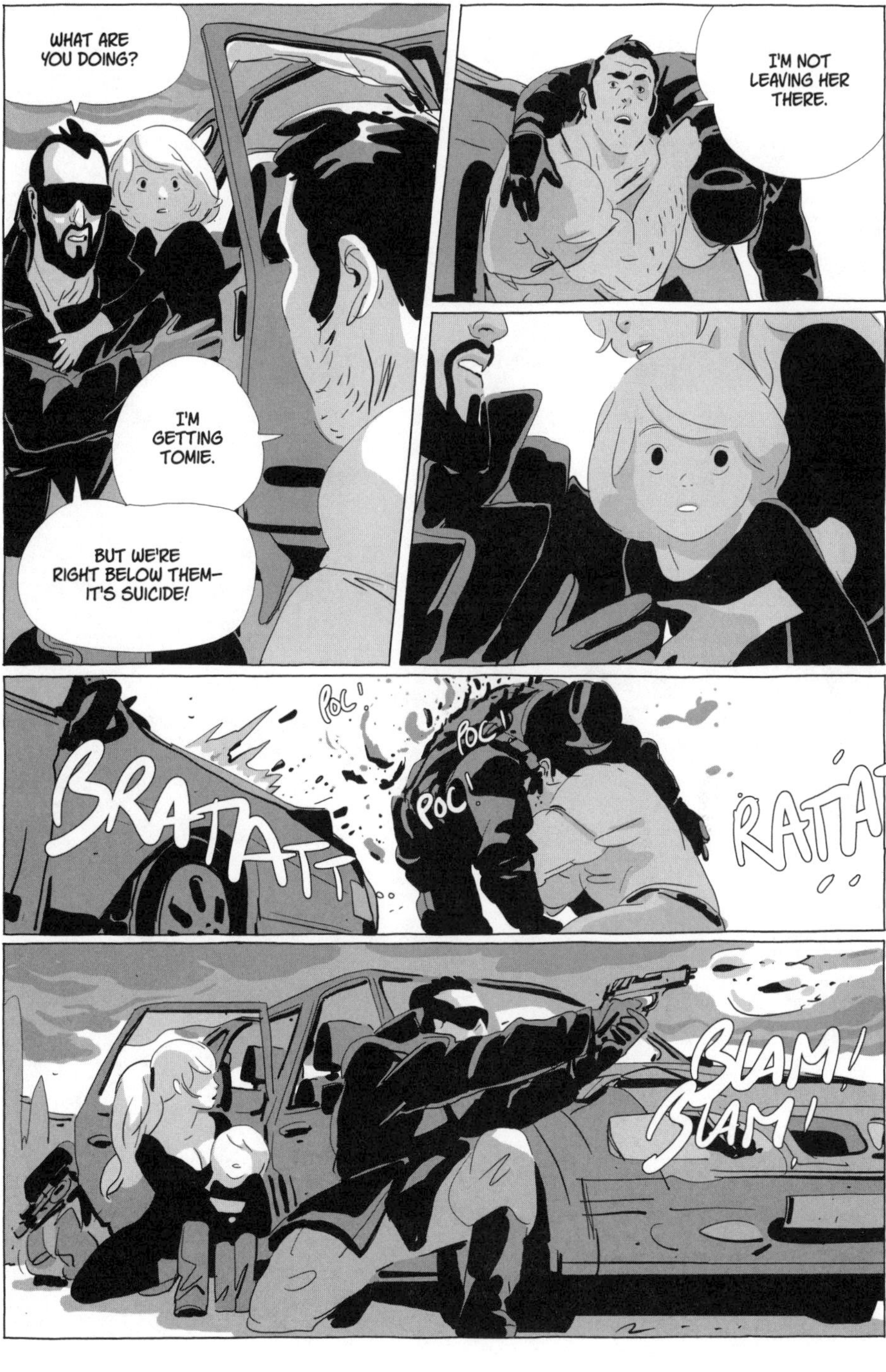
WHAT ARE YOU DOING?
I'M GETTING TOMIE.
BUT WE'RE RIGHT BELOW THEM– IT'S SUICIDE!
I'M NOT LEAVING HER THERE.
BRATATATT
POC!
POC!
POC!
RATAT
BLAM! BLAM!

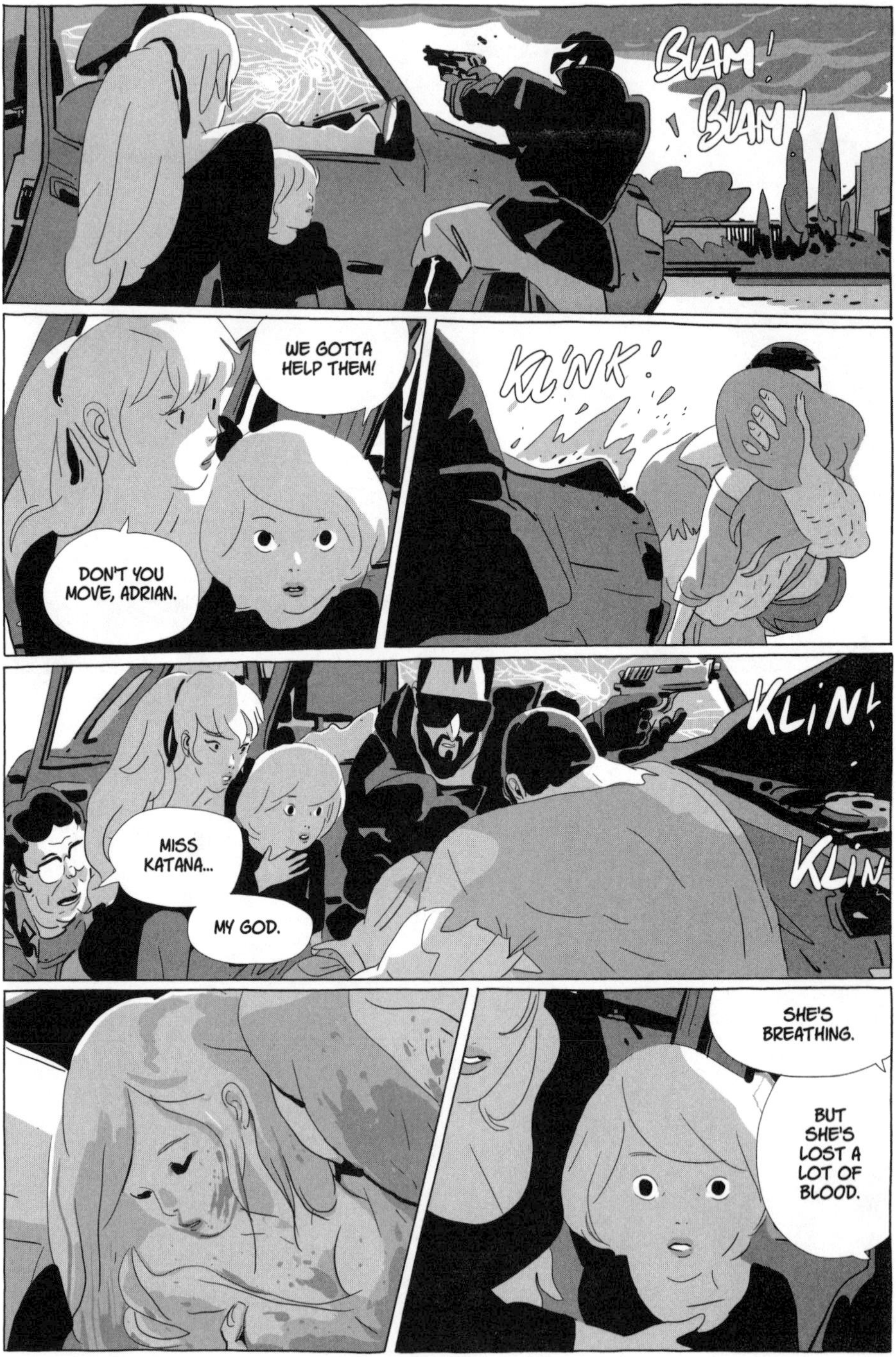
BLAM! BLAM!
WE GOTTA HELP THEM!
DON'T YOU MOVE, ADRIAN.
KLINK!
KLIN!
KLIN
MISS KATANA...
MY GOD.
SHE'S BREATHING.
BUT SHE'S LOST A LOT OF BLOOD.

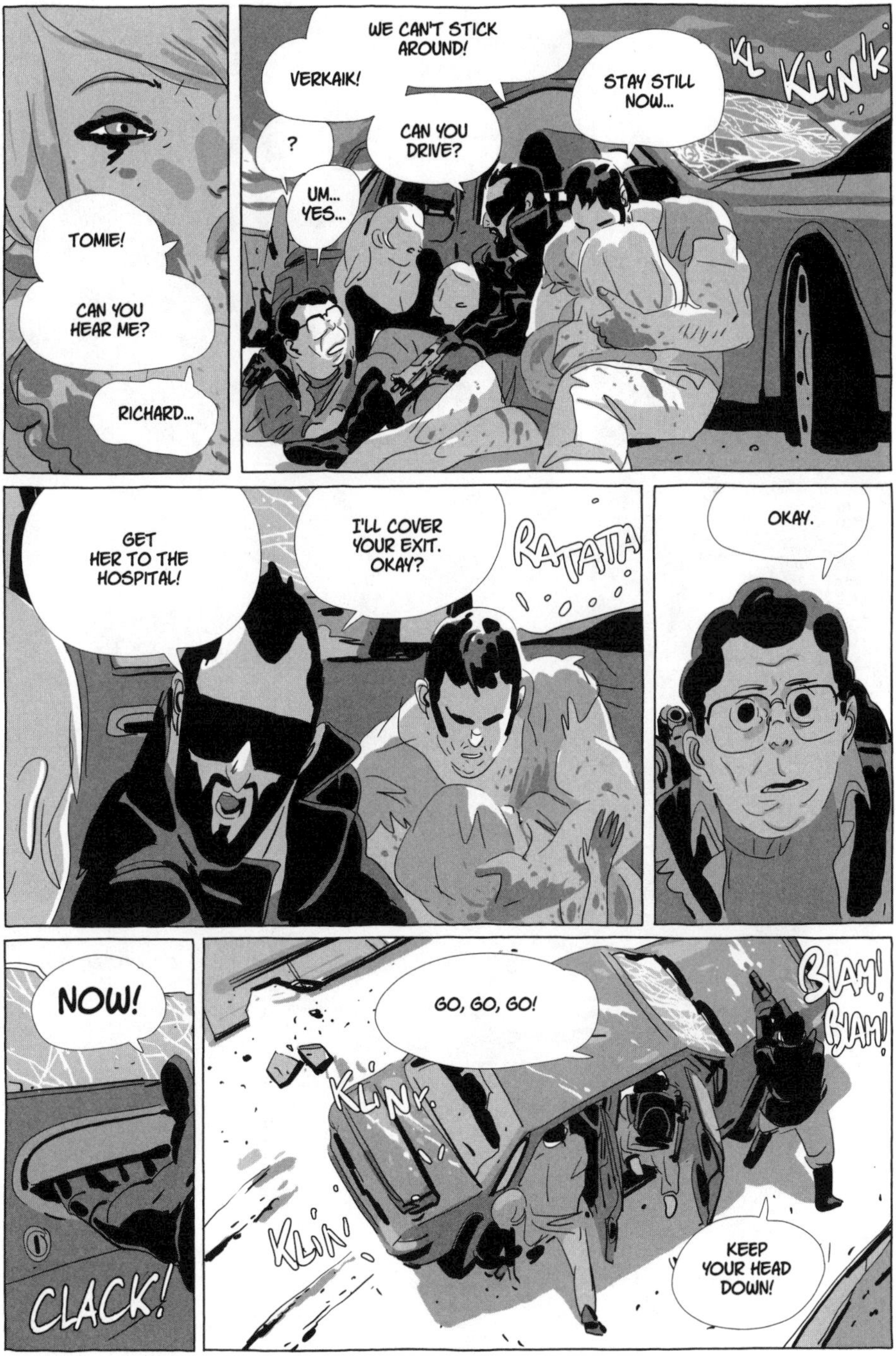
TOMIE!
CAN YOU HEAR ME?
RICHARD...
VERKAIK!
WE CAN'T STICK AROUND!
CAN YOU DRIVE?
?
UM... YES...
STAY STILL NOW...
KL' KLIN'K
GET HER TO THE HOSPITAL!
I'LL COVER YOUR EXIT. OKAY?
RATATA
OKAY.
NOW!
CLACK!
GO, GO, GO!
BLAM! BLAM!
KLINK.
KLIN'
KEEP YOUR HEAD DOWN!

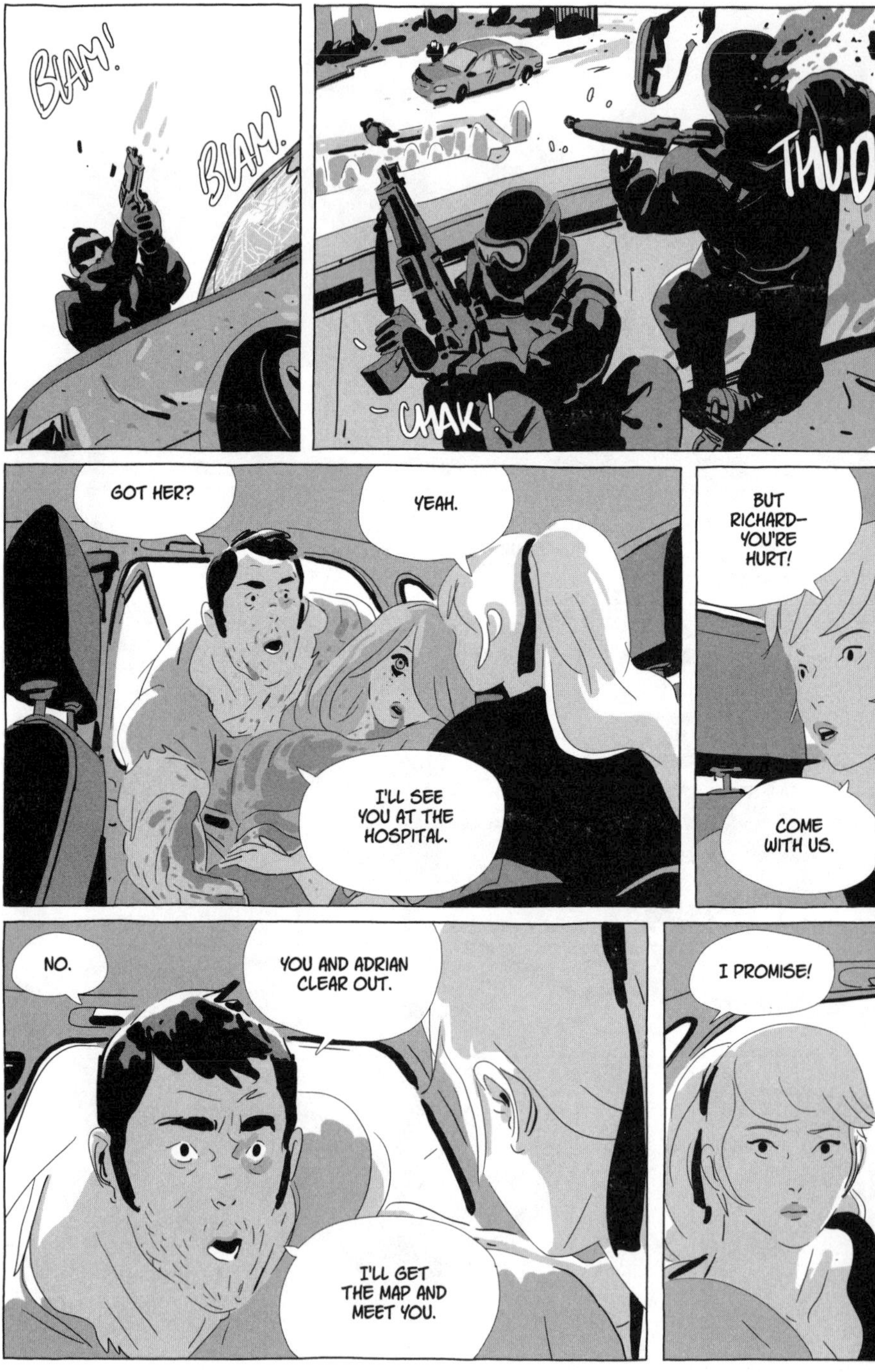
BLAM!
BLAM!
THUD!
CHAK!
GOT HER?
YEAH.
I'LL SEE YOU AT THE HOSPITAL.
BUT RICHARD— YOU'RE HURT!
COME WITH US.
NO.
YOU AND ADRIAN CLEAR OUT.
I'LL GET THE MAP AND MEET YOU.
I PROMISE!

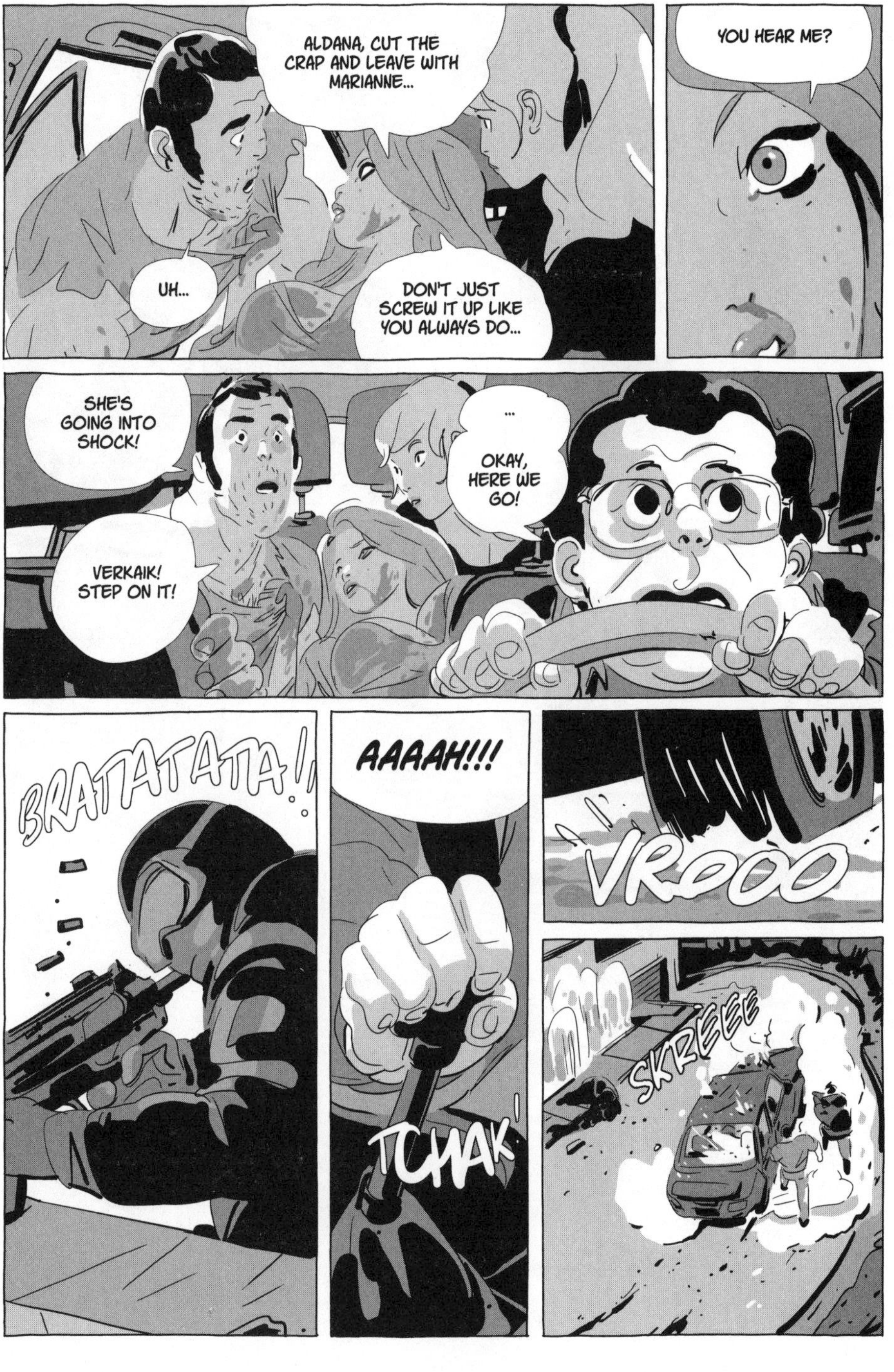
ALDANA, CUT THE CRAP AND LEAVE WITH MARIANNE...
UH...
DON'T JUST SCREW IT UP LIKE YOU ALWAYS DO...
YOU HEAR ME?
SHE'S GOING INTO SHOCK!
VERKAIK! STEP ON IT!
...
OKAY, HERE WE GO!
BRATTATATTA!!
AAAAH!!!
TCHAK
VROOO
SKREEE

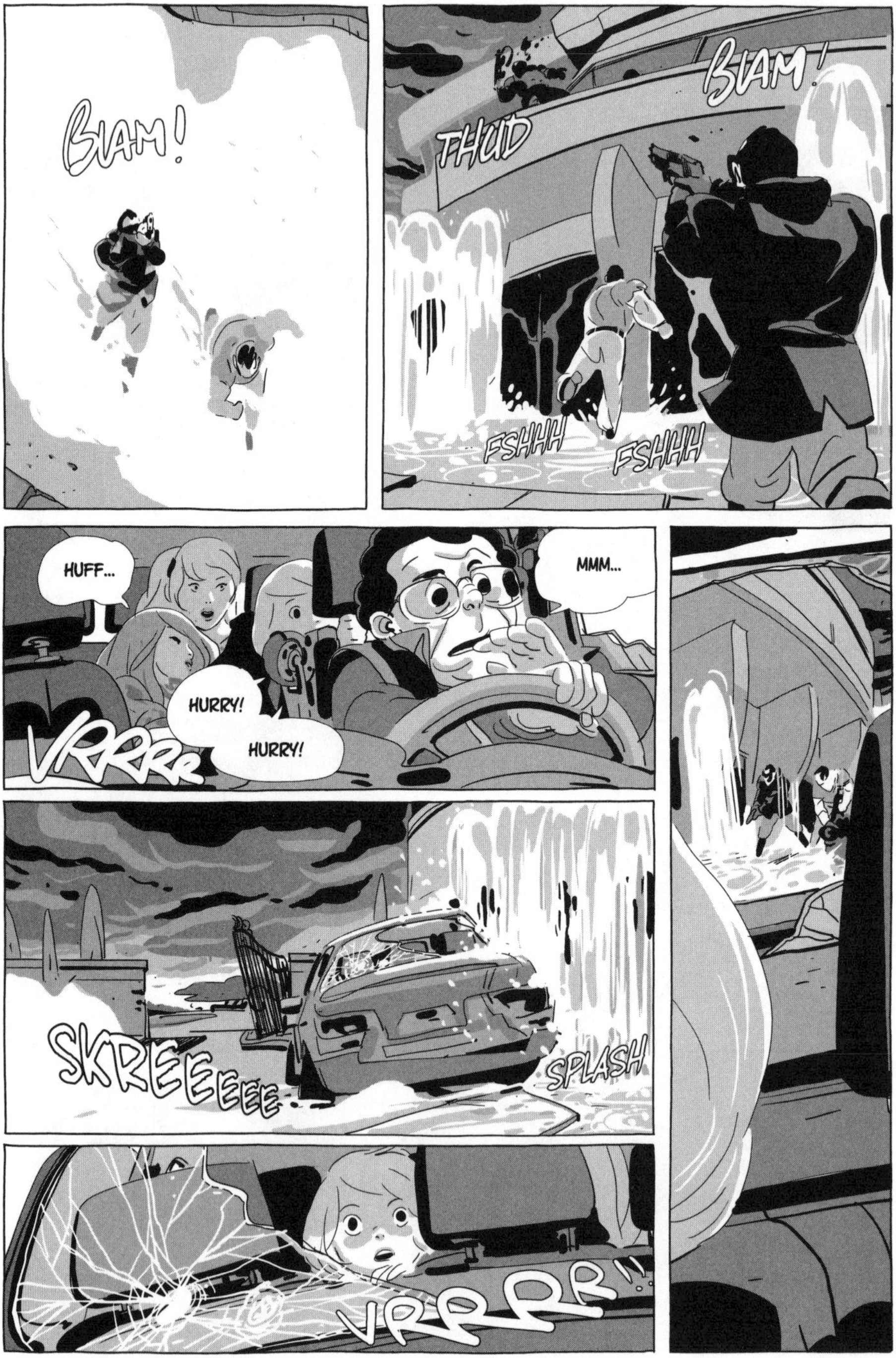
BIAM!
BIAM!
THUD
FSHHH
FSHHH
HUFF...
MMM...
HURRY!
HURRY!
VRRRR
SKREEEEEE
SPLASH
VRRRR!!

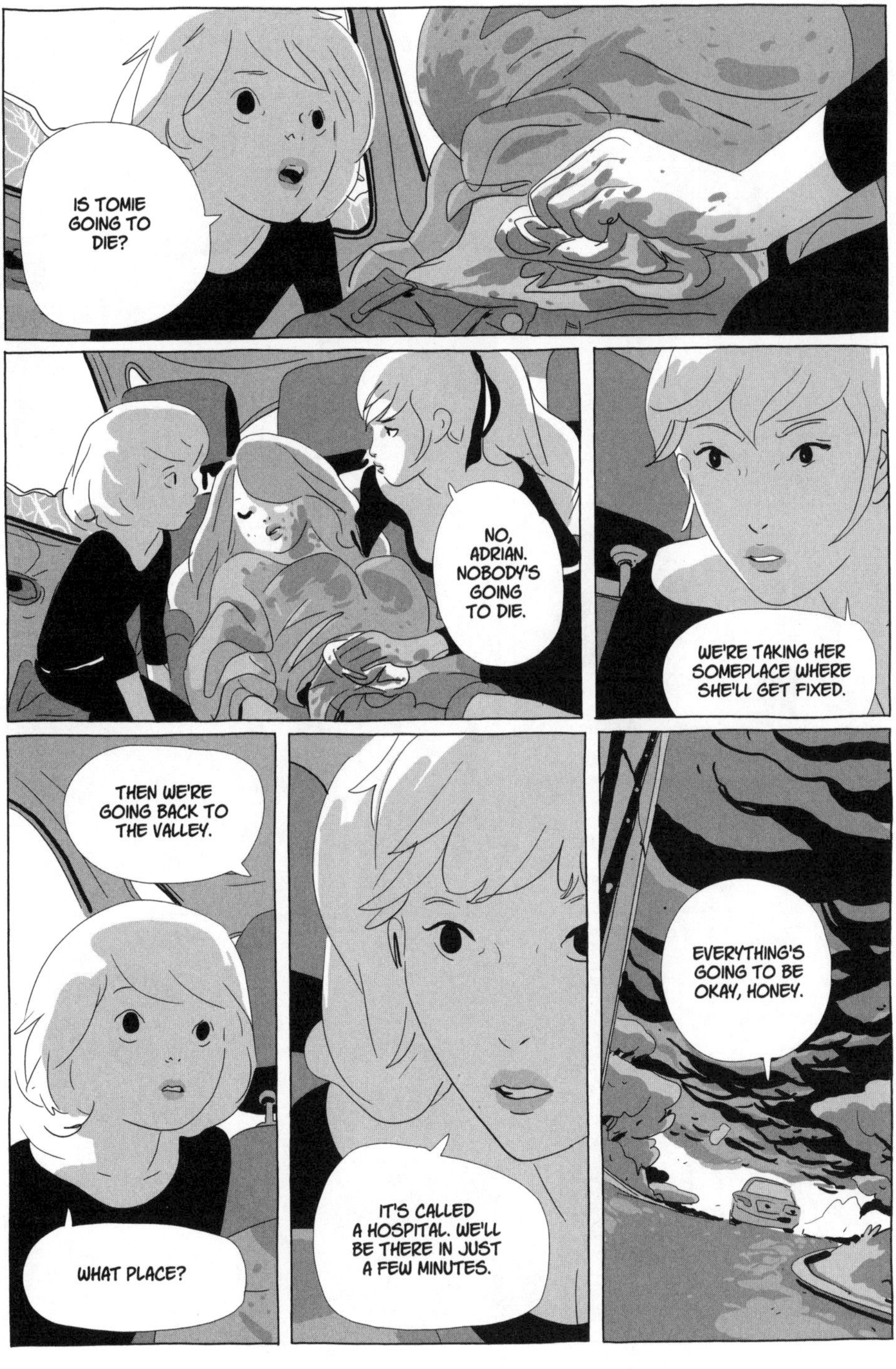
IS TOMIE GOING TO DIE?
NO, ADRIAN. NOBODY'S GOING TO DIE.
WE'RE TAKING HER SOMEPLACE WHERE SHE'LL GET FIXED.
THEN WE'RE GOING BACK TO THE VALLEY.
WHAT PLACE?
IT'S CALLED A HOSPITAL. WE'LL BE THERE IN JUST A FEW MINUTES.
EVERYTHING'S GOING TO BE OKAY, HONEY.

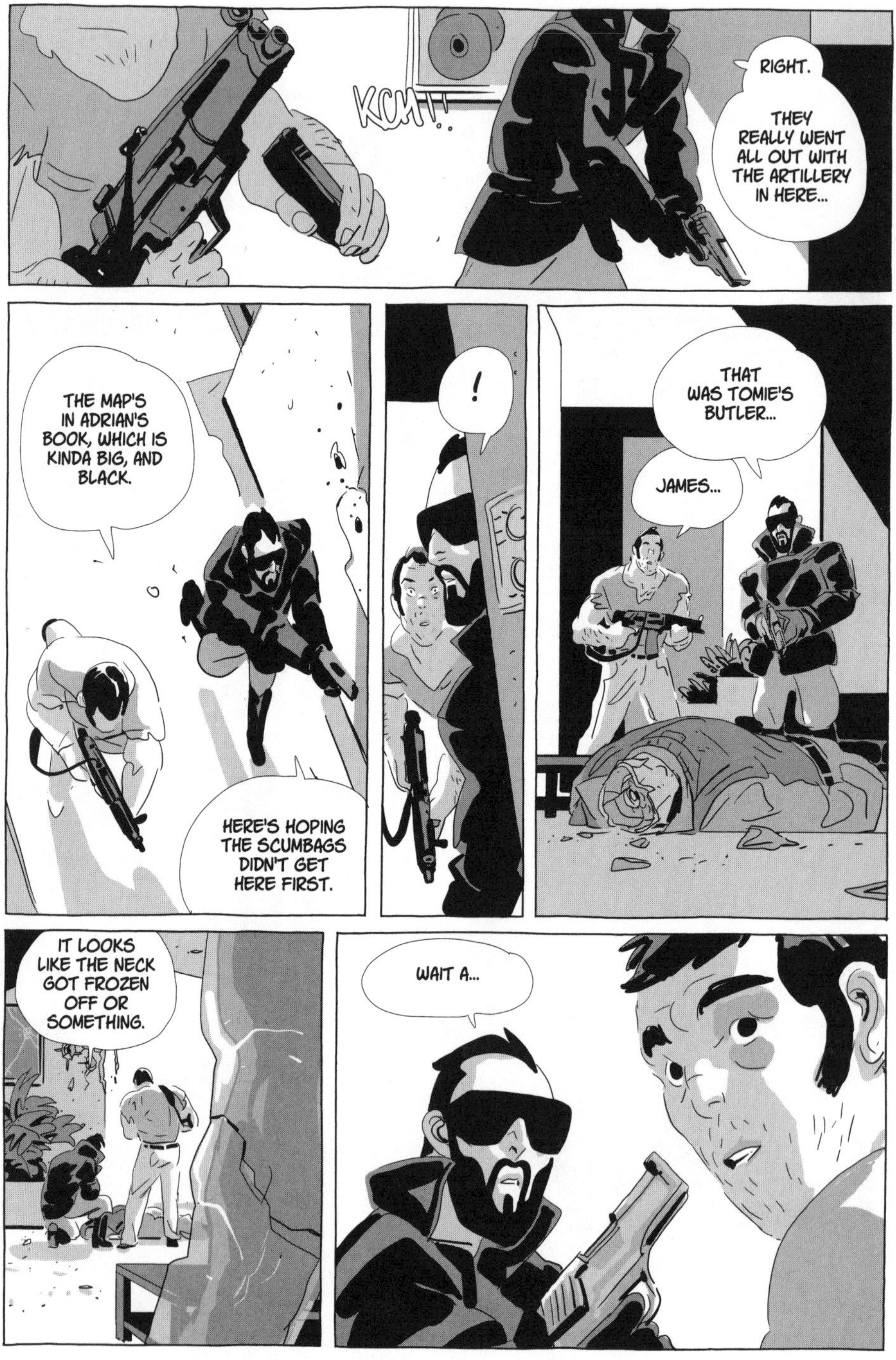
KCLIK!!
RIGHT.
THEY REALLY WENT ALL OUT WITH THE ARTILLERY IN HERE...
THE MAP'S IN ADRIAN'S BOOK, WHICH IS KINDA BIG, AND BLACK.
HERE'S HOPING THE SCUMBAGS DIDN'T GET HERE FIRST.
!
THAT WAS TOMIE'S BUTLER...
JAMES...
IT LOOKS LIKE THE NECK GOT FROZEN OFF OR SOMETHING.
WAIT A...

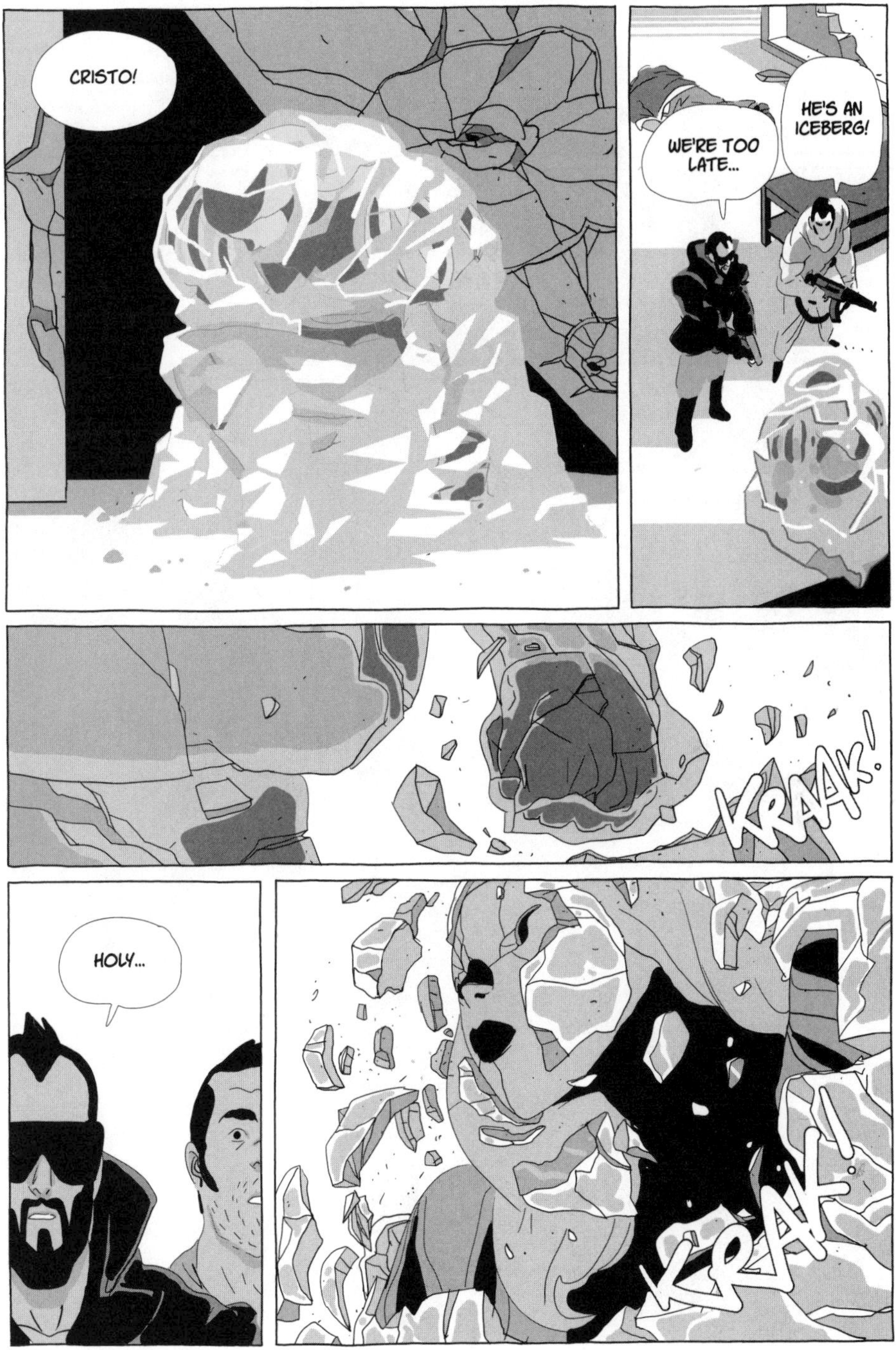
CRISTO!
WE'RE TOO LATE...
HE'S AN ICEBERG!
KRAAK!
HOLY...
KRAK!

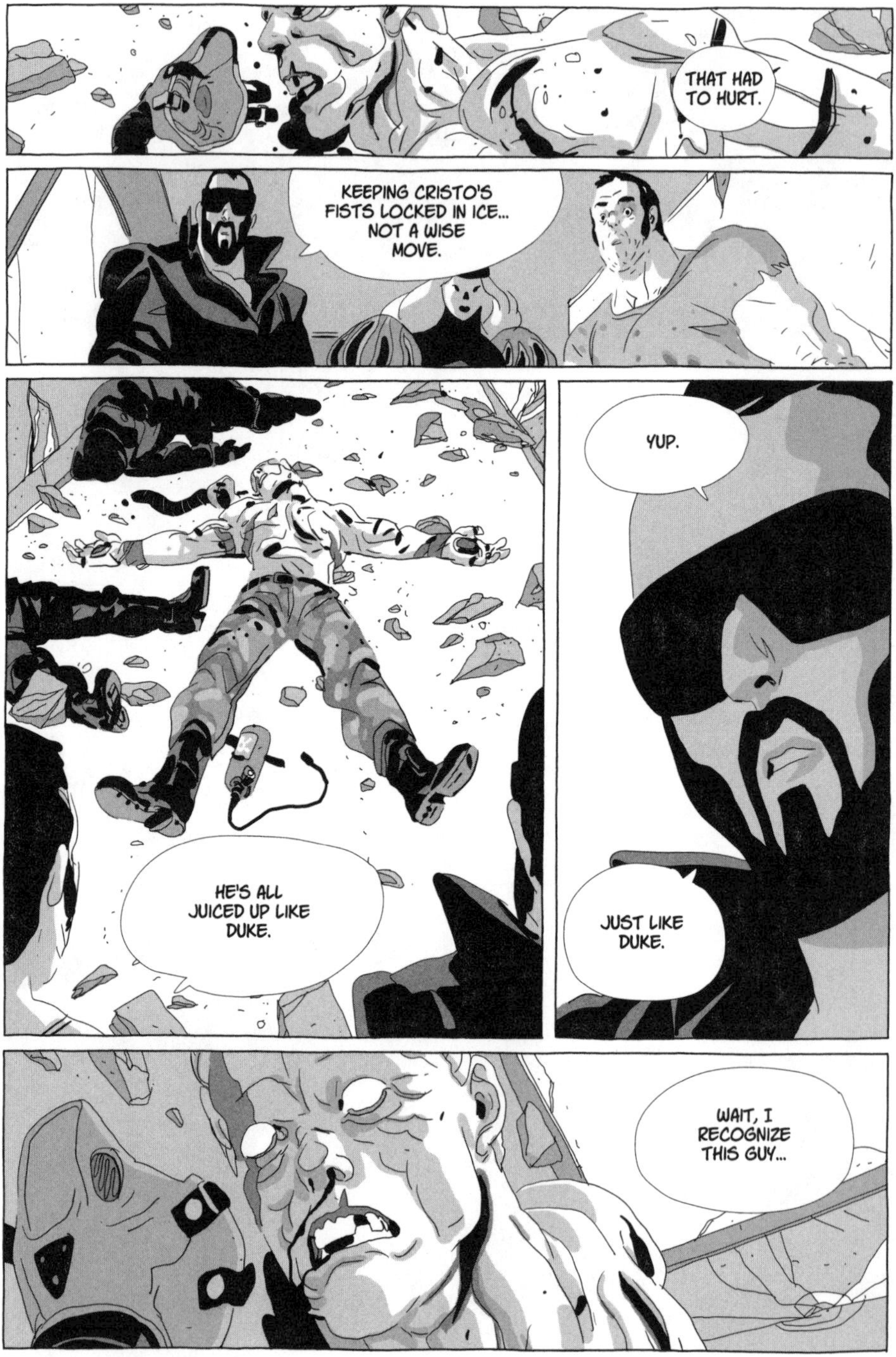
THAT HAD TO HURT.
KEEPING CRISTO'S FISTS LOCKED IN ICE... NOT A WISE MOVE.
HE'S ALL JUICED UP LIKE DUKE.
YUP.
JUST LIKE DUKE.
WAIT, I RECOGNIZE THIS GUY...

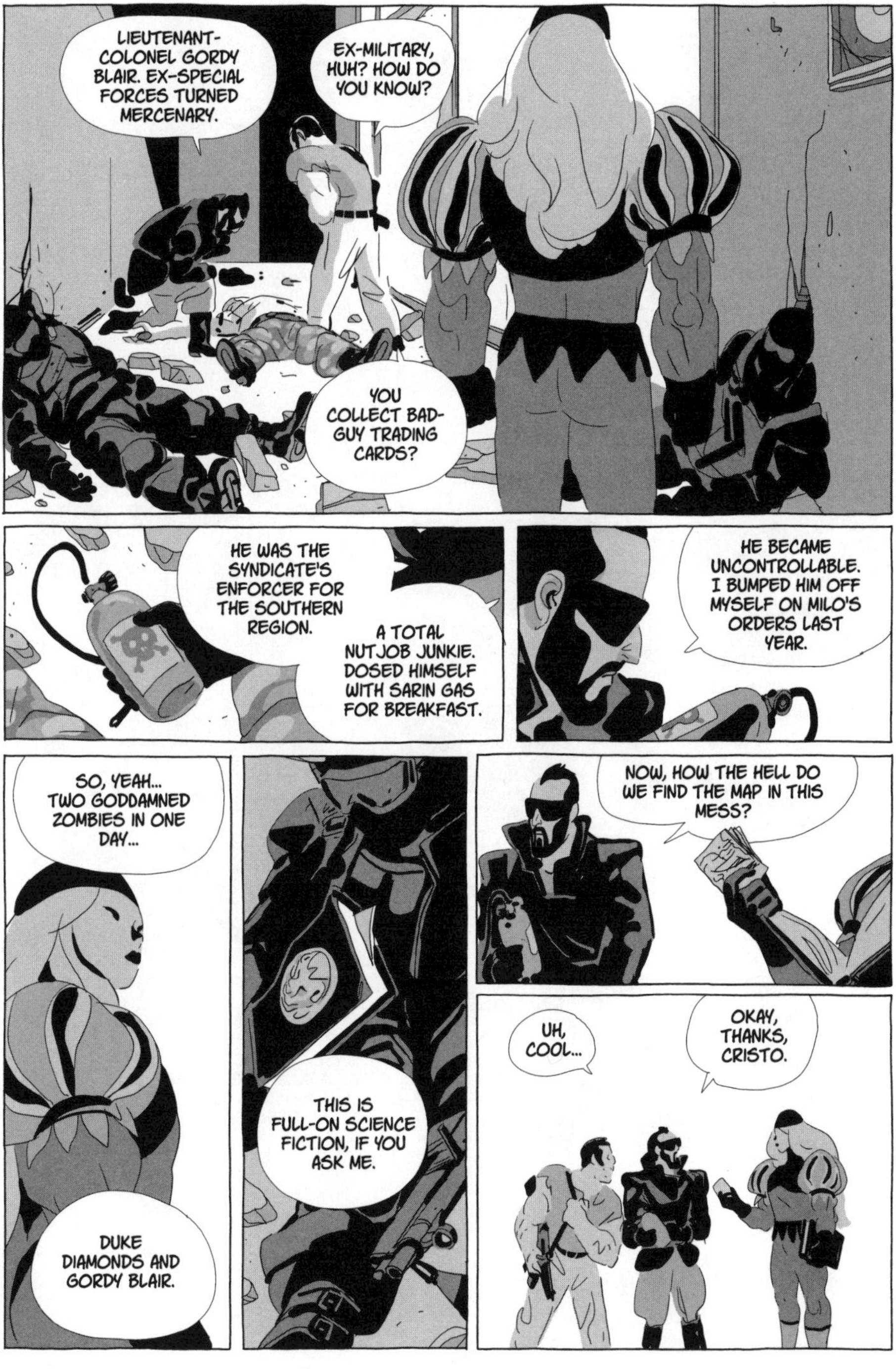
LIEUTENANT-COLONEL GORDY BLAIR. EX-SPECIAL FORCES TURNED MERCENARY.
EX-MILITARY, HUH? HOW DO YOU KNOW?
YOU COLLECT BAD-GUY TRADING CARDS?
HE WAS THE SYNDICATE'S ENFORCER FOR THE SOUTHERN REGION.
A TOTAL NUTJOB JUNKIE. DOSED HIMSELF WITH SARIN GAS FOR BREAKFAST.
HE BECAME UNCONTROLLABLE. I BUMPED HIM OFF MYSELF ON MILO'S ORDERS LAST YEAR.
SO, YEAH... TWO GODDAMNED ZOMBIES IN ONE DAY...
DUKE DIAMONDS AND GORDY BLAIR.
THIS IS FULL-ON SCIENCE FICTION, IF YOU ASK ME.
NOW, HOW THE HELL DO WE FIND THE MAP IN THIS MESS?
UH, COOL...
OKAY, THANKS, CRISTO.

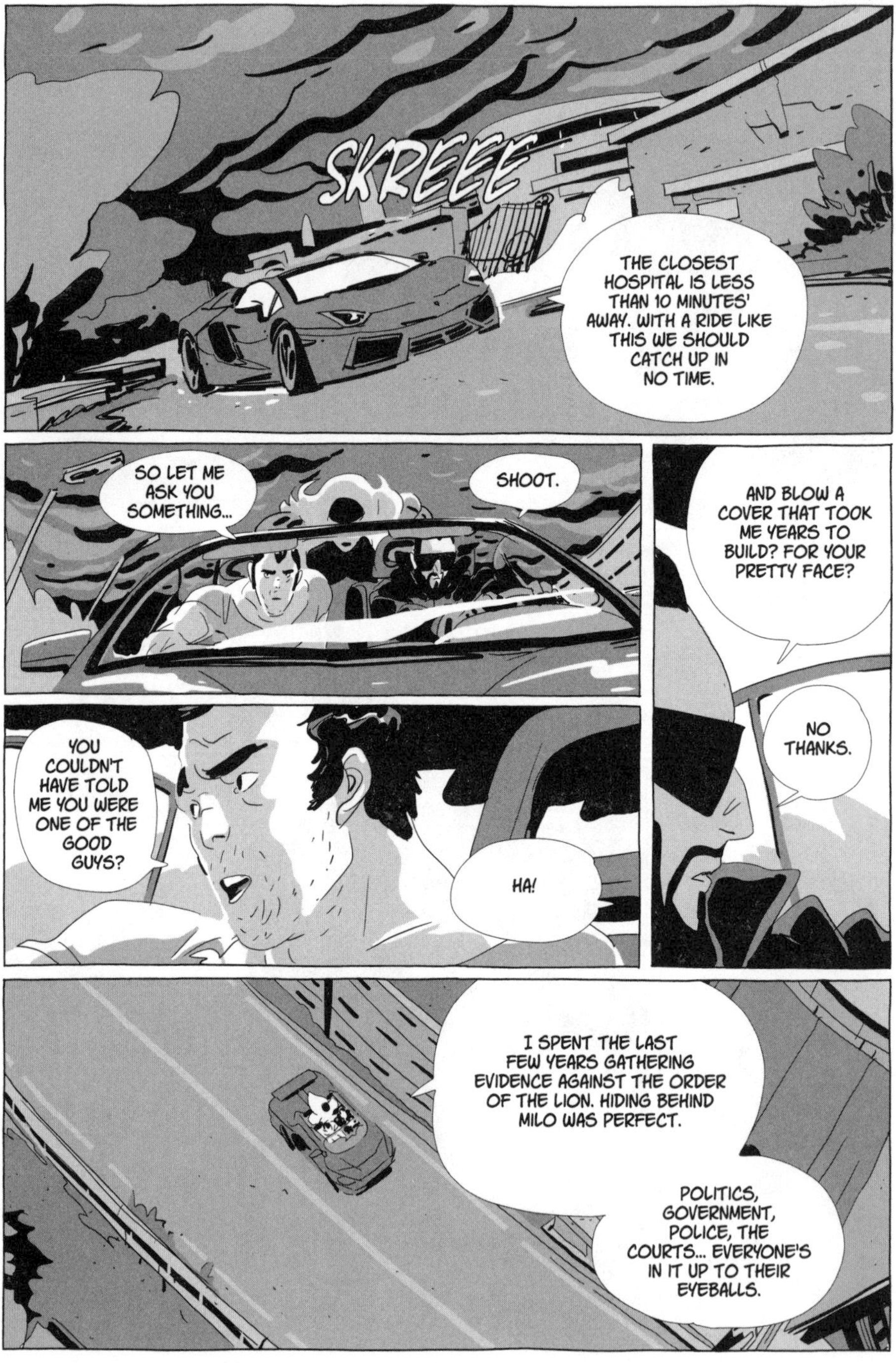
SKREEE
THE CLOSEST HOSPITAL IS LESS THAN 10 MINUTES' AWAY. WITH A RIDE LIKE THIS WE SHOULD CATCH UP IN NO TIME.
SO LET ME ASK YOU SOMETHING...
SHOOT.
AND BLOW A COVER THAT TOOK ME YEARS TO BUILD? FOR YOUR PRETTY FACE?
YOU COULDN'T HAVE TOLD ME YOU WERE ONE OF THE GOOD GUYS?
HA!
NO THANKS.
I SPENT THE LAST FEW YEARS GATHERING EVIDENCE AGAINST THE ORDER OF THE LION. HIDING BEHIND MILO WAS PERFECT.
POLITICS, GOVERNMENT, POLICE, THE COURTS... EVERYONE'S IN IT UP TO THEIR EYEBALLS.

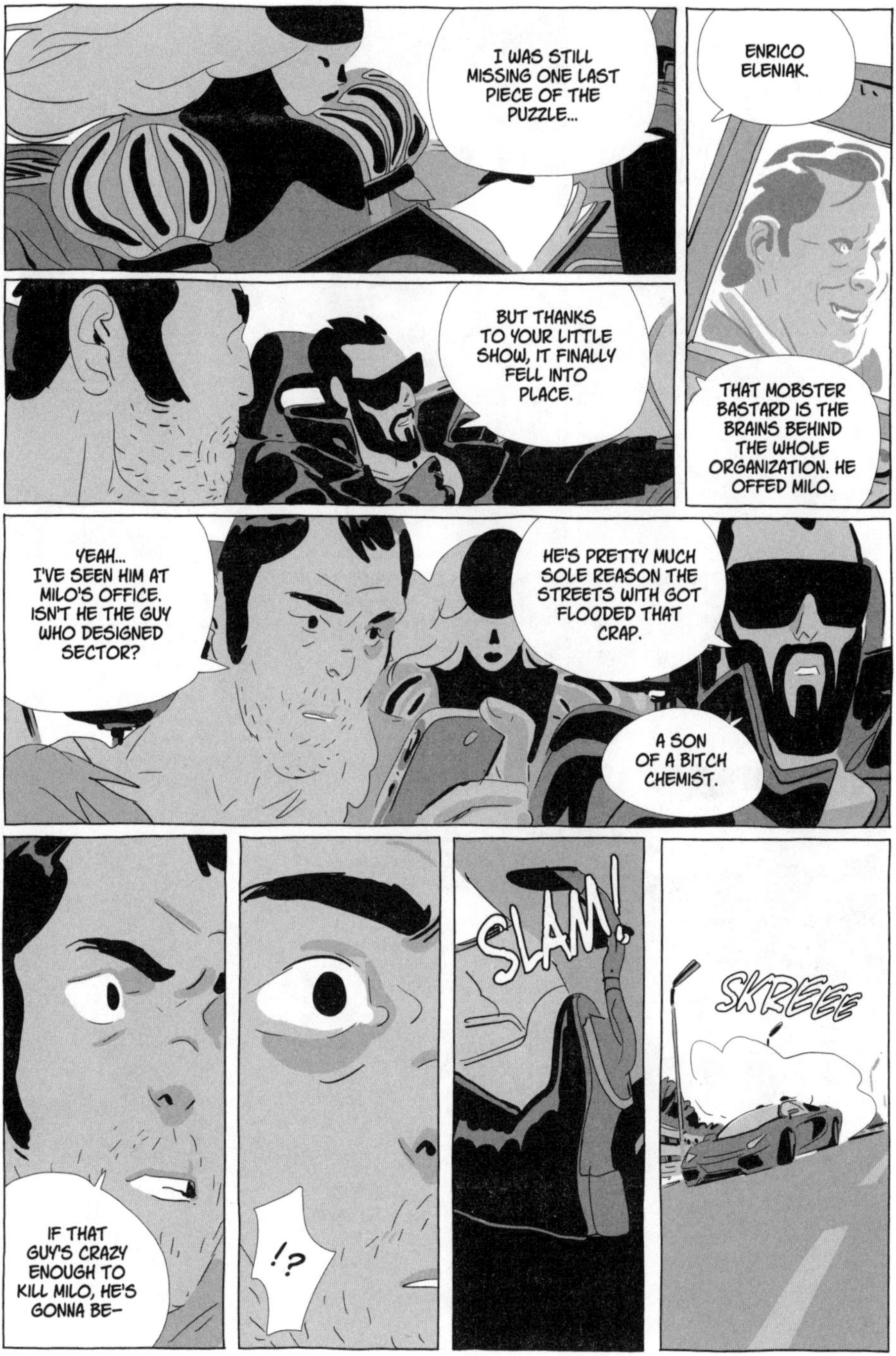
I WAS STILL MISSING ONE LAST PIECE OF THE PUZZLE...
ENRICO ELENIAK.
BUT THANKS TO YOUR LITTLE SHOW, IT FINALLY FELL INTO PLACE.
THAT MOBSTER BASTARD IS THE BRAINS BEHIND THE WHOLE ORGANIZATION. HE OFFED MILO.
YEAH... I'VE SEEN HIM AT MILO'S OFFICE. ISN'T HE THE GUY WHO DESIGNED SECTOR?
HE'S PRETTY MUCH SOLE REASON THE STREETS WITH GOT FLOODED THAT CRAP.
A SON OF A BITCH CHEMIST.
IF THAT GUY'S CRAZY ENOUGH TO KILL MILO, HE'S GONNA BE-
!?
SLAM!
SKREEE

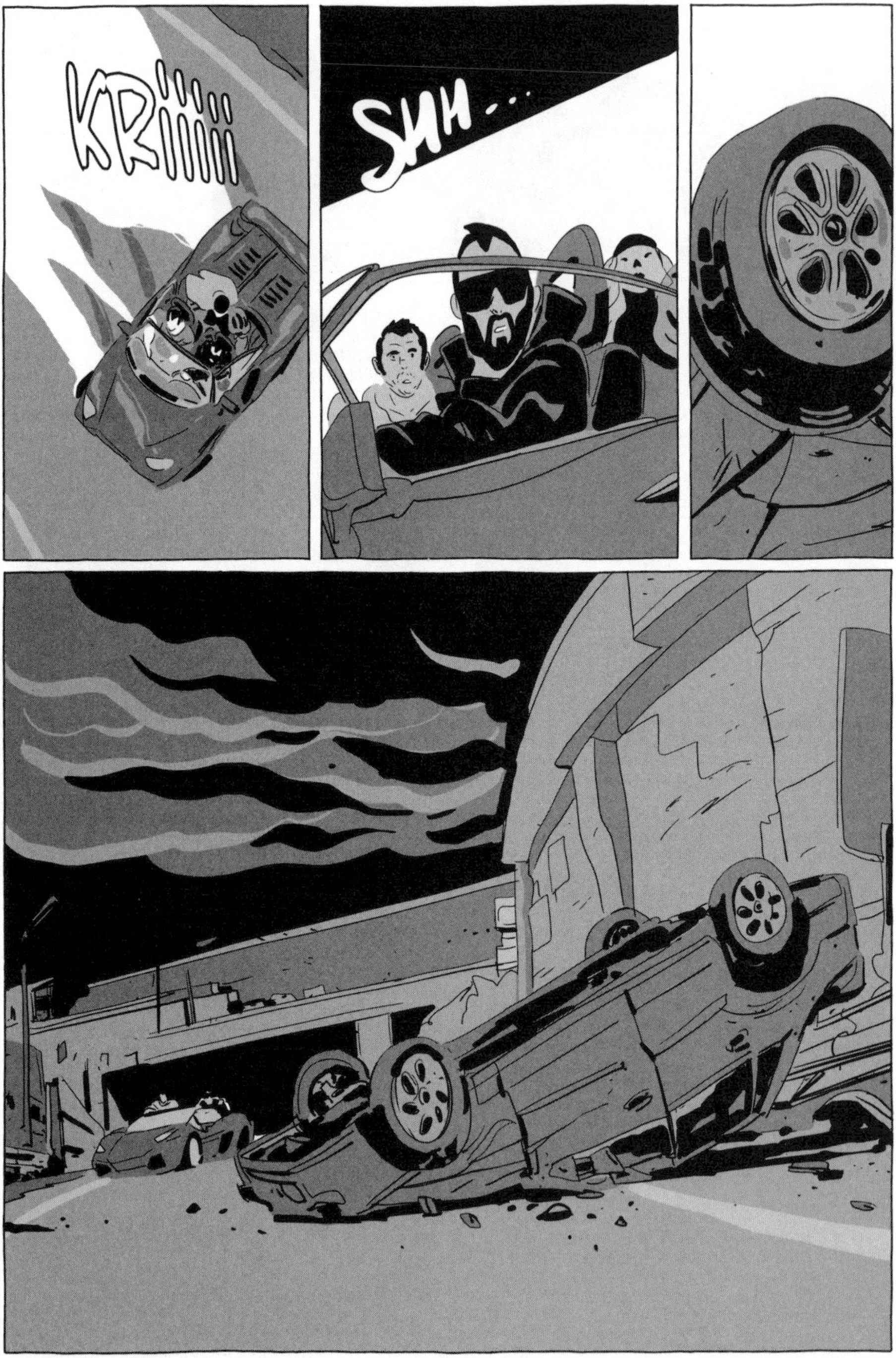
KRiiiii
SHH . . .

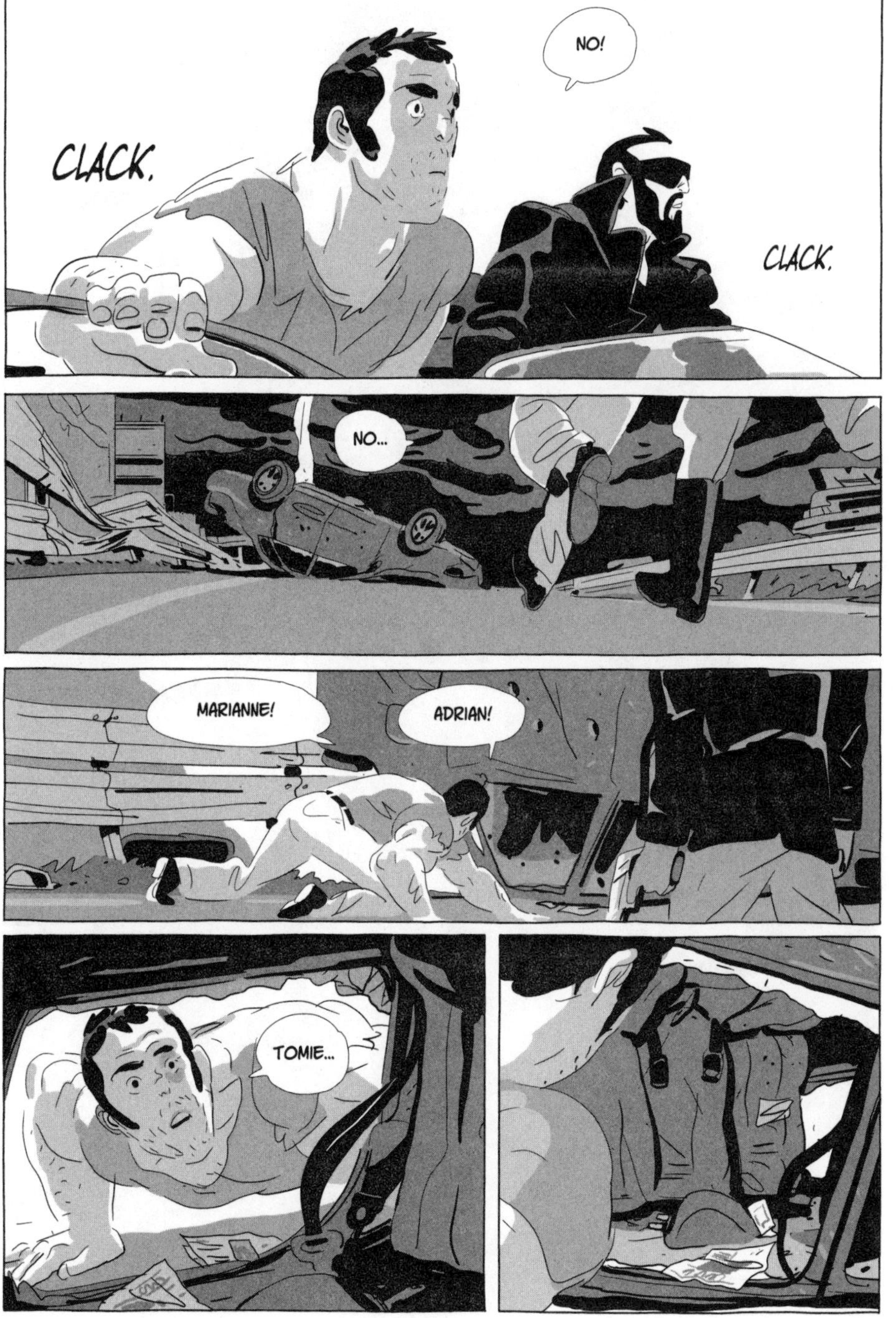
NO!
CLACK.
CLACK.
NO...
MARIANNE!
ADRIAN!
TOMIE...

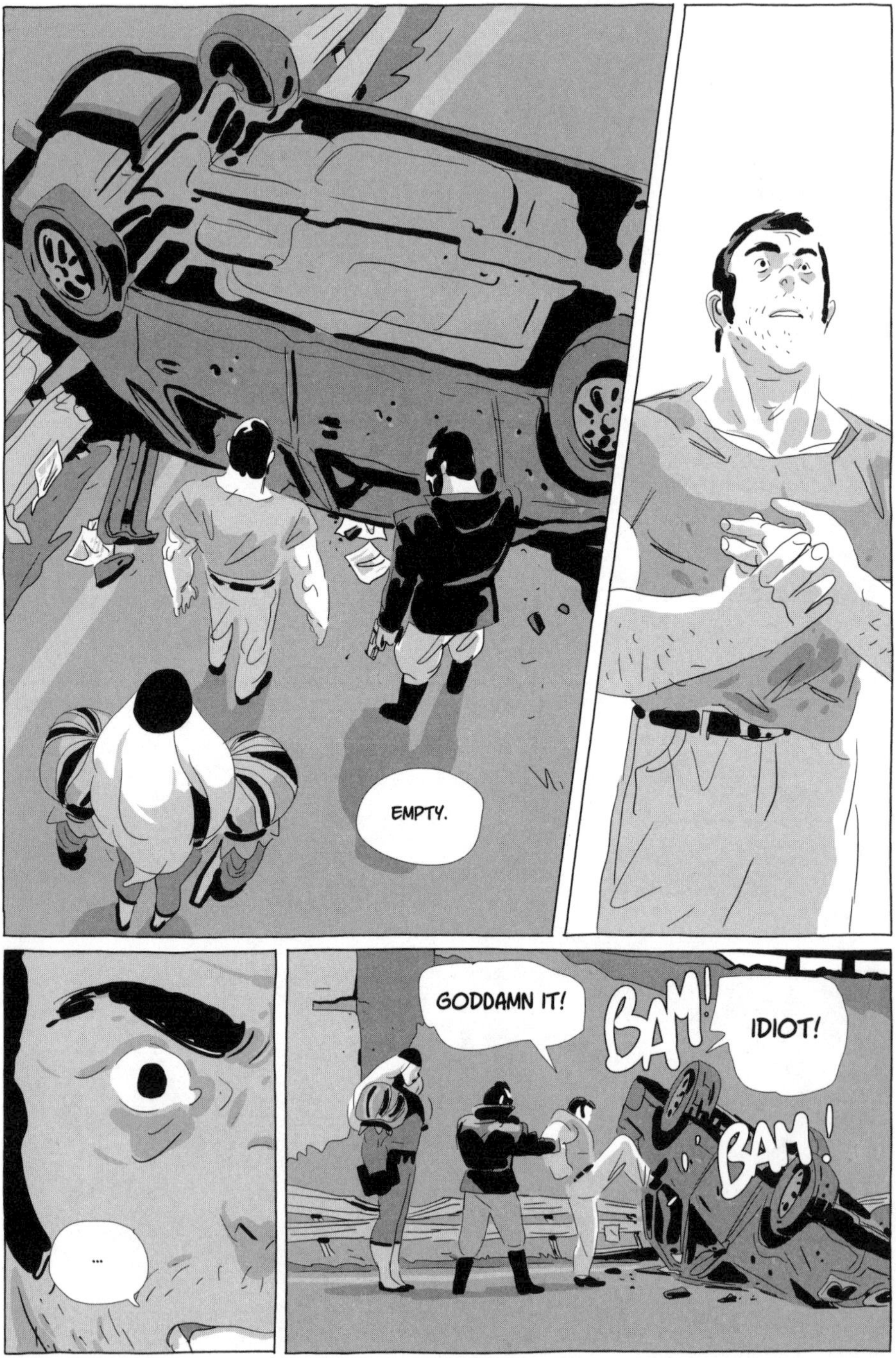
EMPTY.
...
GODDAMN IT!
BAM!
IDIOT!
BAM!

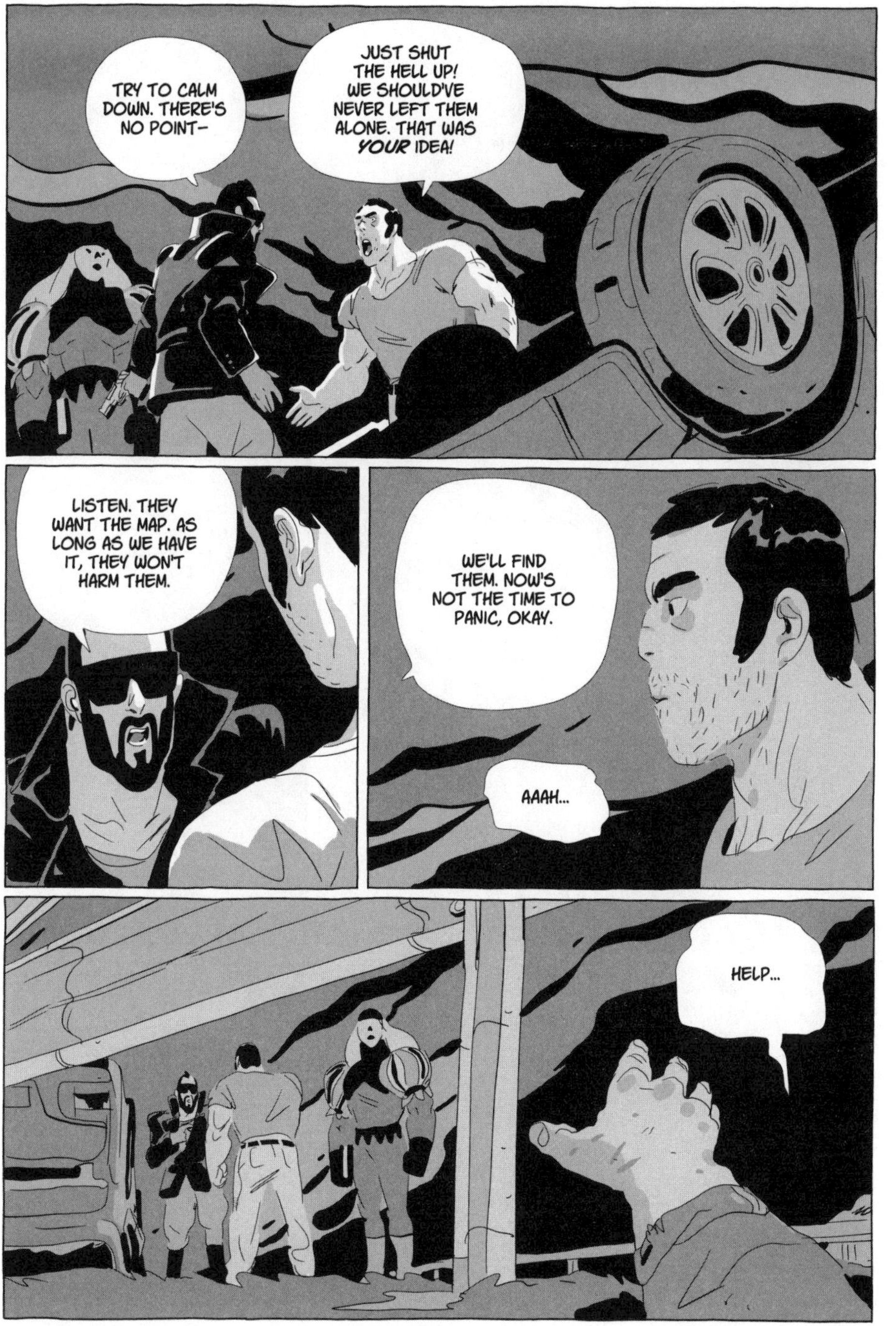
TRY TO CALM DOWN. THERE'S NO POINT-
JUST SHUT THE HELL UP! WE SHOULD'VE NEVER LEFT THEM ALONE. THAT WAS YOUR IDEA!
LISTEN. THEY WANT THE MAP. AS LONG AS WE HAVE IT, THEY WON'T HARM THEM.
WE'LL FIND THEM. NOW'S NOT THE TIME TO PANIC, OKAY.
AAAH...
HELP...

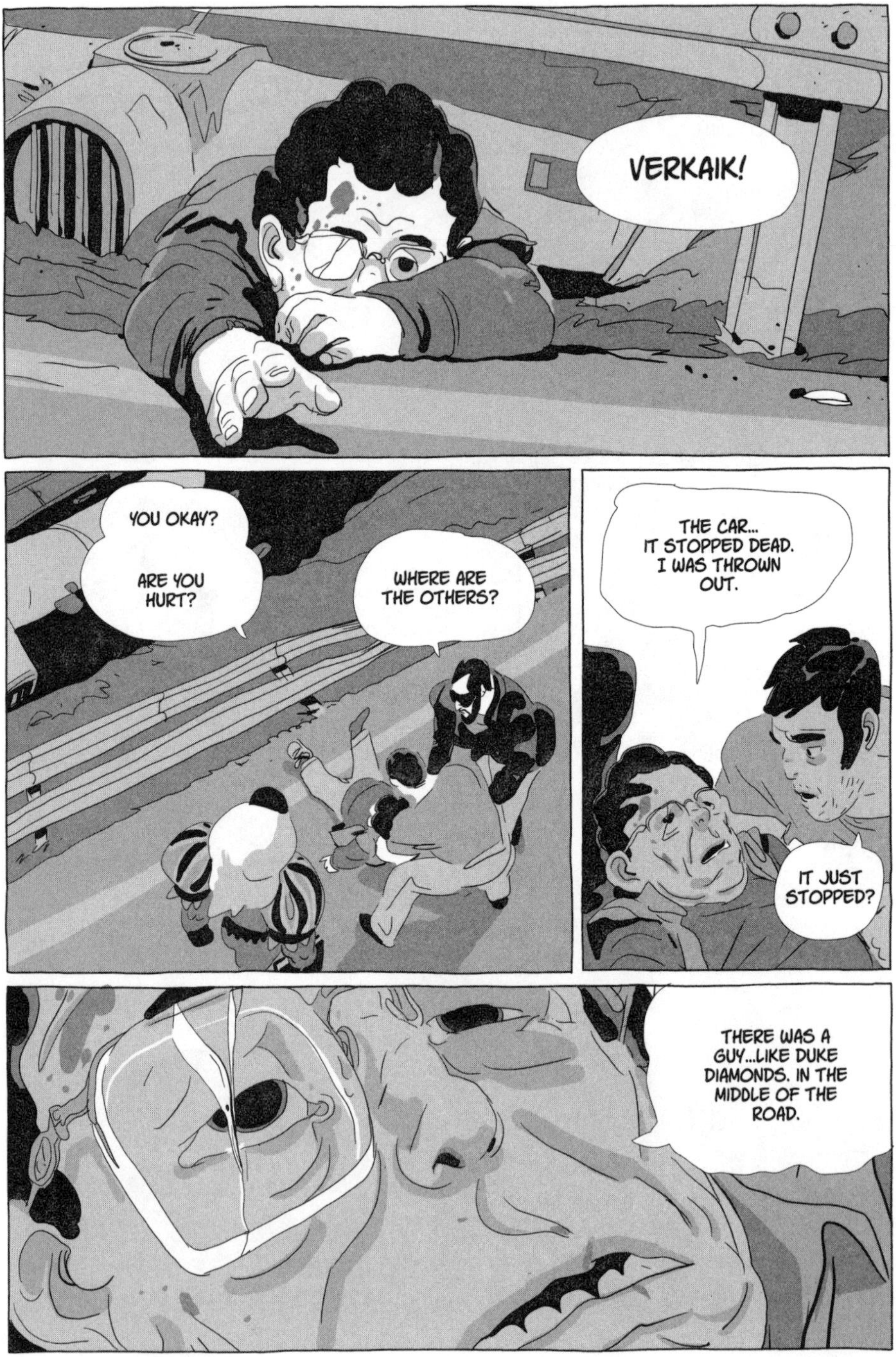
VERKAIK!
YOU OKAY?
ARE YOU HURT?
WHERE ARE THE OTHERS?
THE CAR... IT STOPPED DEAD. I WAS THROWN OUT.
IT JUST STOPPED?
THERE WAS A GUY...LIKE DUKE DIAMONDS. IN THE MIDDLE OF THE ROAD.

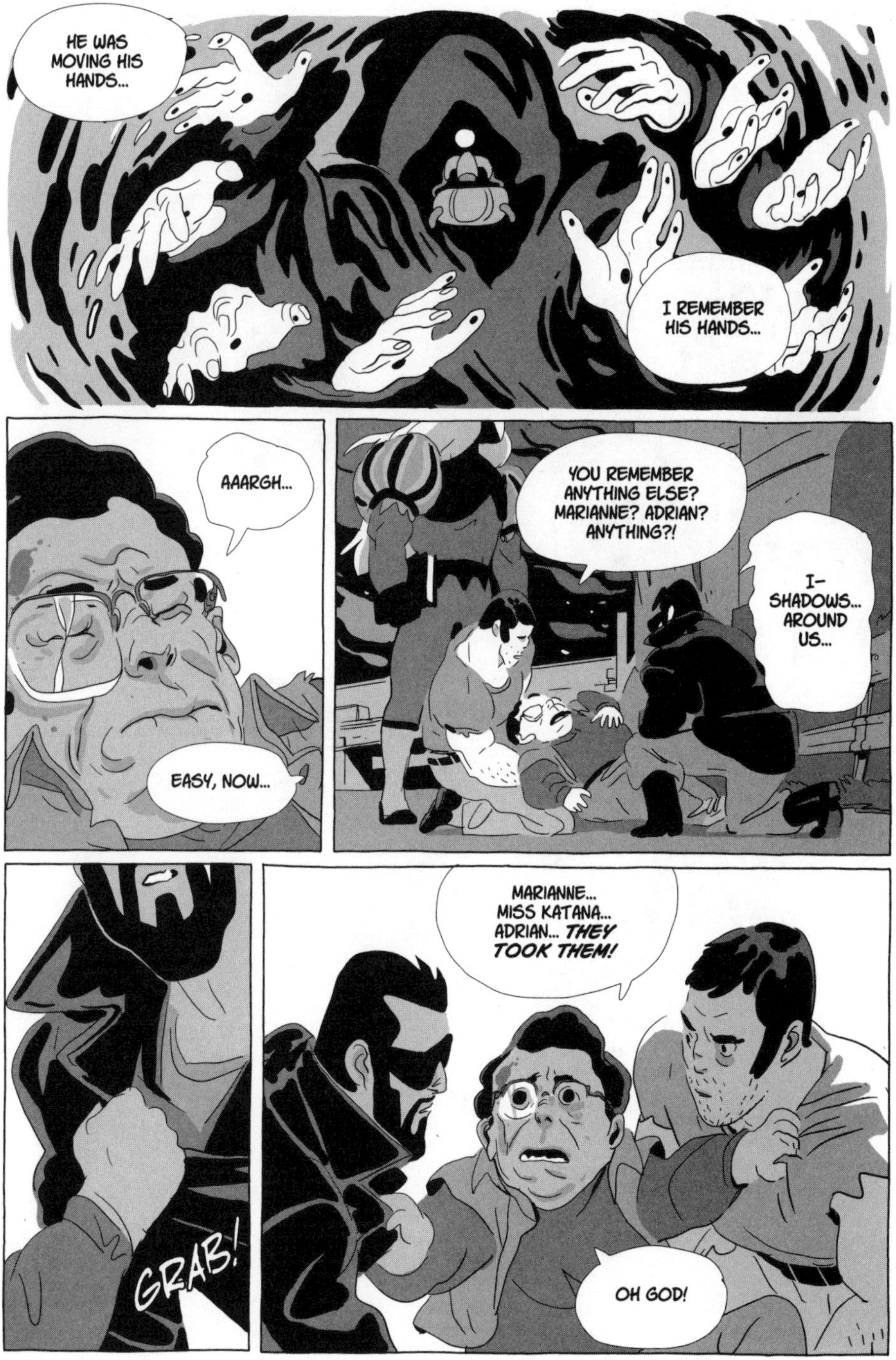
HE WAS MOVING HIS HANDS...
I REMEMBER HIS HANDS...
AAARGH...
EASY, NOW...
YOU REMEMBER ANYTHING ELSE? MARIANNE? ADRIAN? ANYTHING?!
I– SHADOWS... AROUND US...
GRAB!
MARIANNE... MISS KATANA... ADRIAN... *THEY TOOK THEM!*
OH GOD!

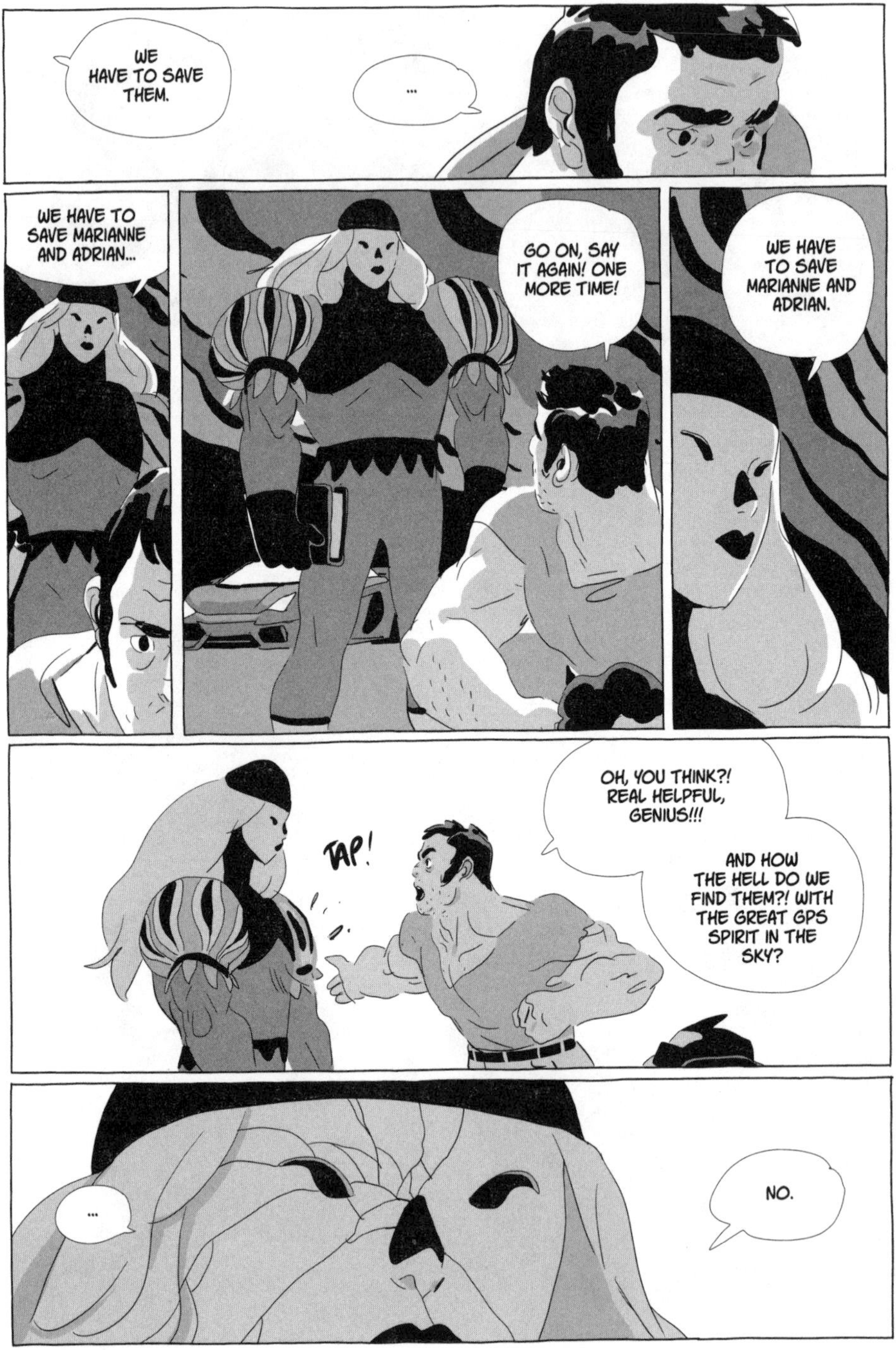
WE HAVE TO SAVE THEM.
...
WE HAVE TO SAVE MARIANNE AND ADRIAN...
GO ON, SAY IT AGAIN! ONE MORE TIME!
WE HAVE TO SAVE MARIANNE AND ADRIAN.
TAP!
OH, YOU THINK?! REAL HELPFUL, GENIUS!!!
AND HOW THE HELL DO WE FIND THEM?! WITH THE GREAT GPS SPIRIT IN THE SKY?
...
NO.

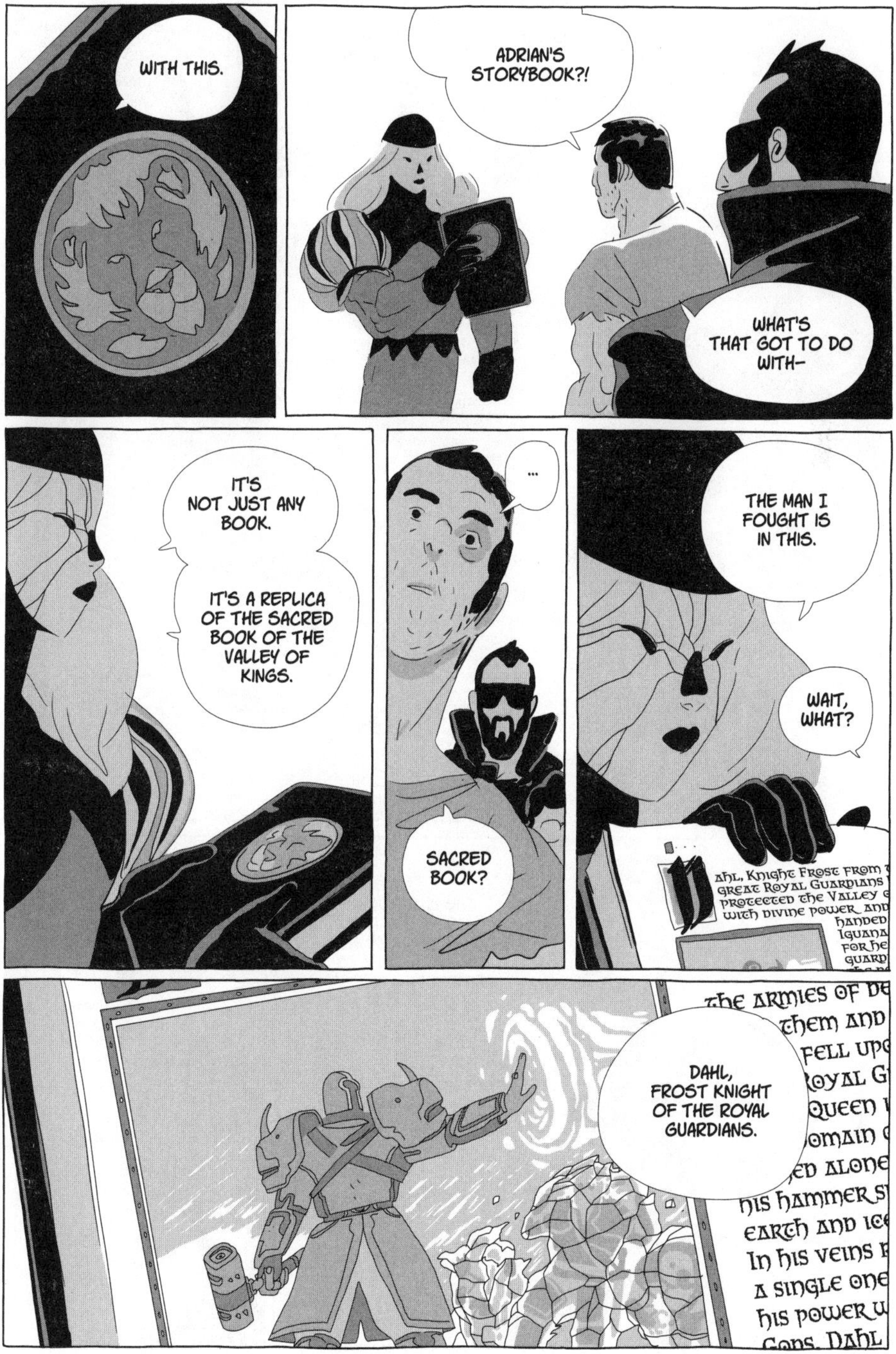
WITH THIS.
ADRIAN'S STORYBOOK?!
WHAT'S THAT GOT TO DO WITH–
IT'S NOT JUST ANY BOOK.
IT'S A REPLICA OF THE SACRED BOOK OF THE VALLEY OF KINGS.
...
SACRED BOOK?
THE MAN I FOUGHT IS IN THIS.
WAIT, WHAT?
DAHL, FROST KNIGHT OF THE ROYAL GUARDIANS.

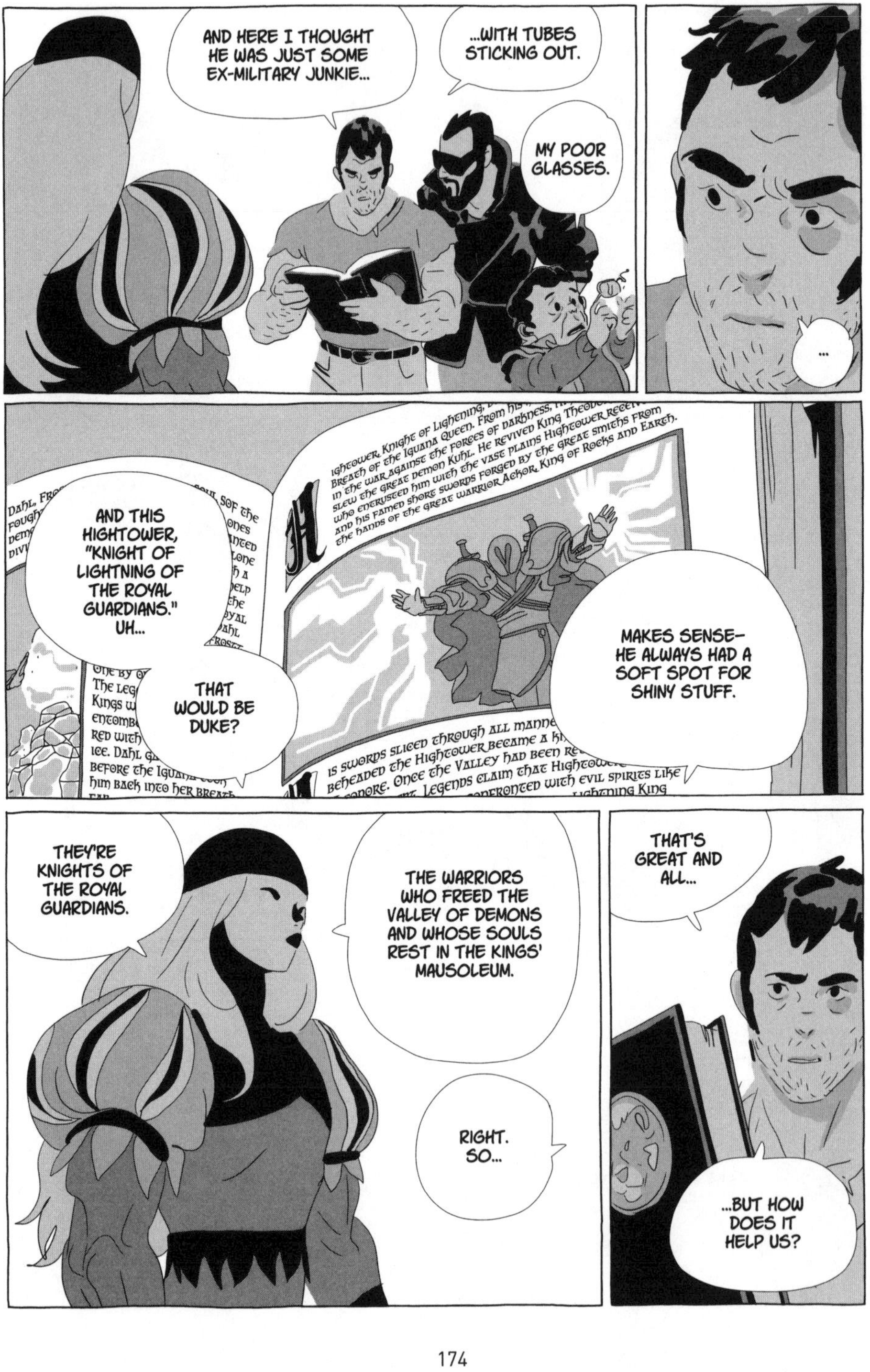
AND HERE I THOUGHT HE WAS JUST SOME EX-MILITARY JUNKIE...
...WITH TUBES STICKING OUT.
MY POOR GLASSES.
...
Breath of the Iguana Queen. From his
in the war against the forces of darkness,
slew the great demon Kuhl. He revived King Theod
who entrusted him with the vast plains Hightower
and his famed short swords forged by the great smiths from
the hands of the great warrior Aekor, King of Rocks and Earth.
AND THIS HIGHTOWER, "KNIGHT OF LIGHTNING OF THE ROYAL GUARDIANS." UH...
THAT WOULD BE DUKE?
MAKES SENSE— HE ALWAYS HAD A SOFT SPOT FOR SHINY STUFF.
is swords sliced through all manne
beheaded the Hightower became a kn
Once the Valley had been re
Legends claim that Hightower
with evil spirits like
THEY'RE KNIGHTS OF THE ROYAL GUARDIANS.
THE WARRIORS WHO FREED THE VALLEY OF DEMONS AND WHOSE SOULS REST IN THE KINGS' MAUSOLEUM.
RIGHT. SO...
THAT'S GREAT AND ALL...
...BUT HOW DOES IT HELP US?

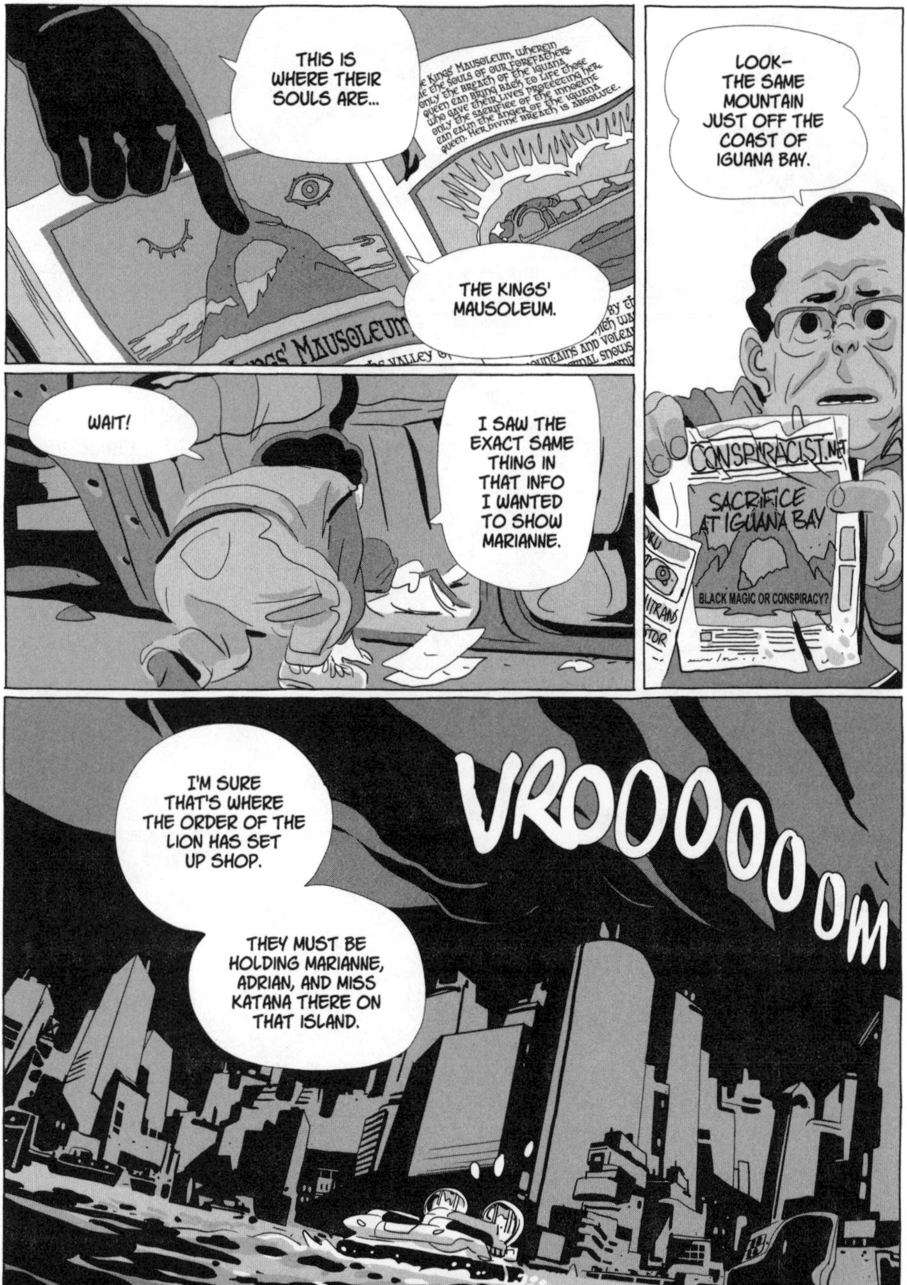
THIS IS WHERE THEIR SOULS ARE...
THE KINGS' MAUSOLEUM.
WAIT!
I SAW THE EXACT SAME THING IN THAT INFO I WANTED TO SHOW MARIANNE.
LOOK– THE SAME MOUNTAIN JUST OFF THE COAST OF IGUANA BAY.
CONSPIRACIST.NET
SACRIFICE AT IGUANA BAY
BLACK MAGIC OR CONSPIRACY?
I'M SURE THAT'S WHERE THE ORDER OF THE LION HAS SET UP SHOP.
THEY MUST BE HOLDING MARIANNE, ADRIAN, AND MISS KATANA THERE ON THAT ISLAND.
VROOOOOOOM

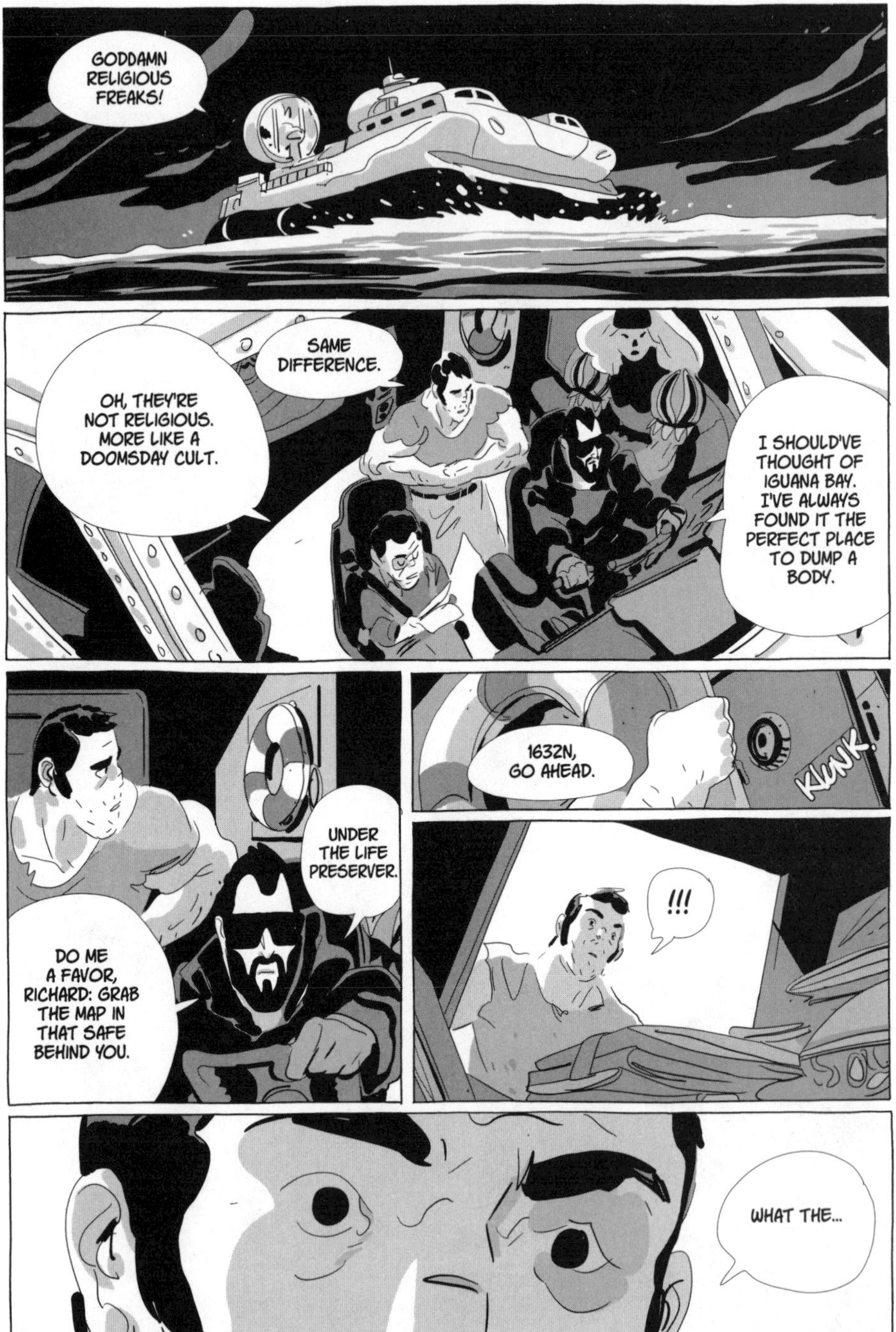
GODDAMN RELIGIOUS FREAKS!
OH, THEY'RE NOT RELIGIOUS. MORE LIKE A DOOMSDAY CULT.
SAME DIFFERENCE.
I SHOULD'VE THOUGHT OF IGUANA BAY. I'VE ALWAYS FOUND IT THE PERFECT PLACE TO DUMP A BODY.
DO ME A FAVOR, RICHARD: GRAB THE MAP IN THAT SAFE BEHIND YOU.
UNDER THE LIFE PRESERVER.
1632N, GO AHEAD.
KLUNK!
!!!
WHAT THE...

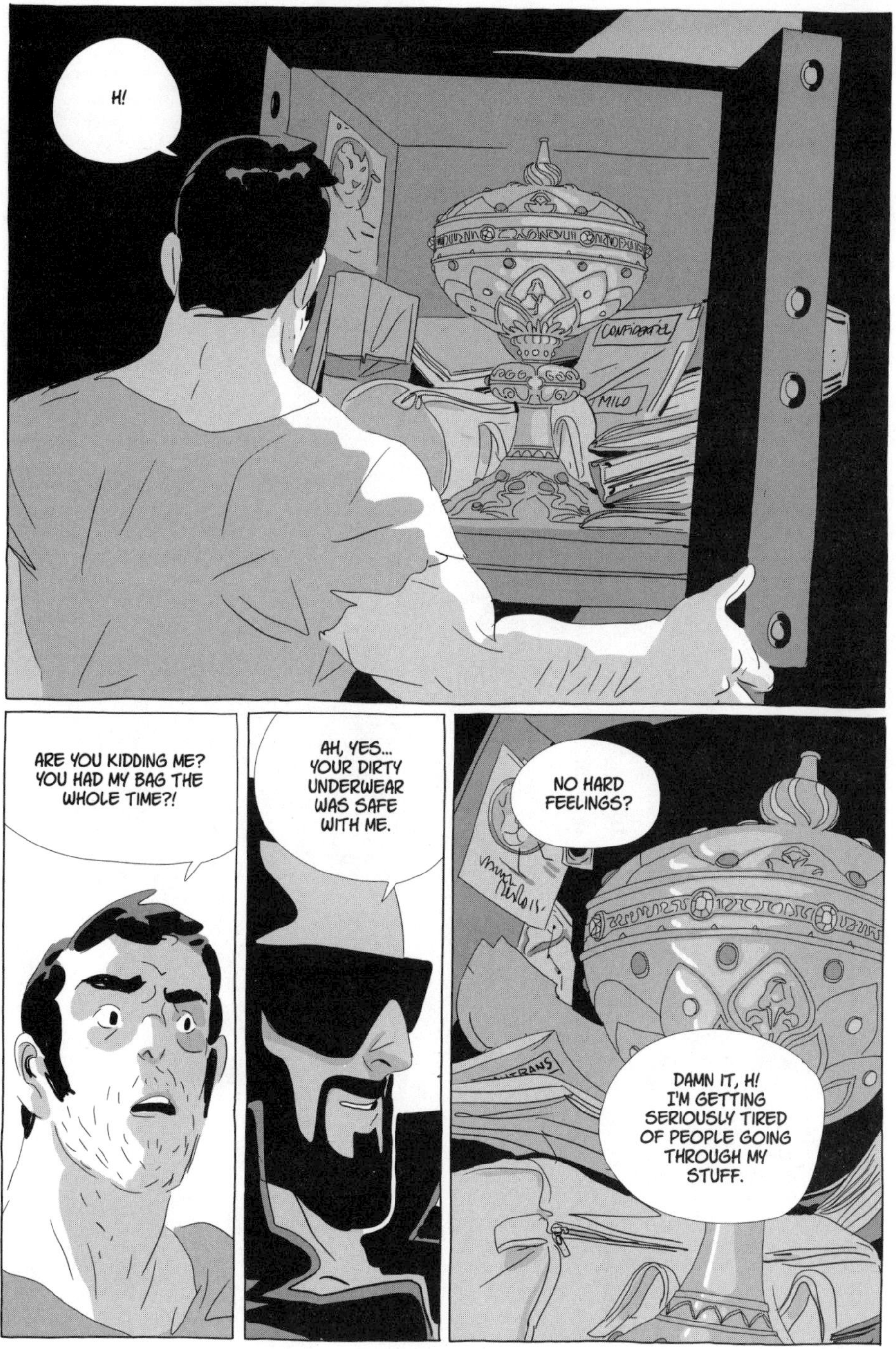
H!
ARE YOU KIDDING ME? YOU HAD MY BAG THE WHOLE TIME?!
AH, YES... YOUR DIRTY UNDERWEAR WAS SAFE WITH ME.
NO HARD FEELINGS?
DAMN IT, H! I'M GETTING SERIOUSLY TIRED OF PEOPLE GOING THROUGH MY STUFF.

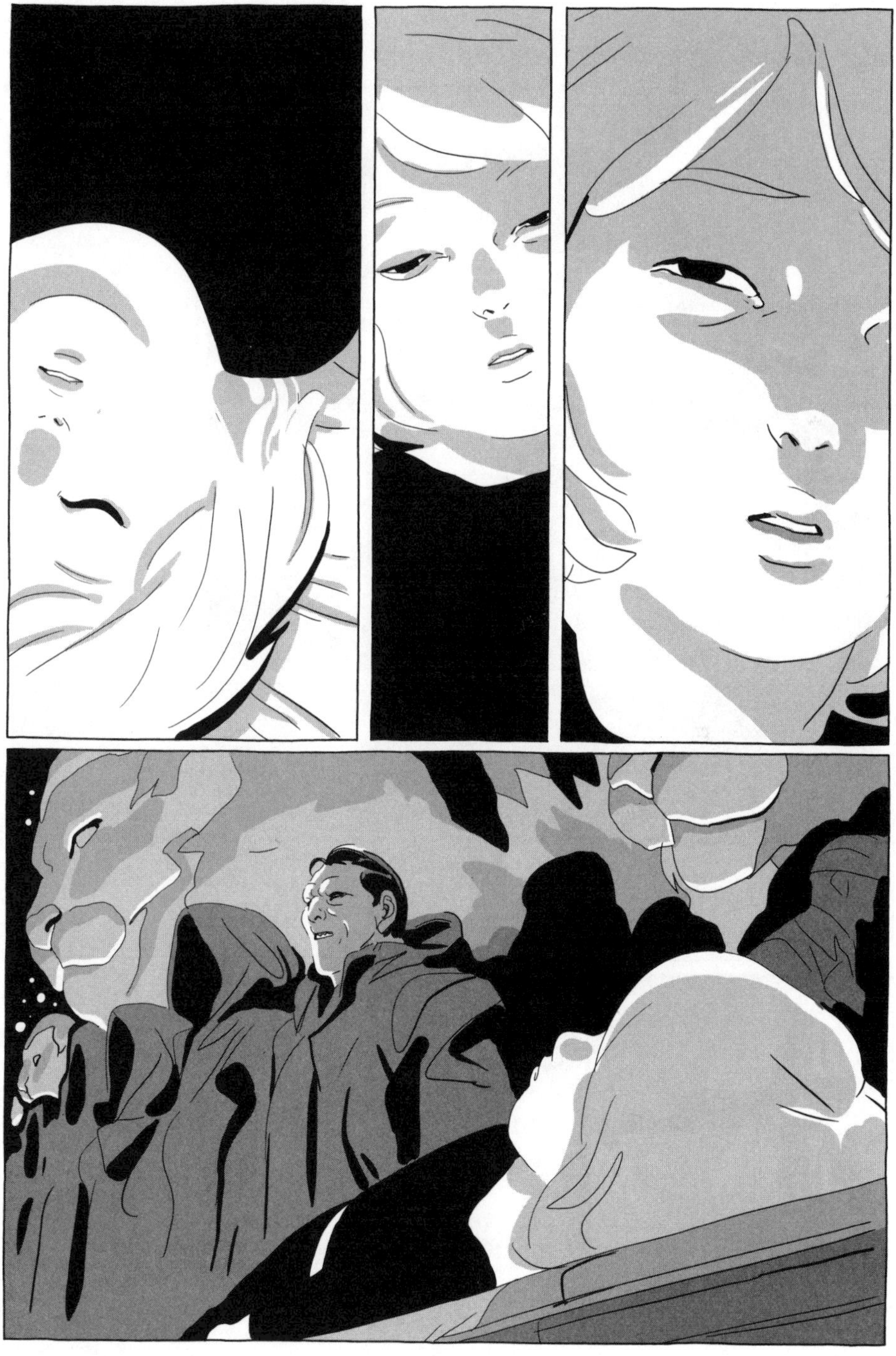

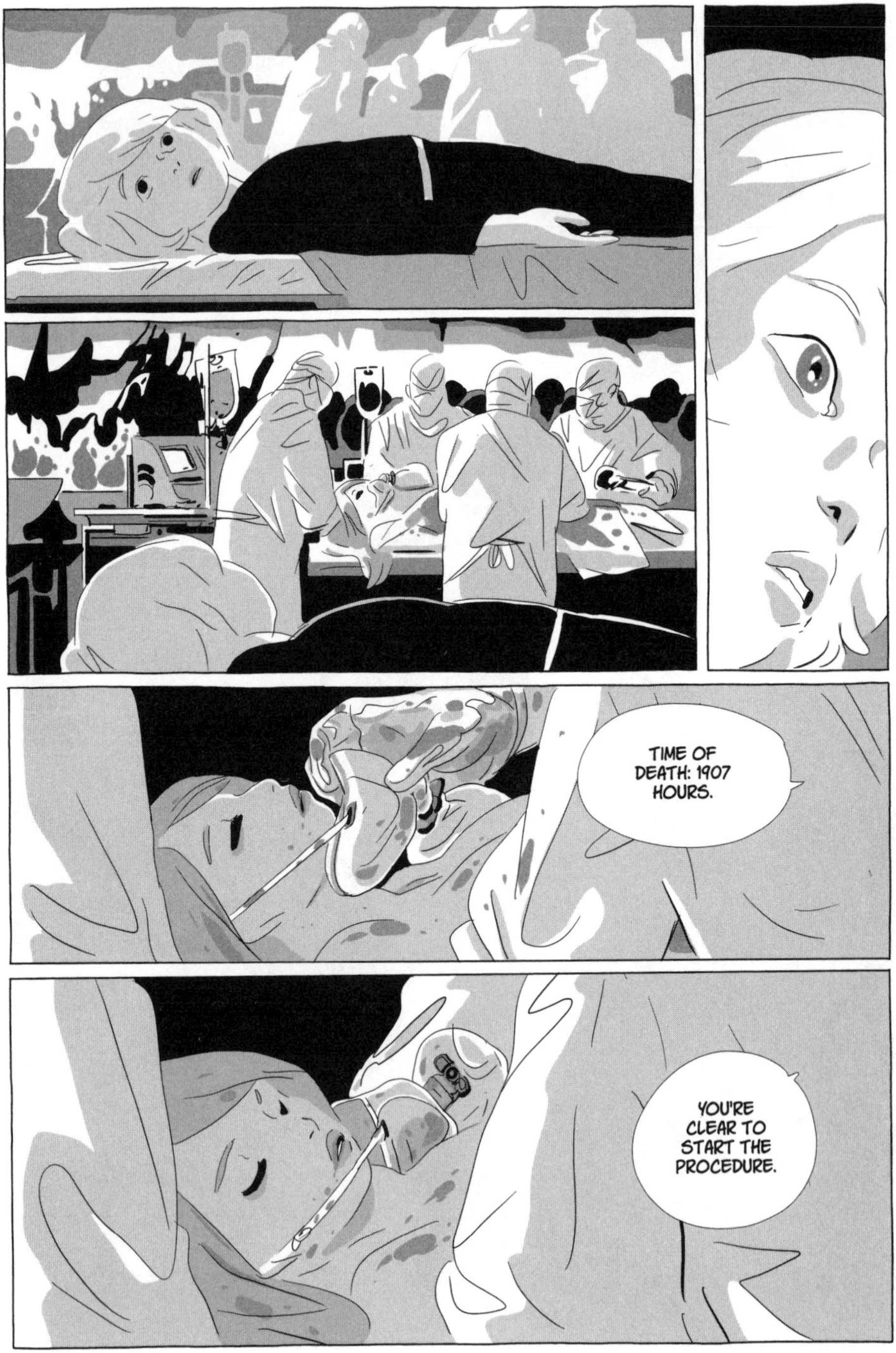
TIME OF DEATH: 1907 HOURS.
YOU'RE CLEAR TO START THE PROCEDURE.

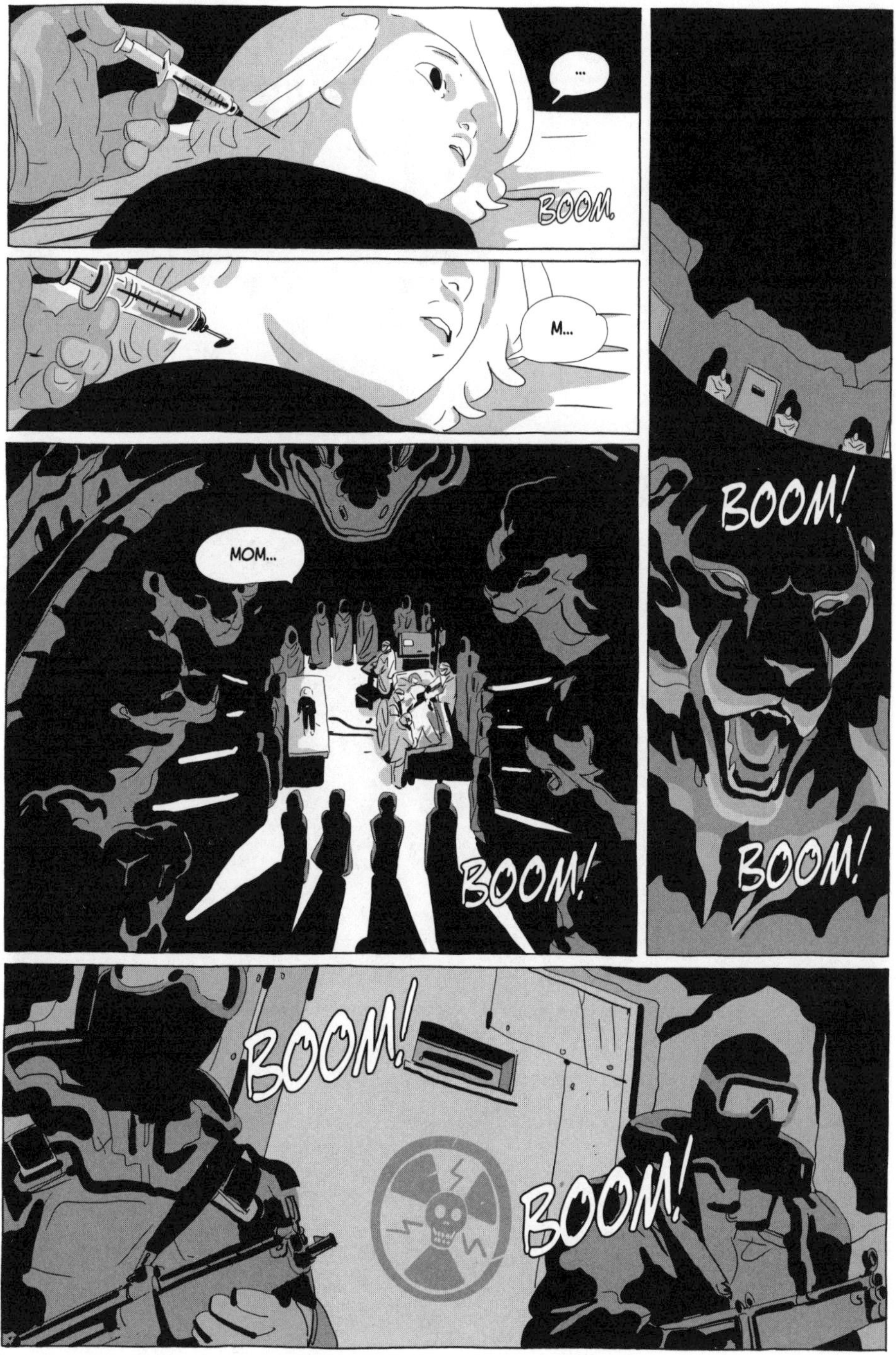
...
BOOM.
M...
MOM...
BOOM!
BOOM!
BOOM!
BOOM!
BOOM!

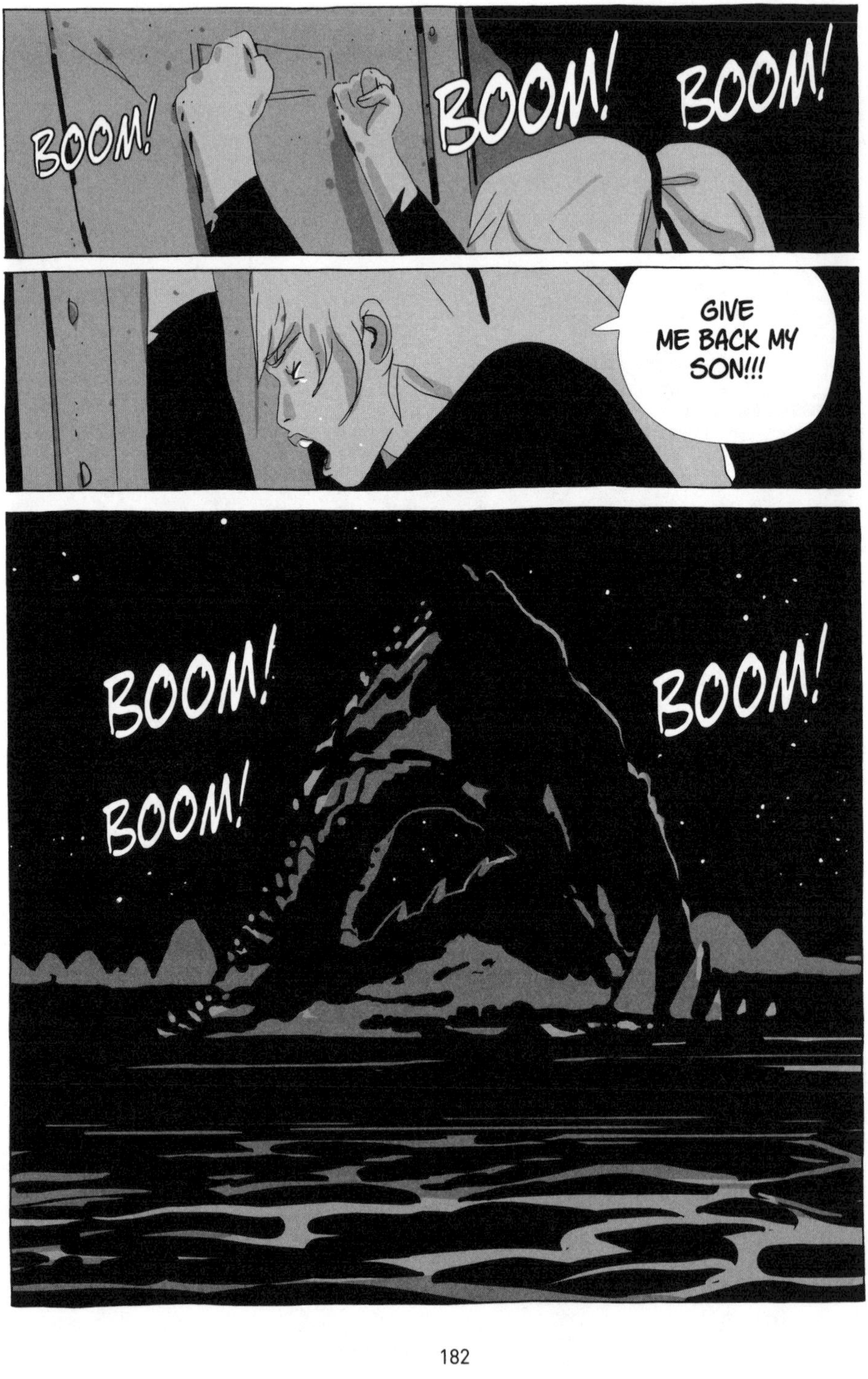
BOOM!
BOOM!
BOOM!
GIVE ME BACK MY SON!!!
BOOM!
BOOM!
BOOM!

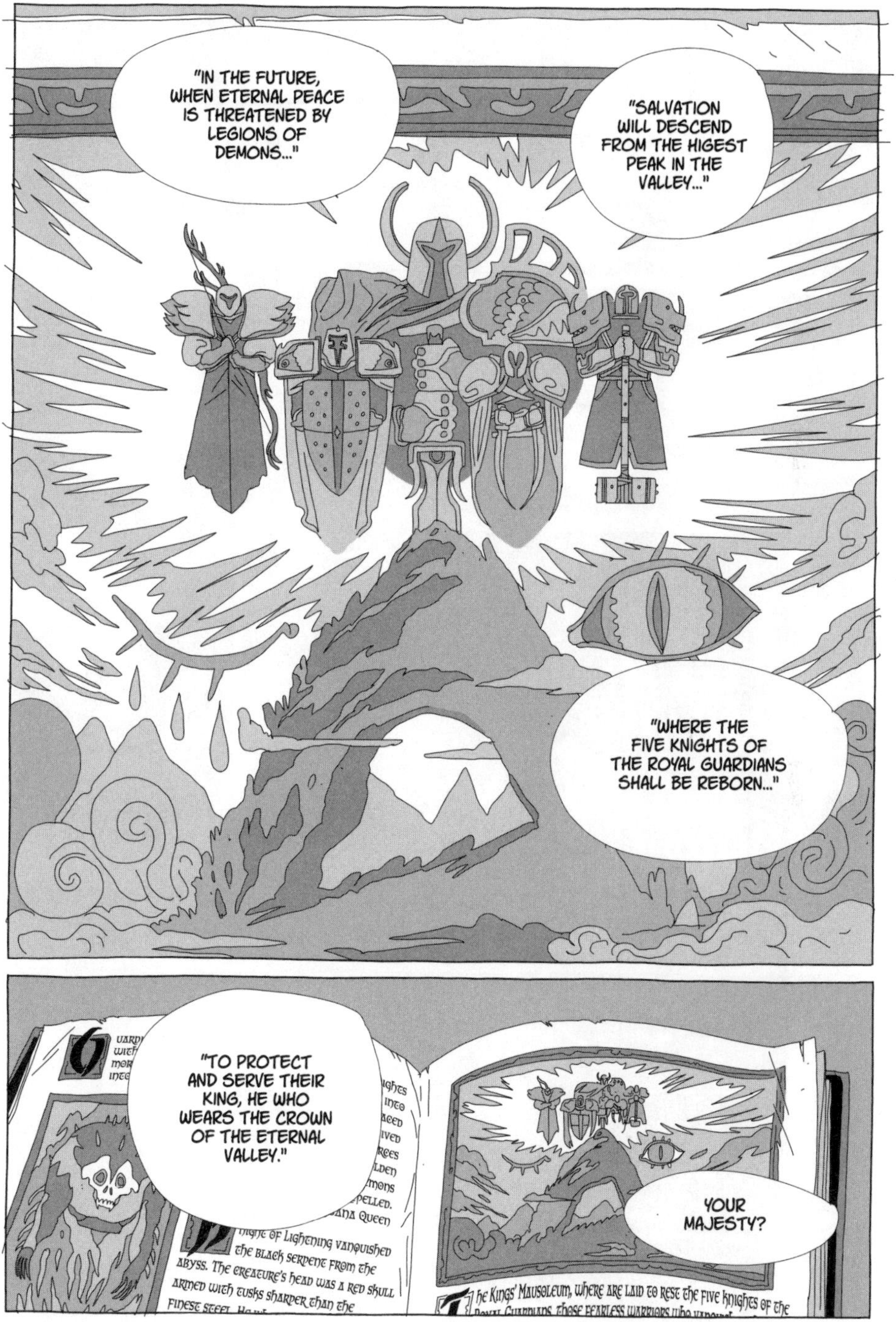
"IN THE FUTURE, WHEN ETERNAL PEACE IS THREATENED BY LEGIONS OF DEMONS..."
"SALVATION WILL DESCEND FROM THE HIGEST PEAK IN THE VALLEY..."
"WHERE THE FIVE KNIGHTS OF THE ROYAL GUARDIANS SHALL BE REBORN..."
"TO PROTECT AND SERVE THEIR KING, HE WHO WEARS THE CROWN OF THE ETERNAL VALLEY."
YOUR MAJESTY?
night of Lightning vanquished the black serpent from the abyss. The creature's head was a red skull armed with tusks sharper than the
The Kings' Mausoleum, where are laid to rest the five knights of the

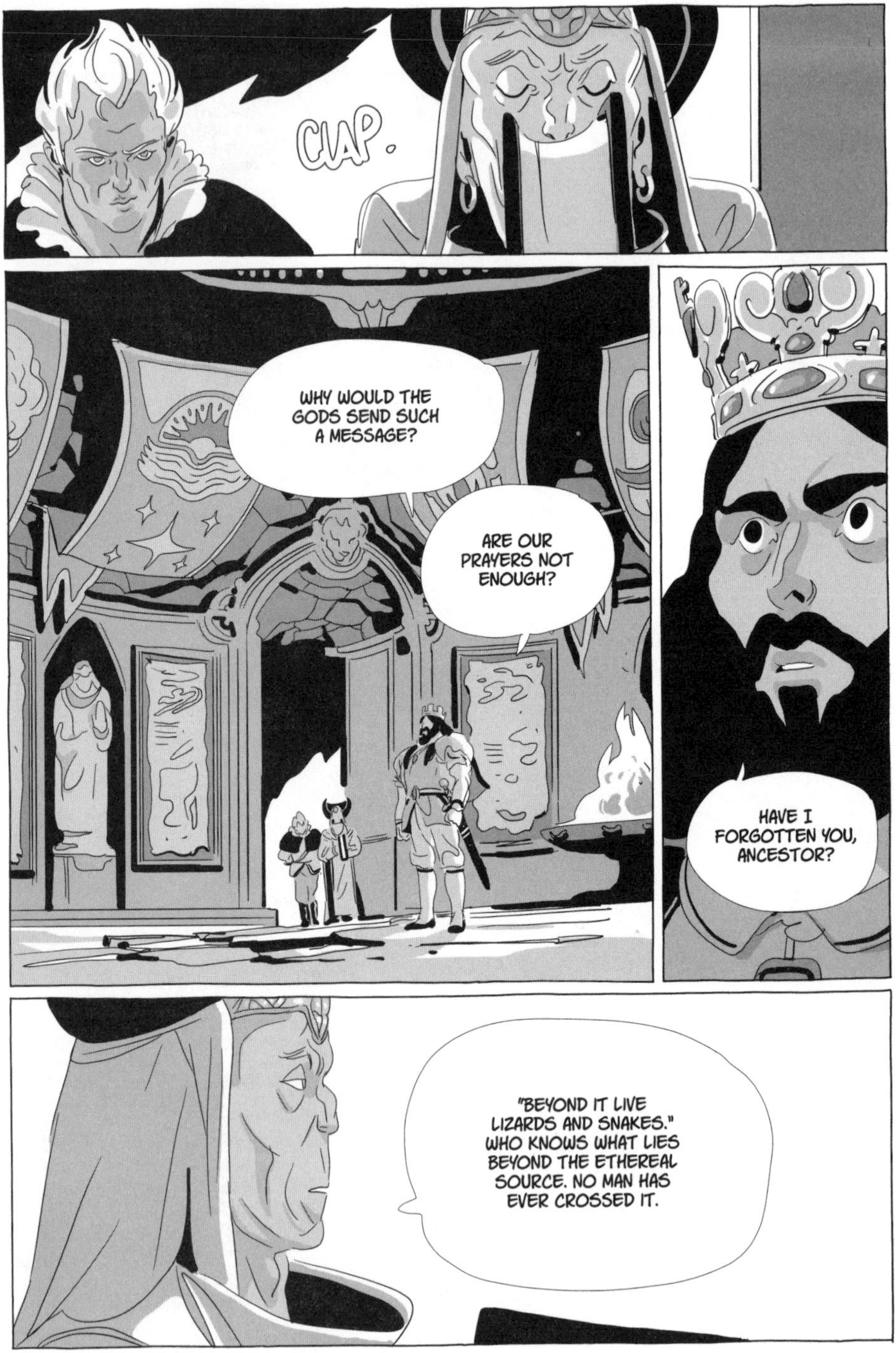
CLAP.
WHY WOULD THE GODS SEND SUCH A MESSAGE?
ARE OUR PRAYERS NOT ENOUGH?
HAVE I FORGOTTEN YOU, ANCESTOR?
"BEYOND IT LIVE LIZARDS AND SNAKES." WHO KNOWS WHAT LIES BEYOND THE ETHEREAL SOURCE. NO MAN HAS EVER CROSSED IT.

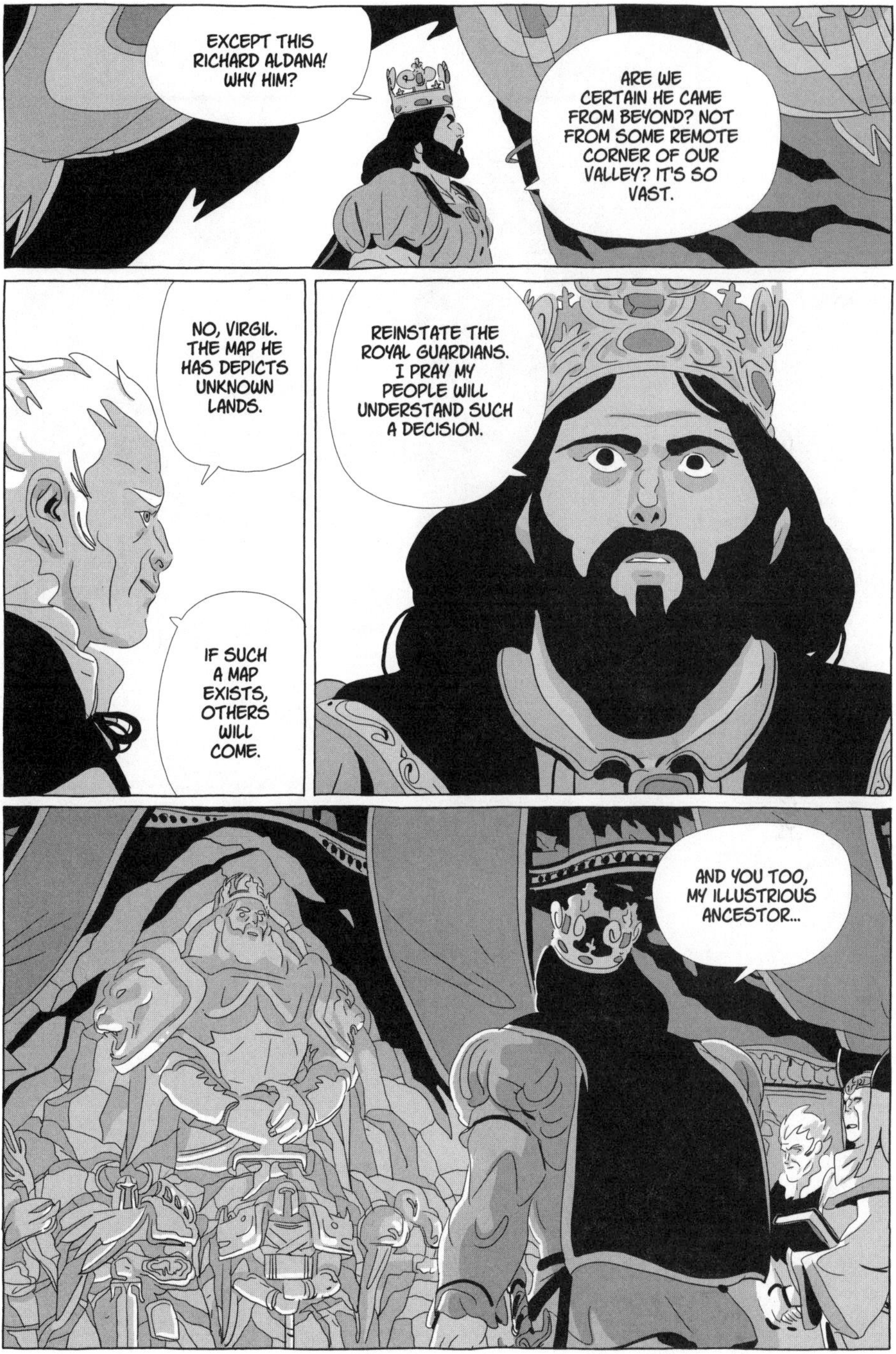

EXCEPT THIS RICHARD ALDANA! WHY HIM?
ARE WE CERTAIN HE CAME FROM BEYOND? NOT FROM SOME REMOTE CORNER OF OUR VALLEY? IT'S SO VAST.
NO, VIRGIL. THE MAP HE HAS DEPICTS UNKNOWN LANDS.
IF SUCH A MAP EXISTS, OTHERS WILL COME.
REINSTATE THE ROYAL GUARDIANS. I PRAY MY PEOPLE WILL UNDERSTAND SUCH A DECISION.
AND YOU TOO, MY ILLUSTRIOUS ANCESTOR...

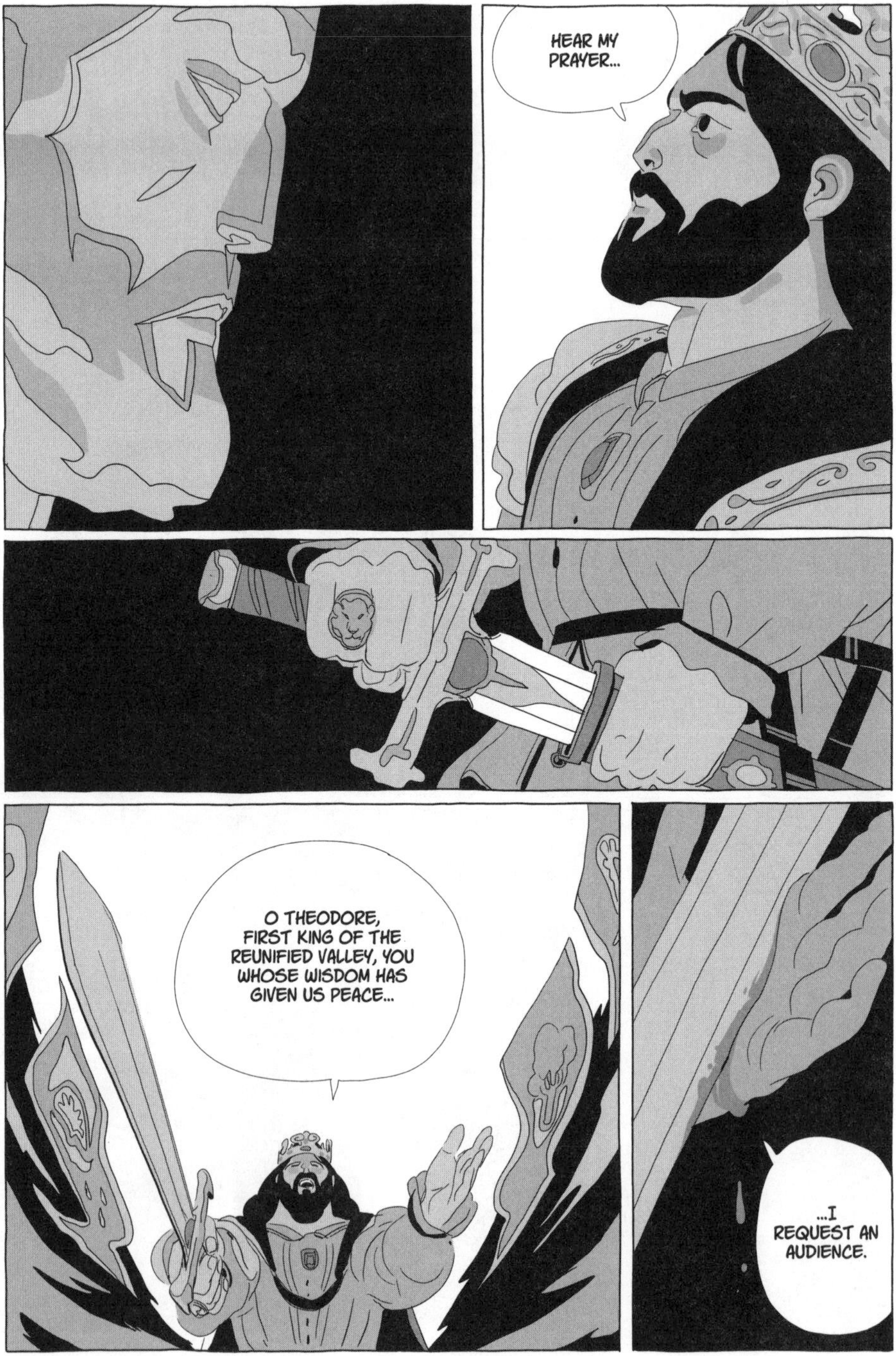
HEAR MY PRAYER...
O THEODORE, FIRST KING OF THE REUNIFIED VALLEY, YOU WHOSE WISDOM HAS GIVEN US PEACE...
...I REQUEST AN AUDIENCE.

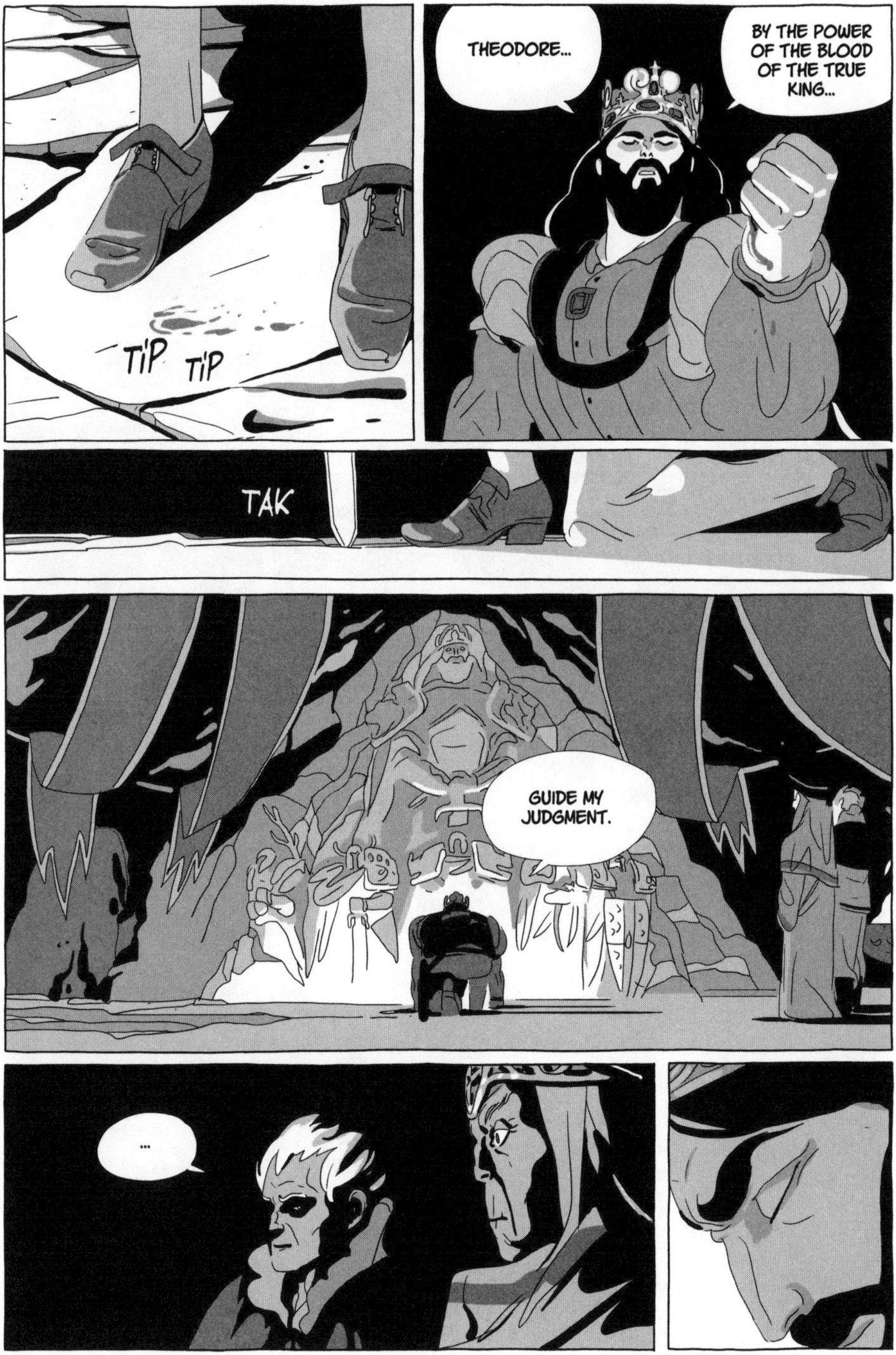
TIP TIP
THEODORE...
BY THE POWER OF THE BLOOD OF THE TRUE KING...
TAK
GUIDE MY JUDGMENT.
...

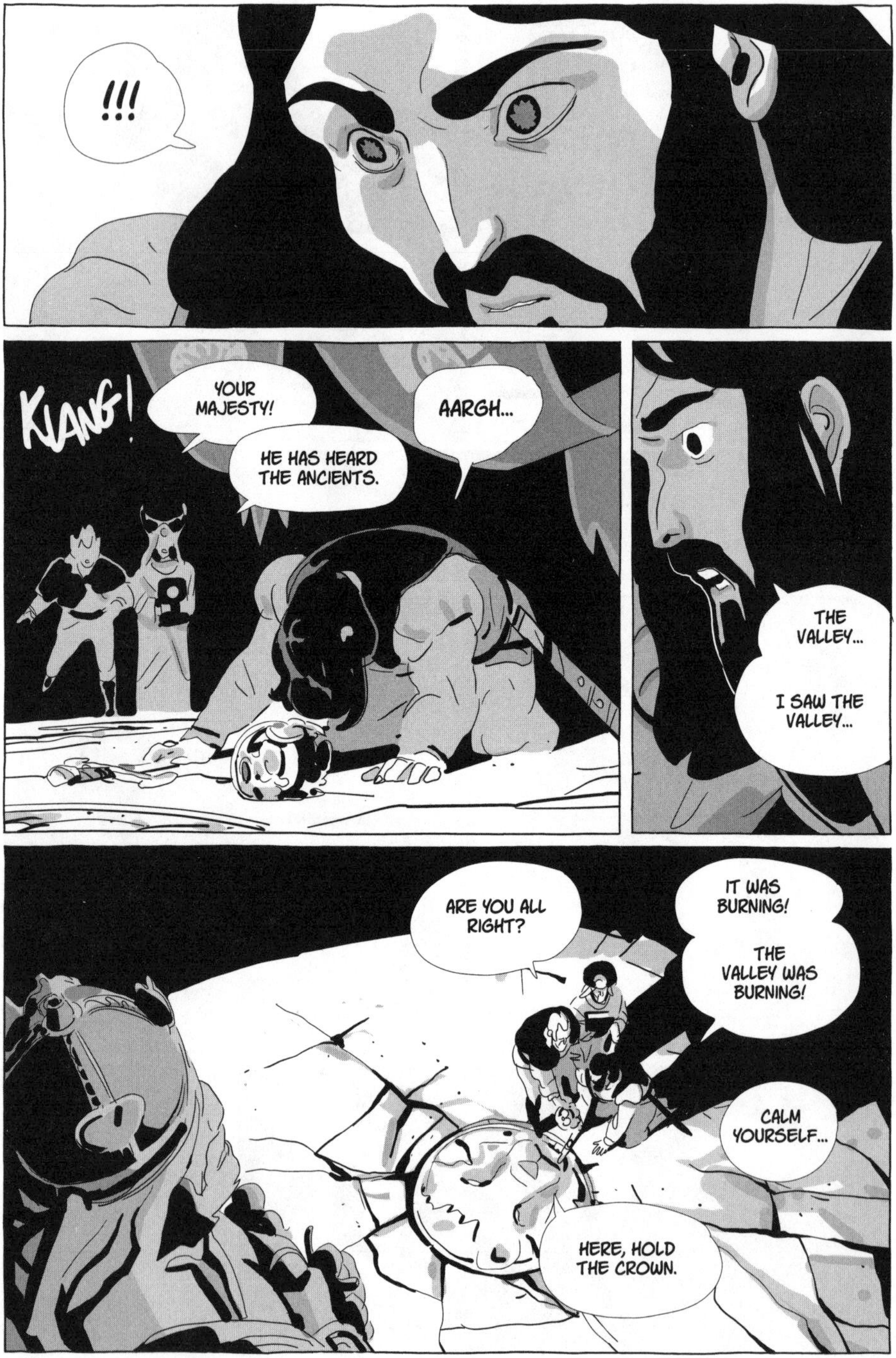
!!!
KLANG!
YOUR MAJESTY!
HE HAS HEARD THE ANCIENTS.
AARGH...
THE VALLEY...
I SAW THE VALLEY...
ARE YOU ALL RIGHT?
IT WAS BURNING!
THE VALLEY WAS BURNING!
CALM YOURSELF...
HERE, HOLD THE CROWN.

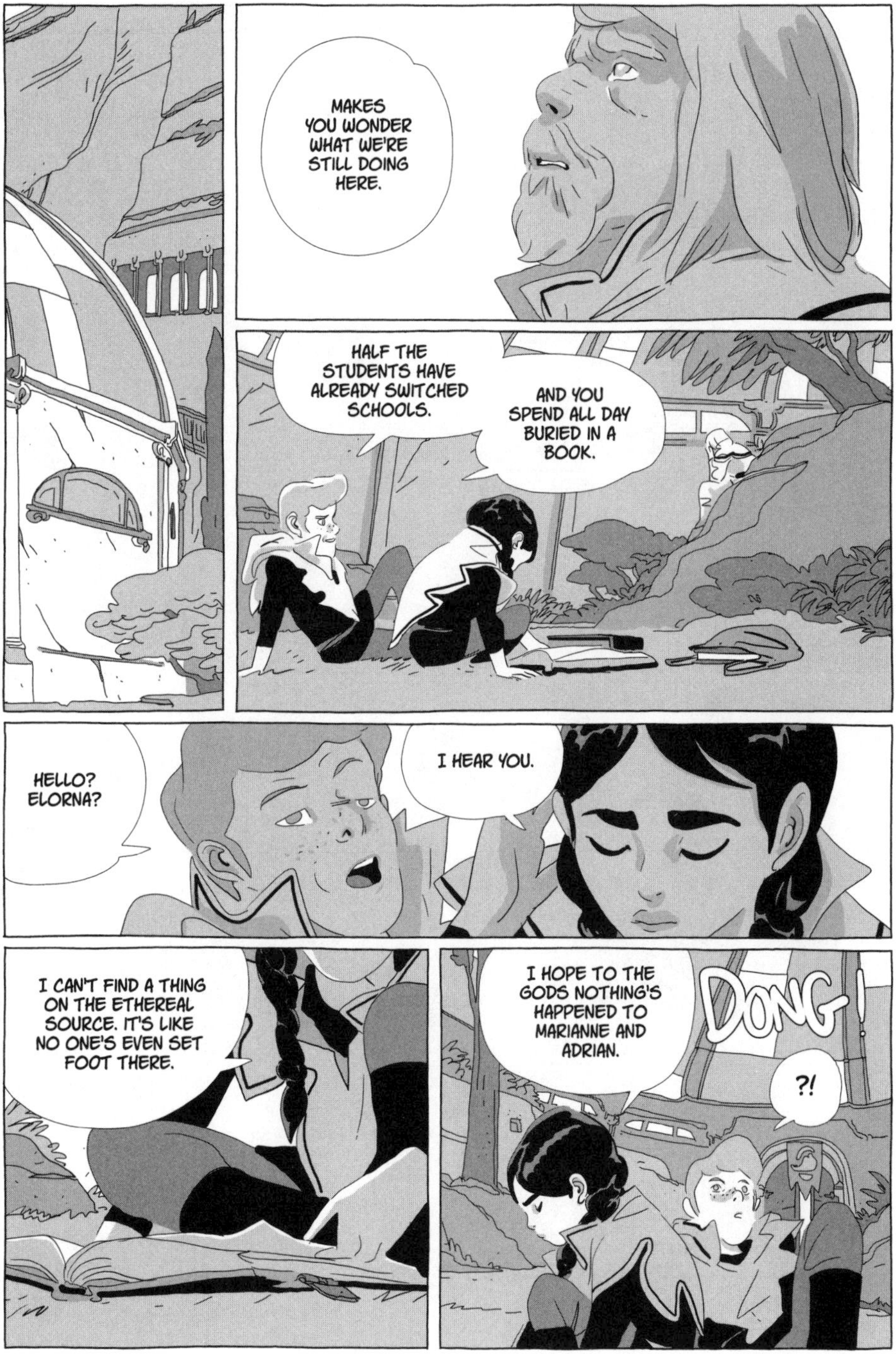
MAKES YOU WONDER WHAT WE'RE STILL DOING HERE.
HALF THE STUDENTS HAVE ALREADY SWITCHED SCHOOLS.
AND YOU SPEND ALL DAY BURIED IN A BOOK.
HELLO? ELORNA?
I HEAR YOU.
I CAN'T FIND A THING ON THE ETHEREAL SOURCE. IT'S LIKE NO ONE'S EVEN SET FOOT THERE.
I HOPE TO THE GODS NOTHING'S HAPPENED TO MARIANNE AND ADRIAN.
DONG!
?!

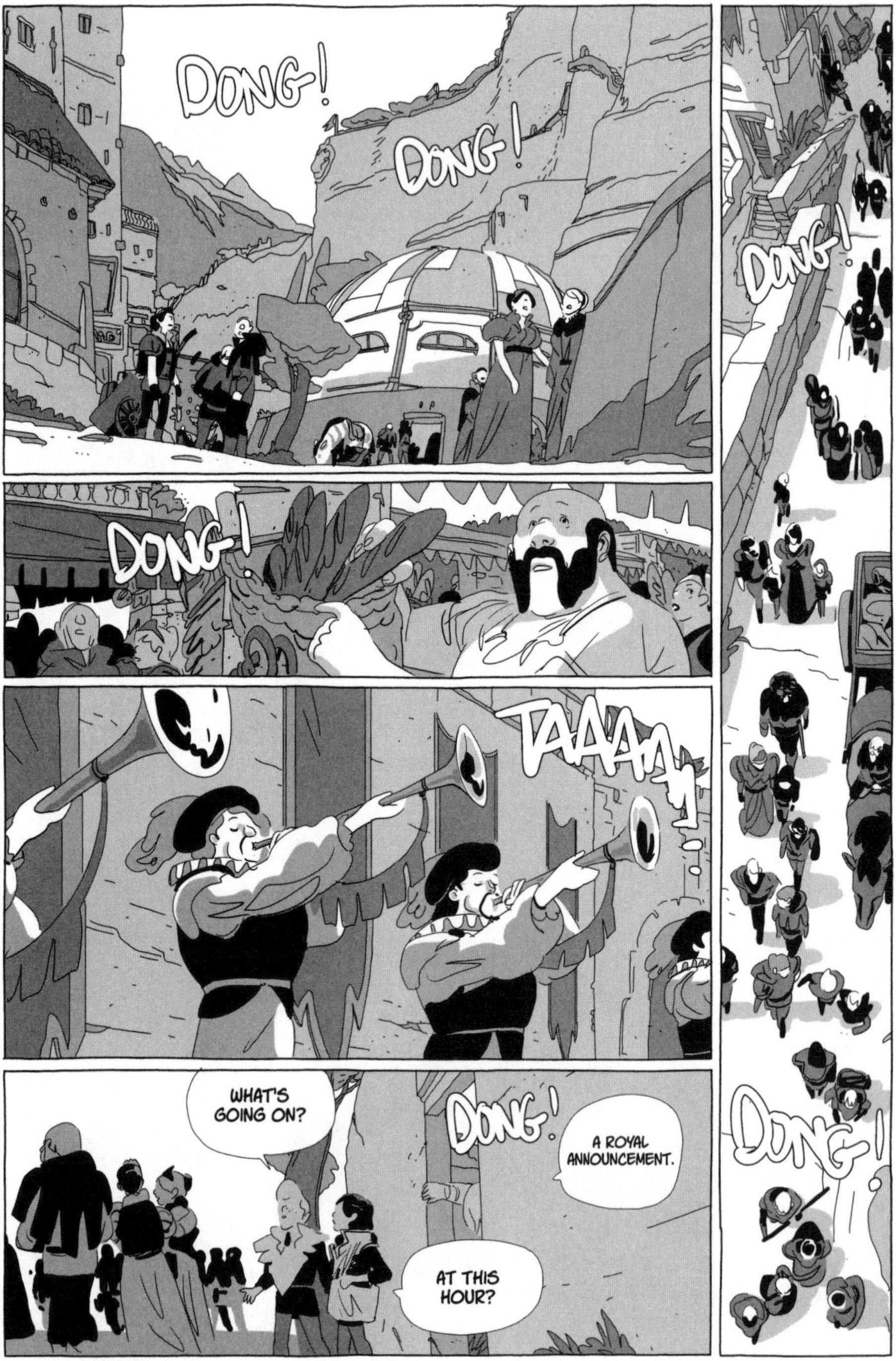
DONG!
DONG!
DONG!
TAAAAA!
WHAT'S GOING ON?
DONG!
A ROYAL ANNOUNCEMENT.
AT THIS HOUR?
DONG!
DONG!

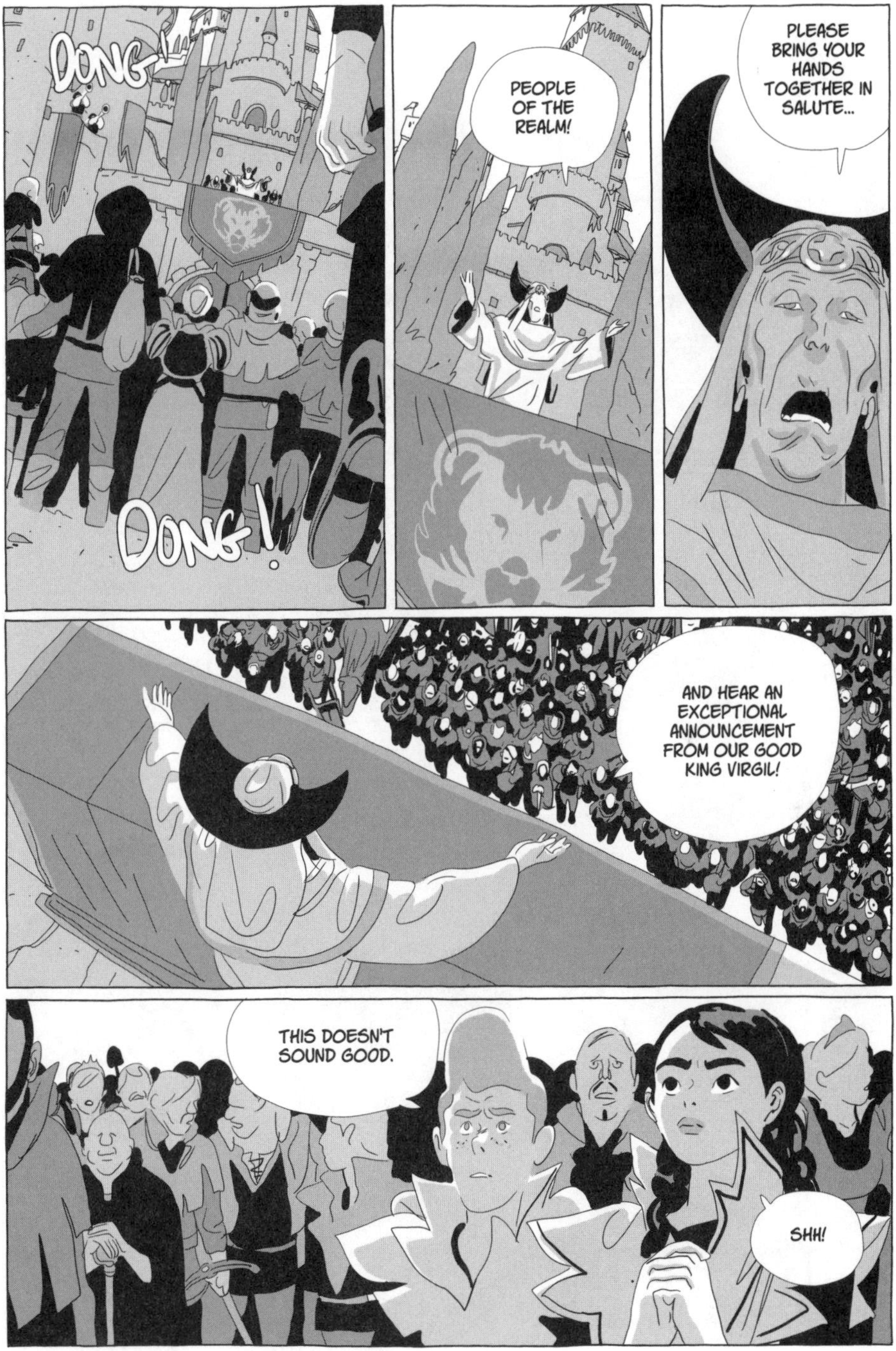
DONG!
DONG!
PEOPLE OF THE REALM!
PLEASE BRING YOUR HANDS TOGETHER IN SALUTE...
AND HEAR AN EXCEPTIONAL ANNOUNCEMENT FROM OUR GOOD KING VIRGIL!
THIS DOESN'T SOUND GOOD.
SHH!

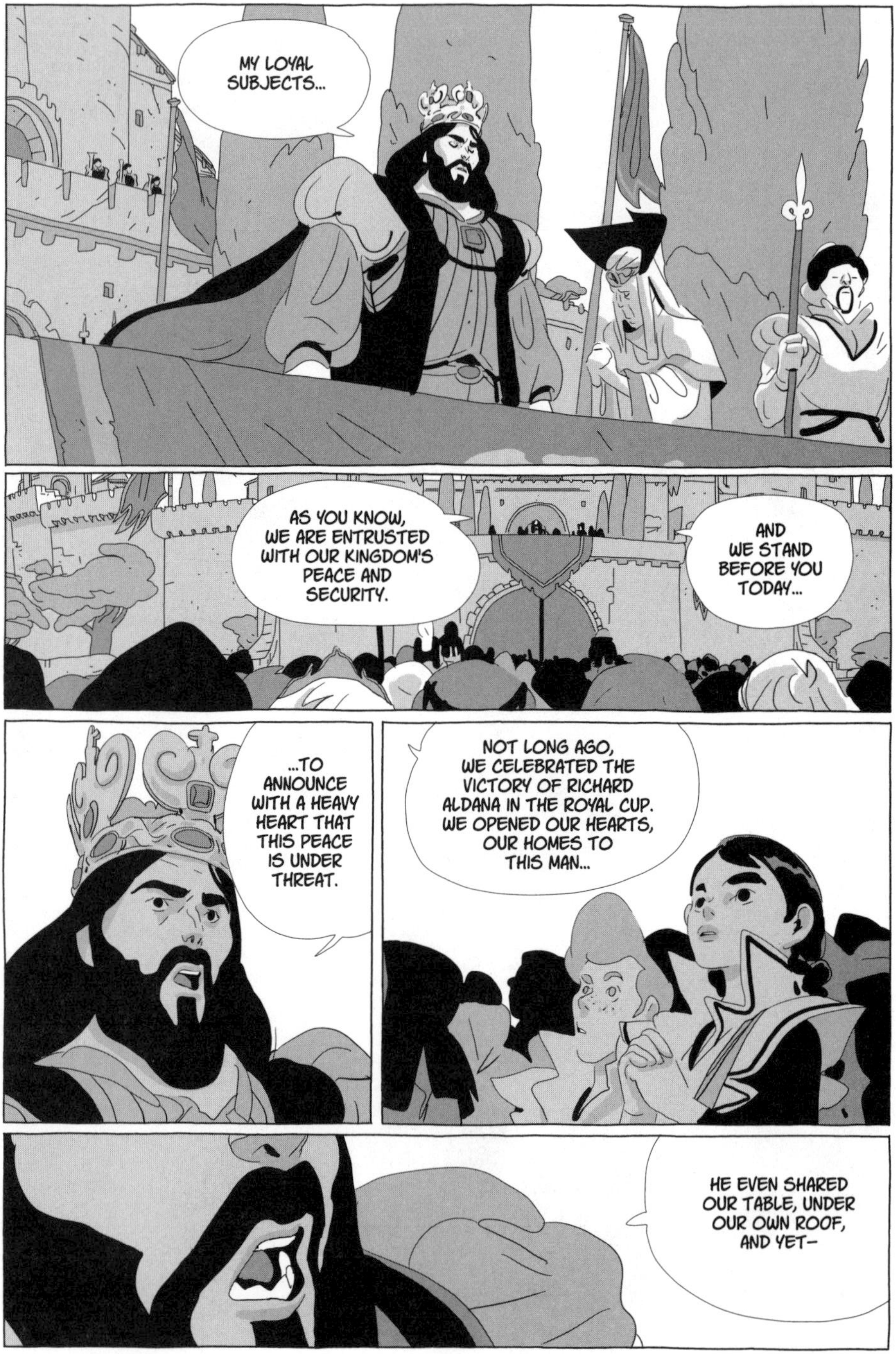
MY LOYAL SUBJECTS...
AS YOU KNOW, WE ARE ENTRUSTED WITH OUR KINGDOM'S PEACE AND SECURITY.
AND WE STAND BEFORE YOU TODAY...
...TO ANNOUNCE WITH A HEAVY HEART THAT THIS PEACE IS UNDER THREAT.
NOT LONG AGO, WE CELEBRATED THE VICTORY OF RICHARD ALDANA IN THE ROYAL CUP. WE OPENED OUR HEARTS, OUR HOMES TO THIS MAN...
HE EVEN SHARED OUR TABLE, UNDER OUR OWN ROOF, AND YET—

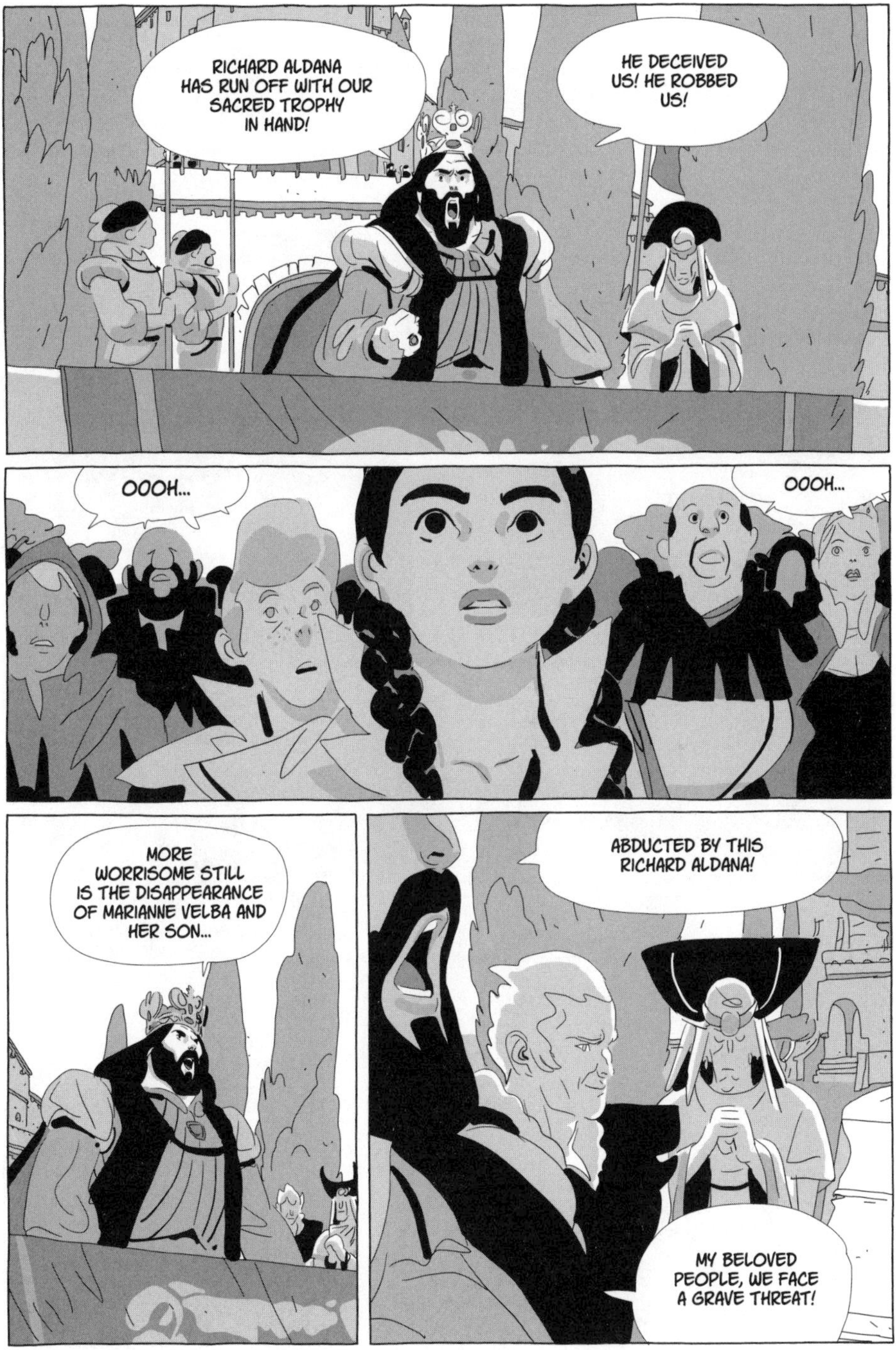
RICHARD ALDANA HAS RUN OFF WITH OUR SACRED TROPHY IN HAND!
HE DECEIVED US! HE ROBBED US!
OOOH...
OOOH...
MORE WORRISOME STILL IS THE DISAPPEARANCE OF MARIANNE VELBA AND HER SON...
ABDUCTED BY THIS RICHARD ALDANA!
MY BELOVED PEOPLE, WE FACE A GRAVE THREAT!

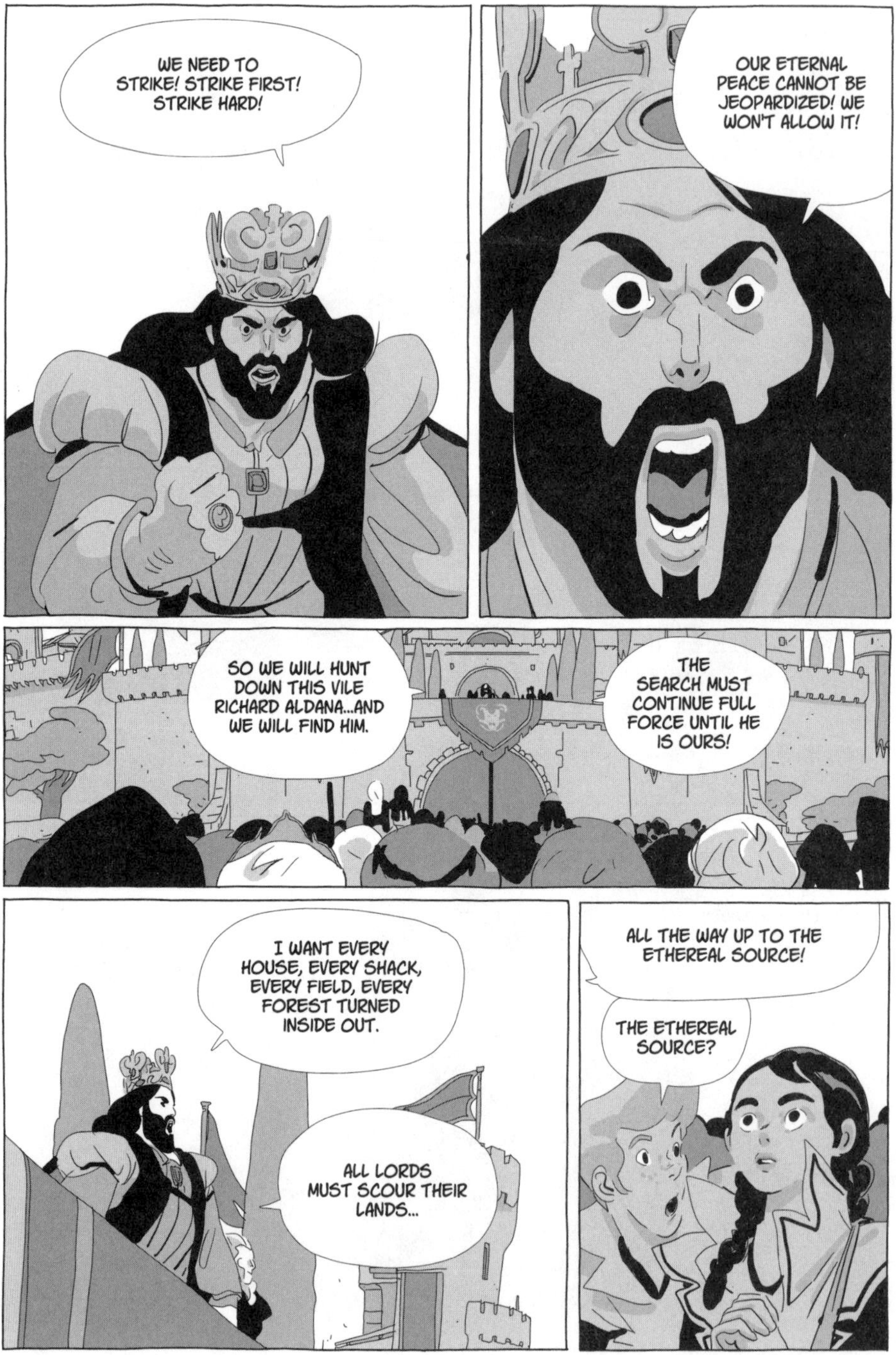
WE NEED TO STRIKE! STRIKE FIRST! STRIKE HARD!
OUR ETERNAL PEACE CANNOT BE JEOPARDIZED! WE WON'T ALLOW IT!
SO WE WILL HUNT DOWN THIS VILE RICHARD ALDANA...AND WE WILL FIND HIM.
THE SEARCH MUST CONTINUE FULL FORCE UNTIL HE IS OURS!
I WANT EVERY HOUSE, EVERY SHACK, EVERY FIELD, EVERY FOREST TURNED INSIDE OUT.
ALL LORDS MUST SCOUR THEIR LANDS...
ALL THE WAY UP TO THE ETHEREAL SOURCE!
THE ETHEREAL SOURCE?

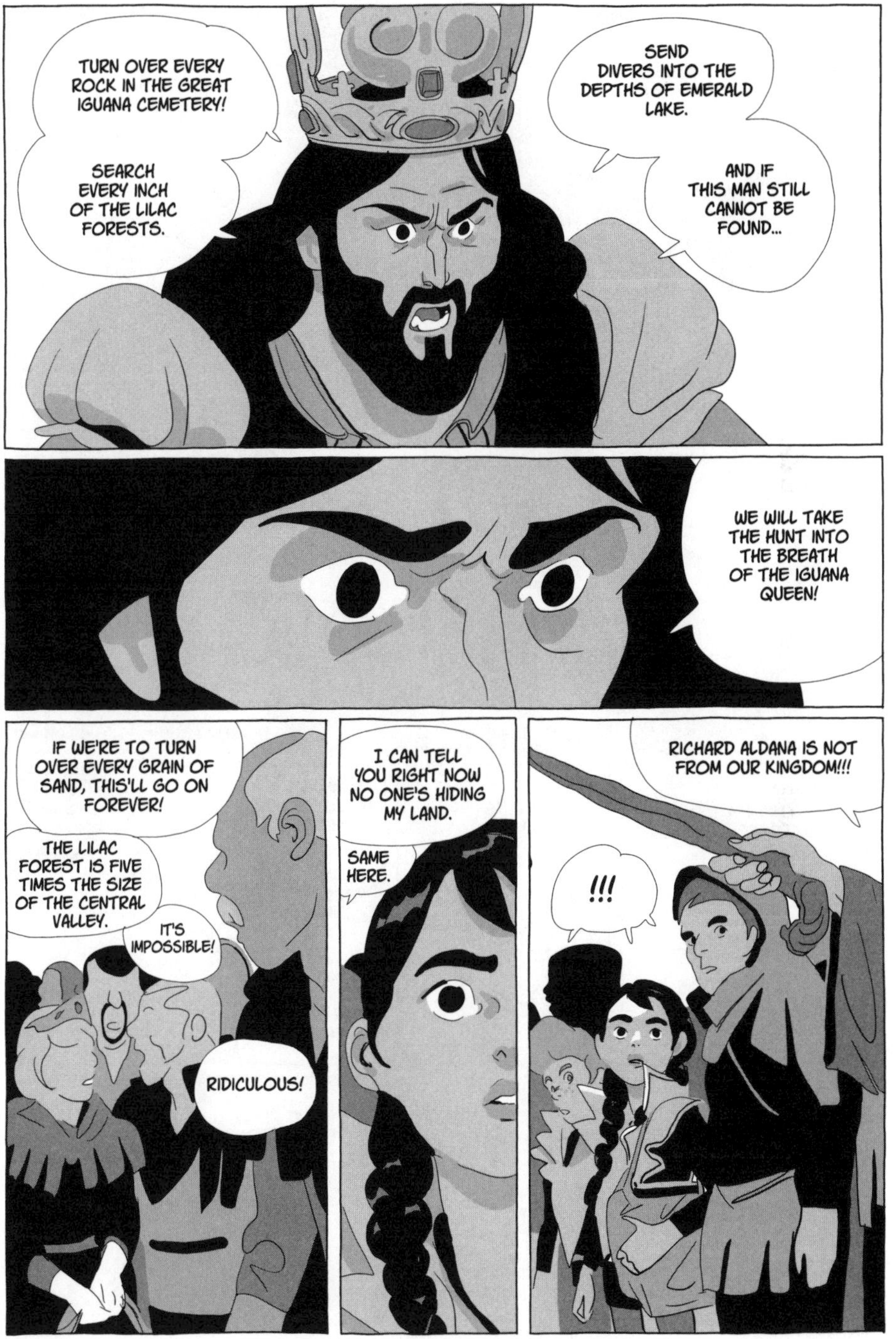

TURN OVER EVERY ROCK IN THE GREAT IGUANA CEMETERY!
SEARCH EVERY INCH OF THE LILAC FORESTS.
SEND DIVERS INTO THE DEPTHS OF EMERALD LAKE.
AND IF THIS MAN STILL CANNOT BE FOUND...
WE WILL TAKE THE HUNT INTO THE BREATH OF THE IGUANA QUEEN!
IF WE'RE TO TURN OVER EVERY GRAIN OF SAND, THIS'LL GO ON FOREVER!
THE LILAC FOREST IS FIVE TIMES THE SIZE OF THE CENTRAL VALLEY.
IT'S IMPOSSIBLE!
RIDICULOUS!
I CAN TELL YOU RIGHT NOW NO ONE'S HIDING MY LAND.
SAME HERE.
RICHARD ALDANA IS NOT FROM OUR KINGDOM!!!
!!!

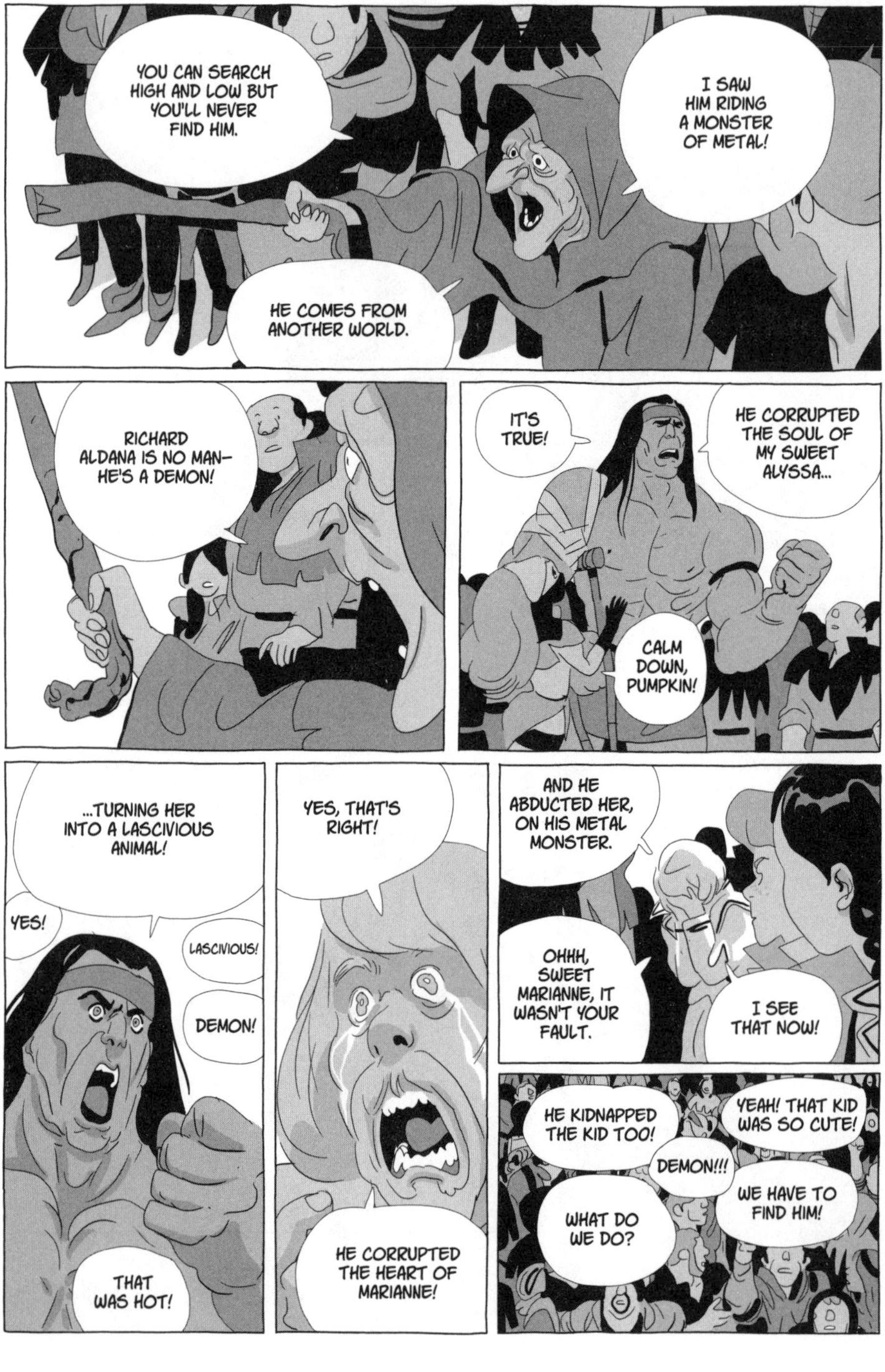
YOU CAN SEARCH HIGH AND LOW BUT YOU'LL NEVER FIND HIM.
I SAW HIM RIDING A MONSTER OF METAL!
HE COMES FROM ANOTHER WORLD.
RICHARD ALDANA IS NO MAN-HE'S A DEMON!
IT'S TRUE!
HE CORRUPTED THE SOUL OF MY SWEET ALYSSA...
CALM DOWN, PUMPKIN!
...TURNING HER INTO A LASCIVIOUS ANIMAL!
YES!
LASCIVIOUS!
DEMON!
THAT WAS HOT!
YES, THAT'S RIGHT!
HE CORRUPTED THE HEART OF MARIANNE!
AND HE ABDUCTED HER, ON HIS METAL MONSTER.
OHHH, SWEET MARIANNE, IT WASN'T YOUR FAULT.
I SEE THAT NOW!
HE KIDNAPPED THE KID TOO!
YEAH! THAT KID WAS SO CUTE!
DEMON!!!
WHAT DO WE DO?
WE HAVE TO FIND HIM!

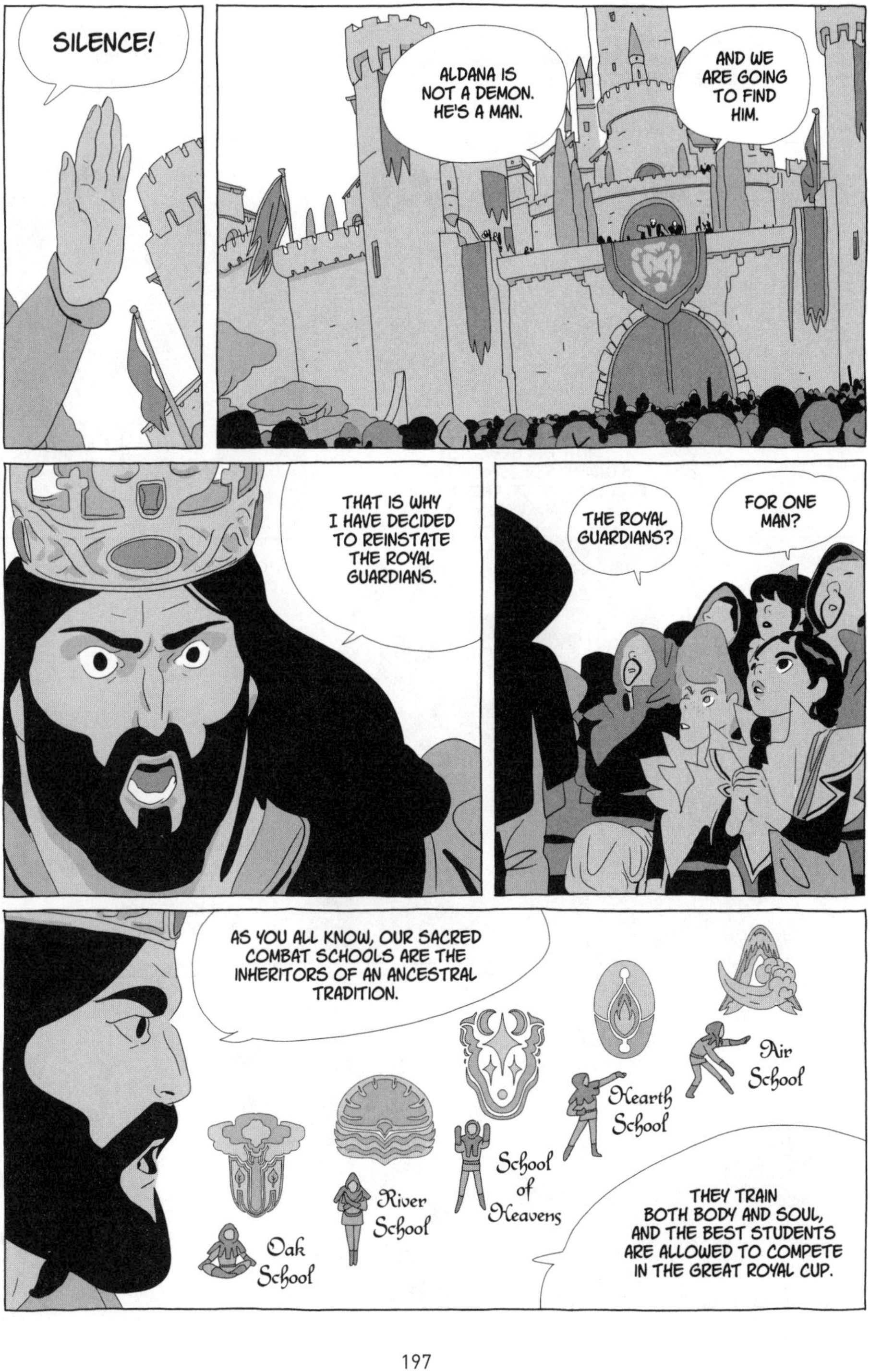
SILENCE!
ALDANA IS NOT A DEMON. HE'S A MAN.
AND WE ARE GOING TO FIND HIM.
THAT IS WHY I HAVE DECIDED TO REINSTATE THE ROYAL GUARDIANS.
THE ROYAL GUARDIANS?
FOR ONE MAN?
AS YOU ALL KNOW, OUR SACRED COMBAT SCHOOLS ARE THE INHERITORS OF AN ANCESTRAL TRADITION.
Oak School
River School
School of Heavens
Hearth School
Air School
THEY TRAIN BOTH BODY AND SOUL, AND THE BEST STUDENTS ARE ALLOWED TO COMPETE IN THE GREAT ROYAL CUP.

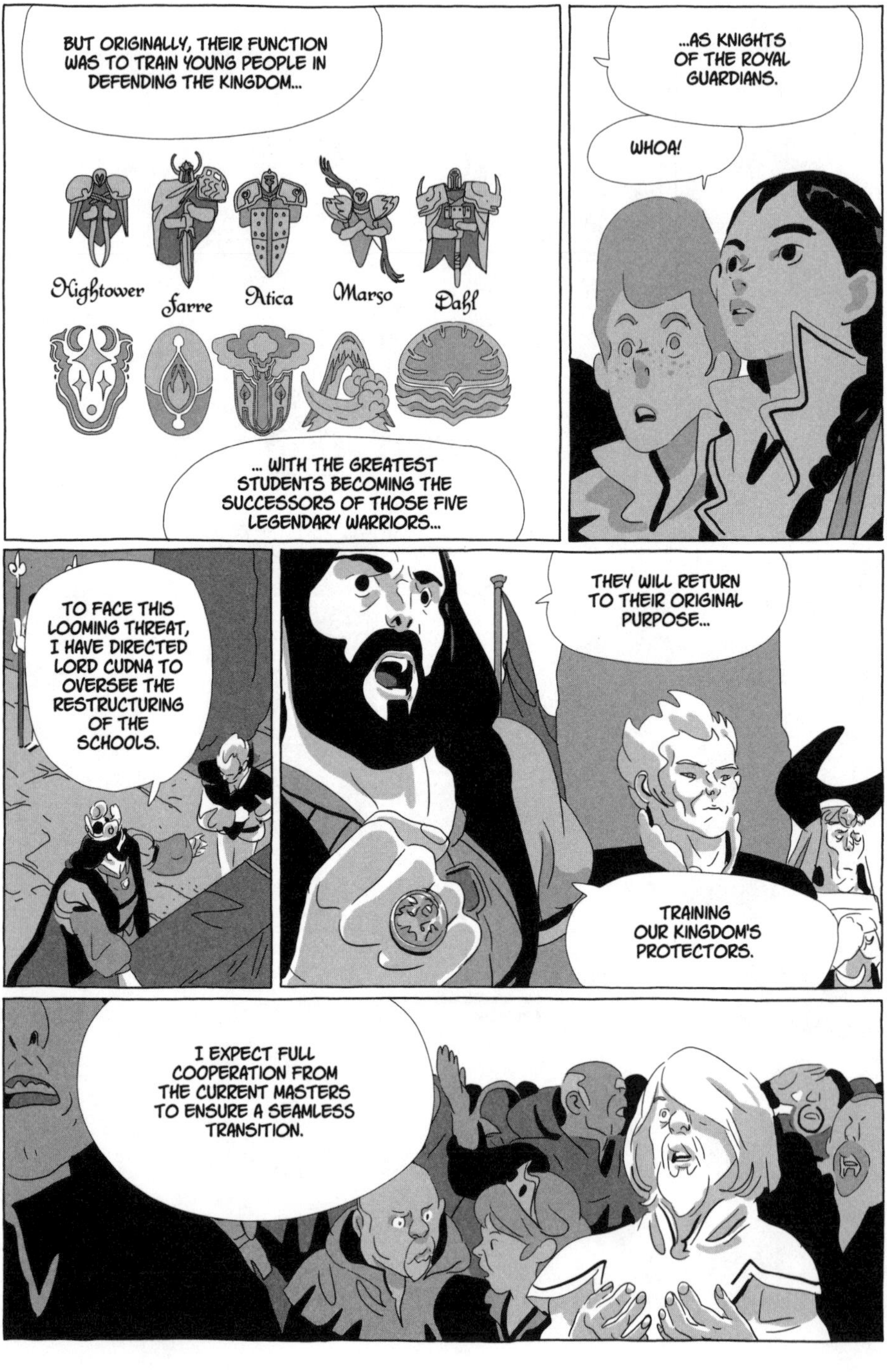
BUT ORIGINALLY, THEIR FUNCTION WAS TO TRAIN YOUNG PEOPLE IN DEFENDING THE KINGDOM...
Hightower
Farre
Atica
Marso
Dahl
... WITH THE GREATEST STUDENTS BECOMING THE SUCCESSORS OF THOSE FIVE LEGENDARY WARRIORS...
...AS KNIGHTS OF THE ROYAL GUARDIANS.
WHOA!
TO FACE THIS LOOMING THREAT, I HAVE DIRECTED LORD CUDNA TO OVERSEE THE RESTRUCTURING OF THE SCHOOLS.
THEY WILL RETURN TO THEIR ORIGINAL PURPOSE...
TRAINING OUR KINGDOM'S PROTECTORS.
I EXPECT FULL COOPERATION FROM THE CURRENT MASTERS TO ENSURE A SEAMLESS TRANSITION.

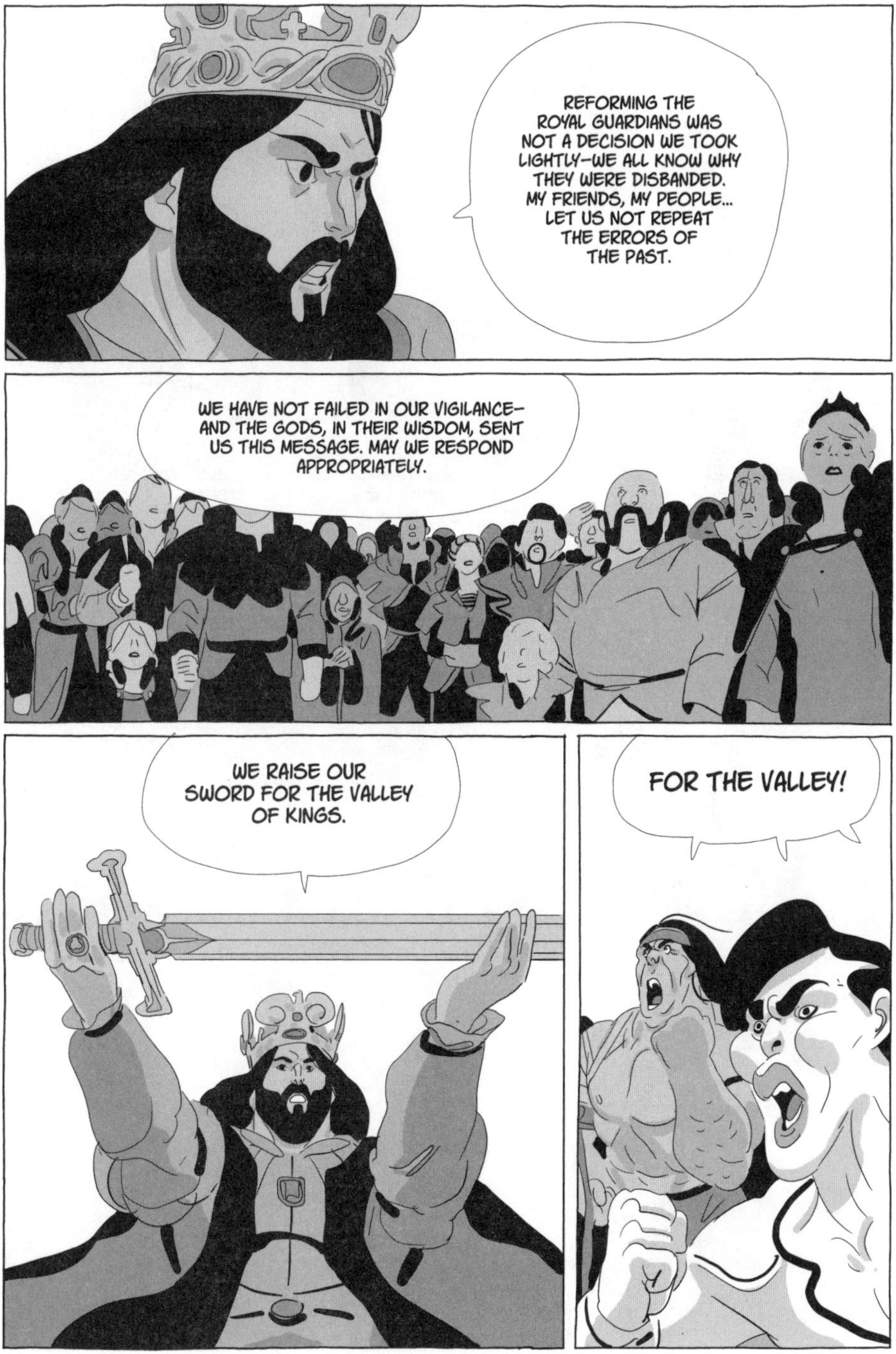
REFORMING THE ROYAL GUARDIANS WAS NOT A DECISION WE TOOK LIGHTLY—WE ALL KNOW WHY THEY WERE DISBANDED. MY FRIENDS, MY PEOPLE... LET US NOT REPEAT THE ERRORS OF THE PAST.
WE HAVE NOT FAILED IN OUR VIGILANCE—AND THE GODS, IN THEIR WISDOM, SENT US THIS MESSAGE. MAY WE RESPOND APPROPRIATELY.
WE RAISE OUR SWORD FOR THE VALLEY OF KINGS.
FOR THE VALLEY!

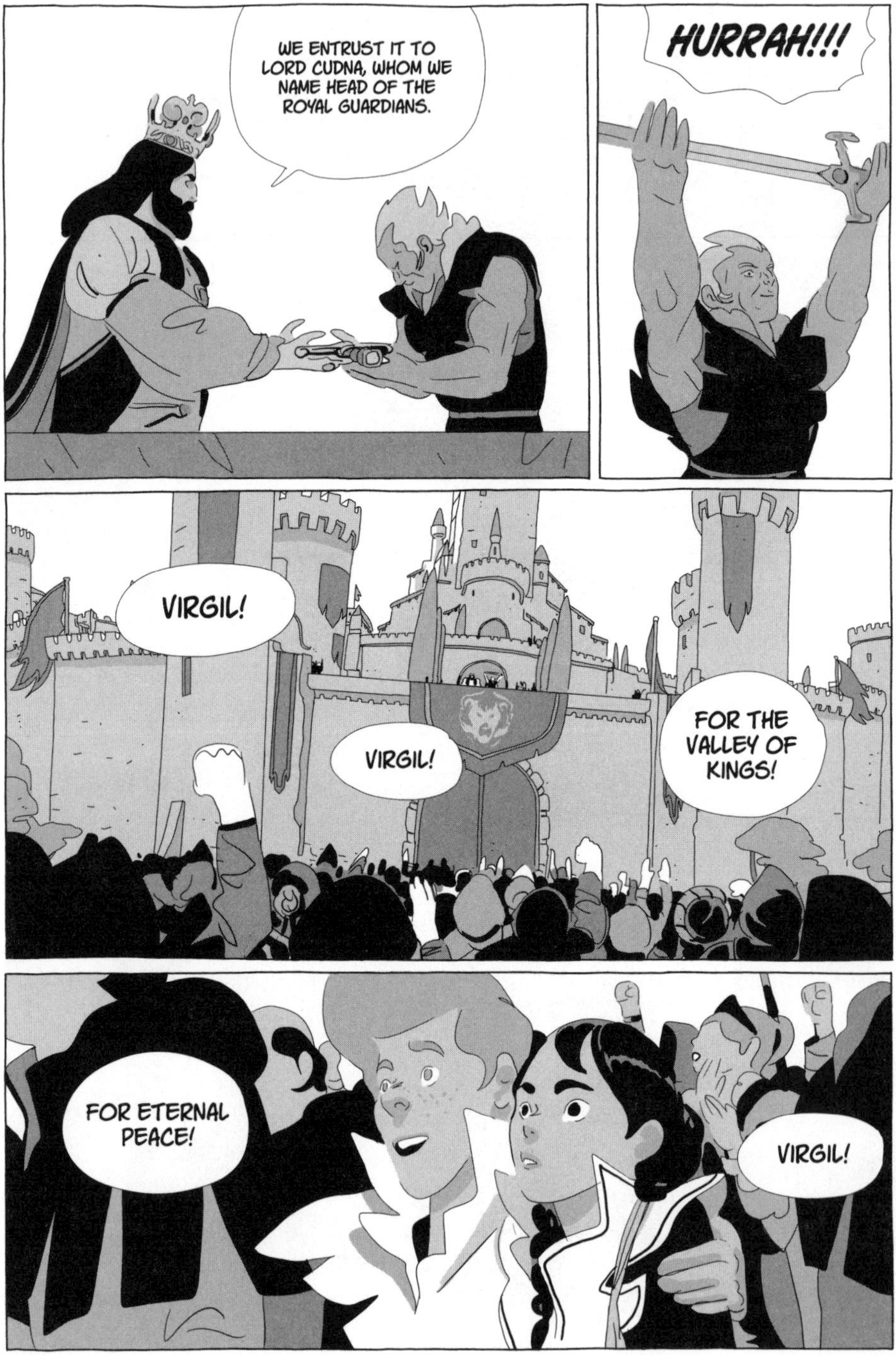
WE ENTRUST IT TO LORD CUDNA, WHOM WE NAME HEAD OF THE ROYAL GUARDIANS.
HURRAH!!!
VIRGIL!
VIRGIL!
FOR THE VALLEY OF KINGS!
FOR ETERNAL PEACE!
VIRGIL!

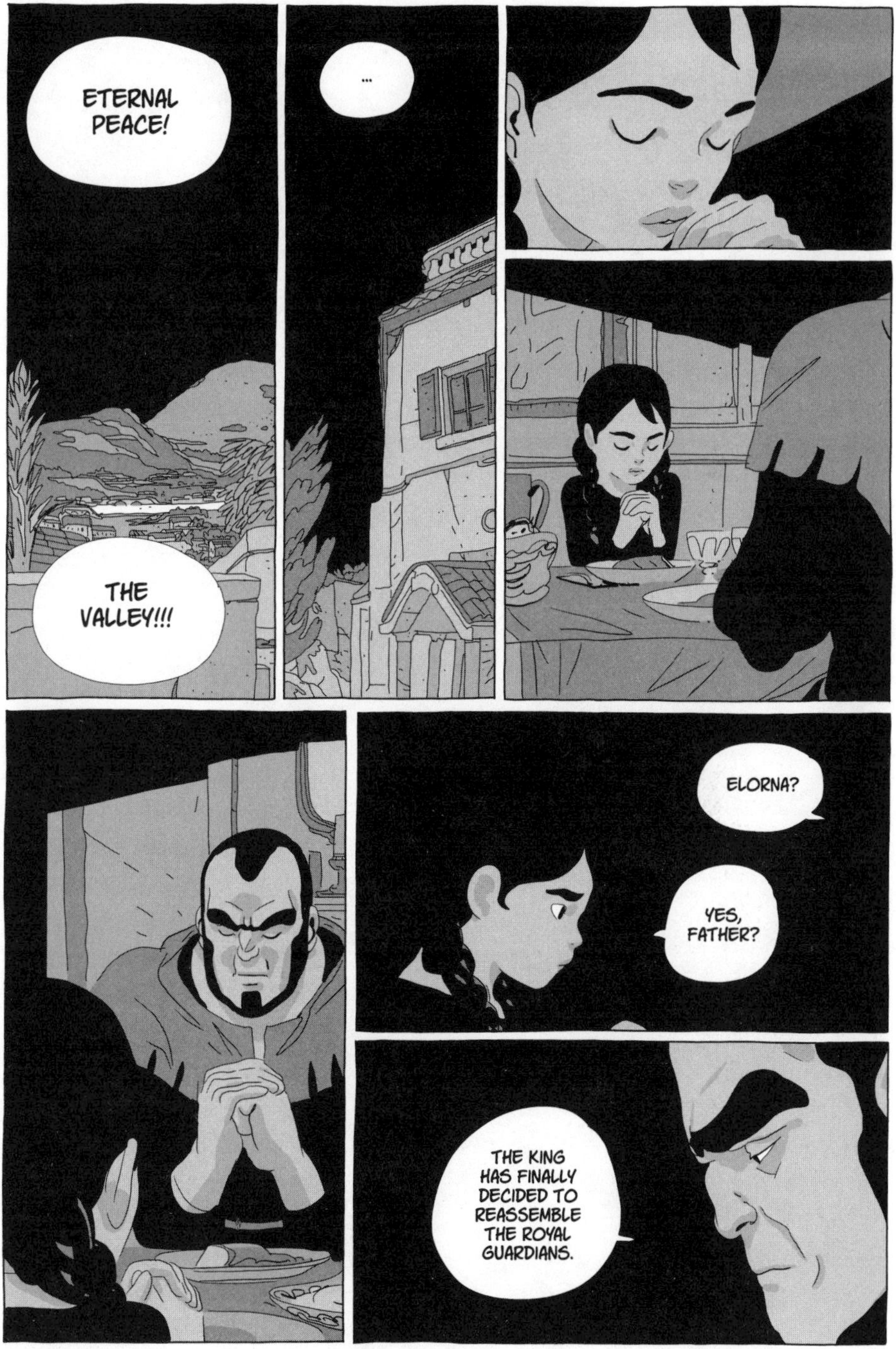
ETERNAL PEACE!
THE VALLEY!!!
...
ELORNA?
YES, FATHER?
THE KING HAS FINALLY DECIDED TO REASSEMBLE THE ROYAL GUARDIANS.

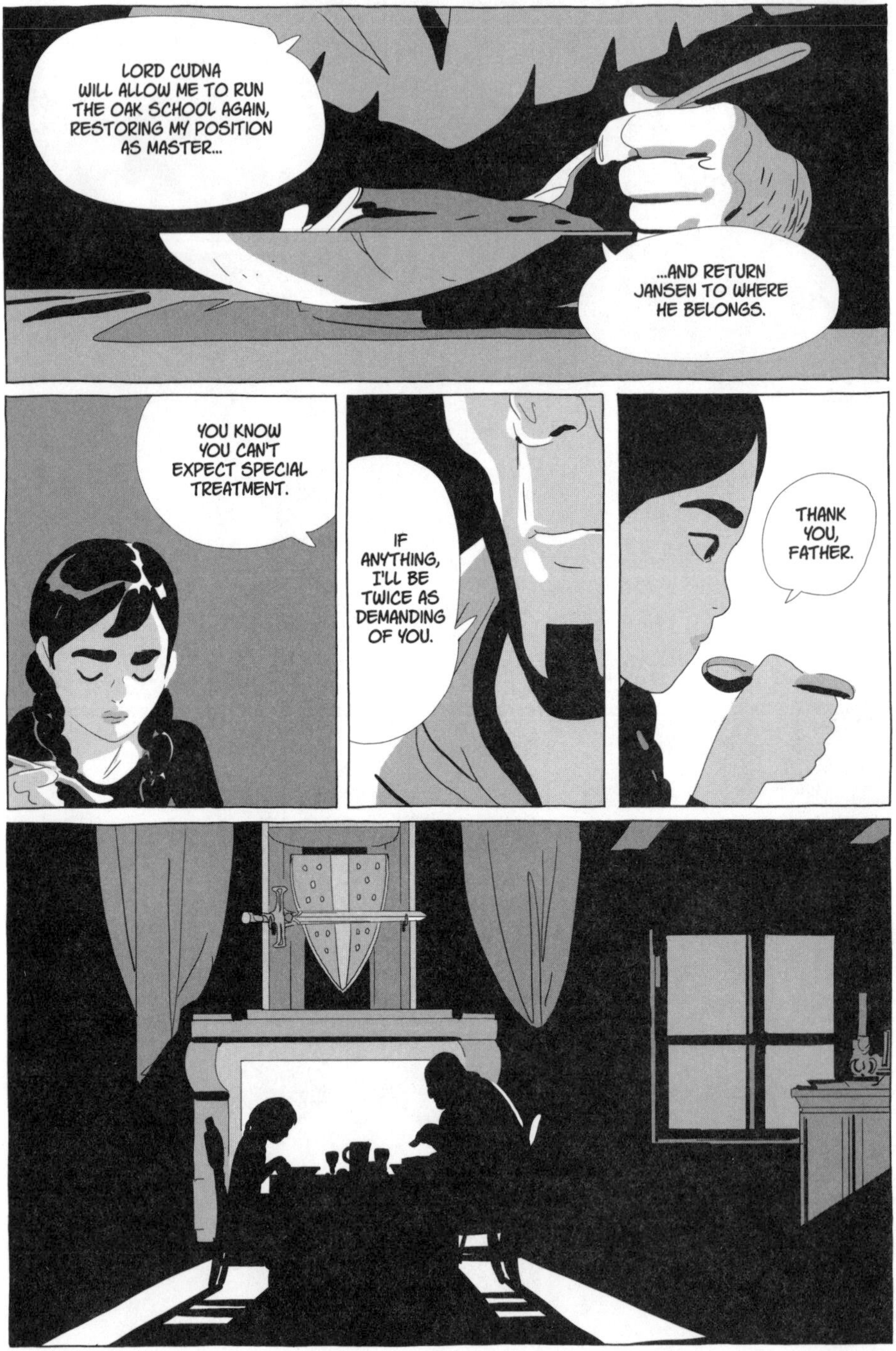
LORD CUDNA WILL ALLOW ME TO RUN THE OAK SCHOOL AGAIN, RESTORING MY POSITION AS MASTER...
...AND RETURN JANSEN TO WHERE HE BELONGS.
YOU KNOW YOU CAN'T EXPECT SPECIAL TREATMENT.
IF ANYTHING, I'LL BE TWICE AS DEMANDING OF YOU.
THANK YOU, FATHER.

Read on for a preview of

LAST MAN

6

The Rescue

Balak + Sanlauille + Uiuès

Available in November 2016 by First Second Books

:01

First Second

ISBN 978-1-62672-051-0

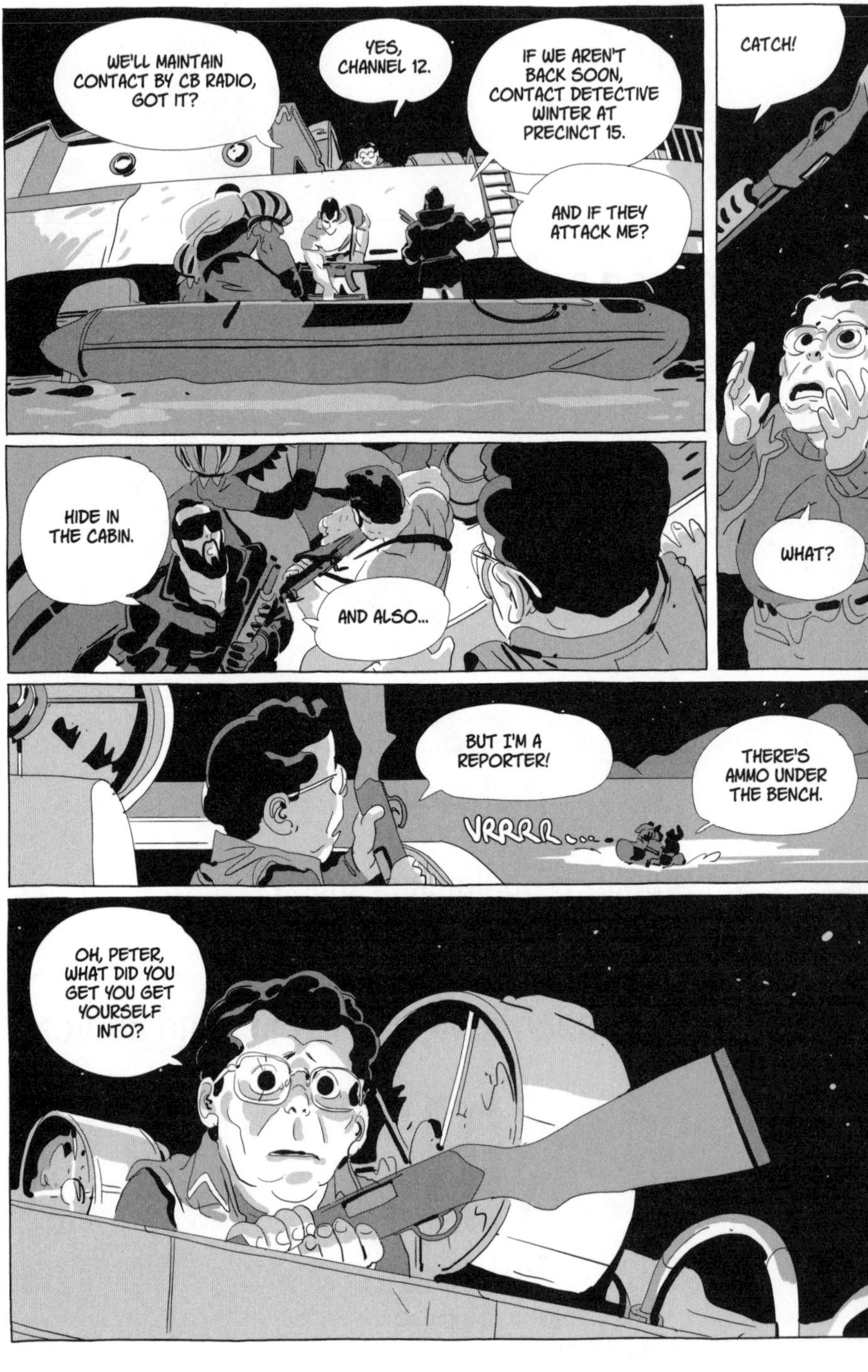

WE'LL MAINTAIN CONTACT BY CB RADIO, GOT IT?
YES, CHANNEL 12.
IF WE AREN'T BACK SOON, CONTACT DETECTIVE WINTER AT PRECINCT 15.
AND IF THEY ATTACK ME?
HIDE IN THE CABIN.
AND ALSO...
CATCH!
WHAT?
BUT I'M A REPORTER!
VRRRR...
THERE'S AMMO UNDER THE BENCH.
OH, PETER, WHAT DID YOU GET YOU GET YOURSELF INTO?

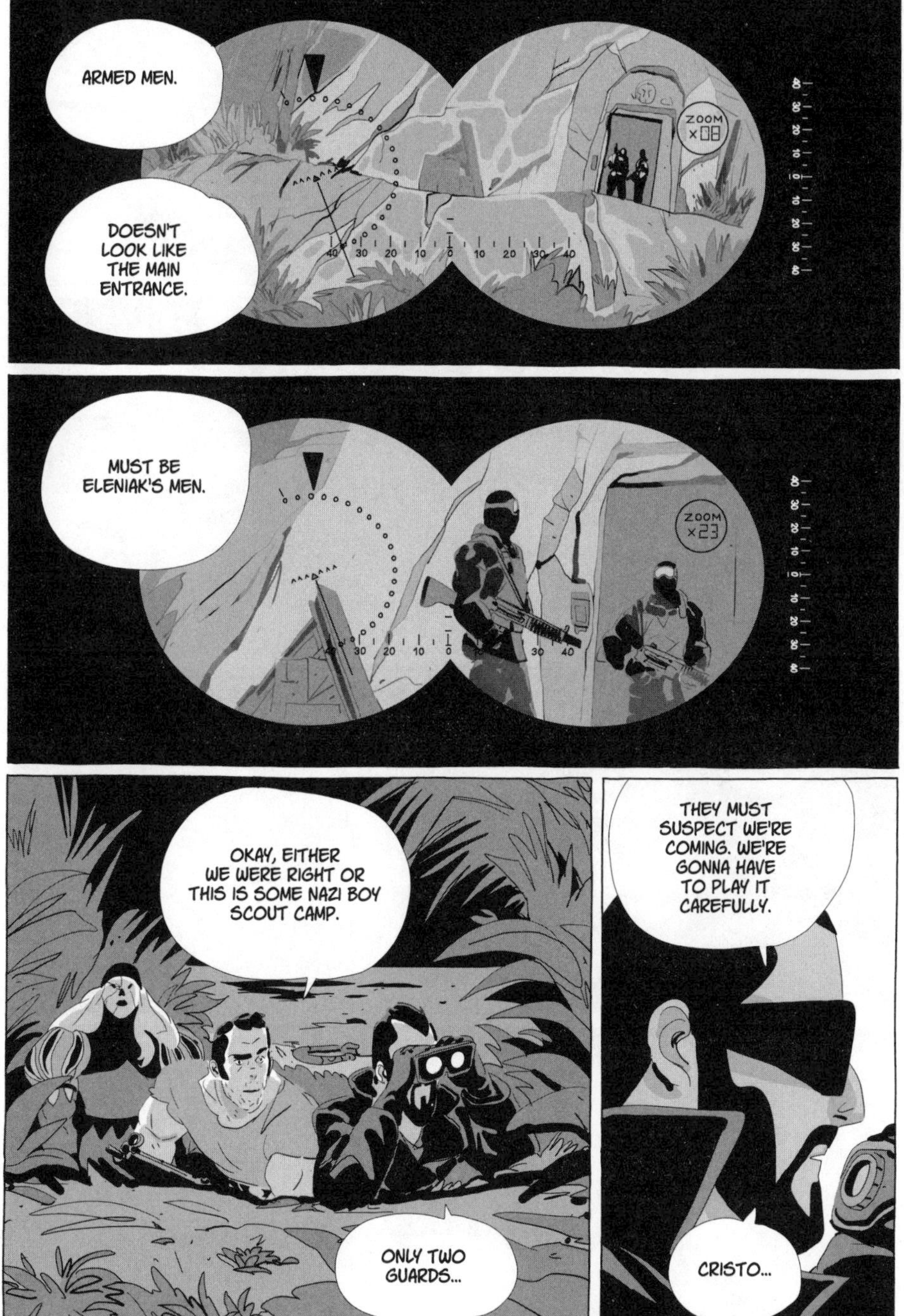

ARMED MEN.
DOESN'T LOOK LIKE THE MAIN ENTRANCE.
ZOOM ×08
MUST BE ELENIAK'S MEN.
ZOOM ×23
OKAY, EITHER WE WERE RIGHT OR THIS IS SOME NAZI BOY SCOUT CAMP.
ONLY TWO GUARDS...
THEY MUST SUSPECT WE'RE COMING. WE'RE GONNA HAVE TO PLAY IT CAREFULLY.
CRISTO...

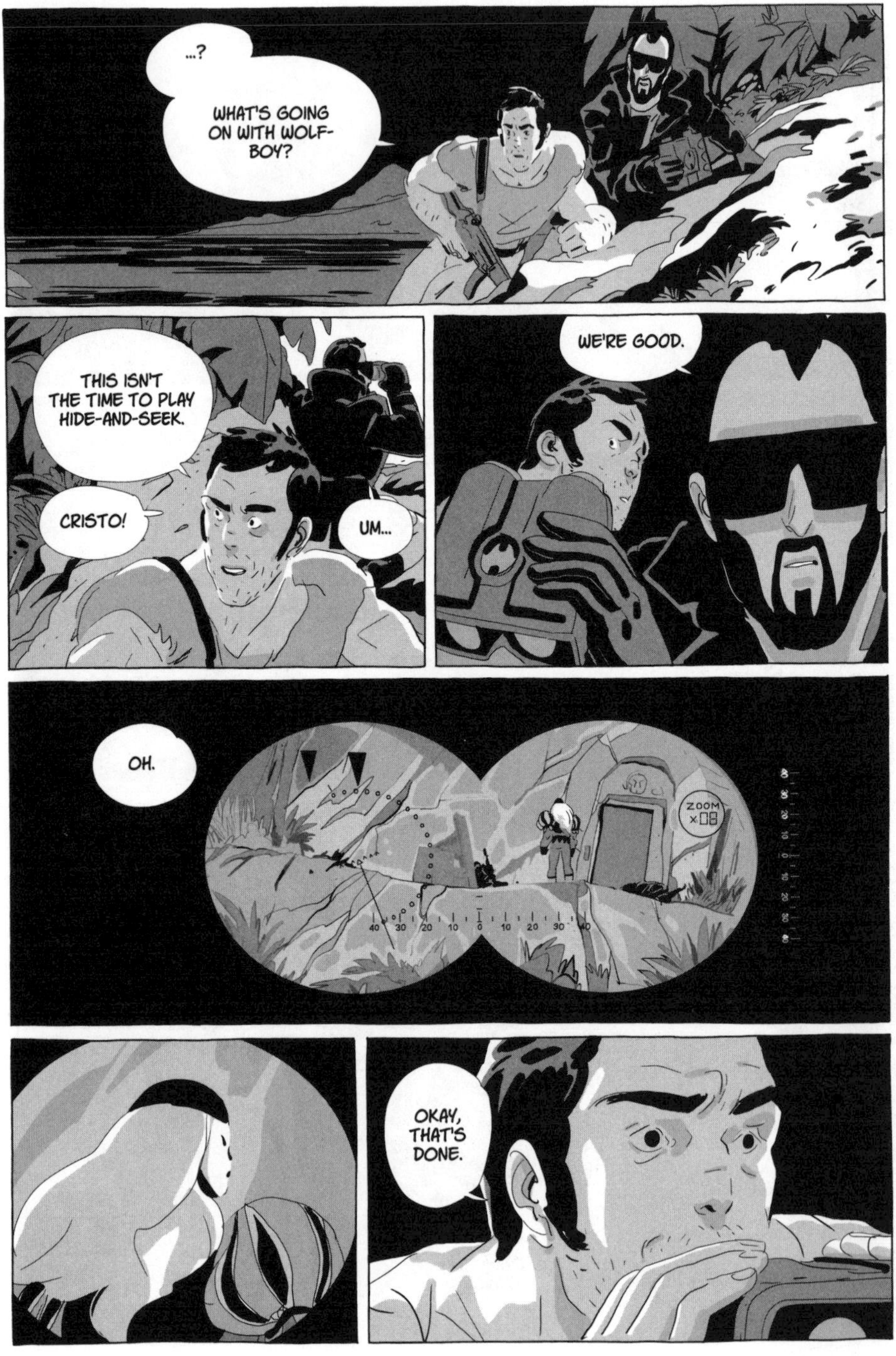
...?
WHAT'S GOING ON WITH WOLF-BOY?
THIS ISN'T THE TIME TO PLAY HIDE-AND-SEEK.
CRISTO!
UM...
WE'RE GOOD.
OH.
ZOOM ×08
OKAY, THAT'S DONE.

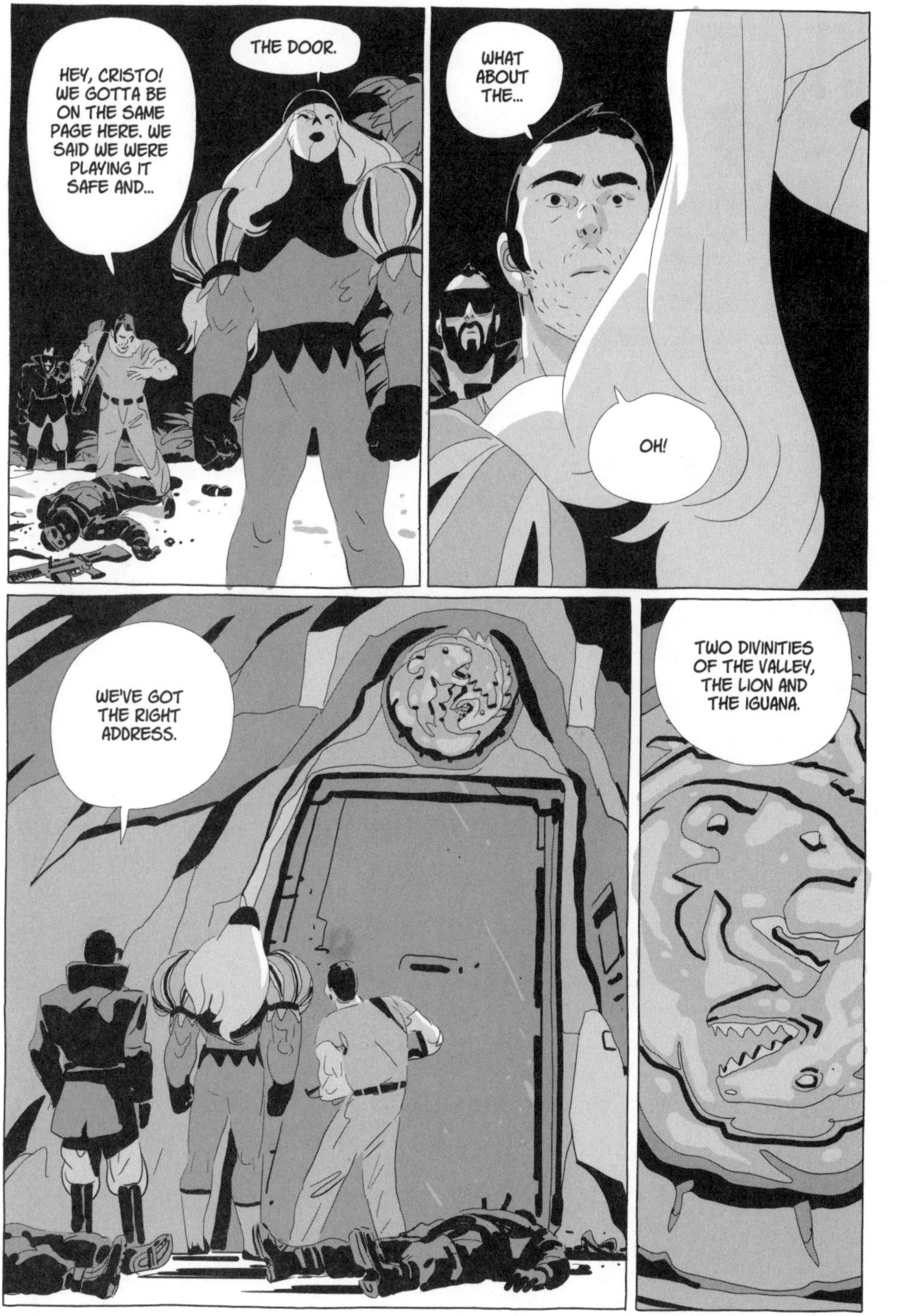
HEY, CRISTO! WE GOTTA BE ON THE SAME PAGE HERE. WE SAID WE WERE PLAYING IT SAFE AND...
THE DOOR.
WHAT ABOUT THE...
OH!
WE'VE GOT THE RIGHT ADDRESS.
TWO DIVINITIES OF THE VALLEY, THE LION AND THE IGUANA.

First Second

New York

Lastman tome 5 copyright © 2014 Casterman
English translation by Alexis Siegel
English translation copyright © 2016 by First Second

Published by First Second
First Second is an imprint of Roaring Brook Press,
a division of Holtzbrinck Publishing Holdings Limited Partnership
175 Fifth Avenue, New York, New York 10010

Library of Congress Control Number: 2015944939

ISBN: 978-1-62672-050-3

Our books may be purchased in bulk for promotional, educational,
or business use. Please contact your local bookseller or the Macmillan Corporate
and Macmillan Premium Sales Department at (800) 221-7945 ext. 5442
or by email at MacmillanSpecialMarkets@macmillan.com.

Originally published in France by Casterman as *Lastman tome 5*.

First American edition 2016

Book design by Rob Steen

Printed in the United States of America

10 9 8 7 6 5 4 3 2 1